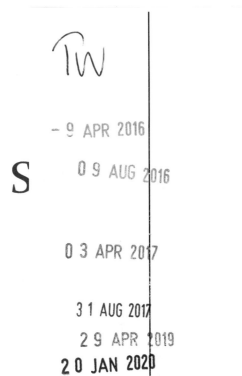

For my sister,
Patricia Anne Clifton.
She also inherited green fingers,
and has the responsibility
for passing them on.

STIRLING MACOBOY'S
What
Shrub
is
That?

Published in 2014 by
New Holland Publishers
London • Sydney • Cape Town • Auckland
www.newhollandpublishers.com

First published in 1989.
Reprinted 1992, 1994, 1997, 2009.

The Chandlery, Unit 114 50 Westminster Bridge Road London SE1 7QY United Kingdom
1/66 Gibbes Street Chatswood NSW 2067 Australia
Wembley Square First Floor Solan Road Gardens Cape Town 8001 South Africa
218 Lake Road Northcote Auckland New Zealand

A catalogue record of this book is available at the National Library of Australia

ISBN: 9781921517259

Publisher: Fiona Schultz
Project Editor: Simon Papps
Designer: Kimberley Pearce
Production director: Olga Dementiev
Printed in China through Asia Pacific Offset Ltd

10 9 8 7 6 5 4 3 2 1

Follow New Holland Publishers on
Facebook: www.facebook.com/NewHollandPublishers

CONTENTS

INTRODUCTION

What would our gardens be like without shrubs? Far less interesting and appealing places, that much is certain, for shrubs are the eye-level plants that give a garden form, function and much of its colour and beauty. Without them, how could we create sheltered suntraps or screen ourselves from neighbours? Shrubs can deflect winds or block out unsightly buildings while accentuating attractive views. They can even add mystery and interest to the garden simply by allowing paths to disappear behind banks of dense foliage. And how else would we fill the gap between the foliage canopies of our trees and the low-growing flowers and groundcovers below?

No, a garden without shrubs is scarcely a garden at all, and no matter where in the world you live there are literally hundreds, even thousands, of shrub species and varieties that would be suitable for your climate. All bear flowers, and while it's true that not all shrubs are spectacular in bloom, the majority are at least quite pretty. A few species bear insignificant flowers but make up for their poor floral show with an outstanding display of foliage or fruit, sometimes both.

But shrubs don't just exist to appeal to gardeners. In nature, they feed, shelter and house a huge range of small creatures, and they can do the same job in your garden. Their pollen, nectar and fruit draw birds and butterflies and a host of less desirable insects which, in turn, attract insectivorous birds. These are well worth having in the garden, for they'll happily keep caterpillars and other unwanted insects down. The more shrubs you have, the more birds you'll attract, since reliable sources of food and good nesting sites can be in short supply in the suburbs. And, naturally enough, our conservative feathered friends prefer flowers that are native to their own country.

Shrubs in general are fast-growing, and can fulfil the particular function for which they were chosen in just a few years. So long as you provide them with good soil in the first place and don't ignore their continuing need for food and water, they'll usually give you a lifetime of trouble-free pleasure.

If you have a large garden or are on a tight budget, you can still enjoy the effect of massed shrubs without a big cash outlay. Virtually all shrubs can be easily propagated by even the novice gardener, and cuttings received from friends and neighbours can be quickly converted into healthy new plants. You'll find more details on taking cuttings and other methods of propagation on the following pages, but first let's define more clearly exactly what a shrub is.

This may seem fairly straightforward, but it's actually not so simple. After all, some plants defined as shrubs really do look like small trees, while others are so small and soft, they could be mistaken for perennials. So where do we draw the line? What *is* a shrub? Most authorities would agree, it's a woody rather than succulent-stemmed plant and these stems remain in place throughout the year. They may lose their leaves, but the stems themselves do not die back completely as in the case of herbaceous perennials. Shrubs may have a single, short trunk which soon divides into a framework of branches, or they may produce many stems from a crowded base. And, as already mentioned, while some shrubs may grow to the size of a small tree, that's as far as they go in height. The vast majority would be under 15 ft/4.5 m tall.

Depending on where in the world they come from, shrubs can be deciduous, part-deciduous or evergreen. As a rule, those from cold climates are deciduous while the evergreen species hail from areas where winters are mild. Of course, there are exceptions to the rule and you'll find some evergreens that can endure frigid winters and a few from the tropics that like to drop their leaves during the warm, dry season. Generalizing again, deciduous shrubs often put on a spectacular but relatively brief floral display, usually in spring or early summer; and in autumn, most can be relied on to produce a second display — this time from the foliage as it turns scarlet and gold in reaction to the chilly autumn nights.

Evergreens, especially those from warmer regions, often make up for their lack of autumn foliage with a prolonged flowering period that sometimes lasts right through the warmer months. Both deciduous and evergreen shrubs can produce colourful, decorative berries or seed pods and this should be kept in mind when choosing shrubs, too. Flowers are important, but they're only one aspect of the beauty of shrubs.

PLANNING FOR SHRUBS

Before you plant anything at all in your yard, you should develop a plan for the finished garden. By doing so, you'll be able to gather your thoughts together and in seeing them down on paper, you'll almost certainly develop new or better ideas as you proceed. Your initial vision of the proposed garden is bound to be too grand for the space you have available but by drawing up a plan, you'll get a very clear idea of what will fit where and how many of each you will need to fill the allotted space. Most gardeners make the mistake of putting in too many shrubs too close together, and this results in an untidy tangle that has to be thinned out all too frequently. At the planning stage, you don't have to know exactly what shrubs you want, only their shapes, growth habits and potential sizes, and that will be determined by the effect you are trying to achieve.

For example, if you want to screen out a dividing fence but not your neighbour's tree, choose shrubs that are densely foliaged to ground level and grow to about fence height. If you want a lawn specimen, choose a shrub with an attractive silhouette. For a windbreak, you'll want fairly dense, compact growth, while to shelter delicate groundcovers a taller, more open shrub might be needed. There'll be hundreds that fit any set of criteria, and you can get down to the job of choosing species after you have a clear idea of what you want them to do.

While there are thousands of species of shrubs in the world, they have only a few basic shapes between them. In fact, you'll find that virtually all shrubs adopt a variation of one of these seven shapes.

1. Bun-shaped

A broad or narrow hemisphere of foliage, either open or dense, supported by a framework of branches that arise from a short, central trunk. Bun-shaped shrubs vary from low to quite tall and are usually at least as wide as they are high, often wider.

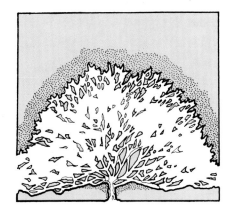

A hemispherical or *bun-shaped* shrub.

2. Vase-shaped

A short trunk soon divides into a series of branches that grow upwards and outwards. Vase-shaped shrubs are not usually foliaged right to the ground and they can be quite tall.

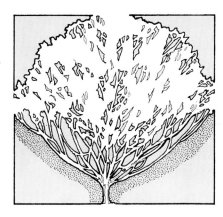

Vase-shaped shrub, growing up and out.

3. Fountain-shaped

Many stems arise from the ground, the central stems more or less erect while those towards the outer edges arch gracefully outwards. Such shrubs are usually densely foliaged and make good screens.

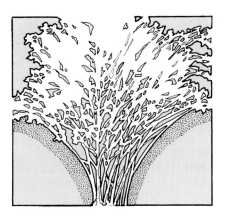

Fountain-shaped shrubs make a good screen.

Tree-like shrubs support a canopy of foliage on a framework of branches.

4. Tree-like

A canopy of foliage supported by a framework of branches which become thicker and fewer towards the base until they join the short main trunk. Tree-like shrubs can be amongst the tallest of shrubs but many small shrubs also adopt this habit. Large, tree-like shrubs can be good shade 'trees' in small gardens.

Horizontally branched shrubs are often quite picturesque.

5. Horizontally branched

One or more trunks support several main branches which lie in a horizontal plane. These shrubs are often fairly open and quite picturesque. They are usually much broader than they are tall.

6. Prostrate

Prostrate shrubs either creep along the ground or produce a series of low, horizontal branches that usually take root where they touch ground. They are excellent erosion controllers and make handsome, large scale ground-covers.

Prostrate shrubs creep along the ground, rooting where they touch.

7. Conical

Densely foliaged to the ground, conical shrubs have a central stem from which all other stems branch. Their shape makes them a good choice for the formal garden or for use as accent or lawn specimens.

Conical shrubs are usually foliaged to the ground, make good formal specimens.

CHOOSING SHRUBS

As we've said before, flowers are wonderful but they shouldn't necessarily be the sole reason for choosing one shrub over another. Most shrubs spend much of their lives out of bloom, so take other things into account when choosing between them. What other things? Well, the size, shape, texture and colour of the leaves for a start.

Unusually coloured leaves can be just as eye-catching as flowers and you have the benefit of them for at least seven to eight months of the year, twelve in the case of evergreens. If they change colour with the seasons, count that as another point in their favour. Colourful fruits are yet another source of interest that shouldn't be ignored. They usually appear in autumn, and with many species they'll persist right through the winter, adding a bright splash of colour to what, in some climates, can be a drab time of year.

But for whatever reason you'd like to grow a particular shrub, let your climate be the final arbiter. True, many shrubs are highly adaptable and will grow in climates dissimilar to their natural ranges, but clearly, the best and most reliable results will be had from shrubs whose natural temperature range and rainfall matches yours. If you live in a dry area, you'll be giving yourself a job for life and paying dearly for the water if you plant rainforest natives. Similarly, those who live where winters are mild shouldn't plant deciduous shrubs in the hope of enjoying a blaze of autumn foliage. It simply won't happen!

Other points to consider are the amount and distribution of your rainfall. Some shrubs like an even distribution of rain year round while others can take a long dry season. Mediterranean climates have dry summers and wet winters but monsoonal regions experience the opposite. Shrubs from one rarely do well in the other.

Your soil is another important factor. Most shrubs will do well in deep, fertile, moist but well-drained soil. Sadly, that's not a description of what lies under most gardens. You can decide to grow only those shrubs that will thrive in your type of soil (natives to your area would be the obvious choice) or to improve the drainage and condition of your soil in order to grow a wider range. The latter may be the preferable option but it is also the hardest.

When you have narrowed down your list to shrubs that are suitable to your climate and soil (and that list will still be vast), select for size, shape and timing of flowers and fruit. If you get to know what shrubs do before buying them, you'll be sure that they will fit into your garden plan and you will be able to arrange the display to suit yourself. You might like a massed display in spring, or perhaps you'd prefer flowers all year round. Whatever you want you can have, so long as you get to know your shrubs first.

AT THE NURSERY

When the time comes to buy, check each shrub carefully before you part with any money. They should look healthy and lush and be free of insects and damaged or distorted foliage. Avoid large shrubs in small containers or any that have a mass of roots protruding from the drainage holes. Such shrubs are likely to be pot bound and may never recover, remaining stunted and weak even when planted into good soil.

Where winters are cold, deciduous shrubs are sometimes sold bare-rooted, but of course, only when they are leafless in late autumn and winter. Though not in pots, the roots of bare-rooted shrubs must still be wrapped to prevent desiccation. Don't buy them if the roots have been exposed to the air. Bare-rooted shrubs must be planted out immediately.

Container-grown shrubs are available year round and where winters are mild, they can be planted out at any time. In cold-climate gardens, plant them any time but late autumn and winter.

HOW TO PLANT SHRUBS

Good, fertile, well-drained soil is the key to success in gardening, and you should improve one area at a time, planting only after it has been thoroughly worked over. Dig the area to at least the depth of a spade, breaking up clods as you go. Work in a generous amount of compost or well-rotted manure, as organic matter is an important soil conditioner.

If you find that you are digging down into heavy, sticky clay that is just beneath the surface, you will have a hard time establishing any sort of garden on it without major improvement. Clay drains poorly, is badly aerated and often quite infertile. It is also difficult to dig, so incorporating organic matter is no easy task. A rotary-hoe will make the job easier, but an alternative way to garden on clay is to raise beds 12 in/30 cm above the surrounding soil behind small retaining walls. Break the surface of the clay before filling the beds with top quality, humus-rich, well-drained soil and a dressing of dolomite.

After you have improved your soil, dig the planting holes twice as wide and deep as the shrub's root ball. Half-fill the hole with enriched soil and firm down. Unpot the shrub by punching down on the rim at several places with one hand while grasping the shrub by its trunk with the other. Alternatively,

Planting a *container-grown* shrub.

cut the container with snips and pull it away. Place the root ball in the hole and either add or remove soil so that the shrub's trunk will be the same depth in the soil as it was in the pot. Water the roots and soil in the half-filled hole, then fill completely with the remaining soil. Firm down and water again. If you form the surface soil into a depression around the trunk, you will direct water to where it is most needed.

Bare-rooted shrubs should be planted in a slightly different way. Place them on a cone-shaped mound of soil in the planting hole and spread their roots downwards and outwards. Be sure that the trunk will not be deeper in the soil than it was previously, and do press soil *firmly* around the roots when filling the hole, as air pockets are undesirable. Once the hole is filled, water deeply.

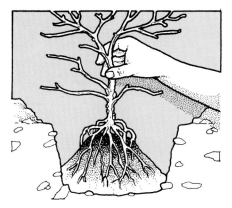

Planting a *bare-rooted* shrub.

Shrubs that are sold with their root balls wrapped in hessian or burlap can be planted as if they were container-grown but there is no need to remove the wrapping. It will quickly rot away in the soil.

Planting a balled and burlapped shrub.

KEEPING YOUR SOIL RICH

In the wild, animal and plant wastes fall to the ground and rot away, enriching the soil as they do. You can utilize this natural cycle, too, and get rid of bulky garden and household vegetable wastes in the process by first composting the organic waste and then spreading it back onto the garden in the form of mulch. A layer of mulch replenishes vital organic matter washed out by rain and watering, adds nutrients to the soil, encourages beneficial organisms such as worms, retains soil moisture and suppresses weeds. You can make compost from leafy kitchen waste, coffee grounds, tea leaves, the contents of the vacuum cleaner dust bag, grass clippings, fallen leaves, prunings, etc. In a matter of weeks, all this material breaks down into rich, dark, sweet-smelling compost that makes the ideal mulch.

In summer, mulch keeps the soil cool and moist while in winter it can prevent the ground from freezing, thus enabling you to grow a wider range of shrubs. Apply mulch in a layer at least 4 in/10 cm deep over all garden beds. If you don't have enough to go round, apply it only beneath the foliage canopies of shrubs, but take care not to build it up around the trunks as this can lead to collar rot. With azaleas and other surface-rooting shrubs, apply a thin layer only or you may encourage the roots to grow upwards, leading to the death of the lower root system.

WHEN AND HOW MUCH SHOULD YOU WATER?

If the soil around your shrubs is kept evenly moist at all times, you'll never lose one through lack of water. But how do you know that it is evenly moist? One way is to stick your finger into the soil. If it feels dryish a finger's length down, water deeply. Deep soakings encourage strong, healthy water-seeking roots but light sprinklings keep the plant's roots at the surface. Deep-rooted plants will survive a shortage of water, while those with surface roots will drop dead at the slightest hint of drought. After a few 'feeling' sessions, you'll know how long your soil takes to dry out and you should water accordingly.

DO GARDEN PLANTS NEED FEEDING?

Yes they do, but if you prepared the soil well in the first place and regularly apply organic mulches, you could safely assume that no further feeding was necessary. However, gardeners mostly like to apply fertilizer, and a ration of complete plant food broadcast in early spring, with a follow-up dose in early summer, won't do any harm. Apply as directed, for fertilizers can acidify and salinate soils if used to excess and there's just no way of boosting plant growth beyond the maximum possible by applying extra fertilizer. You are more likely to kill your plants than see them grow.

Don't feed during the second half of autumn or in winter, and never apply fertilizer to dry soil. Always water first, feed, then water again.

WHEN TO PRUNE SHRUBS

Pruning has something of an image problem among gardeners and next to weeding, it is probably the most hated of gardening chores. But really, there's no need to recoil in horror. Pruning is a simple task that takes little more than clean, sharp secateurs and common sense. And you don't have to prune every shrub every year, though some will undoubtedly benefit from this.

You should prune when shrubs have grown too big for their allotted spaces or when flowering or fruiting is deteriorating due to overcrowded branches or too much tired, old wood. Some shrubs, especially those with naturally neat, compact habits, need no pruning at all; but for most of your shrubs, selective pruning will mean healthier, lusher growth, neater and more compact plants, and many more flowers over the coming year!

Since all shrubs are grown for their flowers, fruit or foliage, the main object of pruning should be to maximize those displays. That means getting to know the growth and flowering habits of your shrubs. Some are best pruned before bloom while others prefer a trim afterwards.

Deciduous shrubs that flower on new growth which only begins to appear in late winter or early spring may be pruned any time after the leaves have fallen in autumn.

Evergreens with a similar flowering habit can also be pruned during the cooler weather, but not usually until very late when all danger of frost has passed.

Deciduous shrubs that flower in early spring on stems that already exist should be pruned as soon as possible after flowering has finished.

HOW TO PRUNE

Before making your first cut, take a few moments to study the shrub's natural shape. Your aim should be simply to reduce its size, not to alter its form. Some shrubs have a definite main framework from which smaller and smaller branches are produced. *Hibiscus*, *Fuchsia* and *Azalea* are examples. This framework should be left intact unless it is damaged, dead or diseased, for on many plants it is not quickly replaced and results in gaping holes for months or years. Rather, pruning

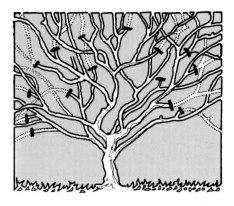

Reduce a shrub's size by pruning, but
don't alter its natural shape.

should be confined to the outer
branches, though these can be
shortened quite dramatically if need
be.

Shrubs that produce many erect or
arching canes from the base are best
pruned by completely removing about
one third of the oldest stems and
shortening the remainder, also by
about one third.

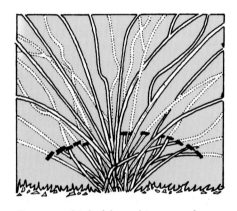

Remove a third of the arching canes from
a multiple-trunked shrub.

Dense, compact shrubs frequently
need no pruning at all, but if it is desirable to slow their spread, a light, all-
over shearing immediately after bloom
is usually all that's needed.

Young shrubs can be encouraged to
produce dense, twiggy growth by regularly pinching out the growing tips;
this may delay the need for harder
pruning by years.

When you prune, use only clean,
very sharp secateurs. Always remove
dead, diseased or damaged growth
first, then weak or spindly stems and
any branches that are growing in
towards the centre of the plant. If

two or more branches are rubbing
together, retain only the stronger, provided it is growing in a desirable direction. Make all cuts as close as possible
on the outer sides of growth buds
(usually found where leaves join
stems). Don't leave stubs, for they will
only die back, making easy entry
points for pests and diseases in the process.

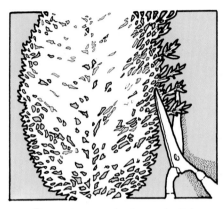

Dense, compact shrubs need a light
all-over shearing after bloom.

Most pruning cuts will quickly heal
but it is advisable to treat larger
wounds (say, 1 in/3 cm in diameter)
with special tree wound sealant.

Very old or straggly shrubs can be
revitalized by cutting every branch
almost to the ground in earliest spring.
Masses of new shoots will emerge and
grow quickly into a dense plant.
Clearly, such drastic pruning should
not be undertaken very often.

PROPAGATING YOUR OWN SHRUBS

At today's prices, planting out a whole
garden can be astonishingly expensive.
Even just a few new shrubs can make
a fair-sized hole in your wallet, but
there's an easy way round this
expense, for most shrubs are a snap to
propagate at home. Naturally, you'll
first need to find the plants you want;
but you'll soon discover that friends,
relatives, even complete strangers are
usually willing to let you take seeds or
a few cuttings from their gardens. Just
ask them first!

There are several ways to propagate
shrubs and methods that have proved
successful are suggested in the entries

for each plant in this book. Some
shrubs are best propagated from seeds,
but as a rule vegetative means, i.e., cuttings, layers or division are recommended. This is because seeds have a
number of disadvantages. Firstly, they
can take anything from a few days to
many months to germinate and the
result may be a tiny seedling that is not
large enough to plant out for three or
four years. It may then be several more
years before the first flowers are seen.
Moreover, seedlings may not come
true to type, especially if the parent
plant is a hybrid — a highly likely
prospect with many of today's favourite flowering shrubs. Such seedlings
often lose all the features that distinguish the prized hybrid from its
much inferior ancestor. So, to be sure
of getting an identical plant to the one
you have admired, and getting it to a
reasonable size and in bloom as
quickly as possible, use one of the vegetative methods of propagation
outlined here.

Taking cuttings

Cuttings are described in three ways
depending on the age of the material
taken: soft-tip, semi-hardwood and
hardwood.

Soft-tips are taken in spring and
summer from the top couple of inches
of new growth. The stems are bright
green, not woody looking and snap
easily when bent. As they are the
growing tips, they are full of plant
growth hormones and usually root
quickly. If the stem does not snap, it is
too sappy and will not root anyway.

Semi-hardwood cuttings are taken
in summer when the spring growth has
matured somewhat. They will be
beginning to turn brown and woody,

Taking a semi-hardwood cutting with a
heel for propagation.

and stems will bend before snapping. Many gardeners like to tear these cuttings away from the parent material with a heel of older wood attached. Semi-hardwood cuttings usually take a little longer to form roots but are more robust and better able to survive the sudden hot days of summer.

Both these types of cutting should be taken in the early morning when shoots are firm and full of sap. But as they wilt quickly and must be processed immediately, it is advisable to have everything ready before you start.

First organize a table in a shady place and have small pots or trays filled with a moist, 50/50 mix of coarse sand and peat-moss. Hygiene is important, so ensure that used pots are thoroughly clean. You will also need: a pair of very sharp, clean secateurs or a small, sharp pruning knife; a thin stick; some straightened coathanger wire; large clear plastic bags; bleach or disinfectant; and hormone rooting powder.

Select the strongest, healthiest looking growth and cut off more than you will need. (If you are a long way from home, wrap cuttings in wet newspaper, seal in a plastic bag and place in an ice-filled portable cooler.) Wipe secateurs with bleach or disinfectant before moving to another plant.

Halve areas of leaves on cuttings to reduce water loss while roots form.

Soft-tip cuttings should be 2–3 in/5–8 cm in length; semi-hardwood cuttings can be 6–8 in/15–20 cm long. Snip off the lower leaves carefully so as not to damage the stem and reduce any large leaves by cutting in half crosswise. This reduces water loss through the leaves while the new roots are forming. Dip the stem tip only into the hormone rooting powder, shake off the excess and insert the cutting into a small hole made in the soil with the thin stick. Insert the cutting just deep enough so that it can support itself. Don't overcrowd your pots or trays or you will damage the new roots when the time comes to repot them individually.

If you have one, place the cuttings in a propagating box or make a passable substitute by enclosing the pots in clear plastic supported over a framework of coathanger wire. Place in a bright but shaded spot and keep the soil consistently moist.

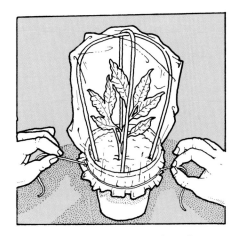

Enclose pots of cuttings in clear plastic supported on coathanger wire.

After about three weeks, the cuttings should have begun to form their own roots and can be slowly introduced to the outside world. Start by piercing the plastic bags or half removing the cover of the propagating box. After about a week remove the cover or plastic entirely but keep the cuttings humid by regularly misting them and wetting the surrounding area. After another week, repot cuttings individually into small containers and grow on until large enough to plant out.

Hardwood cuttings are taken from deciduous shrubs in late autumn or winter when all the leaves have fallen. Remove 2 ft/60 cm lengths from strong, healthy branches and cut these into 4–6 in/10–15 cm sections, ensuring that there are at least four buds on each. The lower cut should be made about 3 in/8 cm below a leaf junction and the top cut about 1 in/3 cm above one.

Bundle the cuttings together with all their tops at one end and note which is the top. Stand them in a box of moist sand/peat mix and cover with more of the mix. Cover the box and store in a cool, dark spot that remains above freezing point all winter. By spring, the cuttings will have formed roots and may be potted up individually so that only the top bud protrudes above soil level. Grow on until large enough to plant out — but be patient: this can take 2–3 years!

Layering

Layering is a process that causes a stem to form roots while still attached to the mother plant. Once rooted, the stem is detached and planted out. Layering is a good way to get a few large shrubs and there are a number of ways of going about it. Common to all methods is the need to exclude light from the section of stem you wish to take root. In shrubs that produce many cane-like stems from the base (such as *Abelia*, *Azalea*, *Forsythia*, *Japonica*, Gooseberries and Raspberries) this is achieved by burying a part of the cane (tip layering).

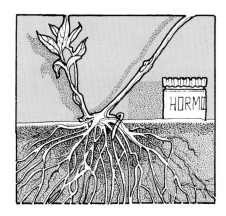

Tip layering forms roots near the tip of the new season's growth.

Tip layering

Roots are made to form near the tips of the new season's growth, resulting in new but small plants quickly. Stems are pegged down in late winter with their tips in a hole, pointing at a downward angle. The hole is filled and as stem growth is always upwards, a new shoot appears above ground. Roots form at the bend in the buried stem and the young plant should be advanced enough to be detached in autumn.

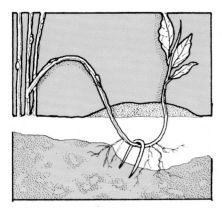

Simple layering is best carried out in early spring.

Simple layering

With this method, the growing tip remains above ground level while a portion of the stem is first cracked then buried to form roots. Tough stems may have to be partially cut through. Cover the cracked or cut section with up to 6 in/15 cm of soil and secure in place with a wire peg or two. Simple layering is best carried out in early spring.

Multiple layering

Use this method on plants that produce long, sinuous stems. It is very similar to simple layering except that instead of burying just one section, the stem is made to snake in and out of the soil. The stem must be partially sliced through wherever it is buried, and the above-ground sections should include one or more growth buds.

Air layering

Where it is not possible to tie a branch down, roots may still be induced to

Air-layering can induce roots to form high in a shrub's branches.

form on the aerial parts of many shrubs. Choose old rather than new season's growth and after making a slit in the bark, tear and remove a 1 in/ 3 cm wide strip of bark all the way round the branch (use a small, sharp knife for this). Cover the wound with a wad of moist sphagnum moss then enclose the moss in plastic. It is essential that the moss stay moist for about six weeks so ensure that the plastic is tied firmly at each end. After about six weeks you will be able to see roots growing through the moss, indicating that the branch can be removed and planted out. Air layering is most successful if carried out during the summer.

Grafting

This is probably the most difficult form of propagation, but all in all the most successful, for it provides a cutting with a ready-made root system. There are several means of carrying this out — but do remember, grafts can be performed only be inserting a cutting (scion) into a larger plant that is closely related (the stock). Three of the most popular methods are illustrated.

In a bark graft, a scion is inserted directly below the bark of the stock.

In the *bark graft*, the stock is sawn straight across, and with a sharp pruning knife, the bark is loosened from the top edge. A piece of the scion is cut to a slender chisel point, and inserted parallel to the cut bark so that as much as possible of the cambium (growth) layers of both scion and stock can be brought into contact. The two pieces can be sealed together with tape or grafting wax. Watch for shoots that

A cleft graft can quickly produce two or more scions on a single stock.

appear *below* the graft, cut them away.

The *cleft graft* is similar, but after cutting across horizontally, the stock is then split an inch or two vertically with a chisel. Insert a wedge to keep the cleft open, then insert two scions cut with a chisel point, one at each side of the cleft stock, again making sure the cambium layers match. Seal with grafting wax.

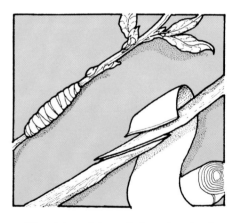

The whip graft is used where the scion is the same diameter as the stock.

In the *whip graft* both scion and stock of the same diameter are cut, but each on the diagonal so that their cambium layers match. The two pieces are then bound tightly together to completely seal the wound. When the pieces have grown together, and new growth is apparent from the scion, the tape can be removed to allow the stock to expand.

Do remember that grafting can only be used to combine two closely related plants, e.g., a rose onto a rose, a camellia onto a camellia. It will rarely work without this relationship.

HOW TO USE THIS BOOK

The shrubs in this book are arranged in the only practical way, by the alphabetical order of their scientific names — names which are used and recognized throughout the world. These are usually in Latin or Ancient Greek, which have the advantage of being internationally understood, which popular names in any modern language are not.

If you already know the botanical name of a shrub you want to look up, just turn through the alphabetically arranged pictorial section until you find the right heading.

If you don't know the botanical name, or what the shrub looks like, turn to the index at the back of the book, where you'll find the more common English-language names listed, also alphabetically, with cross reference to the correct botanical name. Be warned, however: one popular name may apply to several different plants.

The botanical names are also listed in the comprehensive index, together with all known synonyms.

Each main entry in the pictorial section is headed with the botanical name of the shrub *genus*, which corresponds to your family name, e.g., **Genista**. These generic names are printed in *italic* type in their main entry. In the heading, they are often followed by one or more synonyms, where these exist; they are printed in CAPITALS, and bracketed. Following a fine ruled line, and within parentheses, is a simple phonetic guide to the pronunciation of the generic name; a key to this pronunciation is on page 14.

Underneath the phonetic pronunciation you will find some popular names of the most prominent shrubs in the genus — one or more of them according to usage.

These are followed by one or more abbreviated words, e.g., Spr.-Sum., to indicate the season in which the shrub presents its maximum display. Next to this are figures, e.g., 1½-10 ft/50 cm-3 m, indicating the height to which the plant grows (or its height range) in both imperial and metric measure. The figures converted from imperial to metric have been rounded off and are therefore approximate. There is also a description of the shrub's habit of growth, and whether it is evergreen or deciduous.

Finally, in CAPITALS, is the name of the botanical family to which the shrub belongs. In the case of *Genista* it is FABACEAE, the peas or beans. In botany, the family is a .larger group including many related species with similar characteristics.

Each heading also includes a group of symbols.

☼ indicates the shrub does best in full sun. These are good as lawn specimens.

☀ shows the shrub prefers sun for only part of a day. These could be ideal on the east or west side of your home.

☀ (the rarest) shows the plant will flower in full shade. Ideal for use among trees.

Ⓒ shows that the shrub blooms well in cold-winter areas (but it may also grow elsewhere).

Ⓣ that it flowers in cool-temperate climates (though range may be wider).

Ⓦ that it flowers in warm-temperate climates.

Ⓗ that the plant does well in the tropics. Few cold-climate plants bloom in the tropics as well.

As some shrubs are quite adaptable, the symbols may appear in many different combinations.

Within many dictionary entries, you will find reference to some of the most popular species of the genus in cultivation. *Specific* or *species* names correspond to our given or personal names. Specific names are also printed in *italic* type, but without an initial capital. Where several species are described, the generic name is abbreviated after its first usage to its initial *italic* capital with a full stop, to save space.

Sometimes, the genus and species names will be followed by a third name. This is either a varietal or a cultivar name, which further identifies the flower when two varieties have the same generic and specific names.

Varietal names are used when it is necessary to distinguish some small natural point of difference — a flower colour or leaf marking, or a particular habit of growth that reproduces constantly from seed. Varietal names are also printed in *italic* type.

Cultivar names fall in the same position when it is necessary to refer to some characteristic or sport of the shrub that seems capable of cultivation only by means of cuttings (raised from seed it might revert to the original). Cultivar names are usually in a modern language instead of Latin or Greek. They are printed in roman type and enclosed in quotes. Sometimes they are further identified by the abbreviation CV.

Another word you'll run across is *hybrid* or *hybrida*. This is used when each of a plant's parents is of a different species. Hybrids are often raised by nurseries to produce superior new strains just as breeders of horses and cattle try to improve their stock. A hybrid is often indicated by X between the generic and specific names.

When the X appears before the generic name, the plant is a bigeneric hybrid or cross between two different genera. These are quite rare.

Two abbreviations are sometimes confusing: *spp.*, which is short for more than one species, and *ssp.*, which is short for *subspecies*.

Individual generic entries give all sorts of additional information for the home gardener: e.g., the plant's spread and speed of growth; its flowering time, country of origin, methods of propagation, soil requirements, minimum necessary winter temperature, ideal position or light intensity, natural pests and diseases, uses in medicine, commerce or history and many other things.

Under every photograph is a brief caption giving the illustrated shrub's botanical name, one or more of its popular names, and its country of origin.

Later in the book you'll find a useful glossary of botanical terms, and an illustrated listing of genera included in the most popular botanical families — yet another useful way of deciding just where a particular plant belongs by its family relationships.

Nothing, we hope, has been overlooked that would help you identify (at least partially) any shrub you are likely to run across.

And you'll never be stuck for an answer when somebody asks, *What Shrub is That?*

Clerodendrum nutans

Clerodendrum ugandense

Clerodendrum paniculatum

Pictures tell the story best: the three exotic shrubs above share the generic name *Clerodendrum* — but have individual specific names to describe their differing habits and origins.

Clerodendrum nutans bears its flowers in a nodding, or drooping head.

Clerodendrum ugandense is a very tropical species from Uganda and is often called Blue Butterfly Bush for obvious reasons.

Clerodendrum paniculatum bears its scarlet flowers in an upright pyramid or panicle; it is sometimes called the Pagoda Flower.

KEY TO THE PHONETIC PRONUNCIATION

Each flower entry in this book is headed by that flower's generic name, followed immediately by a simple phonetic guide to its pronunciation. There are still many differences of opinion as to how these botanical names should be pronounced, but the phonetic guide below should help set you on the right track. The spelling will often differ from the normal spelling of the generic name, because English vowels, and some consonants, can be pronounced in many different ways. (Look at the vowel 'a' in f*a*t, f*a*te, f*a*ther and f*a*re or the consonant 'c' in *c*at and a*c*e.) In a phonetic guide each letter or group of letters represents one sound only. But because there are more sounds in English than there are letters in the English alphabet or its recognized diphthongs, we also use one extra symbol (ə) to represent the many indeterminate vowel sounds heard in words like *a*lone, syst*e*m, terr*i*ble, gall*o*p and circ*u*s.

Beyond that, we have separated each syllable from the next by a hyphen, and printed the syllable to be stressed in **bold** type.

Each separate letter or letter combination is always pronounced according to the following:

a	f*a*t
ae	p*ay*, f*a*te, sl*eigh*
ah	m*ar*k, f*a*ther
ai	*i*ce, h*i*gh, b*uy*, c*y*cle
ə	*a*lone, syst*e*m, terr*i*ble, gall*o*p, circ*u*s
e	d*ea*f, d*e*n
ee	t*ea*ch, s*ee*
eə	*air*, d*are*d
i	f*i*t, t*i*ff, g*y*m
o	s*o*t, t*o*ss
oh	*oa*th, b*o*th, cr*ow*
oi	b*oy*, r*oy*al
oo	pr*o*ve, p*oo*l, gl*ue*
or	*ough*t, m*ore*, r*oar*
ou	c*ow*, cr*ou*ch, sl*ough*
u	s*u*ck, s*o*n, r*ou*gh
ur	*err*, c*ir*cus
b	*b*at, ta*b*
ch	*ch*ip, pa*tch*
d	*d*o, co*d*
f	ree*f*, rou*gh*, *ph*one
g	*g*as, ba*g*
h	*h*elp, a*h*oy
j	*j*aws, *g*em, ra*ge*

k	*c*at, sa*ck*
l	*l*imb, mi*ll*
m	*m*ore, rum*m*y
n	to*n*, *t*o*n*ight
p	*p*al, la*p*
r	*r*ot, t*r*ot
s	*s*ale, la*ce*
sh	*sh*ade, mo*ti*on
t	*t*one, no*t*e
th	*th*in, bo*th*, loa*the*
v	*v*at, ca*v*e
w	*w*in, t*w*in
y	*y*ellow
z	*z*ip, toe*s*, ro*se*
zh	mea*s*ure, inva*si*on

Remember, the sound of each phonetic letter or letter-group remains constant. As examples, here are five consecutive generic names and their phonetic pronunciations.

Adenandra (ad-en-**an**-drə)
Adenanthos (ad-en-**an**-thos)
Adenium (ae-**den**-ee-əm)
Adenostoma (a-den-o-**stoh**-mə)
Adina (a-**dee**-nə)

PICTURE DICTIONARY A–Z

Abelia schumannii. Schumann's Abelia. China

from the prevailing winds. Popular species include Mexican *A. floribunda* with rounded leaves and tubular carmine blooms 2 in/5 cm long. Hybrid of several Chinese species, *A. X grandiflora* is most widely seen, with shining, deep green foliage and pink-flushed bells only one-third as long. The entire bush has a distinctly reddish tone at various times of the year—when there is new foliage, or when the pale flowers have fallen to leave the red bracts behind. Its variety *tricolor* (CV 'Francis Mason') has the green foliage brilliantly variegated with red and gold. *A. schumannii* (Schumann's Abelia) is from China. It has vivid red stems and larger flowers of a deeper mauve-pink tone than *A. X grandiflora*. It has a dense habit and trims to a neat hedge sprinkled with blossom. Indian *A. triflora*, the Himalayan Abelia, has slender, hairy, pointed leaves and clusters of rosy-budded blooms that

Abelia floribunda. Mexican Abelia. Mexico

Abelia

(a-**beel**-ee-ə)　☼ ☀ C T W
Abelia
Summer; 3–6 ft/1–2 m; arching; evergreen

CAPRIFOLIACEAE　　　FRAGRANT

Less fragrant than the honeysuckles, but still closely related to them, *Abelias* are one of the most widely cultivated genera of shrubs in all temperate climates. Native to Japan, the Himalayan areas of China and India, and with a species or two found in Mexico, they are happy in a wide range of temperatures, although often turning deciduous in cold or frosty climates. They are at their best when they have plenty of room to adopt a graceful, arching habit and produce panicles of fragrant bell flowers at the tip of arching canes. All species may be planted out in autumn or early spring in any leaf-rich soil. Give them plenty of sun and a generous hand with the water and they'll reward throughout the warmer months with seemingly endless masses of bloom, finally being decorated in autumn with a sprinkling of deep red bracts. In really cold areas, they'll need the shelter of a wall or larger bushes to protect them

Abeliophyllum

(a-**beel**-ee-oh-fil-əm) ☼ ☀ C T
White Forsythia
Early spring; 3 ft/90 cm; wide; deciduous

OLEACEAE   FRAGRANT

With leaves like an Abelia, flowers like a Forsythia, yet a member of the olive family, the gentle *Abeliophyllum distichum* sounds like it has something for everybody! And indeed it should be grown more often in the cool temperate climate range which it loves. Best multiplied by layering in early spring, this Korean beauty can also be propagated from 4 in/10 cm cuttings, taken in midsummer and struck in a sand/peat mixture. A sparsely branched, deciduous shrub, *Abeliophyllum* rarely passes 3 ft/90 cm in height but is inclined to sprawl more widely. Like the look-alike Forsythia, it blooms very early in spring on bare wood, opening its ½ in/1 cm white flowers in small, fragrant clusters at branch tips. Twigs of unopened buds may be cut for decoration and will open indoors. Autumn is the best planting time (the earlier the better) but very early spring is also good. Soil should be acid, fast-draining and rich in leaf mould. Light cutting for decoration is sufficient pruning.

Abelia triflora. Deciduous Abelia. Himalayas

open 5 pure white lobes each at the tips of short twigs. This is the most fragrant variety.

Propagate all species from summer cuttings, struck at a temperature of about 61°F/16°C. Thin out the canes from time to time, taking one in three right back to the ground. In addition, trim lightly all over during winter.

The ease of trimming, and the fine growth that follows will rightly suggest that *Abelias* make most decorative hedges.

Abelia CV 'Francis Mason'. Variegated Abelia

Abeliophyllum distichum. White Forsythia. Korea

Pamela Harper

Abutilon

(a-**byew**-til-on)   ☼ ☀ T W H
Flowering Maple,
Chinese Lantern,
Chinese Bellflower
Spr-Aut; 8 ft/2.5 m; leggy; evergreen

MALVACEAE

Grown as much for the beauty of their exquisitely marked, maple-like leaves as for their colourful, lantern-shaped flowers, *Abutilons* are for the most part untidy, leggy shrubs, needing constant care to look at their best. In the northern hemisphere they are raised more often than not in a glasshouse or conservatory as they are not frost hardy, but sometimes they're used outdoors during summer in hanging baskets or window boxes. In the southern United States, Australia, South Africa and other subtropical zones, *Abutilons* can be spectacular, open garden plants, particularly when trained up columns or against sunny walls, so the beauty of their hanging flowers and fascinating foliage can be enjoyed all through the warm weather. While they like a position in full sun, they also enjoy a rich, moist soil, so compromise is often necessary. Heavy feeding makes them bolt to leaf, so they are best given only enough fertilizer to replace nutrients leached out of the soil by heavy summer watering. Flower yield can be improved by regular pinching back to ensure branching, and thus, more

Abutilon X 'Cannington Peter'.
Variegated Abutilon. Hybrid

Abutilon megapotamicum variegatum. Trailing Abutilon. S. Brazil

buds. Most widely grown are the many colourful cultivars grouped as *Abutilon* X *hybridum*. These include white 'Boule de Neige', rose pink 'Delicatum', red 'Emperor', pale yellow 'Golden Fleece' and orange-red 'Brilliant'. All have variably toned, heart-shaped leaves with a furry texture, while the flowers are borne at the leaf axils. *Abutilon* can be raised from seed sown any time at a temperature of 75°F/24°C. These will germinate in three weeks or less and should flower within 12 months. Named varieties may come true only from cuttings. These are normally taken from firm, new tips late in the

Abutilon X 'Brilliant'. Hybrid Bellflower

season and struck with heat in a sand/peat mixture.

Some hundred natural species are also grown, including the sprawling Big River Abutilon, A. *megapotamicum* from Brazil. In its variegated form, this may be used as a dense groundcover or trained as a wall shrub. Sometimes it even decides to climb by itself and is by far the hardiest of the genus. Its narrowly ovate leaves are lightly toothed and variegated with yellow blotches. The pendent, tubular flowers rather resemble Fuchsias, but in red and yellow. Its hybrid, A. X *milleri*, has larger leaves and more open, red-veined blooms. A. *pictum* has deeply lobed, maple-like leaves of a smoother texture with orange flowers veined in red. Its variegated form 'Souvenir de Bonn' is quite spectacular. In cold climates, *Abutilons* are often raised as indoor plants, blooming best when rootbound. The mauve flowered A. *vitifolium* and its hybrids have been reclassified and will be found in this book under Corynabutilon.

Abutilon X 'Orange King'. Chinese Lantern. Hybrid

Abutilon X 'Boule de Neige'. Snowball Abutilon. Hybrid

Acacia

(a-**kae**-shə) ☼ ☀ T W H
Mimosa, Wattle, Myall
Varied; 1½–12 ft/50 cm–4 m; evergreen
FABACEAE

Mostly short-lived plants of a rather scrawny appearance, the *Acacias* or wattles are completely transformed into a softly glowing, golden mass when their flowering season comes around, which may be any time at all, dependent on variety. The vast majority of more than 1000 species are trees, but there is also a respectable number of shrubby, sprawling types native to Africa, North America and most of all to Australia, which is home to seven out of ten wattle species. The illustrated shrub types vary in height from 1½ ft/ 50 cm (species A. *acinacea* and A. *drummondii*) through 3 ft/1 m (A. *suaveolens*) to 12 ft/4 m for the others. The silver-spined Karroo Thorn (A. *karroo*) is South African, the others Australian. All are very adaptable as to soil but really prefer a position that is well-drained to arid.

Acacia boormannii. Snowy River Wattle. Victoria, N.S.W.

Acacia karroo. Karroo Thorn. South Africa

Acacia drummondii. Drummond Acacia. Western Australia

Acacia acinacea. Gold-dust Acacia. E. Australia

Their flowering time varies from winter (*A. drummondii* and *A. boormannii*) through summer (*A. karroo*) to autumn (*A. suaveolens*).

Alas, the flowering glory of the *Acacia* is all too brief. If rain doesn't make a sodden mess of the golden puffballs, wind will blow them away to be succeeded by a mass of dry, rattling pea pods if the bees have done their work.

Yes, these remarkable plants are members of the legume family, Mimosaceae, though very untypical members it is true. They have no pea flowers, no petals at all, just a dense mass of stamens which may be arranged in the form of puffballs, bottlebrushes or even pipe cleaners. All wattles love full sun, but *A. drummondii* seems to prefer midday shade, perhaps because of its dark, pinnate leaves from which moisture can readily evaporate. Most other wattles have no leaves at all, only phyllodes which are either needle-like or flattened stalks resembling leaves. All species need light watering during dry seasons and a very light pruning after bloom. Propagation is relatively easy from seed, cuttings or, in the case of *A. boormannii*, from the suckers which often appear around the main trunk.

Acacia suaveolens. Sweet Wattle. E. Australia, Tasmania

Acalypha reptans. Summer Love. Subtropics

Acalypha wilkesiana 'Java White' Jacob's Coat. Pacific Islands

Acalypha

(a-**kal**-i-fə)   ☼ Ⓦ Ⓗ

Jacob's Coat, Beefsteak Plant,
Fijian Firebush, Match-me-if-you-can,
Red Hot Cat's Tail
*Summer; to 10 ft/3 m but less wide;
evergreen*

EUPHORBIACEAE

'Match-me-if-you-can.' What a stunning name for this remarkable group of hot-climate plants from the Malaysian archipelago and various western Pacific islands. For indeed you would find it difficult to match leaves from any two plants as they are quite variable in shape and size. In cold-winter areas you'll need to avoid frost by moving them into a glasshouse where you can strike cuttings, taken with a heel. Set them outdoors again when the weather warms up. They enjoy a rich, leafy compost and need endless supplies of water.

Acalypha wilkesiana has almost as many cultivars as it has leaf patterns. 'Java White' is a green/white bicolour, 'Tricolor' includes pink, 'Macrophylla' has larger leaves in various shades of red. Closely related A. *hispida* (known variously as Red Hot Cat's Tail, Chenille Plant or Philip-

Acalypha wilkesiana 'Macrophylla'. Match-me-if-you-can. Pacific Islands

Acalypha hispida. Red Hot Cat's Tail. Malaysia

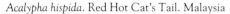

Acalypha pringlei. Three-seeded Mercury. Baja California

Acer

(ae-sər)   ☀ C T
Cutleaf, Japanese Maple
Spr-Aut; 4 ft/120 cm; spreading; deciduous

ACERACEAE

pine Medusa) is a generally upright plant with plain green foliage and strongly weeping effect in summer as the chenille-like clusters of tiny red flowers spill towards the ground. All tropical *Acalyphas* grow fast during the warm weather, often need pruning back several times a season and very hard in late winter. The dense foliage has a slightly furry effect.

A leaf of a different colour (and size) is found on *A. pringlei*, the Three-seeded Mercury, a native of Baja California. This is an interesting plant for arid areas with small, ovate furry leaves of a reddish hue and short racemes or catkins. It is normally propagated from seed and likes gravelly soil. A recent introduction to the house-plant market is *A. reptans*. This shrubby groundcover, promoted under the name of 'Summer Love', makes a spectacular hanging basket.

Though maples are among our most spectacular cool-climate trees (over 200 species of them) the ingenious gardeners of Japan have raised decorative shrubby varieties since time immemorial. These are mostly cultivars of the Full-moon Maple (*Acer japonicum*) with seven or more leaf lobes and the famous cut-leafed cultivars of the Japanese Mountain Maple, *A. palmatum dissectum*. These have leaves like lace and rarely pass 4 ft/120 cm in height. Most of these dwarf, shrubby maples are among the most expensive plants you can buy for they can only be propagated by grafting and are remarkably slow to achieve any size, though they tend to spread horizontally rather than vertically. Several months' salary is cheap for a mature specimen!

These dwarf maples need mountain growing conditions: a deep, leafy

Acer palmatum dissectum. Cut-leaf Maple. Japan

Acokanthera oblongifolia. Wintersweet.
S.E. South Africa

Acokanthera oblongifolia. Bushman's Poison.
S.E. South Africa

compost with free drainage; protection from full sun as the fine leaves burn very badly. As they mostly colour magnificently in the autumn, they are best planted where some sunlight shines through the fine foliage and since this is nearer eye-level, it behoves us to discover their many other fascinating features, such as tiny red flowers on drooping stems and the winged seeds which can glide for miles.

Acokanthera

(ak-o-**kan**-thur-ə)　☼ W H
Wintersweet, Bushman's Poison
*All year; 10 ft/3 m; dense; spreading;
evergreen*

APOCYNACEAE　　　FRAGRANT

Like so many members of the Dogbane family, Apocynaceae, including Alstonia, Carissa, Cerbera, Mandevilla, Nerium, Plumeria, Thevetia and many others illustrated in this book, the South African *Acokanthera* or Wintersweet can have a most disagreeable effect on those foolish enough to eat any part of it. South African Bushmen, in fact, used a concentration from its plum-like fruit in which to dip the tips of their arrows.

Acokanthera is found from Arabia right down through the East African coast to Natal. It grows happily in poor soil, by the sea or in other exposed positions. There it grows in full sun up to 10 ft/3 m and can be trimmed as a dense hedge. Summer water will help it produce an all-year show of fragrant, pale pink flowers, set off to perfection against reddish-purple foliage. The plum-sized fruits appear in the colder months and *Acokanthera* is hardy down to 28°F/ −2°C. Propagate from seeds, cuttings or by grafting.

Actinidia

(Ak-tə-**nid**-ee-ə)　☼ ◐ T W
Kolomikta
*Summer; 14–20 ft/4–6 m; climbing;
deciduous*

ACTINIDIACEAE　　　FRAGRANT

Bees should find no trouble at all in navigating towards the mildly fragrant, white flowers of the remarkable climbing or leaning shrub *Actinidia*

Actinidia kolomikta. Kolomikta.
Temperate East Asia

Actinodium

(ak-tin-**oh**-dee-əm)   ☼ T W
Swamp Daisy, Albany Daisy
Win-Spr; 3 ft/1 m; spreading; evergreen
MYRTACEAE

Short-lived *Actinodium cunninghamii* and closely related species are a challenge for Australian native plant fans who can give them the damp, acid, coastal soil they enjoy, but plantsmen elsewhere can grow them in containers in a sharp sand/peat mixture. Good drainage is essential but extra water round the roots is appreciated during the winter flowering cycle.

Rather sparse, brittle plants, the *Actinodiums* have tiny, aromatic, stem-clasping leaves and are raised from cuttings. Ho-hum, you'll say, just another daisy; but in fact the inflorescence only looks that way—it is a fully fledged member of the myrtle family which includes Australia's many Eucalypts. Prune lightly to shape after bloom.

Adenandra

(ad-en-**an**-drə)   ☼ ☀ W H
Enamel Flower, China Flower
Spring; 1½ ft/50 cm; spreading; evergreen
RUTACEAE   FRAGRANT

South African equivalent to Australia's Boronias and belonging to the

kolomikta, for leaves in the vicinity of the blooms only are variegated with brilliant white or pink to show the way. Humans who follow the bees' example later may be surprised to find small fruits resembling the Yang Tao or Chinese Gooseberry but the Kolomikta is first cousin to that fruit which is known botanically as *A. chinensis* and commercially as kiwi fruit.

The Kolomikta loves a deep, rich soil, permanent moisture and, of course, a stout wall or pergola to lean on. It can be propagated from spring-sown seed or cuttings of half-ripened wood in summer and should be fertilized regularly. Kolomikta likes a cool temperate or maritime climate to colour well and even then you'll need both a male and female plant to turn on a reliable display.

Actinodium cunninghamii. Albany Daisy.
Western Australia

Adenandra uniflora. Enamel Flower.
South Africa

same family, the 30-odd species of *Adenandra* are ubiquitous among the Cape's winter and early spring flowers. Raised from autumn cuttings, the *Adenandras* are slow growers and you can expect a long wait for the shiny 1 in/2.5 cm flowers with an enamel-like finish.

Flowers of *A. uniflora* are snowy white, occasionally with a pink streak in the centre of each petal. Larger growing *A. fragrans* blooms in pink and there are also red varieties. New stems of *Adenandras* are lightly hairy, the tiny, dark leaves are paler on the reverse and distinctly aromatic. Mountain plants, most species demand really good drainage and are hardy down to 23°F/−5°C. Light watering is adequate.

is claimed to attract nectar-feeding birds. Few are in cultivation, except in the gardens of specialists. The principal exception is the Jugflower, *A. obovata*, so named because its small leaves are widest towards the tips.

A. obovata is exceptional in another way too, for whereas all the other species enjoy well-drained, gravelly soil, the Jugflower likes moist, even boggy conditions and a light dose of slow release fertilizer in autumn. Propagation is relatively easy from either seed or summer cuttings. Prune with a light hand any time after bloom. *Adenanthos* prefers dappled shade, especially around midday, and is suited to all areas with mild winters.

Adenium obesum. Desert Rose.
E. Africa—S. Arabia

Adenium

(ae-**den**-ee-əm)   ☼ ☀ W H
Desert Rose, Desert Azalea,
Impala Lily, Sabie Star
*Win-Spr; 3–10 ft/1–3 m; sparse;
deciduous*

APOCYNACEAE

A small group of gorgeously flowering succulents, the handful of *Adenium* species are named for the former British colony of Aden, where they were first discovered, though Arabia is only the northern limit of their territory, which stretches right down to southern Africa. All *Adeniums* resemble stunted, grotesquely

dwarfed Plumerias, to which they are closely related. They are quite intolerant of frost, bloom from midwinter on and are thoroughly drought resistant. Propagate them from dried-off branches struck in damp sand, but they'll never adopt the swollen trunk habit of natural seedlings. Leaves are glossy, oval and widest at the tip. Though desert plants, you'll see them in the gardens of many tropical resort hotels, for they like a dry winter.

Adenanthos obovata. Jugflower.
Western Australia

Adenanthos

(ad-en-**an**-thos)   ☼ ☀ C T W
Jugflower, Woollybush
Aut-Sum; 3 ft/1 m; spreading; evergreen

PROTEACEAE

Some 30 species of *Adenanthos* have been described, almost all of them in the far south-west corner of Western Australia and almost all of them with flowers in some shade of red, which

Adenium obesum laetanum. Impala Lily. E. Africa—S. Arabia

Adenostoma

(a-den-**o**-stoh-mə) ☼ T W
Ribbonwood, Greasewood,
Redshanks, Chamise
Spring; 2–12 ft/60 cm–4 m; upright;
evergreen

ROSACEAE

Rather unlikely members of the rose family, the two species of *Adenostoma* (A. *fasciculatum* and A. *sparsifolia*) are natives of the dry hill country of southern California and northern Mexico and indispensable in the dry hillside garden with gravelly soil. Both species have red, shreddy bark on their sparse branches and aromatic, flammable, needle-like foliage that gives them something of the appearance of a conifer. But in spring, small, pinhead-sized, white flowers appear in terminal panicles, giving the game away. Overall, however, their brilliant green colouration makes them very attractive in their dry, desert milieu. Propagation is by seed or from cuttings taken in spring. Soil must be fast-draining and winter rain is welcome.

Adenostoma fasciculatum. Chamise, Greasewood. California

Adina pilulifera. Chinese Buttonbush. S. China

Adina

(a-**dee**-nə) ☼ ☀ C T W H
Chinese Buttonbush
Summer; 10 ft/3 m; evergreen

RUBIACEAE

Related to such subtropical favourites as Bouvardia, Gardenia and Luculia, southern China's Chinese Buttonbush (*Adina pilulifera*) deserves to be more popular in our subtropical gardens. A slender evergreen shrub that enjoys deep, rich soil, it has particularly dense wood in trunk and branches that was used by the Chinese in carving small items, including buttons. Presumably this apparently useless piece of information shows us how the shrub got its name!

Adina should be kept moist at all times and can be hard pruned for shaping after the summer blooming season, at which time cuttings may be struck. The flowers are an interesting globular shape with projecting stamens—something like a pincushion.

Aeonium canariense. Velvet Rose, Pinwheel. Canary Islands

Aeonium

(*syn.* AICHRYSON, SEMPERVIVUM)

(ae-**oh**-nee-əm) ☼ T W
Canary Island Rose, Pinwheel
Win-Spr; 1½–5 ft/50 cm–1.5 m;
spreading; evergreen

CRASSULACEAE

Startlingly architectural in their appearance, the several species of

Aeonium arboreum. Canary Island Rose. Morocco

Aeschynanthus
(syn. TRICHOSPORUM)

(ees-kin-**an**-thus)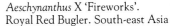
Royal Red Bugler, Lipstick Plant
Summer; 2 ft/60 cm; weeping; evergreen

GESNERIACEAE

Just why these gorgeous tropical plants are classified as shrubs I am not quite sure, though they have woodier stems than other Gesneriads. Yes, *Aeschynanthus* are closely related to the African Violets, and flower in midsummer. They have waxy leaves, and tend to arch their stems with the weight of flowers. From South-east Asia, they are generally grown in baskets of moist, acid compost and hung in a warm, humid position in semi-shade. They need plenty of water in the warm-weather growing season. The flowers look like an orange-scarlet lipstick poking out of a dark green holder. Propagate in spring or late autumn from hardened stem-tip cuttings. Illustrated variety is A. X 'Fireworks' whilst others include A. *lobbianus* with glossy light green foliage, yellow-lined red flowers; A. *marmoratus*, the Zebra Basket Vine, with handsome dark leaves veined with yellow and backed with purple, and has brown-spotted green flowers.

Aeschynanthus X 'Fireworks'.
Royal Red Bugler. South-east Asia

Aeonium are succulent shrubs from North Africa and various nearby Atlantic islands. They grow beautifully in coastal areas of California and Tasmania, provided the soil is poor, sandy and includes a ration of limestone chips. They are, unfortunately, frost tender (50°F/10°C winter minimum), but can stand up to the full fury of coastal salt spray. Propagate them from brittle cuttings (they just snap off) set into damp sand in spring or early summer. They will soon develop formal rosettes of waxy, green, simple leaves, sometimes tinged red. The early spring flower display consists of a many-branched pyramid of tiny blooms—chrome yellow in the case of A. *arboreum*, whitish-green in A. *canariense*. As these plants are xerophytic, light watering is advisable to develop the flower spikes.

Agapetes
(syn. PENTAPTERYGIUM, THIBAUDIA)

(ag-ə-**pee**-tees)　☀✺ T W H
Flame Heath
Early spring on; 5 ft/1.75 m; arching;
evergreen

ERICACEAE

Beloved by gardeners and beloved by name (Agapetes *means* beloved) this curious family of shrubs is native to many parts of the Himalayas and enjoys a curious mixture of montane and tropical climatic features. Of the few species in cultivation, only the Flame Heath, *Agapetes serpens*, is widely seen. It is a rather squat plant, semi-epiphytic and sending out slender, arching branches from a tuberous rootstock. These are furnished with evergreen leaves, red-tinged on the upper side only, which are joined from late winter on with bright red, tubular flowers hanging in loose pairs. These unusual plants are propagated from tip cuttings struck in a sand/peat mixture during summer.

Leafy, acid soil is ideal with perfect drainage and regular water. They love high humidity and semi-shade. The 'Ludgsten's Cross' hybrid has dull pink flowers with horizontal red stripes.

Agathosma
(syn. BAROSMA)

(ag-ath-**os**-mə)　☀ T W
Buchu
Spring; 2–5½ ft/60–175 cm; spreading;
evergreen

RUTACEAE　　　　　FRAGRANT

With South Africa's *Agathosmas*, it's a case of not being able to see the leaves for the flowers, so profusely do they appear in the spring months. Small, spreading shrubs that grow well in a dryish but peaty compost, they are suitable for outdoor or rock garden use in temperate climates or under glass where winters are cold. The name *Agathosma* is a compound of the Greek *agathos* (pleasant) and *osma* (smell), which may be in reference to the odour of the tiny flowers, but more certainly applies to the aromatic foliage which is fragrant all year and has caused the plants to be grown commercially for medical use.

These small, densely foliaged plants can be struck from soft-tip cuttings which may be taken when they are sheared after bloom has faded. Many species of *Agathosma* are known (over 100) but few are called on to do garden service. *A. villosa* is probably the most spectacular. Most others are white or pale lilac.

Agathosma villosa. Buchu. South Africa

Aglaia

(ag-**lae**-ə)　☀✺ W H
Mei-sui-lan, Chinese Riceflower,
Mock Lime, Chulan
Spr-Aut; 8–10 ft/2.3–3 m; dense;
evergreen

MELIACEAE　　　　　FRAGRANT

Appropriately named for *Aglaia*, one of the Graces in Greek mythology, this charming plant has never enjoyed popularity in the West to the same degree as in its native China. There it is much sought after to scent tea, perfume clothes and decorate the house. Easily grown from soft-tip cuttings struck in a sharp mixture, it enjoys a rich, well-drained compost and should be kept moist all year. Not a spectacular plant, it does well in a mixed shrubbery where it can get full sun for at least part of the day. It has a densely branched habit, shiny pinnate evergreen foliage and small, individually insignificant yellow flowers which appear in showy panicles from spring to autumn. The perfume is almost overpowering in this charming shrub for subtropical gardens.

Agapetes serpens. Flame Heath. Himalayas

Allamanda neriifolia. Bush Allamanda. South America

Aglaia odorata. Mei-sui-lan, Mock Lime. China

8 cm tip cuttings taken in spring, it grows into a compact bush in well-drained soil. Light watering is sufficient in colder weather, but step it up through the warmer months and alternate with liquid manure to produce dazzling clusters of medium trumpet flowers. All *Allamandas* may drop a few leaves in cooler areas, where they can be used as greenhouse specimens. A minimum winter temperature of 50°F/10°C is said to be advisable, but I've found *A. neriifolia* can cope with less. Prune heavily in spring to improve shape.

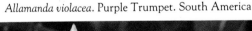

Allamanda violacea. Purple Trumpet. South America

Allamanda

(al-la-**man**-də) ☼ ☀ W H
Golden Trumpet, Bush Allamanda
Summer; 6½ ft/2 m; spreading

APOCYNACEAE

Showy South Americans that lie around in the sun most of the time, *Allamandas* sprawl untidily, are used in the tropics for informal fences. They might best be described as *leaning* shrubs. The most dazzling kinds are *A. cathartica* and its varieties *schottii* and *hendersonii*, all of which have large golden trumpet flowers. Another vining type, *A. violacea*, with pinkish mauve flowers, is commonly grafted onto rooted cuttings of *A. cathartica*. One species, *A. neriifolia*, is content to remain as a true shrub and can make a spectacular specimen in sunny gardens of temperate climates, especially in its variegated form. Propagated from 3 in/

Allamanda cathartica. Golden Trumpet. South America

Alonsoa

(a-lon-**soh**-ə)   ☼ ☀ T W
Maskflower
Summer; 1–2½ ft/30–75 cm; sparse;
evergreen

SCROPHULARIACEAE

Only considered half hardy, in spite of their mountain origins in various parts of South America, the seven species of *Alonsoa* are most variable plants—sometimes classed as shrubby perennials, sometimes as proper shrubs, their habit apparently varying according to the climate in which they are grown. They may be raised from seeds sown under glass in cold winters, or from soft-tip cuttings taken a little later and set out in spring. Any ordinary garden soil seems to suit, provided it is a little on the sandy side and well drained. The plants certainly have a family resemblance to the Antirrhinums and Nemesias to which they are related. Flowers of all seven species are the same Chinese lacquer red, and the corolla of each flower falls after a day or so.

Alöe speciosa. Aloe. South Africa

Alonsoa warscewiczii. Maskflower. Peru

Alöe

(a-**loh**-ae)   ☼ T W
Aloe, Aalwyn
Spr-Sum; 2–10 ft/60 cm–3 m; branched,
upright

XANTHORRHOEACEAE

South Africa's *Alöes* include more than 200 species varying wildly in size from 2 ft/60 cm in height up to 60 ft/20 m in the tree species *Alöe bainesii.* Almost all have thick, succulent, spiky leaves attractively blotched, banded or spotted with grey. When not in bloom, they are often mistaken for the American Agaves, but they belong to a different botanical family and are all native to Africa. Both genera have toothed leaf margins, but unlike Agaves, *Alöes* bloom every year and do not die back after flowering. *Alöes* produce tall candelabra spikes of tubular flowers in scarlet, pink, orange and yellow. They tolerate drought and salt sea air, but are affected by mealy bug, which are best destroyed by regular application of a recommended insecticide.

Aloysia citriodora. Lemon-scented Verbena. Chile, Argentina, Uruguay

moist and plant it where you can pick and crush those beautiful leaves. The panicles of minute purple flowers are, frankly, nothing to remark on.

Alstonia

(al-**stoh**-nee-ə)   ☼ W H
Bitter Bark
Summer; 7 ft/2 m; spreading; evergreen

APOCYNACEAE   FRAGRANT

Another lovely but semi-poisonous shrub in the Dogbane family (Apocynaceae), *Alstonia* shares both its beauty and its bad habits with Acokanthera, Frangipani, Oleander, Rauwolfia, Thevetia and many other semi-tropical plants with white, sticky sap. A fast grower in the warm to tropical climates which it loves, *Alstonia* strikes easily from cuttings rooted in sand, then set out in a compost of peat, loam and sand. The 8 in/20 cm leaves are shiny, with rippled edges, and turn yellow with age, finally dropping to leave the base of the trunk and branches bare, though the plant is supposed to be evergreen. The 5-petalled flowers are very fragrant and borne in terminal clusters. They are smaller than those of most of the other plants in the family. Keep it moist at all times.

Alstonia venenata. Bitter Bark. India

Aloysia

(*syn.* LIPPIA, VERBENA)

(a-**loy**-see-ə)   ☼ C T W
Lemon-scented Verbena,
Lemon Plant
Summer; 3–8 ft/1–2.5 m; dense; semi-deciduous

VERBENACEAE   FRAGRANT

If the Lemon-scented Verbena were only a *little* more attractive, it would be among the most widely grown shrubs in our gardens. As it is, it inclines every whichway, and no amount of regular pruning seems to straighten it out or make it neat. But just pick a leaf, crush it between your fingers and who cares how it looks! The dramatic lemon fragrance is overpowering and makes it an essential ingredient of potpourri and cool drinks for lazy summer days. *Aloysia* was named either for Maria Aloysia, a queen of Spain, or for Maria Louisa, Napoleon's widow. The first seems more likely. It prefers sandy soil and is easy to strike from soft-tip cuttings, taken in spring. Keep it

Alyogyne huegelii. Blue Hibiscus. Southern and Western Australia

Alyogyne

(*syn.* HIBISCUS)

(al-ee-**oj**-ə-nee)   ☼ T W H
Sand Hibiscus, Blue Hibiscus
Spr-Sum; 3–10 ft/1–3 m; spreading; evergreen

MALVACEAE

Split off some years ago from the genus Hibiscus, the handful of *Alyogyne* species are now perhaps more widely grown than any of the true Australian Hibiscus species. They are easily propagated from cuttings or seed (which stays viable for years), and need only a warm dry climate and protection from wind to give of their best. Humidity is anathema; normal rainfall will usually take care of their water needs. *Alyogynes* have all the usual lookalike features of the Malvaceae, so why are they no longer Hibiscus? The reason is a simple difference in the style or female organ, which is undivided in these desert plants. Best known *A. huegelii* is called the Blue Hibiscus for obvious reasons. It has furry, divided

Alyogyne cuneiforme. Sand Hibiscus.
Western Australia

Alyogyne hakeifolia. Red-centred Hibiscus.
Southern and Western Australia

Alyxia

(a-**lik**-see-ə)   ☼ W H
Native Holly, Moonya
*Spr-Sum; 3–10 ft/1–3 m; spreading;
evergreen*

APOCYNACEAE   FRAGRANT

Though known principally from their native Australian species, the *Alyxias* are in fact quite a numerous genus. Some 50 species have been found from Madagascar to Fiji and well up into South-east Asia. They are members of the Dogbane family, Apocynaceae, widely represented in the tropics.

Alyxia was a native name for one of the Indian species and has been adopted for the whole genus. Grown from seed or slow-to-strike cuttings, A. ruscifolia has the sharply tipped,

Alyxia ruscifolia. Native Holly.
Queensland, N.S.W.

Amelanchier ovalis. Snowy Mespilus.
Central and Southern Europe

Amelanchier

(am-el-**an**-chee-ər)   ☼ ☀ C T
Shadblow, Shad Bush, Sugarplum
*Spr-Aut; 3–25 ft/1–8 m; spreading;
deciduous*

ROSACEAE

Dainty, fruiting members of the rose family, like the plums and apples, *Amelanchiers* (there are some 25 species) are found almost exclusively in the North American continent, with rare outliers in Asia and

Amelanchier X *grandiflora.* Hybrid
Shadblow. Hybrid

leaves. *A. cuneiforme* has red-centred white flowers with somewhat wedge-shaped leaves. Less common *A. hakeifolia* with needle-like leaves is described by many authorities as having mauve flowers, but as our picture reveals, they were yellow, at least on this bush. All *Alyogynes* are from Western Australia, where the naturally dry climate has developed them to be suited to South Africa and California.

glossy leaves of the Ruscus plant for which it was named (see Ruscus). It is widely found in rainforest areas of eastern Australia but is sufficiently hardy to flourish in all but the most frost-bitten gardens. It is slow to grow but makes a handsome specimen in gardens or containers. The tiny flowers, borne in terminal clusters, are scarcely ½ in/1 cm in diameter and are followed by glossy, holly-size berries.

Murray Fagg

Pamela Harper

Amelanchier americana. Eastern Shadblow. North America

Amomyrtus luma. Chilean Myrtle. Chile

Europe. They are mostly stoloniferous shrubs, that is to say, they spread from suckers, forming dense colonies which are most attractive when smothered in narrow-petalled, pale pink or white spring blossom. Flowers are followed by small, edible fruit and joined by relatively small broad leaves which turn on a great colour display in autumn. *Amelanchiers* are frost hardy and can be propagated from stratified seed, from suckers or by budding.

Amicia

(a-mee-**chee**-ə) ☼ ☀ T W H
(No popular name)
Autumn; 8 ft/2.5 m; spreading; deciduous

FABACEAE

Since they are the largest of all botanical groups, it seems amazing that we have gone so far into this book without striking a single, typical member of the pea family—typical, that is, in producing a recognizable pea flower with keel and standard. Anyway, here one is at last, and it grows on a most unusual shrub. The blooms of *Amicia zygomeris* are yellow

Amicia zygomeris. Amicia. Mexico

with an occasional splash of purple and they appear in groups of five or six among the deciduous leaves, which are composed of four heart-shaped leaflets.

A. zygomeris is a native of the Mexican mountains and only two other relatives are found, also in mountainous areas from Mexico to Bolivia. All grow from young spring cuttings and none is frost hardy.

Amomyrtus

(am-oh-**mur**-təs) ☀ C T
Chilean Myrtle
Spring; to 30 ft/9 m; dense; upright; evergreen

MYRTACEAE

Typical members of the family Myrtaceae, the two species of *Amomyrtus* were once included among the true myrtles until the discovery of a slight difference in the ovary structure, which is presumably of importance only to the plants themselves. Their small leaves are shiny and appear in opposite pairs—just like a true myrtle. The tiny creamy flowers appear in dense racemes from the leaf axils. New foliage is bronze when young and yes, the bark of both *Amomyrtus* species is smooth and of a particularly rich cinnamon colour. Propagation is from cuttings or ripened seed and plants enjoy a humid, coastal atmosphere with rich soil.

Amorpha fruticosa. Bastard Indigo.
North America

Amorpha

(am-**or**-fə)   ☼ ☀ⓒⓉⓦ
Bastard Indigo, False Indigo,
Indigo Bush
*Late Spr-Sum; 6–16 ft/2–5 m; dense;
deciduous*

FABACEAE

'Deformed by name and deformed by
nature' has been said of the Bastard
Indigo, *Amorpha fruticosa. Amorpha* is
the Greek adjective for deformed it is
true, but as to the plant itself, it
seems to me that it is more over-
crowding than deformation that is
the root of the trouble. The compound, pinnate leaves may bear up to
33 leaflets and the tiny, purplish pea
flowers are absolutely packed into
long, cylindrical spikes that spring
from the leaf axils.

The plants enjoy a light, well-
drained soil, yet should be kept
lightly moist. They are easy to propagate from seed, by layering, or from
autumn hardwood cuttings which
may take a year to strike. The plants
are particularly useful in damp, low-
lying areas or by pools so long as they
can get plenty of sun. They are from
North America and moderately frost
resistant.

Andersonia

(an-der-**soh**-nee-ə)   ☼ ☀ⓦ Ⓗ
Foxtails
*Winter; 3–6 ft/1–2 m; procumbent;
evergreen*

ERICACEAE

Named for William Anderson, a botanist on Cook's second and third
voyages, the 20-odd species of
Andersonia are all native to Western
Australia and were thus never seen in
life by their namesake. They belong
to the southern heath family, Epacridaceae, and share their love of sandy,
well-drained soil together with a
touch of moisture found around
natural rock shelves. None of the
species grows much more than 6 ft/
2 m in height. They are all inclined
to be dense, low-growing, spiky
plants with minute, stem-hugging
leaves so typical of the heaths. In *A.
coerulea*, the small blue flowers are
enclosed in pink sepals. Other species
have sepals varying from red to
greenish-white. Grow them from soft-
tip cuttings struck in sand and peat
and do try them in containers where
the atmosphere is not humid.

Andersonia coerulea. Foxtails.
Western Australia

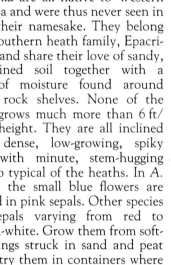

Murray Fagg

Andromeda polifolia. Bog Rosemary.
N. Europe, UK, North America

Andromeda

(an-**dro**-me-də)   ☼ ☀ⓒⓉ
Bog Rosemary
*Late spring; 12 in/30 cm; spreading;
evergreen*

ERICACEAE

A native of sub-arctic regions,
Andromeda polifolia grows naturally
in peat bogs and is suitable only for
cool-climate or mountain regions,
unlike the many related plants that
are often sold under the name
Andromeda. These have generally
been reclassified over the years as
Enkianthus, Leucothoë, Pieris and
Zenobia, to name just a few synonyms. But the name *Andromeda*
seems to have powers of survival, like
her mythical namesake, who, as you
may remember, survived the murder-
ous attentions of a sea monster. The
genus *Andromeda* now consists of the
plant in our illustration, and a pretty
little thing she is.

A. polifolia can be propagated from
seed, division or rooted runners. It is
perfect at the sheltered base of rock
gardens—that is, of course, assuming
you live in the right climate and have
the right soil—acid and slightly
boggy.

Angophora

(an-**gof**-or-ə) ☼ T W
Dwarf Apple Gum
Summer; 10–12 ft/3–4 m; evergreen

MYRTACEAE

The *Angophoras* or Apple Gums are a small Australian genus greatly resembling the Eucalypts, but with opposite leaves. Popular in other dry areas such as California and South Africa, they are native to the fast-draining sandstone of eastern Australia. They have elegant orange or pink bark which peels unevenly, and two types of leaf: pale green, heart-shaped juvenile foliage and long, drooping adult leaves up to 5 in/12 cm in length. The summer flowers, invariably cream, are very largely a mass of stamens, but unlike the Eucalypts, they also have some petals. The gumnut type fruits are ribbed.

Angophora hispida. Dwarf Apple Gum.

The only species of interest to this book is *A. hispida*, the Dwarf Apple Gum, which has a rugged, spreading appearance but rarely exceeds 12 ft/4 m in height.

Anthocercis

(an-thoh-**kur**-kis) ☼ ☀ W H
Sticky Rayflower
Spr-Sum; 6–10 ft/2–3 m; densely branched; evergreen

SOLANACEAE   FRAGRANT

Though it may not seem that way to you, most botanical names are chosen for their descriptive powers. Callistemon for instance, means 'beautiful stamens' which is a fine description when you think about it. But the experts must have been having a rough day when they decided to name this genus of 25 shrubs *Anthocercis* which means merely that the petals radiate from the flower. That would probably apply equally to half the flowers in this book!

Flowers of most species are white or whitish and though they largely come from Western Australia, most

Angophora hispida. Dwarf Apple Gum. Eastern Australian coast

Anthocercis viscosa. Sticky Rayflower. Western Australia

species do occur in other states in a variety of soil types including lime and coastal sand. *A. viscosa* grows quickly from cuttings of firm, new growth treated with a rooting hormone, and produces its fragrant 2½ in/6 cm blooms in late spring and early summer. Its leaves have a sticky feel about them.

Anthyllis

(an-**thil**-ləs) ☼ ☀ C T
Jupiter's Beard, Kidney Vetch
*Spring; 4 ft/1.25 m; heavily branched;
deciduous*

FABACEAE

Anthyllis is a widely distributed genus around the Mediterranean area—north Africa, southern Europe and the Middle East—but almost all of the species are pink or white flowering, and are classified as annuals or perennials. What makes this species different is the fact that it is a shrub and blooms in yellow.

It is a dainty, mounded plant with spiny stems that are well hidden most of the year under a dense covering of trifoliate leaves. These are joined in spring by a mass of golden pea flowers which have caused the plant to become a popular rock-garden subject in cool-temperate climates. You'll grow it mainly from seed or cuttings.

Anthyllis hermanniae. Jupiter's Beard.
Corsica

Aotus

(ae-**oh**-təs) ☼ ☀ T H
Golden Pea, Bacon and Eggs
*Spring; 1½–3 ft/50 cm–1 m; spreading
from base; evergreen*

FABACEAE

Low growing members of the pea/bean family, found in all states, the 15 or so species of *Aotus* are a spring

Aotus ericoides. Common Aotus.
S.E. Australia.

feature of Australian bushland as their showy pea flowers appear in long, ground-hugging spikes. These are normally a dazzling yellow, but combined in some species with purple, red or orange. *A. ericoides* (with leaves like a heath) is the most widespread of the clan—easily grown from seed or soft-tip cuttings. Grow in any moist, sandy loam or even in low-lying, boggy areas. *Aotus*, with several similar pea genera, are often known collectively as Bacon and Eggs.

Aphanopetalum

(a-fan-oh-**pet**-ə-ləm) ☼ ☀ W H
Bush Clematis
Spring; to 7 ft/2 m; spreading; evergreen

APHANOPETALACEAE

A native of the Australian rainforests, *Aphanopetalum resinosum* is perhaps more widely cultivated in California than in its native land. Quite a curiosity, it retains its shrubby habit when grown in the open as a lawn specimen or in a rock garden in full sun, but develops the straggly habit of a Clematis when given a larger plant on which it can lean, or in full shade. It is closely related to several better-known plants of the Australian rainforest such as Callicoma (Blackwattle) and

Ceratopetalum (NSW Christmas Bush) and like the latter its floral display consists not of petals but of four greenish sepals which enlarge in spring.

Aphanopetalum has most attractive, lustrous leaves—up to 4 in/10 cm in length—and is easy to propagate from seed or soft-tip cuttings. It enjoys continuous moisture and is a most attractive plant for semi-shaded areas in the subtropical garden.

Aphanopetalum resinosum. Bush Clematis.
E. Australia

Aphelandra

(af-el-**an**-drə) ☼ ☀ W H
Zebra Plant, Golden Spike
*Summer; 1½–5 ft/50–150 cm; pyramidal;
evergreen*

ACANTHACEAE

Most familiar as indoor or greenhouse shrubs, the Zebra Plants or *Aphelandras* can turn on a miraculous outdoor display in warm-climate gardens with rich, moist soil. They belong to the Acanthus family and produce typical terminal spikes of showy, tubular flowers. These are orange-scarlet in the species *A. aurantiaca*, *A. tetragona* and *A. nitens*. *A. sinclaireana* grows much taller and flowers in pink and orange, while the many varieties of *A. squarrosa* have

Aphelandra sinclaireana. Red Aphelandra.
Tropical America

Arbutus unedo (fruit). Irish Strawberry. S. Europe, Ireland

dazzling golden blooms and zebra-striped foliage in various patterns. For indoor use, it is customary to raise new plants each season. Just break off a side shoot with a heel, dip in rooting hormone and insert in damp sand. Keep under cover in a bright position till growth is apparent.

Arbutus

(ar-**byoo**-təs)   ☼ C T W
Irish Strawberry, Madrone
Autumn; 15 ft/5 m; dense; evergreen

ERICACEAE   FRAGRANT

Though probably a tree in the wild, like the other members of its genus,

Aphelandra X 'Rembrandt'. Zebra Plant. Tropical America

Arbutus unedo. Irish Strawberry.
S. Europe, Ireland

Arbutus andrachne, A. canariensis and *A. menziesii,* the colourful *A. unedo* or Irish Strawberry is content to remain large shrub-size in cultivation, and turns on a magnificent display of fragrant, lily-of-the-valley type flowers in autumn. These are followed by the Chinese-chequer-type fruit which ripen from green through yellow to a vivid scarlet over the period of a year. They are edible but not very exciting to eat, except for the birds.

Arbutus is most easily propagated by layering low-hanging branches in winter or by sowing seed in early spring. The young plants do not move readily and should be set into their permanent positions as soon as possible in either autumn or spring. Arbutus turns up its toes at any trace of lime, does best in a moist, peaty soil.

Arctostaphylos

(ark-toh-**staf**-il-os)   ☼ C T
Manzanita, Bearberry, Kinnikinnick
Spring; 1–3 ft/30–100 cm; dense; evergreen

ERICACEAE

North America's bear population has a light-fingered reputation but I cannot imagine their clumsy paws making much of these berries which they are said to adore. I rather think the Indians were having the early settlers on when they told them that tale.

There are around 50 species of Bearberries or *Arctostaphylos*. Mostly low and spreading shrubs, they are easy to grow from seed, autumn cuttings or by separation of self-layered branches. Young plants should be set out as soon as possible into a moist, peaty soil and not disturbed again. Light watering only is required, along with regular pruning to control shape. All species are good bee plants and the profusion of white or pink heath flowers really keep them humming all through the spring.

Arctostaphylos 'Vancouver Jade'. Bearberry. N.W. North America

Arctostaphylos densiflora. Sonoma Manzanita. California

Ardisia humilis. Spiceberry. E. India

Arctostaphylos uva-ursi. Kinnikinnick. N. Europe, N. Asia, North America

Ardisia

(ah-**dis**-ee-ə)   ☼ ☀ T W H
Coralberry, Spiceberry
All year; 1½–3 ft/50 cm–1 m; erect; evergreen

MYRSINACEAE   FRAGRANT

Unique in appearance, the *Ardisias* are widely seen as a component of Japanese gardens where the whorled

and layered arrangement of scarlet berries seems to last the entire year. There are about 250 species of them, all native to subtropical climates right round the world, but most commonly found in the East Indies and up to Japan and Korea. *A. crispa*, the most popular type, usually flowers in

Ardisia crispa. Coralberry. Japan, Korea, China

Aronia arbutifolia. Chokeberry. Nova Scotia

summer but the red, white or pink berries that follow last a year or more. When a layer of these has ripened the vertical growth continues, developing into a second whorl of dark, shiny foliage. *A. humilis* is a taller-growing, tropical type for hot climates. Its red berries ripen to black. Moist, leaf-rich soil is the go in a position with plenty of shade.

Aronia

(a-**roh**-nee-ə) ☼ C T
Chokeberry
Spr-Aut; 12 ft/3.6 m; open; deciduous

ROSACEAE

Tending to form colonies in open, swampy ground, the Chokeberries (*Aronia* spp.) were for many years considered a sub-group within the pear genus, Pyrus, though the fruit are only a fraction of the size. They make attractive specimens for the cool-climate garden (hardy to −10°F/−22°C) and can be propagated from ripe seed, suckers or cuttings struck under glass. In spite of their preference for swamps in nature, they are not fussy as to soil and even tolerate a heavy clay. The early show of spring blossom does

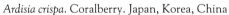

Ardisia X 'Coconut Ice'. Variegated Coralberry

Aronia melanocarpa. Chokeberry. Newfoundland—Tennessee

indeed resemble that of the pear and the *Aronias* are also deciduous, putting on a wonderful display of brilliant autumn colour from both foliage and fruit. *A. arbutifolia* is particularly spectacular.

Artemisia

(ah-tem-**ee**-shə)   ☼ ☀ Ⓒ Ⓣ
Sagebrush, Wormwood, Mugwort,
Lad's Love, Absinthe
*Late summer; 1–5 ft/30–150 cm;
spreading; evergreen*

ASTERACEAE

Named for Artemis the Chaste, ancient Greek goddess of the moon, the 200-odd species of *Artemisia* all have a silvery moonlit appearance due to the dense, hair-like covering on the finely divided leaves. They are great favourites for the white border or as a foliage contrast to darker plants. With rare exceptions, they are native to both sea coast and desert areas of the northern hemisphere,

Artemisia absinthium. Absinthe. Europe

where many of them release their aromatic oils into the dry atmosphere. The genus does in fact include many well-known herbs such as Absinthe, Tarragon, Lad's Love and Wormwood. The majority of species are perennial but quite a few fall into the shrub category, including the illustrated *A. absinthium* and *A. pycnocephala.* The tiny yellow or white summer daisy flowers do not always appear in cultivation. Grow from summer cuttings or seed, raise in gravelly, well-drained soil and water only during droughts.

Astartea fascicularis. Astartea.
Western Australia

Astartea

(as-**tah**-tee-ə)   ☼ Ⓦ Ⓗ
Astartea
*Win-Sum; 3–7½ ft/1–2.5 m; spreading;
evergreen*

MYRTACEAE

Named for the Phoenician goddess of fertility, presumably because of their year-round blooming habits, the small genus *Astartea* is found only in Western Australia and the Northern

Territory. Delicate in appearance, they are easily grown from tip cuttings or uncovered seed and are highly adaptable in growth, tolerating frost, salt air, drought and even waterlogged soil. But they need very little water as a rule and definitely dislike humidity. The leaves are adapted to needle form, like many other drought-resistant plants, and the rosy, 5-petalled flowers quickly fade to white.

Asteriscus

(as-tur-**is**-kus)   ☼ Ⓦ Ⓣ
Canary Island Daisy
Summer; 3 ft/1 m; bun-shaped; evergreen

ASTERACEAE   FRAGRANT

Native to the Canary Islands and the Mediterranean climatic region as far east as Iran, the 15 species of *Asteriscus* are mainly annual or perennial—but the shrubby type illustrated is the most widely grown of all. It thrives in Mediterranean climates worldwide. *A. sericeus* is a silver-hairy plant with somewhat sinuate leaves which are completely evergreen. Its rich golden daisy flowers appear from midsummer on, opening both terminally and in the leaf axils. Raised easily from seed or cuttings, it likes a sunny position and soil that's sandy but rich in leaf mould.

Asteriscus sericeus. Canary Island Daisy.
Canary Islands

Asterolasia

(as-tur-oh-**lae**-see-ə) ☼ ❋ T H
Starbush
Spr-Sum; 4 in–6 ft/10 cm–2 m; furry; evergreen

RUTACEAE

Covered in starry hairs (which is the meaning of the botanical name), the five species of the small Australian genus *Asterolasia* are confined almost exclusively to the damp mountain valleys of the eastern states. In cultivation their fibrous roots dry out easily, causing the collapse of the whole plant, so a moisture-retentive compost is essential, together with a good mulch. They are frost tolerant and grown commonly from cuttings of very young growth since seed is hard to germinate. *Asterolasias* spread into showy groundcovers for native gardens, giving a particularly long display. *Asterolasia* species should be watched for collar rot and scale infection.

Asterolasia hexapetalum. Starbush. N.S.W.

Astroloma ciliatum. Candle Cranberry. Western Australia

Astroloma

(as-troh-**loh**-mə) ☼ ❋ T W
Native Cranberry,
Moss-leafed Heath
Win-Sum; 4 in–3 ft/10 cm–1 m; spreading; evergreen

ERICACEAE

Resembling nothing so much as a mass of colourful Christmas candles caught up in an ornamental Yuletide decoration, the 20-odd species of *Astroloma* are scattered through all states of Australia except Queensland. Most species grow easily from soft-tip cuttings struck in damp sand and peat and can later be planted out in well-drained soil. Showiest of all is *A. ciliatum*, the Candle Cranberry, a generally dwarf or prostrate shrub with sharply pointed ½ in/1 cm leaves and dazzling tubular flowers striped in scarlet, black and green, from the base upward. Beware the formation of grey mould in humid weather and move quickly with the fungicide.

Asystasia

(a-sis-**tae**-shə) ☼ ❋ W H
Ganges Bluebell
Spr-Sum; 4 ft/1.3 m; spreading; evergreen

ACANTHACEAE

A curious group of scrambling shrubs in the family Acanthaceae, the 20-odd species of *Asystasia* are almost

Asystasia gangutica. Ganges Bluebell. India, Malaysia, Africa

equally divided between perennial and shrubby species and might be more sensibly referred to as shrubby perennials. They are mostly from India and West Africa and once included the showy *Mackaya bella* which will now be found separately listed.

Asystasias are mostly used as groundcovers and grow particularly well in a leaf-rich, well-drained soil with regular water. They should be propagated from soft-tip cuttings in early spring and will cover quite a distance before summer is through. The flowers appear in erect spikes and will include some degree of violet in their colouration.

Atriplex

(**a**-trip-leks)   ☼ W H
Saltbush
All year; to 10 ft/3 m; dense; fire-resistant
CHENOPODIACEAE

If there's one thing the deserts of Australia and the American southwest have in common, it's a wide selection of saltbush species. Each area has its own native types, though the Old Man Saltbush, *Atriplex nummularia*, is seen on both continents, probably originating in Australia. An invaluable plant for seaside

areas and dryish, alkaline soil, *Atriplex* is often seen lining driveways or along roadsides, for it reflects the glow of headlights. It is also fire-resistant and makes an effective firebreak. Grown easily from cuttings, it is slow to move until a rainstorm sets it off into a dense, erect habit. Stems are brittle and the small, dull reddish flowers appear in dense terminal clusters.

Atriplex nummularia. Old Man Saltbush. Inland Australia

Aucuba

(aw-**koo**-bə)   ☼ ☀ C T W
Japanese Laurel,
Gold-dust Tree
Spring; 3–10 ft/1–3 m; spreading; evergreen
GARRYACEAE

Shrubs that thrive in full shade and produce colourful fruit beneath the dense cover of trees are rare indeed, but such a treasure is *Aucuba japonica*, the Japanese Laurel or Gold-dust Tree, in its many leaf forms. Easy to propagate from semi-hardwood autumn cuttings, it grows fast provided the soil in the chosen position is not totally impoverished. Cool-climate mountain plants, *Aucubas* suffer badly from frost burn though they are otherwise hardy down to 23°F/ −5°C. Before you get too ambitious though, you must understand that *Aucubas* have a sex problem and will not bear fruit unless you arrange for at least one male plant to every two females. How to tell? The fruiting plants are female.

Aucuba japonica (fruit). Japanese Laurel. Japan

Aucuba japonica crotonifolia. Spotted Aucuba.

Aucuba japonica. Gold-dust Tree. Japan

Austromyrtus

(os-troh-**mur**-təs)

Ironwood

Sum-Aut; 3–10 ft/1–3 m; stiff; evergreen

MYRTACEAE   FRAGRANT

Found mostly in semi-shaded bushland areas of Australia's north-east coast, particularly in rainforests, the many *Austromyrtus* species have possibilities beyond measure. Though rather slow from cuttings, they take off quickly from fresh seed if you can get it.

In the rich, damp soil they adore, they'll grow at a great rate, producing a profusion of fragrant pink-tipped white blooms in late summer. They follow up with a crop of small but succulent berries which were used for jam making by early settlers. *A. tenuifolia* is reasonably frost hardy, grows tall enough to make a stiff, protective hedge.

Austromyrtus tenuifolia. Narrow-leaf Ironwood. Queensland, N.S.W.

Azalea

(*syn.* RHODODENDRON)

(a-**zae**-lee-yə)

Satsuki, Azalea, Kurume

Spr-Aut; 1–10 ft/30 cm–3 m; evergreen or deciduous

ERICACEAE   SOME FRAGRANT

There are so many points of con-fusion when it comes to classifying the Azaleas that I have often thought

Azalea mollis (foreground) and *Rhododendron ponticum* (background). Japan and Asia Minor

Azalea 'Tama no Hada'. Macrantha Azalea. Japan

Azalea 'W. J. Crossley'. Mollis Azalea

of writing a book on the subject to clear things up, at least to my own satisfaction. But alas, the amount of research required always seems to sidetrack me onto an easier subject.

The principal problem is, I suspect, in deciding just what is an Azalea in the first place. I think all enthusiastic plantsmen would recognize most Azaleas at first sight, but we might just all be wrong! As far as botanists and taxonomists are concerned, these days there is no such plant as an Azalea at all. They have all been reclassified as *Rhododendron* long since, though few nurseries and even fewer home gardeners recognize them as such. In earlier days there did seem to be adequate reason to separate them, but that was because neither plant was really familiar to European plant collectors. They were an everyday sight only to the aboriginal residents of North America and the Far East, particularly Japan. As the earliest plant collectors brought their beauty back to Europe, these gorgeously flowering plants were named Azalea from the Greek *azaleos* meaning arid, in reference to the type of dry, mountain soil in which they grow. They were deciduous, shallow-rooted plants with five stamens to each flower and a habit of repeat blooming—most heavily in spring, more lightly in autumn and again from time to time. They ranged in height from 1 ft/30 cm to ten times as much.

Around the same time, other plant hunters brought back the first of a series of much larger plants from the mountain villages of China and India. These grew all the way up to tree size, were evergreen, often with large leathery leaves, and had much larger flowers, each with 10 stamens, borne in terminal clusters. They had a heavy demand for water and botanists christened them *Rhododendron* or Tree Rose.

But as the pace of plant exploration increased, the botanists returned with masses of new *Rhododendron* species and suddenly the distinction was no longer clear. It was decided that both Azaleas and *Rhododendrons* were member species of the same genus to be known as *Rhododendron*, irrespective of the stamen numbers.

The botanists have done their best, but experience has taught that the home gardener is very stubborn in the matter of such a major name change. Azaleas the smaller plants were, Azaleas they are, and Azaleas they always will be, one supposes.

Azalea pontica. Yellow Azalea. Species

Indica Azaleas. Sydney, Australia

Azalea X 'Coccinea Speciosa'. Ghent Hybrid Azalea

Few of the Azaleas we grow today are original species, but have been cross-bred from literally dozens of predecessors, and therefore, as they are hybrids, there still seems no valid reason to call them by a name of their own.

As a rule, the species we class as Azalea Indica are descended from *Rhododendron simsii*; the smaller flowered Kurume descend from *R.*

Azalea 'Exquisite'. Variegated Indica Azalea

obtusum; the gold and orange Mollis Azaleas from *R. japonicum*; and the Korean Azaleas from *R. yedoense*. The evergreen Indicas and Kurumes are most commonly grown in warmer climates, the deciduous Mollis and Ghent and Exbury hybrids where winters are cold. Late blooming and cold resistant A. macrantha are popular in both climates, while the Rutherfordiana hybrids are rarely seen outside the United States. Indica Azaleas bloom mostly in shades of pink, mauve and white and may grow 10 ft/3 m both in height and width. A sub-division, the Belgian Hybrid Indicas, includes many double blooms and shades of red, and rarely exceeds 3 ft/1 m in height. They look wonderful in pots.

The small-flowered Kurume Azaleas have daintier blooms and leaves, and are most often seen either in rockeries or mass planted as groundcover. Some reach only 2 ft/ 60 cm in height, and more than most Azaleas they have a second flowering in autumn.

The Gumpo Azalea, also evergreen, rarely grows above 10 in/ 25 cm. Mollis, Ghent and Exbury hybrids are deciduous and often perfumed. They include unusual shades

of cream, beige, green, apricot, orange and yellow.

All Azaleas are surface rooting and can be moved quite easily, even in bloom. They should not be planted too deeply or mulched heavily lest older, deeper roots rot and the plant die. An acid soil with a pH of 5 or 6 is ideal, preferably light, leafy and well drained. Most Azalea cultivars can be grown from 5 cm autumn cuttings struck under glass. Larger plants can be layered in mid-spring, the layers lifted in late autumn. Pruning is not essential, but bloom is more profuse when Azaleas are kept more compact by shearing.

In some countries, a fungal infection known as petal blight is a problem. When this appears, the entire plant must be sprayed with a recommended fungicide at fortnightly intervals from first bud colour. You can help avoid the blight by watering the root area only, and not the whole bush.

Azalea lacefly and thrips are a problem in some areas, but can be controlled by spraying under the foliage in warm weather with a systemic insecticide.

Azalea X 'Schryderi'. Hybrid cultivar

Azalea 'Magnifica'. Indica Azalea

Azalea 'Alba Magna'. Indica Azalea

Azalea 'Nuccio's Lavender Lady'.
Kurume Azalea. American cultivar

Azaleas and Bluebells. Rothschild Exbury Estate. England

Azara

(a-**zah**-rə)   ☼ C T
Oromo, Gold Spire
Spring; 10 ft/3 m; upright; evergreen

SALICACEAE   FRAGRANT

All from Chile, and including both small, slender trees and shrubs, there are about a dozen species of the delightful *Azara*, richly perfumed with a scent reminiscent of vanilla and chocolate. Suitable for any mild, temperate garden, they will thrive in a light soil, but if you're cursed with something heavier, then turn in plenty of peat or compost before planting and fertilize regularly in autumn to help produce plenty of unbelievably fragrant flowers.

Propagate from summer cuttings, each rooted in its own pot and over-wintered under glass. The glossy, finely-toothed foliage is handsome at any time of the year, and useful for cutting.

Azaleodendron

(a-zae-lee-oh-**den**-dron)   ☼ ◐ T
Azaleodendron
Spring; 3 ft/90 cm; spreading; evergreen

ERICACEAE

One can still count on the exotic name of *Azaleodendron* to draw the crowds at many a flower show. The plant illustrated caught my eye at London's Chelsea spectacular about twenty years ago. In modern taxonomic practice, the name is quite old-fashioned and dates from the period when Azalea and Rhododendron were regarded as separate genera. But some botanical genius, not realising that they *were* the same genus, created a great deal of excitement by exhibiting what was believed to be an intergeneric hybrid or X *Azaleodendron*. Before we laugh at silly old him, just think—what if he were correct in his nomenclature? Galileo won his argument by holding out long enough! By the way since they are Azaleas (or Rhododendrons!) they should be treated like one of the family.

Azaleodendron odoratum. Azaleodendron.
Bigeneric Hybrid?

Azara dentata. Oromo. Chile

Baccharis

(**bak**-kah-ris) ☼ T W H
Groundsel Bush,
Coyote Bush
Autumn; 8 in–14 ft/20 cm–4 m; variable

ASTERACEAE

One of the most widespread and popular genera in the daisy family, there are 300 species of *Baccharis* native to all parts of the Americas. The deciduous Groundsel Bush *B. halimifolia*, is grown in the northeastern United States where it is popular in seaside gardens, a legacy of its natural salt-marsh territory. It may grow 14 ft/4 m tall. In California, it's the prostrate Coyote Bush, *B. pilularis*, which is more widely seen as it is suited to dryish soil and a warm climate. Both are easily grown from seed or cuttings and bear masses of uninteresting, white, rayless daisy flowers in late autumn. On female plants these are followed by fluffy white seeds.

Backhousia

(bak-**hou**-see-ə) ☼ ☽ T W H
Lemon-scented Myrtle
Lemon Ironwood
Summer; 10–30 ft/3–10 m; dense; evergreen

MYRTACEAE　　　　　FRAGRANT

When is a tree not a tree? Quite often when it's a Lemon-scented Myrtle, it would seem. Though sometimes found as a forest tree of 60 ft/20 m it is more often seen in cultivation as a rather dense evergreen shrub only a fraction of the height it achieves in its native rainforests. It has become popular world-wide—in southern Africa, southern USA and southern Europe as well as its native Australia. Raise it from half-ripe cuttings taken in spring. It will grow fast in a good, rich, acid soil, complementing its shiny, citrus-scented leaves with clouds of tiny, four-petalled white flowers in early summer. As the weather warms up, these are succeeded by a mass of small, green calyces, the plant's principal display.

Baeckea virgata. E. Australia

Baccharis halimifolia. Groundsel Bush. N.E. United States

Backhousia citriodora. Lemon-scented Myrtle. E. Australia

Balaustion

(bal-**ou**-stee-ən)   ☼ ☀ W H
Native Pomegranate
Spr-Sum; 1 ft/30 cm; wide-spreading;
evergreen

MYRTACEAE

Dwarf shrubs from Western Australia (there are only two species), the *Balaustions* would make a great addition to temperate gardens wherever plants are available. Completely prostrate and with many branches clothed in almost invisible leaves, they both produce dazzling, orange-scarlet flowers like miniature pomegranates. These bloom throughout spring and summer. Easy to grow from seed or soft-tip cuttings, they need a sandy, very well-drained soil rich in leaf mould. They do best in hot, dry areas but make showy container plants in cooler districts. They are completely drought resistant and reasonably frost hardy.

Baeckea ramosissima. Rosy Baeckea. S.E. Australia, Tasmania

Balaustion pulcherrimum. Native Pomegranate. Western Australia

Baeckea

(**bae**-kee-ə)   ☼ ☀ T W
Baeckea
Spr-Sum; 4 in–10 ft/10 cm–3 m; dainty;
evergreen

MYRTACEAE

Though more than 50 of the 70 known species of *Baeckea* are from Western Australia, the remainder are scattered among all the Australian states. They vary from dainty shrublets to quite tall, woody plants and come from areas with vastly different climates and rainfall, from the coast to the mountains. This means that there is a variety of species for most types of garden.

Baeckeas are easy to grow either from young cuttings or ripe seed if you can catch it before it is dispersed. Soil should be well-drained and regular moisture is needed. The Rosy Baeckea, *B. ramosissima*, is a ground-hugging shrub suitable for rockery work or protected seaside areas. The dainty, heath-like foliage can develop copper tones and the typical myrtle flowers vary from white to deep pink in toning and appear for months.

Banksia

(**bank**-see-ə)   ☼ ◐ T W H
Honeysuckle, Bottlebrush
*Varied according to species; 6–17 ft/
2–5 m; erect to spreading; evergreen*

PROTEACEAE

Though the species discovered by Sir Joseph Banks in 1770 (and subsequently named after him) was a tree (*Banksia serrata*, the Red Honeysuckle), most of the more than 60 species discovered since are distinctly shrubby in habit. They are found in all Australian states (with one in New Guinea as well) but the great majority grow naturally only in the southwest corner of the Australian continent. Curiously enough, this is also the natural habitat of the genus Dryandra (see entry *Dryandra*) and is the closest part of the continent to South Africa's Cape of Good Hope which is home to the marvellous and closely related Proteas. To many scientists, this is almost perfect proof of the original jointure of the two continents as the prehistoric super-continent of Gondwanaland.

Strange and wonderful plants, the *Banksias* are extraordinarily variable. The foliage varies from the needle-like in *B. ericifolia*, through the saw-like in *B. baxteri* to the almost round leaves of *B. coccinea*. Habit varies from the almost prostrate Possum Banksia to the densely foliaged Heath-leaf Banksia, but the most interesting variations are in the showy flower heads. Basically, these consist of slender, tubular flowers arranged in neat parallel rows along a spike varying from short to extremely elongated according to species. As the flowers open gradually from the base upward, the coiled stamens emerge one by one and spring out to give the entire inflorescence a fuzzy appearance. *Banksia* flowers are normally rich in nectar, hence the popular name of Honeysuckle.

All *Banksias* prefer a sandy soil rich in organic matter and can be propagated from seed or tip cuttings. They are not fast growers but present a great flower display when quite young, while their spectacular inflorescences persist for years. Of the illustrated species, *B. ericifolia* is usually compact but can grow to 23 ft/7 m in its native eastern bushland. Spreading *B. spinulosa* is found in hilly areas of Australia's eastern states. It closely resembles Western Australia's *B. occidentalis* or Waterbush, although the latter is a swamp dweller. All other species shown on these pages are from Western Australia, though many of them are grown in the western United States and other areas with Mediterranean climates. *B. baxteri* is hardy to light frosts when established. The soft and hairy *B. baueri* or Teddybear makes a popular garden specimen but the more spectacular Albany Banksia, *B. coccinea*, often takes years to flower in strange surroundings. *B. grandis*, the Bull Banksia, is a most adaptable species and gives an additional display with its brightly coloured new growth. The orange and grey flowered *B. prionotes* or Acorn Banksia is often difficult to establish but worth trying in sandy, alkaline soils.

If *Banksias* have a special flowering season it is spring, but there are always some species in bloom at any time of year. They do not enjoy tropical heat and humidity.

Banksia ericifolia. Heath-leaf Banksia. Coastal N.S.W.

Banksia baueri. Teddybear. Western Australia

Banksia spinulosa. Hairpin Banksia. E. Australia

Michael Morcombe

Banksia coccinea. Albany Banksia. S.W. Western Australia

Banksia occidentalis. Waterbush, Swamp Banksia.
Western Australia

Banksia grandis. Bull Banksia.
Western Australia

Banksia prionotes. Acorn Banksia.
Western Australia

Michael Morcombe

Michael Morcombe

Michael Morcombe

Barleria

(bah-**leer**-ee-ə)   ☼ ☀ W H
Philippine Violet
Spr-Sum; 3 ft/1 m; dense; evergreen
ACANTHACEAE

A puzzle to many cool-climate gardeners when they run across them on vacation, the *Barlerias* must be among the most popular of ornamental plant genera in the tropical to warm-temperate garden. There are over 230 species, mostly shrubs, and they are found naturally from Africa to India and on many islands of the Indian Ocean. Where the climate is right they are easy to propagate either from seed or from half-ripe cuttings struck any time other than winter. In summer or in a heated glasshouse, *Barlerias* grow fast, enjoy humidity and an acid soil enriched with leaf mould and manure. They appreciate plenty of water right through the hot weather with some light shade around midday. In borderline areas, you'll need to grow them in containers for they'll need protection under glass when temperatures drop below 45°F/7°C. *B. cristata* is often seen sheared into a neat hedge in warmer climates.

Barleria lupulina. Hop-head Barleria. Mauritius

Barleria cristata. Philippine Violet. India, Burma

Bauera rubioides. River Rose. E. Australia, Tasmania

Bauera

(**bow**-ur-ə)   ☀ T W
River Rose, Dog Rose,
Wiry Bauera
Spring; 8 in–10 ft/20 cm–3 m; spreading; evergreen
BAUERACEAE

Australia's delicate *Baueras* (there are only three species) are normally found clinging to the sandy, peaty soil of mountain stream banks, thriving in areas where the sun hardly

Bauera sessiliflora. Grampians Bauera. W. Victoria

ever reaches. In cultivation, the shaded side of rockeries suits, or even among the stonework of garden walls—but here, please, never a trace of lime.

They are hardy down to 23°F/ −5°C, will withstand periods of waterlogging and can be propagated easily from soft-tip cuttings struck in a sand/peat mixture. The dainty, ¾ in/2 cm flowers of the River Rose (*B. rubioides*) hang from slender stems and may be pink or white. In the Grampians Bauera, *B. sessiliflora*, the blooms are smaller and stemless. The delicate leaves of both species become tinged with red in winter.

Bauhinia

(boh-**hin**-ee-ə)   ☼ ☀ W H
Butterfly Flower,
St Thomas Tree
Spring; to 15 ft/4 m; open; deciduous
CAESALPINIACEAE

Tropical and sub-tropical to the core, the 300-odd species of *Bauhinia* are natives of the American, Asian and African tropics. At one time there were several Australian species listed too, but these have since been reclassified. The most popular species are lightweight trees, but some beautiful shrubs are grown as well.

Members of the pea family, they produce large quantities of seed from which they may easily be grown.

An African beauty, *B. galpinii* (syn *B. punctata*) is probably the most spectacular. Known popularly as the Nasturtium Bauhinia or Pride of de Kaap, it makes a low, spreading bush up to 10 ft/3 m in diameter and covers itself with brick-red flowers, borne in small racemes.

B. glauca (syn. *B. scandens*) is from South-east Asia and particularly effective when spilling over walls or balustrades. Its flowers come in dense, terminal corymbs, and are usually less than 1 in/2.5 cm in diameter, rosy-white with red stamens. If not watered, it tends to develop into a full-blown climber, as is the case with many of the *Bauhinias*.

B. petersiana is another African species, this time from Mozambique. Its flowers are up to 3 in/7.5 cm across with long, white, wavy petals and deep red stamens.

The golden-flowered St Thomas Tree, *B. tomentosa*, is a more erect type of plant with flowers conspicuously marked in brown or deep red, and roundish leaves. It is found naturally from China to India and has become naturalized in the Caribbean area.

Wonderful though the *Bauhinia* flowers are, the plants' most spectacular feature is their leaves. These

Bauhinia glauca. Rosy Bauhinia. South-east Asia

are uniquely twin-lobed, sometimes split right to the stem, and caused the genus to be named for the brothers Bauhin, twin botanists in the 16th century.

Though tropical in origin, most of the *Bauhinias* are hardy enough to survive in warm temperate areas. Once established, they will not suffer from the occasional 27°F/−3°C frost.

All prefer rich, well-drained soil with plenty of organic matter, and benefit from a light pruning of flowered stems when blooms have faded. This has the additional benefit of preventing the formation of the unsightly seed pods.

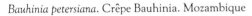

Bauhinia petersiana. Crêpe Bauhinia. Mozambique

Bauhinia galpinii. Pride of de Kaap. Tropical Africa

Beaufortia

(boh-**fort**-ee-ə) ☼ ☀ W H
Swamp Bottlebrush,
Gravel Bottlebrush
*Summer; 1½–12 ft/50–400 cm; sparse;
evergreen*

MYRTACEAE

Though female plant collectors are something of a rarity, there have been any number of women who have made a career as *patrons* of botany, dissipating fortunes in the support of private botanic gardens or plant-hunting expeditions. One of these was Mary, Duchess of Beaufort, whose work in the early 19th century is commemorated in the nomenclature of the Western Australian genus *Beaufortia*. There are 17 species of these Melaleuca relatives, all endemic to that state and with bottlebrush-type flowers in pink, red or purple. They are raised from cuttings of half-ripe stems or seeds from the previous year's capsules. These should be scattered on a damp sand/peat mixture, barely covered. Gravelly, well-drained soil suits best.

Beaufortia sparsa. Swamp Bottlebrush.
Western Australia

Beaumontia grandiflora. Herald's Trumpet.
Himalayas

Beaumontia

(boh-**mon**-tee-ə) ☼ W H
Herald's Trumpet,
Easter-lily Vine
*Early spring; 10 ft/3 m; spreading;
evergreen*

APOCYNACEAE   FRAGRANT

Though technically a climber I suppose, I've often seen this wonderful plant used as a rather leggy shrub or a splendid lawn specimen. The situation is, I imagine, that it needs something to climb on and otherwise remains shrubby. I tried in my own garden (which is all too full of wonderful plants to climb) to grow it in a large pot. Grow it did, flower it did not until I gave it to a friend who set it out in his garden where it now blooms quite heavily, the fragrant flowers set off beautifully against the glossy, deep green leaves.

Beaumontia grandiflora, as I now know, needs rich, deep soil with plenty of food and water. It is not frost hardy at all, nor does it bloom on new wood. Strike it from cuttings taken in summer.

Begonia

(be-**goh**-nee-ə) ☀ W H
Begonia
Sum-Aut; to 3 ft/1 m; succulent; evergreen

BEGONIACEAE

Just why one of the largest genera in all botany (over 1000 species with more than 10,000 listed cultivars) should be named for an obscure 17th century governor of French Canada, I have been unable to discover.

Begonia foliosa CV 'Rosea'. Fern-leaf
Begonia. Colombia, Venezuela

Begonia scharfii. Elephant-ear Begonia. Brazil

Begonia foliosa var *foliosa*. Fuchsia Begonia. Colombia, Venezuela

Begonias are among the world's great families of hobby plants and native to all moist tropical countries except Australia, though some splendid species have been discovered in the highlands of nearby New Guinea.

Begonias are such a vast genus, it is very difficult to say anything general about them except that they have succulent stems and foliage that dissolve into a pulp at the first touch of frost. In the northern hemisphere they are largely greenhouse plants except for the annual *B. semperflorens* and the Tuberous Begonias which are set out in spring and lifted after their summer display. Curiously enough, it is these latter types that are raised under glass in the southern hemisphere while the majority of species are seen in the open garden, though usually in a sheltered position.

A few types are considered shrubs. These include the Elephant-ear Begonia, *B. scharfii*, a fibrous rooted plant covered in reddish hairs. It may reach 3 ft/1 m in height and bears masses of rose-pink flowers in 12 in/ 30 cm cymes.

Another popular shrubby type is *B. foliosa*, the Fuchsia Begonia or Corazon de Jesus. Woody at the base (to which it may die back in cold weather), this dainty plant branches heavily and is covered in the warmer months with glossy, dark green, oblong leaves, often reddish when young. The small flowers are five-petalled if female, four-petalled if male. They are white tipped, backed pink, and hang on slender branched stems through most of summer and autumn. Both described species are easily grown from soft-tip cuttings or seed if available. They should be kept moist and grown in a leaf-rich, mildly acid soil that drains perfectly. Both make good container plants.

Bellendena

(bel-en-**dee**-nə) ☀ⓉⓌ
Mountain Rocket
Summer; 1–3 ft/30–100 cm; spreading; evergreen

PROTEACEAE

If the remarkable *Bellendena* did not already exist in the cool Tasmanian mountains, it would have been necessary to invent it in order to increase the world's botanical wonders. Quite frost tolerant, it is a spreading shrub with almost com-pletely vertical branches clothed with variable blue-grey leaves presenting an astonishing range of shapes and sizes. Not surprisingly, it is a member of the infinitely variable Protea family. The small, stalkless flowers may be either white or pink and are held in dense, terminal racemes well above the foliage. The real display comes later, however, when the flowers are succeeded by a mass of flattened fruits, startlingly red in colour. *B. montana* prefers a consistently moist, light, well-drained soil and should be grown in the dappled shade of taller plants.

Bellendena montana. Mountain Rocket. Tasmania

Berberidopsis

(bur-be-rid-**op**-sis) ☀ⓉⓌ
Coral Plant
Summer; 3–10 ft/1–3 m; sprawling; evergreen

BERBERIDOPSIDACEAE

One of the more remarkable plants from the Chilean forests, *Berberidopsis corallina* is in fact a shrub, though often seen trained against a southward facing wall in English gardens. Left to its own devices in a warmer climate, it is more inclined to

Berberidopsis corallina. Coral Plant. Chile

Berberis nevinii (fruit). Nevin Barberry. S. California

sprawl over banks, or tangle with nearby, larger plants. Though some trouble to keep in good shape, its hanging clusters of coral-red flowers make everything seem worthwhile when they appear in summer.

Berberidopsis offers a wide range of propagation choices. Seed or soft-tip cuttings are most successful in spring while a mature plant is easily layered in early autumn. Moderately frost hardy, *Berberidopsis* enjoys a cool root run in a leafy-rich, neutral soil. Assured moisture is essential.

Berberis thunbergii 'Atropurpurea'. Japanese Barberry. Japan

Berberis

(**bur**-bur-iss)   ☼ C T
Barberry, Piprage
Spr-Aut; 3–10 ft/1–3 m; dense; both evergreen and deciduous types

BERBERIDACEAE

With species originating in Europe, Asia and the Americas, the Barberries are among the most popular shrubs for cool-climate gardens. There are some 500 species, mostly deciduous and with a dense, spiny habit. The leaves are shiny and serrated while the spring flowers of many species have an uncanny resemblance to tiny golden daffodils; and since they are often displayed against dull red or even purple foliage, they produce a remarkably vivid display. This grand show is repeated in late summer and autumn as the foliage of many types changes colour just as the succulent berries, which may be red or blue, appear.

Most Barberries like a rich, well-drained soil but need heavy watering only in dry seasons. They may be grown from seed or cuttings from lateral shoots taken with a heel in late summer. They may be pruned lightly to shape after flowering but this will mean the loss of some berries. South

American *Berberis darwinii* and Chinese *B. julianae* are evergreen. European *B. vulgaris* and the many colour varieties of Japanese *B. thunbergii* are deciduous and hardy down to 12°F/−11°C. Californian *B. nevinii* is drought resistant, so there are species for every climate. Smaller types are suitable for rockeries. Taller species make dense, spiny hedges.

Berberis darwinii. Darwin Barberry. Chile, Argentina

Pamela Harper

Berberis julianae. Wintergreen Barberry. China

Billardiera erubescens. Red Billardiera.
Western Australia

Billardiera longiflora. Purple Apple-berry.
S.E. Australia

agreeable. The best known species, *Billardiera longiflora* (Purple Apple-berry) is found from New South Wales down to Tasmania and is popular in plantsmen's gardens in England and California. It can be allowed to climb some form of trellis but if pruned back regularly will adopt a shrubby habit. Greenish, tubular flowers rather like those of Correa (which see) deck the bush in spring and summer and are followed by metallic purple fruits, ¾ in–2 cm long. *B. erubescens*, the Red Billardiera or Marianthus is from Western Australia but will do well in any temperate area provided the soil is well-drained and rich in compost. Its leaves are a dark, glossy green and the tubular red flowers appear in spring. To force a shrubby habit, grow in the open and tip prune any wayward stems that head towards other, taller plants.

Bocconia

(bok-**koh**-nee-ə) ☼ Ⓦ Ⓗ
Plume Poppy
Spring; to 25 ft/7.5 m; treelike; evergreen

PAPAVERACEAE

The stately *Bocconia arborea* is a giant of the poppy family and best placed at the back of the shrub border in a tropical or subtropical garden. Originating in Central and South America, it needs all the heat it can get to grow tall and produce the crowded

Bocconia arborea. Plume Poppy.
Central and South America

Billardiera

(*syn.* MARIANTHUS)

(bil-ah-de-**eə**-rə) ☼ ◑ Ⓣ Ⓦ
Purple Appleberry
Summer; to 3 ft/1 m; twining; evergreen

PITTOSPORACEAE

Named for the French botanist J. J. de Labillardière, this genus of shrubby climbers are found in limited areas of Australia's cooler southern states. They are grown from seed and though definitely preferring a light shade will find most soils and aspects

branches of greyish, lobed leaves that give such a wonderful tropical effect to the garden. Grow it from seed in a protected position with bottom heat. Prick out seedlings into pots of sand and leaf mould and finally set out in well-drained soil that's rich in rotted organic matter. Keep moist at all times but especially in summer. The tiny petal-less blooms appear in terminal panicles each spring and cut well for arrangements.

Boronia

(bə-**roh**-nee-ə) ☼ T W H
Native Rose
Early spring; 1–5 ft/30 cm–1.5 m; open; evergreen

RUTACEAE	FRAGRANT

It's no wonder *Boronia* flowers smell so good—they are closely related to Citrus and Murraya (which see). One of the most charming and fragrant of Australia's genera, the *Boronia*, in all its 90-odd species, is endemic to the southern continent and rarely grown successfully elsewhere, even by the

Boronia pinnata. N.S.W.

Boronia megastigma. Brown Boronia. Western Australia

Boronia mollis. Lorne Pride. N.S.W.

Boronia muelleri CV 'Sunset Serenade'. Victoria

Boronia microphylla. Dwarf Boronia. N.S.W.

most enthusiastic of plantsmen.

In nature, they are mostly found in lightly covered, sandy bushland so rich in leaf mould it can never dry out. An acid pH balance and perfect drainage are also among its requirements and all species need a cool root run that can be provided by an adjacent boulder or rock shelf.

Western Australian *B. megastigma* is perhaps best known, as much for its unique colouring as for its rich perfume. In the common variety, the tiny, four-petalled, cup-shaped flowers are a warm chestnut brown outside, lime green inside. There are variations in red-brown and pure yellow. The perfume is as we have said, unique, and there is no use trying to compare it with any other flower, though Daphne and violets come to mind. Fortunately, the scent has been captured by the perfumers and is now sold in many Australian tourist outlets and on the national airline. *B. megastigma* has the typical wiry-stemmed, trifoliate leaves of the genus but most of the other species, native to the eastern states, bloom in some shade of pink. Prominent among them is the New South Wales Native Rose, *B. serrulata*. It grows to 3 ft/1 m and is highly protected in the wild. The star-shaped blossoms of the more common *B. pinnata* are frequently seen in Sydney bushland in early spring as is the dwarf *B. pulchella* which blooms in a deeper pink. In the more shaded coastal gullies you may run across the taller growing *B. mollis* which is quite variable in its flower colour and height.

Smaller *B. pilosa* is found right down the eastern face of the continent and often bears double flowers. All *Boronias* are propagated from small, firm-tip cuttings struck in coarse sand. Seed germination tends to be highly erratic.

Boronia pilosa 'Flore Pleno'. Double Boronia. S.E. Australia, Tasmania

Boronia serrulata. Native Rose. N.S.W.

Bougainvillea

(boo-gain-**vil**-ee-ə) ☼ W H
Paper-flower
Spr-Sum; to 30 ft/10 m; scrambling; part deciduous

NYCTAGINACEAE

The nomenclature of *Bougainvillea* is, frankly, in a mess. So popular have they become in recent years that nurserymen have been throwing round their own names like confetti. One grower's 'Thai Gold' is another's 'Hawaiian Gold' is another's 'Acapulco Gold'. Cultivar names have

Bougainvillea. Mixed as hedge

Bougainvillea villosa 'Jamaican White'. Caribbean hybrid

long been Latinized as if they were true species names and a lot of angry customers have departed with a supposedly new variety for their collection and then found they've had it for years under a totally different name. Fortunately, in Hawaii at least, the authorities have taken action to force the nurseries to have their *Bougainvillea* plants correctly named and labelled.

Even so, the group would be con-

fusing . . . authorities believe there are perhaps 14 original species with at least three of these (*B. glabra*, *B. peruviana* and *B. spectabilis*) having between them some dozens of cultivars in shades of red, purple, pink, white, yellow and orange, many either single or double. Sorting these out is the hardest part: they are all relatively easy to grow. Just plant, water and forget them, for more of these gorgeous South American

Bougainvillea glabra 'Magnifica'. Common Purple Bougainvillea. South America

Bougainvillea glabra 'Raspberry Ice'. Variegated Bougainvillea. Brazil

Bougainvillea X *buttiana* 'Thai Gold'. South America

Bougainvillea spectabilis 'Lateritia'. Brazil

plants were killed by kindness than ever died of neglect.

They enjoy a well-drained soil, preferably of a gravelly texture; sun, sun and more sun and a winter minimum temperature of around 55°F/13°C. They should always be planted facing towards the equator, whatever hemisphere you live in, and hard pruning is the key to flowering display. Like Wisteria, each flowering stem should be cut back to several spurs after bloom. And if we didn't mention water it's because too much of it would force them to bolt to leaf at the expense of bloom.

Bougainvilleas are not true vines. They have no tendrils or suckers, but rather *lean* into taller plants or against walls. You'll need to support them with heavy straps at intervals. On a slope, plant at the *top* of a wall to hang down or use them as a large lawn specimen shrub. Grow it as an espalier or train it as a tree—anything goes. Just be sure you plant it in warm weather with the root junction in full sun. The greater the glare, the more bracts will be produced. Oh yes—all those colourful, papery parts are *bracts*, not flowers. The actual flowers are the tiny, whitish, starry appendages you can see in our picture of *B. glabra* 'Magnifica'.

Bougainvillea X buttiana 'Scarlett O'Hara'

Bouvardia leiantha hybrids. Bouvardia. Mexico, Central America

Bouvardia

(boo-**vah**-dee-ə) ☼ ⚛ W H
Trompatella
Aut-Win; to 6 ft/2 m; scraggly; evergreen

RUBIACEAE

Bouvardias have a reputation for perfume which is totally undeserved—well, that is except for the white blooming species *B. longiflora* which smells as good as it looks, but may well belong to a different genus of plants. All other *Bouvardias*, whether single or double and in shades of red,

pink, yellow or white, are without scent. But if sheer floral beauty is your bag, don't hesitate to plant them anyway. Just remember they are cold resistant only down to 45°F/7°C, and are not frost hardy at all, and do need continuous shaping. They'll always be untidy unless you cut them almost to the ground after flowering and then pinch back the growing tips again and again to force a profusion of flower buds. All *Bouvardias* enjoy a rich, well-drained soil, heavy watering in summer and dilute liquid fertilizer during the flowering season.

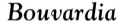

Bouvardia longiflora. Humboldt Bouvardia. Mexico

Bouvardia 'President Cleveland'. Trompetella. Mexico

Brachyglottis

(brak-ee-**glot**-əs) ☼ ⚛ T W
Rangiora
Spring; 8–20 ft/2.5-6 m; treelike; evergreen

ASTERACEAE

A great favourite in New Zealand's North Island where it is found naturally by streams or on the fringes of bushland, the Rangiora (*Brachyglottis repanda*) can be tamed to garden use with regular spring pruning and occasional pinching back. But *regular* is the word, for it can quickly lose the compact shape you'd be after. It is a member of the daisy family although the large evergreen leaves are its most desirable feature and usually more than 6 in/15 cm in length. In the common variety they are pale green above and woolly white beneath. There is, however, a cultivar 'Purpurea' in which the leaves are deep purple. The tiny, greenish flowers appear in spring in much-branched terminal panicles 12 in/30 cm and more in length. Easy to raise from cuttings and fast growing. Damp, compost-rich soil is best.

Brachyglottis repanda. Rangiora. New Zealand

Brachysema lanceolatum. Swan River Pea. Western Australia

Brachysema

(brak-ee-**see**-mə)   ☼ ☀ W H
Swan River Pea,
Scimitar Shrub
All year; 3 ft/1 m; spreading; evergreen

FABACEAE

A showy member of the pea family from Western Australia, *Brachysema lanceolatum* has frankly untidy habits and can only be kept neat with regular shearing after each flush of flowers. Otherwise it flops and will only look good drooping or sprawling over banks. It can also be turned into a semi-climber by tucking the young shoots into a panel of chicken wire. Its branchlets are quite cylindrical, the evergreen leaves sword-shaped with lightly curved tops and silver-silky reverses. *Brachysema* prefers well-drained soil but will stand some waterlogging. Grow it from soft autumn tip cuttings or scarified seed. It is popular in California and is hardy down to 23°F/–5°C.
Brachysema is commonly reassigned to the genus *Gastrolobium* (*G. celsianum* is a synonym for *B. lanceolatum*).

Breynia nivosa. Snowbush. Pacific Islands

Breynia

(**bray**-nee-ə)   ☼ ☀ W H
Snowbush, Foliage Flower,
Lau-kalakoa, Sweetpea Bush
All year; 3 ft/1 m; weeping; evergreen

PHYLLANTHACEAE

Slow to grow in warm temperate areas but very fast in the tropics, the charming Snowbush (*Breynia nivosa*) is a wonderful foliage shrub in warm climates. Propagated from seed, cuttings or offshoots, it does best in rich, well-drained soil and should be kept moist, particularly in hot weather. The simple alternate leaves grow from red zigzag stems in many shades of green, cream and pink, and the bush should be pruned back hard and regularly to force continuous growth of colourful shoots. Check it often for the appearance of invasive suckers. There are small axillary flowers but the foliage is why you grow it and it colours best in dappled shade.

Brugmansia suaveolens. Angel's Trumpets. Brazil

Brugmansia

(brug-**man**-zee-ə)   ☼ ☀ W H
Angel's Trumpets
Sum-Aut; 6–15 ft/2–4.5 m; treelike; part-deciduous

SOLANACEAE   FRAGRANT

Lush and tropical in appearance, the soft-wooded, gorgeously blooming *Brugmansias* look exactly like a South American exotic should look. But I remember as a child, having a beautiful specimen in our Hobart garden where both snow and ice are occasional features of the winter climate.

Close checking reveals, however, that they come from the Andes which explains their tolerance of cool winters.

Leaves are simple and felt-covered, the flowers enormous, trumpet shaped and often night-perfumed. Propagate from heeled cuttings or seed and grow in well-drained, leaf-rich soil. All *Brugmansias* have a narcotic principle in the sap and snails make a terrible mess of them while enjoying a 'high'. Keep moist during the growing season.

Brugmansia sanguinea. Red Angel's Trumpet. Colombia, Chile

Brunfelsia pauciflora var *macrantha.* Brazil Raintree. Brazil

Brugmansia aurea. Yellow Trumpet. Colombia, Ecuador

Brunfelsia
(*syn.* FRANCISCEA)

(brun-**felz**-ee-ə)   ☼ ☀ W H
Yesterday, Today and Tomorrow, Kiss-me-quick, Brazilian Raintree, Paraguay Jasmine
Spr-Sum; 10 ft/3 m; rounded; evergreen

| SOLANACEAE | FRAGRANT |

Exciting South American *Brunfelsias* really sing the blues. And not just one blue, but a whole range of them on the one plant. In spring and autumn, the fragrant violet flowers fade to pale blue and finally a bluish-white over successive days. There are some 30 species with this curious habit, mostly resembling one another except in size and profusion of bloom. All of these tropical beauties enjoy a rich, heavy soil with good drainage and plenty of summer water. They can be grown from summer cuttings which are easily struck at 70°F/21°C and, in tropical gar-

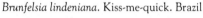

Brugmansia versicolor. Salmon Trumpet. Ecuador

Brunfelsia lindeniana. Kiss-me-quick. Brazil

Brunfelsia americana. Lady of the Night. West Indies

Buddleia globosa. Globe Buddleia. Chile, Peru

Buddleia davidii. Butterfly Bush. China

Buddleia

(**bud**-lee-ə) ☼ C T W
Butterfly Bush, Summer Lilac
Sum-Aut; to 10 ft/3 m; arching; part deciduous

SCROPHULARIACEAE   FRAGRANT

Variously native to Asia, Africa and the Americas, the beautiful Butterfly Bushes (*Buddleia* species) really do attract butterflies from far and wide with their aromatic foliage and spicily fragrant bloom. Having this much in common, the various species are quite different in the style of their inflorescences in which many tiny tubular florets may be arranged in whorls, globes, single spikes or branched racemes. Leaves are all similar: pointed, crepe textured and often quite large—up to 1 ft/30 cm in the illustrated *B. davidii* from China.

Most species are propagated from semi-hardwood cuttings struck in summer and they all grow fast in

Buddleia alternifolia. Weeping-willow Buddleia. N.W. China

dens particularly, the cuttings are often used as a perennial ground-cover and give quite a stunning effect.

A second group of *Brunfelsias*, noted for their night fragrances and blooming in shades of green, white and pale butterscotch, are native to the nearby West Indies where *B. americana* is known as Dama de Noche or Lady of the Night.

rich, well-drained soil but need plenty of water, especially in summer. The weight of bloom pulls branches down towards the ground, so shape should be restored by pruning back by half after bloom or in late winter. Most commonly seen *B. davidii* is available in white, mauve, blue, pink, cream and darkest purple. Many other species have orange blooms. Though cool-growing, *Buddleias* can be damaged by frosts.

Buddleia davidii. Summer Lilac. China

Burchellia bubalina. Buffalo Horn, Wildegranaat. South Africa

Bursaria spinosa. Prickly Box. Australia

Burchellia

(bur-**chel**-lee-ə)   ☼ ☀ Ⓦ Ⓗ
Wildegranaat, Buffalo Horn
Spr-Sum; 10 ft/3 m; spreading; evergreen

RUBIACEAE   FRAGRANT

Not very common away from its native South Africa, the showy Wild Pomegranate *Burchellia* is related to the Gardenia and should do as well in temperate climates. It is hardy down to 28°F/−2°C, will grow splendidly where the soil is well-drained and compost rich.

It is best raised from semi-hardwood cuttings taken in late summer and kept warm until well rooted. The glossy, evergreen foliage resembles that of a Gardenia, the showy orange-scarlet flowers open at branch tips only. They are quite fragrant. The lone species is known variously as *B. bubalina* or *B. capensis*. Plants should be shaped immediately after bloom.

Bursaria

(bur-**sear**-ree-ə)   ☼ ☀ Ⓒ Ⓣ Ⓦ Ⓗ
Prickly Box, Blackthorn, Tasmanian Christmas Bush
Summer; 10–35 ft/3–10 m; sparse; evergreen

PITTOSPORACEAE   FRAGRANT

The viciously spined Australian Blackthorn just has to be included in this book in spite of its terrible reputation among Australian graziers who insist it snags the wool of passing sheep and bloodies cattle with its sharp spines. But in hoping for a world circulation for this book, I have to remember that the English call it 'charming' and the Californians 'delightful'. And if you live in an area where shale is found, you just can't go wrong in planting it—well away from paths, of course!

It propagates easily from seed or half-ripe cuttings and grows fast in well-drained soil. It will thrive in a dry position, though growing spindly, but a light pruning any time will improve matters. The tiny white flowers are very fragrant and are borne in massed panicles towards the ends of branches. They are very long-lasting and followed by attractive reddish seed capsules which contrast well with the small, shiny leaves and look fine in arrangements.

Burtonia scabra. Painted Lady. Western Australia

Burtonia

(bur-**toh**-nee-ə)   ☀ Ⓦ Ⓗ
Painted Lady
Spring; to 5 ft/1.5 m; spreading; evergreen

FABACEAE

One of Australia's most colourful members of the pea family, *Burtonia scabra* belongs to a small genus native mostly to Western Australia. Though all species are attractive in the wild, they are not often seen in gardens as they do not appreciate cultivation and are hard to maintain for more than a season or two. They can be grown from seed or tip cuttings of young growth, and do best in very well-drained soil that is rich in leaf mould to retain moisture. They grow rather slowly, are evergreen with small, 2 in/1.5 cm needle leaves borne in groups of three. Plant them in a sheltered position in at least dappled shade and watch for the gorgeous spring flower display of red-violet, pea-shaped blossoms, which are borne in the leaf axils. The Painted Lady is not frost hardy and must never be allowed to dry out.

Buxus sempervirens variegata. Variegated Box. Europe, N. Africa

Buxus

(**buk**-sus) ☼ ❂ Ⓒ Ⓣ
Box, Boxwood
Spring/all year; 6–20 ft/2–6 m; dense; evergreen

BUXACEAE

Most densely foliaged of evergreen shrubs, *Buxus* species (there are over 30 of them) have been used for centuries for hedges and bed edgings. In the 17th century particularly, they were planted densely and closely clipped to become the dark accent plant in ornamental parterres. Native to Mediterranean Europe, Japan and Central America, they grow in well-drained soil and thrive in semi-shade.

Grow from small, 1–2 in/2–5 cm cuttings struck in a sand/peat mix at any time in the warmer weather. Set them out in early spring or late summer, water regularly and pinch to shape as they grow, which is *very* slowly. Later, as the plants grow together, they can be sheared regularly. Foliage colours include dark green, gold and variegated. The plants are quite hardy and do, of course, bear flowers. These are in tiny axillary clusters, greenish and petalless.

Cadia purpurea. Kadi Bush. S. Arabia

Cadia

(**cae**-dee-ə) ☼ Ⓦ Ⓗ
Kadi Bush
Spr-Sum; 4 ft/1 m; open; evergreen

CAESALPINIACEAE

Shrubs that are native to southern Arabia and the horn of Africa are few and far between—and particularly useful to gardeners in Australia, California and other warm, dry climates.

Kadi Bush (*Cadia purpurea*) is such a plant. The good news is that *Cadia* is not only practical but pretty. It is evergreen and densely covered for most of the year with dull green, pinnate leaves of up to 40 pairs of leaflets each. The charming, bell-shaped flowers, up to 1½ in/4 cm long, hang in axillary clusters. They are a dull purple-pink and heavily veined.

Buxus sempervirens. Common Box. N. Africa, N. Asia

Caesalpinia

(seez-al-**pin**-ee-ə)   ☼ ⚜ W H
Bird of Paradise Bush,
Barbadoes Pride, Dwarf Poinciana
Spr-Sum; to 10 ft/3 m; dense; evergreen

CAESALPINIACEAE

Named for a 16th century Italian botanist, who must have been a very
colourful character, the brilliantly
flowering *Caesalpinia* are a relatively
small genus of tropical and subtropical trees and shrubs, popular
throughout most of the warm climates.

The most commonly seen is C.
pulcherrima, the Barbadoes Pride,

Caesalpinia gilliesii. Dwarf Poinciana.
Argentina, Uruguay

Caesalpinia sepiaria. Mysore Thorn. India

Caesalpinia pulcherrima. Barbadoes Pride. West Indies

Calceolaria integrifolia. Slipper Flower. Chile

which does grow in the Caribbean
area but also in many other parts of
the world. It has pink and yellow
varieties as well as the common scarlet and gold type. Fast growing to
10 ft/3 m, it has a short trunk and
branches almost to the ground. It is
grown from seed in sandy, well-
drained soil, is hardy down to
28°F/−2°C, though it may be
burned by more severe frosts and
drop many of its bipinnate leaves.

In cooler areas such as England,
the Dwarf Poinciana, *C. gilliesii*, is
sometimes seen as a wall shrub. The
Indian Mysore Thorn, *C. sepiaria*,
has a spreading habit which sometimes causes it to climb after a
fashion. It is best suited to a hot, dry
climate and bears long racemes of
lemon yellow flowers striped red on
the upper petals. It is quite viciously
spined and is sometimes used as a
dense hedge.

Calceolaria

(kal-see-oh-**lear**-ee-ə) ☼ ☀ T W
Bush Calceolaria,
Slipper Flower
Summer; 1½–6 ft/.5–2 m; dense;
evergreen

SCROPHULARIACEAE

An evergreen sub-shrub from Chile, *Calceolaria integrifolia* is a larger version of the popular annual flowering pot plants, and more attractive and versatile in every way. It can be grown from spring-sown seed which will germinate in about 10 days in a temperature range of 55–70°F/ 13–21°C. Hardwood cuttings have an even greater chance of survival.

The Slipper Flower prefers an acid, moderately rich soil with only occasional water. It can be grown outdoors in a wide range of climates. It enjoys heat and will survive a light frost with a minimum of damage. It can be grown in a pot and kept trimmed to a manageable shape. This

Calliandra haematocephala. Red Powder Puff

Calectasia cyanea. Blue Tinsel Lily. Australia

Murray Fagg

is done after bloom in autumn. The ¾ in/2 cm pouched, golden flowers are borne in dense cymes.

Calectasia

(kal-ek-**tae**-shə) ☀ W
Blue Tinsel Lily
Win-Spr; 1–2 ft/30–60 cm; spreading;
evergreen

CALECTASIACEAE

Somewhat controversial in its classification, the Blue Tinsel Lily is sometimes described as a shrub, at others as a tufted perennial. Certainly it is not a lily, so the popular name further confuses the matter.

Native to the southern states of Australia, it grows in well-drained, compost-rich soil and is normally propagated from winter divisions, which must be taken with care so as not to damage the fine roots. It should be kept moist but will take heavy, damp soil. It is slow to establish and enjoys the company of other plants. The leaves, small, heath-like and sharply pointed, make a fine contrast to the 6-petalled, metallic blue flowers which may appear profusely at any time over winter or spring.

Calliandra

(kal-lee-**an**-drə) ☼ ☀ W H
Powder Puff, Tassel Flower,
Fairy Duster
Aut-Win; 6–10 ft/2–3 m; horizontal;
evergreen

FABACEAE

From Central to South America, these really spectacular Acacia-relatives were aptly named from the

Calliandra tweedii. Mexican Flamebush. Mexico

Calliandra surinamensis. Fairy Duster.
Caribbean

Calliandra conferta. Tassel Flower.
Central America

the shiny berry show ripens in most cases after leaf fall.

All species are rather ungainly and should be pruned in winter, using the fruiting stems for indoor decoration. American *C. americana* is hardy down to 23°F/–5°C, but other illustrated species are not so cold resist-

Callicarpa rubella. Violet Berry. China, Burma, Assam

Greek *kallos* (beauty) and *andros* (stamens), for their 3 in/8 cm flower heads are quite without petals. There are some 150 species, mostly producing red, white or pink powderpuff blooms.

Calliandras of all types enjoy light soil with heavy water in summer and should be pruned back in late winter to compact them. Propagate from seed in spring or from semi-hardwood cuttings struck in autumn with bottom heat. They will survive some frost with relatively little damage.

C. tweedii, the Mexican Flame Bush, is most spectacular. *C. surinamensis* may be more charming and *C. haematocephala* has the largest inflorescence, in red or white.

Callicarpa

(kal-li-**kah**-pə)   ☼ ☀ T W H
Beauty-berry, Violet Berry,
French Mulberry
*Spr-Sum; 6–10 ft/2–3 m; arching;
deciduous*

VERBENACEAE

Widely scattered around northern Australia, Asia, North and Central America, the stunning Beauty-berries are planted in most warm-temperate to subtropical climates for the sheer luxuriance of their violet-coloured fruit. They have the typical crepe-textured leaves of the Verbena family, uninteresting white flowers and

Callicarpa americana. French Mulberry.
E. USA, West Indies

Callicarpa longifolia. Beauty-berry. N.E. Australia, South-east Asia

ant. Chinese *C. rubella* is a neater, more erect bush with 3 in/8 cm flowers and is sometimes grown in southern England. Australia's *C. longifolia* is not at all frost hardy, has larger, 6 in/15 cm leaves.

All can be grown from seed or winter hardwood cuttings with bottom heat, and enjoy a rich, well-drained soil with regular water.

Callistemon

(kal-**lis**-tem-ən)   ☼ ☀ T W H
Bottlebrush
Varied; 3–20 ft/1–6 m; treelike; evergreen

MYRTACEAE

Probably the most unusual and popular of Australia's shrub genera to be grown in many parts of the world, *Callistemons* of one sort or another are treasured in the USA, England, Ireland, the Mediterranean, Hawaii,

Callistemon viridiflorus. Green Bottlebrush. Tasmania

Callistemon pinifolius. Pine-leaf Bottlebrush. E. Australia

Callistemon 'Western Glory'. Showy Bottlebrush. Cultivar

Hong Kong and South Africa. The 25 natural species and innumerable cultivars have provided at least one type for every climate. Woody or sometimes papery-trunked shrubs, often somewhat weeping in habit, *Callistemon* tips its branches in season (which varies according to species) with exciting brush-like flowers of red, pink, green, white or purple. From the ends of these flower spikes, new leaves grow, by-passing a patch

Callistemon citrinus 'Reeves Pink'. Pink Bottlebrush. Cultivar

Callistemon viminalis. Weeping Bottlebrush. E. Australia

Callistemon salignus. Willow Bottlebrush. E. Australia

of woody seed capsules which persist for years. Foliage varies from almost needle-like to spear-shaped with a silky-hairy texture.

In nature, all prefer a light, deep soil that is well-drained but damp, and are found naturally along the banks of streams in almost pure sand. They may be propagated from spring-sown seed or from short, leafy tips taken in autumn and struck in a humid atmosphere. Most species tol-erate wind and periodic waterlogging. The species *C. montanus* is one of the hardiest, able to tolerate several degrees of frost.

The main flush of *Callistemon* flowers occurs in spring with a sec-ondary blooming in autumn. Flowers may also appear at other times, especially after periods of heavy rain. CV 'Captain Cook' forms a dense, dwarf bush about 6 ft/2 m in height. It flowers prolifically in spring and makes a good tub specimen.

C. viminalis, the Weeping Bottle-brush, has an attractively pendent habit. Green-flowered *C. viridiflorus* will tolerate light frosts, enjoys occasionally flooded soil and more shelter than most. The hybrids 'Western Glory' and 'Harkness' have particularly large and showy brushes, while 'Reeves Pink' and the white 'Anzac' are cultivars of *C. citrinus* and relatively frost hardy.

Callistemon montanus. Mountain Bottlebrush. E. Australia

Callistemon citrinus 'Anzac'. Lemon-scented Bottlebrush. Cultivar

Calluna

(kal-**loo**-nə)   ☼ⒸⓉ
Heather, Ling
*Spr-Aut; 1½–3 ft/.5–1 m; spreading;
evergreen*

ERICACEAE

Not often seen away from the
northern hemisphere, *Calluna* is the
monotypic genus that clothes many a
grouse moor. It is a densely spreading
bush with innumerable varieties of
bloom in shades from white to crimson and with foliage of silver or gold
in addition to the standard green.

Heather prefers a gritty, well-
drained, acid soil with regular water.
A cool root-run is an asset and the
plants do well in rockeries or where
mulched with pebbles. Shear after
spring bloom to keep compact and
stimulate further flowering.

Calluna vulgaris. Scottish Heather.
Europe, Asia Minor

Calocephalus

(kal-oh-**kef**-ə-ləs)   ☼ⓉⓌⒽ
Skeletonbush, Cushionbush,
Snowbush
*Spring; 8 in–7 ft/20 cm–2 m; rounded;
evergreen*

ASTERACEAE

A most useful plant for many a difficult situation, the Cushionbush
(*Calocephalus brownii*) is native to
sand dunes and rock outcrops
around much of the southern Aus-

Calocephalus brownii. Skeletonbush.
South Australia, Tasmania

tralian coast. It has no leaves to speak
of, merely a mass of silvery intertwin-
ing branches, growing so densely it
takes on the appearance of a white,
woolly cushion. The tiny yellow-
green flowers are quite insignificant;
but let's face it, the stems are why
you grow it.

It is a good rock plant, great as a
pathway planting to define edges at
night. It is salt-wind and drought
resistant and a good groundcover.
Grow it from autumn cuttings, plant
in gravelly, well-drained soil (acid or
alkaline will do) and water only during extreme drought.

Calothamnus validus. One-sided Bottlebrush.
Western Australia

Calothamnus

(kal-oh-**tham**-nəs)   ☼ⓌⒽ
Netbush, One-sided Bottlebrush
Spr-Sum; 7 ft/2 m; spreading; evergreen

MYRTACEAE

The 20-odd species of *Calothamnus*
are endemic to Western Australia
and useful wherever climatic conditions approximate its native desert.
Highly drought resistant, they can
be, and are, relied on in poor or
sandy soil as in California. They are
also resistant to wind and salt. Even
light frost is no problem, for while
growing tips may be destroyed,
flowers are invariably produced on
older wood.

Leaves of most types are needle-
like and generally about 1¾ in/4 cm
long. The flowers persist for many
months in one-sided clusters, each
inflorescence consisting of several
bundles of gold-tipped stamens
united at the base. All species grow
from seed or cuttings.

Calothamnus villosus. Woolly Netbush.
Western Australia

Calotropis procera. Bowstring Hemp.
Africa to India

Calotropis

(kal-oh-**troh**-pəs)   ☼ W H
Giant Milkweed, Crown Plant,
Kapal, Bowstring Hemp
Warm weather; 5–15 ft/1.5–4.5 m;
evergreen

ASCLEPIADACEAE   FRAGRANT

As shrubs, the 3 species of *Calotropis*
tend to be rather leggy, their sparse
branches clothed with wedge-shaped,
mealy leaves. But the pink and purple
flowers, which have a charming
fragrance, greatly resemble those of
the related Stephanotis and are used
for lei-making in Hawaii.

Calotropis are easy to grow from
their silky seeds, or from cuttings,
which should be struck under glass
and kept dry. Good drainage is a
necessity and regular heavy pruning
after bloom will promote bushiness
and reduce height.

Native to all of South-east Asia
and Africa, it is a no-no in Western
Australia, where it has been declared
a noxious weed.

Calpurnia

(kal-**pur**-nee-ə)   ☼ ☀ W H
East African Laburnum,
Golden Tassels
Spring; 15 ft/5 m; treelike; evergreen

FABACEAE   FRAGRANT

Popularly named by homesick emi-
grants for its English lookalike, the
East African Laburnum, *Calpurnia
aurea*, belongs to the same botanical

Calpurnia aurea. East African Laburnum.
South Africa

family, but does not flower so profusely, nor do its pinnate leaves have
the hairy surface of the English
Laburnum. It is evergreen, whereas
Laburnum is not. *C. aurea* grows naturally from Ethiopia right down to
South Africa.

It can be propagated from seed or
cuttings, which should be struck
under glass. It will grow happily in
any warm-temperate to subtropical
climate, but further away from the
equator must be entrusted to a greenhouse. It is not frost hardy.

The name *Calpurnia* is a rather
obscure literary allusion to the
Roman writer Calpurnius, who was a
plagiarist of Virgil. What's the connection, you say? Calpurnia is closely
related to another African tree,
Virgilia!

Calycanthus occidentalis. California Allspice.
California

Calycanthus

(kali-**kan**-thəs)   ☼ ☀ T W H
Sweet Shrub,
Californian Allspice,
Pineapple Shrub
Summer; 12 ft/3.5 m; long display,
deciduous

CALYCANTHACEAE   FRAGRANT

The 4 species of this small genus are
all native to North America, but
flower anywhere in a rich, well-
drained soil. Only the illustrated
Californian *Calycanthus occidentalis* is
not reliably frost hardy, but its

cousins do well in a cold winter climate.

All 4 species can be propagated from seed, suckers, divisions or, most reliably, by layering. And while they look remarkably like Magnolias, they are closely related only to the Chinese Wintersweet, Chimonanthus praecox.

Calycanthus are deciduous and bear long glossy leaves that are ovate, pointed and downy on their reverses. The curious flowers, which are quite fragrant, are borne singly on terminal twigs, and are 3 in/7.5 cm in diameter. Their colouring is brown and purple. All species enjoy a maximum of sun.

Calytrix tetragona. Starflower.
Australia wide

use. All species are Australian, but divided into two groups, those from the drier West being more colourful (but also more difficult to grow where the humidity is higher). The species from the eastern states grow like weeds but generally have white or pale pink flowers.

Calytrix strigosa. Blue Fringe Myrtle.
Western Australia

Calytrix

(**kal**-i-triks) ☼ T W
Starflower, Fringe Myrtle
Spring; 1–5 ft/30–150 cm; rounded; evergreen

MYRTACEAE

Not yet common in cultivation, the attractive, heath-like genus *Calytrix* is full of possibilities for general garden

Most species are easily propagated from cuttings, while seed is also successful though in short supply. For all species, a well-drained sandy soil is essential with full sun through most of the day. The habit of most species is spreading and many-branched. The leaves are minute, the flowers 5-petalled and starlike. *Calytrix strigosa*, the Blue Fringe Myrtle, is really quite spectacular.

Camellia

(ka-**meel**-ee-ə) ☼ ☀ ☀ T W H
Tea Plant, Tsubaki,
Japonica, Chinese Rose, Sazankwa
Spr-Aut; 3–20 ft/1–6 m; heavily branching; evergreen

THEACEAE   SOME FRAGRANT

Though *Camellias* will always be associated principally with Japanese culture, some 75% of the 100-odd species originate from China, nearby islands and the Indo-Chinese peninsula. They are woody plants (sometimes trees), generally with handsome, glossy leaves. Their usual habitat is mountainous and subtropical, where they grow in partial shade.

The flowers of the vast majority of the genus *Camellia* are neither large

Camellia 'Great Eastern'. Japonica Camellia. Hybrid

Camellia 'Kuro Tsubaki'. Black Camellia. Japan

Camellia chrysantha. Golden Camellia. China (Sichuan)

Camellia sinensis. Tea Plant. Burma

nor spectacular, but less than 1½ in/ 4 cm in diameter and plain white. Even smaller are the blooms of the most widely cultivated species, C. sinensis. The leaves of this plant make what we know as tea, and it is found over a wide range centring on Burma and Assam, where it has been known to reach 50 ft/16 m. It blooms very early.

When tea reached Europe in the mid-17th century, it was immediately adopted by fashionable society. The British East India Company, sensing a commercial bonanza, tried to export some of the tea plants by bribing Chinese officials. But it seems the Chinese outsmarted the company and substituted plants of the more decorative C. japonica, the leaves of which were useless for tea making. Those first plants of C. japonica arrived in England early in the 18th century, and their blooms immediately caught the fancy of nurserymen. Their rapid growth in popularity may be judged by the fact that the number of C. japonica varieties bred since, from these few, early plants, is estimated to be as high as 30,000.

Far and away the majority of ornamental Camellias are descended from the wild C. japonica, a rather scraggy looking plant of 50 ft/16 m found naturally in Japan, Korea and eastern China. But these have been hybridized with the Snow Camellia (C. rusticana) from Japan's western alps, and with the rare and beautiful Higo Camellias, themselves ancient hybrids from Japan's southern Kumamoto province. Today, the japonica descendants look better, flower better, pruned to a more compact height and width. All japonicas prefer protection from full sun and a deep, neutral to slightly acid soil. Reproduce their natural forest surroundings of shade, good drainage and humidity, and you can't go wrong.

The third most widely cultivated species of Camellia is C. sasanqua, a slender, densely-foliaged shrub or tree to 16 ft/5 m, from southern Japan and nearby islands. Originally white flowered, there is now a wide range of colours. The blooms are smaller and lightly fragrant, but they do not last well. They are naturally suited to higher temperatures, quite enjoy full sun, and bloom in autumn.

The fourth widely grown Camellia species is a relative newcomer, C. reticulata, found naturally in the forests of southern China at altitudes of up to 9800 ft/3000 m. Its leaves are

Camellia transnokoensis. Camellia species. China

Camellia 'Tama no Ura'. Miniature Japonica. Hybrid

Camellia 'Shokko Nishiki'. Higo Camellia.
Japan (Kumamoto)

large and sparsely borne, the blooms are better in full sun and open up to 3½ in/9 cm across in the wild—twice as large in many of the American-raised hybrids. Perhaps as a reaction to this excessive size, many modern

Camellia 'Star Above Star'.
Vernalis Camellia. Hybrid

Camellias have been bred deliberately small. The illustrated 'Tama no Ura', one of today's most popular Japonica Camellias, is yet smaller than a Sasanqua. Other modern interspecific hybrids are little more than 1 in/2.5 cm across. Illustrated C. transnokoensis is typical of many original species, with blooms even smaller, and opening mid-season.

Another parent of many interesting modern Japonica hybrids is 'Kuro Tsubaki', the so-called Black Camellia, the origin of which is quite unknown.

But the newly introduced C. chrysantha is the current sensation of the Camellia world. This 6–16 ft/2–5 m shrub from southern China produces a pure yellow bloom, and hybridizers are caught up in a race to hybridize it with other species and grow the progeny to flowering size. It is hoped that it foreshadows a whole new range of colours in garden Camellias, including yellow, orange, apricot and peach. First results are not promising, though I am happy to say that the lovely C. chrysantha flowered in my own garden in 1988.

Cantua

(**kan**-too-ə) ☼ ◑ T W
Magic Flower,
Sacred Flower of the Incas
Spring; 4–7 ft/1–2 m; weeping; evergreen
POLEMONIACEAE

The more I see of the botanical riches from the east coast states of South America, the more I plan to have a garden growing nothing else—well, some day! Meanwhile I stand transfixed at the sheer beauty of many of their gorgeous plants. The illustrated Magic Flower, for instance, *Cantua buxifolia*. Was it really sacred to the Incas? Why not? It is found in the Andes, is scarce in cultivation and very, very beautiful indeed.

Propagation is through autumn cuttings, struck in sharp sand under glass. It is not really frost hardy, but does show a marked resistance to cold, especially when grown in a sheltered position. It enjoys a light, but leaf-rich soil, a sunny, sheltered position, and is remarkably drought resistant.

Cantua develops a rather leggy habit, with slender, weeping branches bowed down by the weight of the long tubular flowers. These are violet-pink at the flaring tips, with the tubes striped in yellow. They hang in dense, terminal corymbs. The shrub needs support for best display, and flowered stems should be shortened by half their annual growth each year. A light tip-pruning after bloom is also beneficial. *Cantua* makes a dazzling basket plant when young, but must eventually be allowed freedom in the garden.

Cantua buxifolia. Sacred Flower of the Incas. Peru, Chile

Capparis

(**kap**-par-əs) ☼ T W
Caper, Caper-bush
Summer; 5 ft/1.5 m; spreading; evergreen
CAPPARACEAE

Judging by the number of Caper-bushes I saw on a recent visit to the Vatican gardens, somebody in a position of high authority there must be very fond of their tangy pickled flower buds—which are so popular in Russian and Polish cooking.

Shrubby *Capparis spinosa* is a small, spreading shrub with rather fleshy heart-shaped leaves and pretty white flowers that fade by noon. They can be grown from seed in a sandy, well-drained loam. The axillary flower buds are picked, pickled and sold as capers.

Capparis spinosa. Caper-bush. Mediterranean

Caragana

(ka-ra-**gah**-nə) ☼ C T
Siberian Pea-shrub, Caragana
Spring; to 20 ft/6 m; weeping; deciduous
FABACEAE   FRAGRANT

This virtually indestructible shrub from outer Mongolia is ideal for climatic extremes of baking heat or freezing cold. *Caragana arborescens* can, however, be killed with kindness and tends to fade away when the going is too soft and persistently damp. These Siberian Pea-shrubs love an exposed position with sum-

Caragana arborescens 'Lorbergii'.
Caragan. Central Asia

Carissa grandiflora. Natal Plum. South Africa

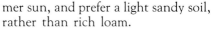

Carissa macrocarpa nana. Anatungulu. South Africa

Carissa grandiflora. Hedge Thorn.
South Africa

mer sun, and prefer a light sandy soil, rather than rich loam.

They are almost too easy to propagate from root cuttings, layers or soft-tip cuttings taken in early summer. Seed is a possibility but must be soaked in boiling water. The *Caragana* grows fast, and needs water only during droughts.

The linear compound leaves resemble fennel, the stems are spiny and the slender yellow flowers are borne singly on long stalks. Try it as a hedge in desert or mountain gardens.

Carissa

(ka-**riss**-ə)   ☼ ☀ W H
Natal Plum, Christ's Thorn,
Hedge-thorn, Anatungulu
*Summer; 7–10 ft/2–3 m; spreading;
evergreen*

APOCYNACEAE   FRAGRANT

Endemic to an area bounded by Australia, South-east Asia and East Africa, the small genus *Carissa* is now

seen throughout warm-climate areas of the world, sometimes as a dense groundcover, more often as an impenetrable hedge. All species are grown from layers or semi-hardwood cuttings struck in winter with heat. They enjoy a sandy, well-drained soil.

The pure white summer flowers resemble related Frangipani, those of the dwarf *Carissa macrocarpa nana* having rounded, overlapping petals. All species bear succulent, oblong fruits which make a good jam. The leathery leaves are glossy and the spines of many species are viciously forked. Older bushes can be pruned hard to rejuvenate growth, and smaller *Carissas* make handsome container plants. They can be clipped into shape as hedges and do well in seaside gardens.

Carpenteria

(kah-pen-**tear**-ee-ə)   ☼ ☀ T W
Tree Anemone
*Summer; 6–8 ft/2–2.5 m; untidy;
evergreen*

SAXIFRAGACEAE   FRAGRANT

Difficult to propagate from cuttings, the lovely Californian *Carpenteria* is best grown from suckers or layers in a damp mixture of sand and peat-

Carpenteria californica. Tree Anemone. California

of the thousands in my library has a word to say about it, but I can be sure it belongs to the Rubiaceae, the same botanical family that includes Bouvardia, Ixora and Rondeletia.

It grows easily from cuttings in a warm climate, the long-stemmed flowers are tiny and white, and I have never noticed a perfume though the plants known to me seem always to be in bloom. *Carphalea kirondron* is its specific name, and its main display is in the showy, brick-red bracts.

Carphalea kirondron. Flaming Beauty. Madagascar

moss. It will really thrive only in full sun (though a semi-shaded position may bring its own reward in a hot climate). *Carpenteria* does not like city air pollution, and is therefore seen at its best in bright, out-of-town gardens. It is evergreen, and like many Californian plants, drought resistant.

You'll grow it best if you can provide a rich, damp, well-drained soil, and keep it longer by withholding water in cold weather. The dark leaves are spear-shaped and leathery; the deliciously fragrant white poppy-like flowers are 3 in/7.5 cm wide and borne singly. *Carpenteria* should be pruned regularly after bloom to correct its rather untidy habits.

Carphalea

(kar-**fae**-lee-ə)　　　　☼ Ⓦ Ⓗ
Flaming Beauty
All year; to 6 ft/2 m; many-branched; evergreen

RUBIACEAE

I don't feel ashamed at being a bit skimpy with the information on this beautiful warm-climate plant. It's not that I haven't seen it, for it is very popular in both Singapore and the Philippines and many Queensland nurserymen sell it in Australia. Like other remarkable plants, it hails from Madagascar, and though it is included in the mammoth reference work *Flore de Madagascar*, the particular volume containing it has not yet been published! No other volume

Cassia

(**kas**-see-ə)　　☼ ❋ Ⓦ Ⓗ
Cassia, Senna-bush,
Buttercup Bush, Golden Wonder
Spr-Sum; 3–12 ft/1–3.5 m; erect; evergreen

CAESALPINIACEAE　　FRAGRANT

The golden flowers on the next page all belong to shrubby species of the most attractive of warm-climate plant genera, the *Cassias*. They are certainly among the most widespread, too, with between 400 and 500 species, native to all subtropical areas of both hemispheres. There are red, orange, white and pink-flowering tree species of *Cassia*—but the shrubs come in any colour you like, so long as it is yellow!

The shrub *Cassias* are mostly easy to raise from seed or from semi-hardwood cuttings struck with winter heat. All like an open, sunny position and seem to do best in well-drained soil in a mild to tropical climate, though some North American species like *C. armata* and *C. lindheimera* are reasonably frost

Cassia corymbosa. Buttercup Bush. Argentina, Brazil

Cassia alata. Candle Bush. Tropics

hardy, as is Australia's *C. ornata*.

All *Cassias* are part of a large subdivision of the pea and bean family, and in spite of their great variety, have a number of points in common. They have pinnate leaves with a quite variable number of leaflets. The flowers are always 5-petalled and open, somewhat resembling buttercups. They have prominent stamens.

Though different *Cassia* species flower in different seasons, almost every one is capable of gorgeous display for weeks or months on end, carpeting the ground beneath with colourful blossoms. Unfortunately, the flowers are followed by long, bean-like pods, and from the gar-

Cassia odorata. Sweet Cassia. E. Australia

Cassia splendida. Golden Wonder. Brazil

dener's point of view these hang in unsightly masses before finally falling.

Cassias are mostly fast growing, and their wide range means there are suitable species for almost all gardening climates. Of the illustrated species, *C. alata*, the Candle Bush, is tropical, growing to 8 ft/2.5 m with brilliant flowers arranged in a spike-like raceme. *C. artemisioides*, the Australian Silver Cassia or Old Man Senna-bush, is a dry-climate plant hardy down to 23°F/−5°C. It will tolerate a wetter climate so long as the soil drains freely and may reach 7–10 ft/2–3 m.

Cassia artemisioides. Silver Cassia. Arid Australia

Cassia biflora. West Indian Cassia. Caribbean

Cavendishia acuminata. Colombian Heath.
Ecuador, Colombia

C. *biflora* is known as the West Indian Cassia, but is widely seen in India. It has clustered flower heads and all parts of the plant are downy when young. Argentinian C. *corymbosa*, the Buttercup Bush, has become naturalized all over the world, and self-seeds regularly. Its flowers have a distinctive nutty odour. The Sweet Cassia, C. *odorata*, is Australian, with rather a pleasant perfume. It tolerates dappled shade, and has dark, linear leaflets. It prefers a rich soil, but is not hardy. Brazil's Golden Wonder, C. *splendida*, bears only 4 large leaflets to a leaf, has the largest of all *Cassia* flowers.

The name *Cassia* is from the Hebrew *quetsi'oth*, an old name for one of the species.

Cassiope
(syn. ANDROMEDA)

(kas-**sai**-oh-pee)   ☼ T
White Heather
Spr-Sum; to 1 ft/30 cm; prostrate; evergreen

ERICACEAE

A charming mountain plant from the western United States, *Cassiope* was once called Andromeda, after the daughter whose beauty the mythical Cassiope extolled above all her rivals. But when a taxonomic split occurred in the botanical Andromedas (which see), the name of *Cassiope* was conveniently revived.

A delightful dwarf member of the heather family, it is a tiny, tufted evergreen with ascending branchlets, on the end of which appear the solitary white bell-flowers about ¼ in/.5 cm across and long.

Cassiope needs peaty, acid soil, and if the climate is right, can be layered at any time. Use it in shaded areas of rockeries in mountain gardens. It will stand frost.

Cassiope mertensiana. White Heather.
W. USA

Cavendishia
(syn. PROCLESIA)

(kav-en-**dish**-ee-ə)   ☼ ☀ W H
Colombian Heath
Spr-Aut; 7 ft/2 m; weeping; evergreen

ERICACEAE

Named in honour of that botanically-minded Duke of Devonshire, William Spencer Cavendish, whose great garden at Chatsworth attracts tourists in their millions every year. The *Cavendishias* are a small genus of evergreen shrubs from the mountains of tropical America, having a great deal in common with Agapetes, Leucothöe and Pieris (all of which see).

They enjoy a rich, mildly acid soil that is well drained, and are propagated from tip cuttings in a misting frame in late summer. Flowered shoots should be shortened after bloom to promote branching, and any upright growth removed that might spoil the weeping habit. *Cavendishia's* new foliage is coral red, as are the bracts that hide the small racemes of green and red heath flowers, just like Agapetes. *Cavendishia* blooms from late spring right through to autumn, but it's the red bracts you'll notice first.

Ceanothus

(see-an-**oh**-thəs) ☼ T
California Lilac, Redroot,
Wild Lilac, Blue Blossom
Spring; 5–9 ft/1.5–3 m; spreading;
evergreen

RHAMNACEAE

Though the majority of *Ceanothus* species originate either in the western United States or in Mexico, the lovely California Lilacs seem to do best in slightly cooler areas. In particular they enjoy a chilly winter, though without too much frost. They do well in many parts of England and Europe. In Australia they do best in Victoria, Tasmania and mountain areas elsewhere.

They are of course not lilacs at all. Certainly they do not share the fragrance, so their popular epithet is probably due to the similarity of flower colour. In fact, they bloom in a wider spectrum than lilacs. Every imaginable shade of blue, violet, mauve, pink and purple can be found among the 40-odd species, and there are whites and greyish tones as well. There are both deciduous and evergreen species, but the latter are the most popular, producing small alternate leaves of roughly oval shape. These are glossy, finely toothed and deeply veined. The tiny flowers (often as small as ⅛ in/3 mm across) develop in showy terminal umbels or panicles.

Grow *Ceanothus* in light, gravelly, well-drained soil in full sun. Propagate from leafy semi-hardwood cuttings taken around summer; keep under glass with humidity until they strike. Tip-prune regularly in early years to force a dense habit, then prune dead flower masses annually.

Ceanothus papillosus. Wartleaf Ceanothus. California

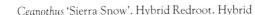

Ceanothus 'Sierra Snow'. Hybrid Redroot. Hybrid

Ceanothus thyrsiflorus repens.
Creeping Blueblossom. W. USA

Cultivars such as the illustrated C. X *edwardsii* are propagated from semi-hardwood cuttings taken in spring or autumn. Bottom heat is helpful. *Ceanothus* looks best against a background of dense greenery or mellow brick walls—but never against a blue sky, which seems to bleach all the colour from it. All species prefer a dry summer to a humid one, but vary in habit from the spreading groundcover of C. *thyrsiflorus repens* (the Creeping Blue Blossom) to tall tree-like plants reaching 25 ft/8 m (C. *spinosus* or Redheart). The hybrid C. X *edwardsii* was produced in Australia, from where it has spread back to Europe and the United States.

Ceanothus X edwardsii. California Lilac.
Australian hybrid

Centradenia grandifolius. Wonder of Peru.
Mexico, Guatemala

Centradenia

(ken-trə-**dee**-nee-ə)   ☼ ☀ W H
Wonder of Peru
Spring; 5 ft/1.5 m; bushy; evergreen

MELASTOMATACEAE

Not very common in cultivation outside European glasshouses, *Centradenia grandifolius* has endless possibilities for the warm-climate garden.
But *warm* is the word. It does not
come from mountainous Peru at all,
but from Mexico. One of a very small
genus of tropical shrubs visibly
related to the Tibouchinas, it is easily
propagated from cuttings taken in
late winter, and will grow fast in a
well-drained soil mix with plenty of
leaf mould.

The stems are strongly 4-angled,
the handsome 6 in/15 cm leaves
backed with red, and the charming
light rose flowers are arranged in
cymes at branch ends. They cut well
for indoor arrangements. The Wonder of Peru has a voracious appetite
for water, especially in summer.

Cephalanthus occidentalis. Buttonbush.
North America

Cephalanthus

(kef-ə-**lan**-thəs)   ☀ T
Buttonbush
Summer; 20 ft/6 m; dense; deciduous

RUBIACEAE

By the look of its curious pincushion-
type flowers, you wouldn't imagine
the showy *Cephalanthus* to be related

to the Gardenia—but according to
the taxonomists it is, it is. A native of
North America, it is found naturally
in swamps and along stream beds,
and is very useful in gardens prone to
flooding or difficult to dry out.

Propagate it from seed, or from
cuttings of green wood taken in
spring. It needs a rich soil and regular
moisture to produce a handsome
crop of glossy, deciduous, lanceolate
leaves, and dense heads of showy
florets in late summer.

Ceratostigma

(*syn.* PLUMBAGO)

(ker-at-oh-**stig**-mə)   ☼ ☀ T W
China Plumbago,
Dwarf Plumbago
*Sum-Aut; 6–40 in/15 cm–1 m;
groundcover*

PLUMBAGINACEAE

The principal difference between
these two species of *Ceratostigma* is
that one (*C. plumbaginoides*) is evergreen, the other (*C. willmottianum*) is
deciduous, and produces quite a display of autumn colour before leaf
drop. Both are fairly drought resistant groundcover plants, and planted

Ceratostigma willmottianum.
Chinese Plumbago. C. & W. China

Pamela Harper

Ceratostigma plumbaginoides. Dwarf Plumbago. W. China

en masse in larger botanic gardens. They will grow in a poor, gravelly soil, but do much better if it is rich and fertile.

Ceratostigmas are propagated from seed, divisions or soft-tip cuttings taken from spring to autumn. They should be pruned in late winter and prunings burned, unless you want seedlings everywhere. The China Plumbago is hardy down to about 41°F/5°C, the dwarf variety may be cut back by frost, but will sprout again in spring. Both produce a stunning display of blue bloom, those of *C. plumbaginoides* being by far the more brilliant. Both plants are endemic to China, and were once classed as Plumbago.

Cercis

(**kur**-kis)　　　　　☼ C T
Western Redbud
Spring; to 15 ft/5 m; many-trunked; deciduous

CAESALPINIACEAE

Gardeners in cool-temperate climates who don't have room for the gorgeously-blooming European Judas Tree (*Cercis siliquastrum*) might well be satisfied with its very much

smaller cousin, the shrubby Western Redbud, from America's western states.

Rarely reaching 15 ft/5 m in the wild, and much less in cultivation, it will grow in any fertile, sandy loam, and can be grown from seed or soft-tip cuttings. It is useful in very dry

Cercis occidentalis. Western Redbud. California

positions, needing water badly only in droughts.

After a respectable display of autumn colour, and some nice cold weather temperatures (say 28°F/ −2°C) the Redbud will burst into spring bloom directly from its trunk and branches, becoming absolutely covered with pale rose pea-blossoms. The interesting leaves are kidney-shaped.

Cestrum endlicheri. Scarlet Jessamine. Central America

Cestrum

(**ses**-trəm)　　　☼ ☀ W H
Night-blooming Jessamine, Jessamine
Spr-Aut; 3–6 ft/1–2 m; arching; evergreen

SOLANACEAE　　　　FRAGRANT

If the night-flowering Jessamine (*Cestrum nocturnum*) were the only member of its family, it would be enough. The rich clouds of perfume exuded after dusk scent a garden for hundreds of yards around, though a bit too strongly for many tastes. My cat, Miss Mouse, ignores that part anyway—she thinks the bush was planted to attract the moths she likes to chase.

Cestrum aurantiacum. Orange Jessamine.
Guatemala

Cestrum parqui. Willowleaf Cestrum.
S. South America

Cestrum nocturnum. Night Jessamine. West Indies

Cestrum newellii. Red Cestrum. Mexico

Plant a C. *nocturnum* in the warm climate it loves and you'll have give-aways to last a lifetime. The green flowers are followed by white berries which drop to start seedlings every-where. And it isn't the only variety. There is orange C. *aurantiacum* from Guatemala; the crimson hybrid C. X *newellii*; scarlet C. *endlicheri*. The golden flowered Willowleaf Jasmine, C. *parqui*; yellowish C. *diurnum* with its black berries, and last but not least C. *purpureum*—plus about 100 more species not commonly seen!

All *Cestrum* species need lashings of water and regular fertilizer during the warmer months. They are easy to grow from soft-tip cuttings in sum-mer, and benefit from cutting a few of the oldest canes out each year. They like a well-drained soil and are not at all frost hardy.

Chaenomeles

(kae-**nom**-ə-leez)   ☼ C T W
Japonica, Flowering Quince
*Winter; 2–7 ft/60 cm–2 m; suckering;
deciduous*

ROSACEAE

Dense, spiny, many-trunked shrubs, often nearly as wide as they are tall, the Japonicas start to bloom in late winter, and continue for months. Members of the rose family, they are invaluable to the flower arranger, particularly in cold climates, as the bare but budded stems will open in water indoors. Four species only are known, but many cultivars have been raised, blooming in shades and combinations of white, pink, red and orange.

Chaenomeles are raised easily from

Chaenomeles japonica. Lesser Flowering Quince. Japan

Chaenomeles 'Apple Blossom'. Pink Japonica.
Cultivar

Chaenomeles X *superba*. Japonica. Hybrid

Chaenomeles speciosa (fruit). China

leafy, semi-hardwood cuttings taken
in summer or autumn, or by division
of the suckering stems. They romp
ahead in any well-drained soil, provided the position is in full sun and
the plants are kept moist during summer. They are hardy down to at least
14°F/ − 10°C, but in such climates
flowering is delayed until well into
spring. Complete removal of at least
one-third of the oldest stems each
year after blooming will ensure a profuse display the following spring.

Flowers appear on bare branches,
and are usually single, though semi-
doubles are also available. The hard
autumn fruit which follow make a
delicious tangy jelly. The original C.
japonica has distinctly orange flowers,
while C. *speciosa* (syn. C. *lagenaria*)
has dozens of cultivars like the white
'Nivalis', pink 'Apple Blossom', deep
red 'Crimson and Gold' and 'Rosea
Plena', a pink semi-double.

Chaenomeles 'Crimson and Gold'. Japanese
Flowering Quince. Japanese cultivar

Chaenomeles speciosa 'Nivalis'.
White Japonica. Cultivar

Chamaedaphne calyculata. Cassandra.
N. Europe, N. Asia, North America

Chamaedaphne

(*syn.* CASSANDRA)

(ka-mae-**daf**-nee)   ☀C T
Leatherleaf, Cassandra
*Spring; 1–5 ft/30–150 cm; many
branched; evergreen*

ERICACEAE

I think I would have preferred this
small plant under its older name of
Cassandra, who was, you may remember, given the gift of prophecy
by Apollo. Perhaps it could have
forecast a flower-filled spring! But
Chamaedaphne? Well, to me it doesn't
look anything like a Daphne, and it
certainly doesn't smell like one. Just a
spreading plant with small leaves and
dainty one-sided spikes of white
flowers like Pieris or Andromeda.

It grows in North America, Asia
and northern Europe and does best
in a boggy, lime-free soil. Grow it easily from seed or summer cuttings and
prune each spring to shape, removing
some of the oldest stems and any
spindly growth. It doesn't like full
sun, so a position in semi-shade
would suit, at the bottom of a rockery perhaps. It prefers a cool to cold
climate, and is monotypic.

Chamelaucium

(kam-e-**lou**-kee-əm)   ☀T W H
Geraldton Wax, Waxflower
*Win-Spr; 2½–10 ft/80 cm–3 m; upright;
evergreen*

MYRTACEAE   AROMATIC

West Australia's sweet *Chamelauciums* should have world-wide popularity, since their 'hard to grow' reputation is really quite undeserved.
They simply prefer a gravelly soil

with a rather alkaline balance, and
given that will grow fast into an
open, twiggy shrub. Acid soil and too
much water are sure to cause prema-
ture death, and as *Chamelauciums*
have very brittle roots they must be
planted with extreme care.

They are propagated from soft-tip
cuttings, are drought and frost resistant down to 37°F/3°C. *Chamelauciums* have tiny aromatic leaves, and
bear honey-rich 5-petalled flowers for
weeks in spring, summer or autumn,

Chamelaucium ciliatum. Western Australia

Chamelaucium megalopetalum.
White Waxflower. Western Australia

Chamelaucium axillare. Esperance Wax. Western Australia

according to species. A light allover trim after bloom compacts the bush, leads to better flowering the following season.

C. *axillare*, the Esperance Wax, is a dense type of plant with white flowers. C. *ciliatum* does well in a container; it rarely reaches 18 in/ 50 cm with white flowers that age to red. C. *uncinatum*, the Geraldton Wax, is the most common species, popular as a cut flower, and has many colour varieties.

Chamelaucium 'Purple Splendour'. Purple Waxplant. Western Australia

Chamelaucium uncinatum. Geraldton Wax. Western Australia

Chilopsis

(kai-**lop**-sis) ☼ T W
Desert Willow
Spr–Sum; 10 ft/3 m; treelike; deciduous

BIGNONIACEAE   FRAGRANT

One of the great floral beauties of the Mexican and south-western USA deserts is a surprising shrub, *Chilopsis*

linearis. It is surprising because it looks so lush with graceful winter foliage, and terminal racemes of exquisite open flowers of pink and yellow—delicately marked with red. These are very fragrant, and bring birds from miles around.

The Desert Willow grows in the most arid of positions, and should be useful in outback gardens in Australia, South Africa and around the Mediterranean. It is easily propagated from hardened cuttings and actually prefers a gravelly, sandy soil. Little water is needed to produce the wonderful warm-weather display. *Chilopsis*, by the way, is deciduous.

Chilopsis linearis. Desert Willow. Nevada, Mexico

Chimonanthus

(*syn.* MERATIA)

(kim-on-**an**-thəs) ☼ ❂ C T
Wintersweet
Winter; 6–15 ft/2–4.5 m; twiggy; deciduous

CALYCANTHACEAE   FRAGRANT

Chimonanthus praecox is one of those shrubs that needs a cold winter to perform well, but even then it mostly looks like a bundle of dead sticks, so nobody in their right mind would ever plant it for display. But if you live in a cold climate, and fancy a rich, mysterious scent in the dead of winter, then it certainly is your shrub. It must be something of a long-range plan, however: seed may take 10 years to flower, autumn layers 3 or 4 years at the least.

Wintersweet demands a friable, well-drained soil, constant moisture, and a light pruning to shape. A native of China and Japan, it is quite deciduous, displaying some autumn colour before it goes to sleep. The dainty flowers, which appear on bare wood, are brown and pale yellow.

Chimonanthus praecox. Wintersweet. China, Japan

Chironia baccifera. Wild Gentian. S. Africa

shaped mass of thin, upright stems and dark, evergreen, fleshy leaves.

In spring and early summer, the flowers appear sporadically for months. They may be solitary or in twos or threes, and are 5-petalled in pinkish-mauve. Reddish orange, berry-like fruits develop later. Ideal for a rockery.

Chironia

(kai-**roh**-nee-ə)   ☼ ☀ W H
Wild Gentian, Bitterbos,
Christmas Berry
Spring; 18 in/45 cm; bunlike; evergreen

GENTIANACEAE

Named for the mythical centaur Chiron, who taught mankind the uses of plants, the *Chironia* are a small South African genus of perennials and shrubs. A charming shrubby species is the dwarf *C. baccifera*, which can be raised from seed or divisions.

It needs a sandy, well-drained soil with an admixture of leaf mould, regular moisture, and protection from midday sun in very hot areas. Given all that, it should develop into a bun-

Chloanthes

(kloh-**an**-thees)   ☼ ☀ W H
Native Penstemon,
Native Lavender
Spring; 1–4 ft/30 cm–1 m; rounded; evergreen

CHLOANTHACEAE

Only 4 species have been discovered of these colourful Australian bush shrubs, but even now they are not much in cultivation. They are not difficult to grow from cuttings of firm, new growth treated with a rooting hormone, and do particularly well in arid areas in a medium-textured soil with good drainage. They need water only in drought periods, and should be tip-pruned regularly to keep them neat.

The red-flowered *Chloanthes coccinea* occurs in a wide range of soils in inland Western Australia, and prefers dappled shade in really hot areas. It has been grown successfully as an indoor plant.

The pale mauve flowered *C. parviflora* found in Queensland and NSW is sometimes known as Native Lavender.

Chloanthes parviflora. Native Lavender. E. Australia

Chloanthes coccinea. Native Penstemon. Western Australia

Choisya ternata. Mexican Orange Blossom. Mexico

Chorizema cordatum (seedling).
Yellow Flame Pea. Western Australia

Choisya

(**choi**-see-ə) ☼ ☀ T W
Mexican Orange Blossom
Spring; 6 ft/2 m; rounded; evergreen

RUTACEAE   FRAGRANT

If it looks like a citrus, smells like a citrus, but has no fruit—well certainly nothing edible—odds on it's the closely related Mexican Orange Blossom, *Choisya ternata*, one of the most popular of garden shrubs in all temperate climates. There is only one species, and it needs a great deal of

Choisya ternata 'Sundance'. Golden Choisya. Cultivar

attention to flourish to perfection. Acid soil, rich in humus, is a good starting point, and the shrub's root junction should be set above the surrounding soil level.

Choisya is propagated from firm-tip cuttings taken in autumn for striking in a peat-sand mixture. A regular pruning keeps the bush neat and producing more bloom. The thin, leathery leaves are aromatic, each consisting of 3 rounded, glossy leaflets. The sweetly fragrant flowers appear in dense axillary clusters, and attract bees from everywhere. It is hardy down to 15°F/−9°C.

The golden-leafed cultivar C. *ternata* 'Sundance' is new, and startlingly attractive, but may not flower so heavily.

Chorizema

(ko-ri-**zee**-mə) ☼ ☀ W
Australian Flame Pea,
Flowering Oak
Spring; 2½–7 ft/.8–2 m; untidy; evergreen

FABACEAE

With the exception of one species, C. *parviflorum*, the colourful genus *Chorizema* is endemic to Western

Australia. But their habit of producing the gaudiest pea-flowers imaginable has brought them world popularity.

Firm-tip cuttings strike easily any time from summer to midwinter if kept warm and humid. Or alternatively, most of them can be raised from seed, which must be scarified or soaked for a day in warm water.

They enjoy a sandy loam, regular water, and an annual pruning to keep them tidy; unpruned, they grow

Chorizema cordatum. Heart-leaf Flame Pea. Western Australia

into a semi-climbing plant. Well-grown *Chorizemas* can be most attractive as sprawling rockery subjects. They are hardy down to 24°F/−4°C and grow well in full sun. The flower colours however are brighter in semi-shade. The yellow-flowered form of *C. cordatum* seems to have great possibilities in the future.

Chorizema ilicifolia. Holly Flame Pea. Western Australia

Chrysanthemoides
(*syn.* OSTEOSPERMUM)

(kris-an-them-**oi**-dees)   ☼ Ⓦ Ⓗ
Bitou Bush, Bone-seed,
Bush Tick-berry
Spring; 10 ft/3 m; invasive; evergreen

ASTERACEAE

'A noxious weed', 'a hated pest'. Two brief quotations give an idea of the popularity of this lovely South African plant in Australia, where it has taken over vast areas of coastal bushland.

This is largely thanks to the miners of coastal sand dunes who have planted it to help restore areas rav-

Chrysanthemoides manilifera. Bitou Bush. South Africa

aged by their operations. For if there's one place the Bitou Bush loves to send down roots it is in coastal sand. It makes a great cover shrub for poor dry banks and cliffside shelves. Anywhere the soil is gravelly or sandy will do, and very little water is required. It can, however, still be grown with safety away from coastal reserves and national parks.

No need to discuss propagation. A couple of seeds and *Chrysanthemoides* is off and away. Please be certain after blooming to prune away all seed heads and burn them or bury them in plastic bags. Lovely though it is, English and American readers should be grateful the Bitou Bush has not yet been introduced to take over their coastlines. Just keep an eye on the developers and check what it is they're planting.

Chrysocoma

(kris-oh-**koh**-mə)   ☼ Ⓦ Ⓗ
Goldilocks
Spring; 2 ft/60 cm; compact; evergreen

ASTERACEAE

Grown and seen in California and Australia as well as its native South Africa, the pretty Goldilocks (*Chryso-*

coma coma-aurea) is closely related to Michaelmas and Easter Daisies. Its botanical name means the same as its popular name, 'hair of gold' and it can put on an almost blinding display in the rock or paved garden.

Chrysocoma enjoys a well-drained soil that is almost gravelly in texture—a generous addition of coarse sand and peat will bring your ordinary garden soil into line. Water with a light hand, but increase the amount as the weather warms up and add a liquid manure at monthly intervals in spring, to force the maximum display of golden pompom flowers. Shear the dwarf bush all over after bloom to keep it compact. Cuttings of half-ripened shoots are easy to strike under glass in late summer.

Chrysocoma coma-aurea. Goldilocks. South Africa

Cistus

(**sis**-təs)   ☼ Ⓒ Ⓣ
Rock Rose
Summer; to 6 ft/2 m; spreading; evergreen

CISTACEAE

Though each flower lasts only a day, *Cistus* species bloom so profusely that the fallen flowers are replaced before you know it.

All of them (some 20 species and innumerable hybrids) are wonderful

Cistus 'Brilliancy'. Brilliant Rock Rose.
Cultivar

Cistus populifolius. Poplar-leaf Rock Rose.
Portugal, France

evergreen shrubs from the sun-baked
shores of the Mediterranean and perfect choices for poor or sandy soil, for
exposed banks or seaside cliffs. Most
remain compact, particularly when
pinched back regularly. They are
remarkably drought resistant, need
little water once established, but as a
corollary, they do not like humidity.
They are hardy down to 15°F/−9°C.

Cultivar 'Brilliancy', the most dazzling in colour, has sage-like leaves.
C. purpureus has red-blotched petals
and willow-like leaves. *C. populifolius*
is twice the size and more open and
erect, with poplar-like foliage.

Cistus purpureus. Rock Rose. Hybrid

X *Citrofortunella*

(**sit**-roh-for-tyew-nel-lə)   ☼ C T
Calamondin, Panama Orange
*Win-Spr; 3–10 ft/1–3 m; treelike;
evergreen*

RUTACEAE   FRAGRANT

One of the less edible of the Citrus
group is the intergeneric hybrid X
Citrofortunella mitis, a cross between a
variety of mandarin and a kumquat.
It is grown largely as an ornamental,
indeed most commonly as a container plant where its shining orange
fruit can be seen throughout the winter. It is not really frost hardy but
seems to flourish anywhere in a climate range from cool to warm-
temperate.

X *Citrofortunella mitis*. Calamondin.
South-east Asia

It is propagated only by grafting,
generally onto Poncirus trifoliata
stock.

Less common outside the United
States is another X *Citrofortunella*
cultivar with a weeping habit and
delicious flavour. It is the Eustis
Limequat, the result of a cross
between the lime and Fortunella
margarita, the Sweet Kumquat.

Citrus aurantium myrtifolia. Chinotto. South-east Asia

Citrus

(**sit**-rəs)   ☼ ☀ W H
Chinotto, Kusai Lime
*Win-Spr; 6–10 ft/2–3 m; treelike;
evergreen*

RUTACEAE   FRAGRANT

Except for the lemons in their infinite variety, the great bulk of *Citrus* species—and there are about 155 of them—are grown in orchards and are definitely trees. There are, however, several borderline cases apart from the related Fortunella and X Citro-

Citrus aurantiifolia. Kusai Lime. S.E. Asia

fortunella which are considered as shrubs.

The first of these is the highly ornamental, spineless Chinotto (*C. aurantium myrtifolia*) which bears very small, myrtle-like, pointed leaves and small, barely edible, bitter fruit. The second is a type of lime called Kusai which bears ping-pong-ball sized, perfectly round fruit (no nipple like other limes) and the most vicious spines.

Like all other *Citrus*, these shrubs are native to South-east Asia but are happy with winter temperatures over 45°F/7°C. *Citrus* enjoys a moist, humid atmosphere, a deep, rich soil that's very well-drained and plenty of manure and other fertilizers during the growing season. Both make good container plants.

Cleome

(*syn.* ISOMERIS)

(klee-**oh**-mee)   ☼ W H
Bladder-bush; Burro Fat
Spr-Sum; 9 ft/3 m; rounded; evergreen

CLEOMACEAE

Quite unlike a number of other *Cleome* species in cultivation, all of

which are annuals, the colourful Bladder-bush is a genuine shrub, and native to the desert area of Baja California and points north.

It can be grown from seed or late winter cuttings struck in sharp sand, after which it can be set out to brighten the most arid position. The leaves are grey and compound; the flowers, borne in upright panicles, are trumpet-shaped and golden, with long, protruding stamens. Regular light watering will produce a happier looking plant, but they are great survivors anyway.

Cleome isomeris. Bladder-bush. California, Mexico

Clerodendrum

(kler-oh-**den**-drum)   ☼ ☀ W H
Glory Bower, Butterfly Bush,
Pagoda Flower, Bleeding Heart
*Spr-Aut according to species; 2–10 ft/
60 cm–3 m; varying; evergreen*

LAMIACEAE   SOME FRAGRANT

Some 300 species of spectacularly-flowering *Clerodendrums* grow mostly in Africa, South-east Asia, Australia, even in the West Indies. Though mostly shrubby, they are very variable in appearance, some tending towards a treeish habit, others starting to climb at the very sight of a nearby wall.

Most can be grown from ripe seed, but are usually propagated from semihardwood cuttings in autumn. They do well in a rich, peaty soil, need

Clerodendrum paniculatum. Pagoda Flower. South-east Asia

Clerodendrum quadriculare. Maidenhair Bush. Philippines

Clerodendrum splendens. Glory Bower. Tropical Africa

year-round water, more generously in summer. Away from the subtropics, grow them against a sunny wall, but where summers are really hot, a light dappled shade will prevent flower fade.

Shrubby *C. paniculatum* grows just over 3 ft/1 m and bears pagoda-like terminal spikes of scarlet bloom which account for the name 'Pagoda Flower'. *C. splendens*, a dwarf climber, can reach 12 ft/3.5 m in equatorial regions, but less in cooler climates. *C. nutans*, a shiny shrub of 2–4 ft/60–120 cm, has airy, drooping panicles of white bloom. The Blue Butterfly Bush, *C. ugandense*, produces blue flowers that are an amazing example of vegetable mimicry, while *C. thomsonii* opens hundreds of white, heart-shaped blossoms that seem to exude drops of blood. The really tropical *C. quadriculare* flowers like a shower of festive fireworks. Even out of bloom, most *Clerodendrums* are decked with handsome foliage. No warm-climate garden should be without one.

Clerodendrum ugandense. Blue Butterfly Bush. Tropical Africa

Clerodendrum nutans. Hanging Clerodendrum. Assam, Himalayas

Gillian Beckett

Clerodendrum thomsonii var *balfourii*. Bleeding Heart. W. Tropical Africa

Clethra arborea. White Alder. Madeira

Cleyera japonica CV 'Tricolor'. Sasaki. Japan

Clethra

(kleth-rə**)** ☼ ☀ Ⓣ Ⓦ
Summersweet,
Sweet Pepper Bush
Sum-Aut; to 10 ft/3 m; bushy; evergreen

CLETHRACEAE FRAGRANT

Clethra was the ancient Greek name for an Alder tree, and it must be confessed the two plants bear lookalike leaves. Native to eastern North America, *Clethra alnifolia* is easily grown from spring seed, soft-tip cuttings struck under heat or, best of all, from suckers, which it produces profusely.

It needs a well-drained, leaf-rich acid soil and year-round water to produce the dense, rounded bush to which we aspire. The leaves are sharply toothed and borne alternately. The tiny white flowers develop as erect terminal racemes, and are spicily fragrant. This *Clethra* should be pruned back after bloom by removing a proportion of the oldest canes.

Another popular *Clethra*, *C. arborea*, is, as the name suggests, tree-like in shape.

Clethra alnifolia. Sweet Pepper Bush. USA, Maine to Florida

Pamela Harper

Cleyera

(syn. EURYA**)**

(klae-ur-ə**)** ☀ Ⓣ Ⓦ Ⓗ
Sasaki
Sum-Aut; 3–15 ft/1–5 m; spreading; evergreen

THEACEAE

Charming evergreen shrubs for the foliage fan. There are 15 or so East Asian species of *Cleyera*, and their glossy elliptical leaves inevitably remind one of closely related Camellias. In Japan, the Shinto priests still cut *Cleyera* branches to sweep out the old year—but who could bear to do that with beautiful *C. japonica* CV 'Tricolor' whose foliage is suffused with rose pink and golden green? The fragrant creamy summer flowers are only thumbnail size, and the black autumn fruits even smaller.

In a warm-temperate climate, *Cleyera* will thrive in semi-shade, with plenty of moisture. In cooler areas, the protection of glass may be needed in winter.

Propagate from cuttings in spring.

Clianthus puniceus. Red Kowhai, Kaka Beak. New Zealand

Clianthus puniceus albus. White Kaka. New Zealand

a little like rosemary's (and equally salt resistant). The sparsely-borne flowers are deep yellow and ½ in/ 1 cm wide. These are followed by brownish-red fruits consisting of three unified segments. Related *C. pulverulentum* is from Tenerife, and rather more tender. Both species will grow easily from cuttings if the climate is right.

Codiaeum variegatum var Duck's Foot Croton. Malaysia

Clianthus

(klee-**an**-thəs)   ☼ ☀ T W

Kaka Beak, Parrot's Bill,
Red Kowhai, Lobster Claw,
Ngutu, Kaka
*Spring; 10–30 ft/3–12 m; weeping;
evergreen*

FABACEAE

Australia's gaudy Sturt Desert Pea may spring to mind when you think of *Clianthus*. But internationally, the more favoured plant is New Zealand's *C. puniceus* or Kaka, commonly flowering in dull red, but with handsome pink and white varieties. Kaka has the pinnate foliage of much of the pea family, and is known to have been cultivated by the Maori people before Europeans came. It has been a popular specimen in England since the early 19th century, usually planted by a sunward facing wall.

Clianthus may be propagated from summer cuttings or from seed, which should be scarified to speed germination. Choose an alkaline soil, water regularly and feed with animal manure. Prune after bloom; watch for snails.

Cneorum

(k'nee-**or**-əm)   ☼ T

Spurge Olive
Spr-Aut; 4 ft/1 m; spreading; evergreen

CNEORACEAE

Not your most sensationally decorative of shrubs, the two species of *Cneorum* are surprisingly useful in light, sandy soil which replicates their native microclimate.

C. tricoccon is the more commonly seen species—a low-growing Mediterranean evergreen, densely branching and with grey-green linear leaves

Cneorum tricoccon. Spurge Olive. S. Europe

Codiaeum

(*syn.* **PHILLAUREA**)

(koh-dee-**ae**-əm)   ☼ ☀ W H

Croton, Variegated Laurel
All Year; 3–25 ft/1–7 m; leggy; evergreen

EUPHORBIACEAE

With leaves as brilliantly coloured as these tropical beauties, who needs flowers? Native to South-east Asia, and established right across the Pacific, Crotons are seen in warm-climate gardens everywhere, displaying gaudy foliage in every colour except blue.

Away from the tropics, they are normally raised in containers and kept in sunny, sheltered positions. Some leaf loss may be expected in

Codiaeum variegatum. 'Emperor Alexander'. Cultivar

Codiaeum variegatum.
'Baronne de Rothschild'. Malaysia

Coffea

(kof-fee-ə)　　　　　　☼ ☀ W H
Arabian Coffee Tree
Spr-Sum; 15 ft/4.5 m; slender; evergreen

RUBIACEAE　　　　　　FRAGRANT

Though referred to in several of its
popular names as a tree, *Coffea
arabica* is in reality a shrub, and is
often pruned lower than its natural

Coffea arabica. Coffee blossom.
Tropical Africa

Codiaeum. Croton blossom. Malaysia

winter, though the modern cultivar
'Norma' has flourished for me for
three years, with never a leaf out of
place. Crotons are inclined to be
leggy unless regularly pruned to a
dense, shrubby shape.

　Which of the myriad leaf shapes or
colours you choose is purely a matter
of taste—but remember that the less
green they include, the more light
will be needed.

　Crotons will grow from seed, but
fancy-leaf varieties must be raised
from cuttings. Growth is fairly slow.

　Pests include thrips, mealybugs
and spider mites which are hard to
see on the colourful leaves. Spray
with Maldison for the first two, and
a recommended miticide for the last.
Fertilize regularly and wear gloves
while pruning, as the whitish sap may
irritate the skin.

Coffea arabica. Arabian Coffee Tree. Tropical Africa

pruning, they can be trained as a low, informal hedge, though flower loss will inevitably result. Winter moisture stimulates bloom, but mature plants will endure drought. Propagate *Coleonemas* from soft summer tip-cuttings. Prune lightly three or four times during the growing season. They are hardy, by the way, down to 23°F/ – 5°C.

Coleonema album. Confetti Bush. South Africa.

height to make berry-picking easier. As the source of all the coffee we drink, it is obviously of great value in commerce, but we don't suggest you grow it for economy's sake. It takes a whole lot of coffee beans to keep one family in coffee for a year!

But if you live in a warm-temperate climate we certainly suggest you grow it for ornament. The leaves are shiny like those of related Gardenias, and the flowers are fragrant and snowy white as well. The green berries that follow turn a brilliant red, and each contains two coffee beans. Grow them from semi-hardwood cuttings in well drained, leaf-rich soil. Water regularly to maintain high humidity.

family, though they certainly have heath-like foliage.

They grow best in a rich but well-drained soil, are favourites for planting on banks, or in groups as lawn specimens. With continuous light

Coleonema X 'Sunset Gold'. Golden Diosma. Cultivar

Coleonema

(koh-lee-oh-**nee**-mə) ☼ ✹ Ⓦ Ⓗ
Diosma, Breath of Heaven,
Confetti Bush
Win-Spr; 2½ ft/75 cm; bun-shaped; evergreen

RUTACEAE   AROMATIC

Neat little evergreen shrubs that preview spring with a shower of tiny pink or white stars, the *Coleonemas* are native to South Africa and, surprisingly, do *not* belong to the heath

Coleonema pulchrum. Breath of Heaven. South Africa

Colletia paradoxa. Anchor Plant. S.E. Brazil

Colquhounia coccinea. Silver Shrub. Himalayas

Colquhounia

(kol-**koo**-nee-ə)   ☼ ◑ T W
Silver Shrub
Autumn; 10 ft/3 m; spreading; evergreen

LAMIACEAE

A handsomely textured shrub from the Himalayas, *Colquhounia* was named after a former patron of the Calcutta Botanic Garden, Sir Robert Colquhoun.

Easy to grow from cuttings, it is not frost hardy, but can be grown against a sunward facing wall in cooler areas. It is a sprawling plant with large felty leaves that reveal its relationship in the mint family, Lamiaceae. The downy stems are 4-angled, another mint characteristic. In late summer and autumn, the shrub sends up the typical terminal flower heads. These may be yellow, pink, or in the most common type, a pale orange-red.

Colletia

(kol-**let**-ee-ə)   ☼ T W
Anchor Plant
Autumn; 7–10 ft/2–3 m; open; evergreen

RHAMNACEAE   FRAGRANT

Looking like a zig-zag modern sculpture, *Colletia* seems to have no specific shape in mind. A very vigorous plant, originally from Uruguay and southern Brazil, it needs well-drained but rich soil to remain in a healthy state.

It is usually grown from semi-hardwood cuttings struck in a sand/peat mixture. Its water needs are minimal, but you should prune it lightly in spring, just to control its size. *Colletia* is not a handsome plant, but its curiosity value is enormous. The cruelly shaped segments are actually adapted spines, and the mature plant is totally without leaves. Tiny creamy flowers appear at the base of most spines in autumn.

Colutea

(kol-oo-**tee**-ə)   ☼ T W
Bladder Senna
Spr-Aut; 7–14 ft/2–4 m; rounded; deciduous

FABACEAE

A small genus of shrubs found westwards from the Himalayas to southern Europe and North Africa, the *Coluteas* are particularly useful in

Pamela Harper

Colutea arborescens. Bladder Senna.
N. Africa, S. Europe

Comarostaphylis diversifolia. Summer Holly. California, Baja California

drier climates (where they flower for months) as they sprawl over banks or frame a view.

Easy to propagate from spring seed or autumn cuttings, they flourish in any soil so long as it is well drained. Prune hard in late winter, almost to last year's wood, they'll shoot immediately and always flower on new season's growth.

The group's popular name comes from the bladder-like seed pods that follow the mass of gaily coloured pea flowers. These are bright yellow in *C. arborescens*, orange-red in those of its hybrid *C.* X *meadia*. Of interest to Australian gardeners who have trouble growing the weak-rooted Sturt Desert Pea, European gardeners have long discovered that it can be successfully grafted onto a seedling of strong-rooted *Colutea*. The compound leaves of both *Colutea* species are deciduous.

Comarostaphylis

(ko-mah-roh-**staf**-ə-lis)   ☼ W
Summer Holly
Spring; 20 ft/6 m; many-branched; evergreen

ERICACEAE

Closely resembling, and in fact, closely related to the Irish Strawberry (see Arbutus), *Comarostaphylis diversifolia* is an ideal shrub for the dry climate.

An erect, many-trunked native of California and Mexico, it is decked out with evergreen leaves, dark and shining above, woolly-white beneath, with the leaf-margins generally rolled inward. In spring, small terminal panicles of white lily-of-the-valley type flowers develop. These are mildly fragrant and are followed by

clusters of bright red, warty fruits, rather like those of Arbutus, which ripen midsummer, and give the tree an out-of-season festive look.

Grow from cuttings, and plant in well-drained lime-free soil. Should be more widely grown in Mediterranean areas, and in Australia.

Comarostaphylis diversifolia. Spring flowers. California

Combretum coccineum. Scarlet Paintbrush. W. Africa

Combretum fruticosum. Paintbrush Plant. Tropical Africa

many uses for the plants they saw around them. The *Commersonias* were especially valued for their strong bark fibres which were used for tying and weaving. They are attractive plants, as the illustrated *Commersonia pulchella* reveals.

A member of the Western Australian sandplain community, it bears irregularly-lobed leaves with brown reverses, and small white flowers with purple markings. Grown from seed or cuttings, it prefers a compost-rich, well-drained soil.

Commersonia pulchella. E. Australia

Comptonia peregrina. Sweet Fern. E. North America

Combretum

(kom-**bree**-təm)   ☼ ⚘ W H
Paintbrush Plant
Spr-Aut; climbing; evergreen
COMBRETACEAE

Many subtropical shrubs, in their search for light and the energy they derive from it, turn themselves into climbers. No matter that they lack tendrils or spines or claws, they are able to lean into other plants and appear to be climbing with a life of their own. Such a group are the *Combretums*, splendid southern hemisphere shrubs with branched inflorescences.

They are grown from stiff cuttings of heeled side shoots in a sandy mix under glass. They can be transferred to a well-drained leaf-rich soil with regular moisture and will grow at a great rate. Evergreen, blooming in warm weather, they are ideal for spilling over banks or leaning against walls.

Commersonia

(kom-ur-**soh**-nee-ə)   ☼ W H
Brush Kurrajong
Spr-Sum; 7–20 ft/2–6 m; compact; evergreen
MALVACEAE

In the days before white settlement, the Australian Aboriginal people had

Comptonia

(komp-**toh**-nee-ə)   ☼ ⚘ C T
Sweet Fern
Spring; 5 ft/1.5 m; many-branched; evergreen

MYRICACEAE   FRAGRANT

Closely related to North America's fragrant Bayberries, Waxberries and Candleberries (Myrica spp.) the curious *Comptonia peregrina* forms a monotypic shrub genus from the eastern states of the USA. It is greatly valued in American country gardens for its fragrant fern-like foliage and spring display of interesting inflorescences (male in the form of catkins,

female of globular form as in our illustration). Both are found on the same plant.

Propagation is by seed or division. It enjoys an arid, sandy soil and light watering, and will grow with moderate speed into a compact, many-branched shape. The foliage makes a splendid subject for arrangements.

Congea

(**kon**-jee-ə)   ☼ H
Pink Sandpaper Vine,
Shower Orchid
Win-Sum; 13–30 ft/4–10 m; climbing shrub; evergreen

VERBENACEAE

Though sometimes grown outside a glasshouse in a mild temperate climate, the *Congea* or Sandpaper Vine is really seen at its best only in fully tropical parts of the world.

Soft-tip cuttings strike well and should be grown in a compost-rich, fast-draining soil. Both water and fertilizer should be applied lavishly during its warm-weather growing season.

The leaves are velvety and 5 in/12 cm long; the insignificant white flowers make way for a showy display of bracts which change from grey to a rich pink as they age. In Californian terminology, *Congeas* need their own space—and plenty of it.

Congea velutina. Sandpaper Vine. Thailand

Conradina verticillata. Pineleaf Mintbush. USA East Coast

Conospermum

(kon-oh-**spur**-məm) ☼ W H
Smoke Grass, Smokebush
Spring; 4–7 ft/1.5–2 m; bun-shaped; evergreen

PROTEACEAE

Common xerophytic plants in the outback of Australia, 30-odd species

Conospermum stoechadis. Smoke Grass.
Western Australia

of *Conospermum* belong to the Protea family. Not often grown in the home garden, even in their native land, they are sold widely as cut flowers, and last for months. They are, however, useful in drought-prone gardens with dry, gravelly soil, where they may be raised from summer cuttings, and need little water except in the hottest of weather.

Bun-shaped and shrubby, *Conospermums* mostly grow 7 ft/2 m in height, though illustrated *C. stoechadis* is barely half that size. The curious, woolly flower heads are mostly grey and look like a puff of smoke when seen from afar.

Conradina

(kon-rad-**ee**-nə) ☼ ☀ T W
Pineland Mintbush
Spring; 1–3 ft/30 cm–1 m; many-branched; evergreen

LAMIACEAE   AROMATIC

Australian visitors to the Florida hinterland are sometimes surprised to find what is apparently one of the Australian native Mintbushes (Prostanthera spp.) growing in the coastal pinelands. The resemblance is strong,

but misleading; the Florida plant is *Conradina verticillata*, one of 4 American species, all very similar.

Struck from cuttings in a damp sand-peat mix, the American Mintbushes push ahead in sandy soil, providing a charming though sporadic display over the warmer months. Reaching from 1 to 3 ft in height (30 cm to 1 m), *C. verticillata* becomes a compact, heavily branched shrub with smooth grey linear leaves that disguise its membership in the mint family.

Convolvulus

(*syn.* RHODORRHIZA)

(kon-**vol**-vyoo-ləs) ☼ W H
Bush Morning Glory,
Silverbush, Canary Glory Bird
Spring; to 6 ft/2 m; dense bush; evergreen

CONVOLVULACEAE

Think of *Convolvulus* and you normally visualize the pink or blue-flowered Morning Glory vines, twining around cottage doors. But there are better blooming shrubs in the genus as well.

Southern European *C. cneorum* is a compact, bushy plant 2–4 ft/60–120 cm tall and almost as wide. It

Convolvulus floridus. Canary Glory Bird. Canary Islands

Coprosma

(kop-**roz**-mə)
Mirror Plant, Taupata,
Looking-glass Plant
*Summer; 7–10 ft/2–3 m; spreading;
evergreen*

RUBIACEAE

Half a century ago and more, I lived in Tasmania, where many New Zealand plants grow to perfection. I remember that one of the first plants to catch my eye was the Mirror Plant, *Coprosma repens*, which grew on my way to school. Towards autumn, it was covered with light red berries. But in later years, whenever I came across a similar plant it was bare of fruit. And then I learned that to bear fruit there must be both male and female plants in proximity . . . even among *Coprosmas*. So unless you're planning to plant them in bulk, learn to plant *Coprosmas* for the beauty of their foliage alone.

All varieties grow well from cuttings set in a warm, humid place, and flourish in well-drained soil that is not too rich. Heavy watering is needed in summer, and a regular light pruning to keep some sort of shape. Leaf varieties of *C. repens* are many, sometimes on the same plant.

The smaller-leafed hybrid C. X

Coprosma repens argentea. Mirror Bush. New Zealand

Convolvulus cneorum. Silverbush. S. Europe

may be propagated from seed, but is easier to grow from heeled cuttings of basal shoots taken in summer for striking in a damp mixture of peat and sand.

The Silverbush likes to sunbake in a light, sandy soil where it will grow into a compact, densely foliaged plant in no time at all. The leaves have a silvery-silky texture and the 1 in/2.5 cm trumpet flowers are flushed in pale pink and appear in terminal spring clusters.

Out in the Atlantic, the Canary Islands are home to a related species curiously known as the Canary Glory Bird. This is a taller plant, simply massed with ½ in/1 cm morning glory flowers of white or pale pink. Its magnificent display during the warmer months has brought the plant great popularity. It is easily grown from soft-tip cuttings.

Coprosma repens 'Picturata'. Looking-glass Plant. New Zealand

kirkii is also variable, and used as a dense groundcover. At its most attractive, the leaves are a bright, glossy green.

All species and varieties do exceptionally well in a seaside environment, and are salt resistant.

Cordia

(**kor**-dee-ə) ☼ Ⓣ Ⓦ
Anacahuita
*Summer; to 25 ft/7.5 m; spreading;
evergreen*

BORAGINACEAE

Many *Cordias* are showy tropical relatives of the temperate gardener's forget-me-nots and Heliotrope, and are as easy to grow. The tropical species have mostly orange or yellow flowers and are of tree size.

But in the deserts of both Old and New Mexico and Texas, there is a horse of a different colour. To be precise, it is *Cordia boissieri*, a compact, spreading shrub with velvety grey-green leaves and golden-centred flowers of purest white. Most commonly raised from seed, it grows very well (if not very large) in completely arid conditions. In richer soil, it may grow to small tree size.

Coprosma X *kirkii variegata*.
Coprosma hybrid. New Zealand

Coprosma repens (fruit). New Zealand

Cordia boissieri. Anacahuita. New Mexico, Texas

Cordyline terminalis. Ti. Pacific Islands

What Queensland's *C. manners-suttoniae* lacks in leaf colour, it makes up for with some of the most gorgeous berries around. These are about ½ in/1 cm in diameter and crowded in long hanging panicles. *Cordylines* are easily propagated by laying pieces of stem in a sand-peat mix, kept warm, moist and humid, or by seed or division. They are only for frost-free gardens, but make colourful indoor specimens with central heating to help them along.

Cordyline manners-suttoniae. Native Cordyline. Australia

Cordyline terminalis. Tree of Kings (in fruit). Pacific Islands

Cordyline
(*syn.* DRACAENA)

(**kor**-də-lain, kor-də-**lai**-nee) ☼ ☀ W H
Ti, Tree of Kings, Dracaena
All year; 5–12 ft/1.5–3.5 m; unbranched; evergreen

ASPARAGACEAE

In the Pacific islands, Polynesia fire-walkers attach the flame-red leaves of the Ti plant to their ankles to ensure painless passage across the glowing embers. Western gardeners are also drawn to the shrub *Cordyline terminalis* because of its leaves, which can be strikingly coloured: bright green, dark red and mixtures of scarlet, white, yellow, purple and orange. Insignificant white or mauve flowers are followed by berries which ripen from green to red.

Cornus
(**kor**-nəs)   ☼ ☀ C T
Dogwood, Redtwig,
Bunchberry, Cornel, Clusterberry
Spring; 1–15 ft/30 cm–4.5 m; twiggy; deciduous

CORNACEAE

The best known Dogwood of all, *Cornus florida*, exquisitely blooming in white or pink, is a tree. But there are around 100 other species found in cool-winter parts of the USA and Asia, many of them shrubs with brilliantly coloured winter bark. Thus they perform the gardener's hat-trick, following spring bloom with autumn foliage and fruit display.

The illustrated species range from 1 ft/30 cm in height for creeping C.

Cornus stolonifera CV 'Aurea'. Yellowtwig. North America

Cornus officinalis. Japanese Cornel.
Japan, Korea

Cornus kousa. Chinese Dogwood.
Japan, Korea

canadensis through 15 ft/4.5 m high for the golden-flowered Japanese variety and brilliant American Redtwig Dogwood, to around 21 ft/7 m for the Chinese *C. kousa*. The display of all Dogwood is in the bracts which surround a cluster of small flowers. These later develop into clustered fruit, hence the name, Clusterberry. The bracts are 4 in number and may vary in colour.

All shrubby Dogwoods are easy to propagate from seed or rooted layers struck in a sand-peat mixture with high humidity. The Japanese *C. officinalis* will tolerate limy soil; the others prefer an acid balance of damp, leafy-rich compost. *C. canadensis* is a groundcover, *C. stolonifera* a multi-stemmed shrub; *C. officinalis* and *C. kousa* may be treelike or heavily branched from around ground level. All are deciduous and make a presentable display of autumn colour. The showy red *C. stolonifera* is classed as rampant, but can be kept within bounds by lopping the underground stems with a sharp spade.

Favourite shrubs for the cold to cool-temperate climate.

Cornus alba. Tartarian Dogwood.
Siberia, China

Corokia cotoneaster. Wire-netting Bush.
New Zealand

Coronilla glauca variegata. Crown Vetch.
Mediterranean

Cornus canadensis. Creeping Dogwood.
Greenland, Alaska, E. Asia, California

Corokia

(kə-**roh**-kee-ə)   ☼ T W
Wire-netting Bush
Spr-Sum; to 10 ft/3 m; sparse; evergreen

ARGOPHYLLACEAE   FRAGRANT

New Zealand's dainty Wire-netting
Bush makes an interesting informal
groundcover, growing every which

way but where you want it. The wiry
stems zig and zag in all directions,
sparsely furnished with tiny, roundish leaves and, in season, a veritable
cloud of bright yellow, star-shaped
flowers at the leaf axils. They can be
borne singly or in small clusters but
always exude a mild, elusive
fragrance.

Corokia may be propagated from
seed or, more usually, from 3 in/8 cm
cuttings taken in late spring or
autumn and kept cool and humid in
a mixture of sharp sand and peat.
Corokia is hardy down to 23°F/−5°C
and is probably more effective when
sheared regularly after bloom to force
denser growth.

Coronilla

(ko-ro-**nil**-lə)   ☼ T
Crown Vetch
Spr-Sum; to 4 ft/1 m; dense; evergreen

FABACEAE   FRAGRANT

The 20-odd species of *Coronilla*
bloom (as Henry Ford might have
said) in any colour you like as long as
it's yellow! Their name is very old,
Coronilla meaning 'little crown'. The
Crown Vetch, *C. glauca*, is most
commonly seen, often in its vari-

egated form. It is a dense, evergreen
bush with glossy, compound leaves
(always with an odd number of leaflets on either side of the stem). The
yellow pea-flowers appear both at
stem ends and in leaf axils and are
quite fragrant by day.

Grown from seed, cuttings, layers
or division, these dainty shrubs just
have to be among the most obliging
of garden plants, provided they are
set in open, well-drained soil.

Correa alba. White Correa.
S.E. Australia, Tasmania

Correa reflexa var reflexa. Hybrid Correa

Correa pulchella. Beautiful Correa.
South Australia

Correa reflexa. Common Correa.
Mainland Australia

Correa

(**kor**-ree-ə) ☼ T W H
Australian Fuchsia,
Native Fuchsia
Win-Spr; 1–16 ft/30 cm–5 m; dense;
evergreen

RUTACEAE   FRAGRANT

Though the entire genus *Correa* is
endemic to Australia (mainly the east
coast) it is named for the 18th century Portuguese botanist José Correa
de Serra. There are 11 species ranging
from groundcovers to tree-like plants
in some areas.

Though dainty in appearance,
they are not difficult to grow (except
from seed) and have become popular
in many countries. Young cuttings
root readily in an alkaline sandy mixture. It is also recommended that

before planting out, the chosen area
should be sprinkled with powdered
limestone. They prefer soil that is
light, well-drained and moist at first,
though drier conditions are acceptable to mature plants.

Belonging to the same family as
Boronia and Citrus (which see) it is
not surprising to find that the long
bell-like flowers are rich in honey and
mildly fragrant. They do best in part-
shade, except in very cool climates.
All *Correas* can be pruned to keep
them reasonably compact. They com-
mence blooming in late winter, generally as a mixture of red, green and
white.

Corylopsis

(ko-ril-**op**-sis) ☼ ☀ C T
Winter Hazel
Winter; 5–6 ft/1.5–2 m; spreading;
deciduous

HAMAMELIDACEAE   FRAGRANT

This very small genus of winter-
flowering shrubs is endemic to East
Asia and the Himalayas, and is therefore quite hardy in Britain, Australia
and New Zealand, though a little tender for central parts of the United
States.

A many-stemmed, deciduous plant, it can be propagated from soft-tip cuttings, divisions or layers and does best in a mildly acid to neutral soil rich in leaf mould. Growth is slow but worth the wait when the small, lemony-green flowers appear in drooping racemes in late winter. They are very fragrant, open on bare wood and are followed almost immediately by toothed, grey-green foliage that often seems to have a pinkish tinge at first.

Corylopsis is most effective in dappled shade, with back lighting if it can be arranged.

Corylopsis spicata. Winter Hazel. Japan

Corylus avellana 'Contorta'. Harry Lauder's Walking-stick. Japanese cultivar

Japanese cultivar *C. a.* 'Contorta' known as the Twisted Filbert, or sometimes, with a nod to an old-time variety star, Harry Lauder's Walking-stick. Its branches, twigs and male catkin flowers are curled and twisted in a remarkable fashion and look stunning at any time of year. This curious cultivar, which can only be propagated by grafting, grows to 4 ft/1.25 m, or just a third of the height of the parent species.

It needs a deep, rich soil that is particularly well-drained, though moisture is still needed. It is hardy down to 18°F/−8°C. The lovely, toothed leaves turn butter yellow in autumn. The Twisted Filbert bears edible nuts, just like its parent plant.

Corylus

(co-**rai**-ləs)   ☼ Ⓒ Ⓣ
Corkscrew Hazel, Filbert,
Harry Lauder's Walking-stick
Win-Spr; 4 ft/1 m; globose; deciduous

CORYLACEAE

One of Europe's favourite nuts is produced on the common *Corylus avellana*—you'll see them in English shops as Hazelnuts or Kentish Cobs. But keen gardeners prefer the bizarre

Corynabutilon X *suntense*. Blue Bellflower. Hybrid

Corynabutilon

(syn. ABUTILON)

(kor-**ai**-nə-byoo-til-ən)   ☼ ☀Ⓣ Ⓦ
Chilean Bellflower,
Blue Bellflower
Summer; 10–25 ft/3–7 m; tall, open; evergreen

MALVACEAE

Almost identical to the Abutilon (which see) the small genus *Corynabutilon* consists of only three Chilean species. The technical difference is in the details of the style or female organ which is malformed, as described in the generic name: *coryn* means 'a club'. More obvious, though, is the flower colour. All *Corynabutilons* are bluish in tone.

Tall shrubs for an open, sunny position (except in hot climates where some shade is a blessing), they may reach 25 ft/7.5 m in an open, vase shape. Leaves are maple-like, with 3, 5 or 7 lobes. Flowers are flat, 5-petalled and borne in axillary clusters. Propagate from semi-hardwood cuttings in summer. They are not really frost hardy but resist cold surprisingly well. They do well in any good garden soil where drainage is beyond doubt.

Corynabutilon vitifolium. Chilean Bellflower. Chile

Cotinus

(koh-**tee**-nəs)   ☼ C T W
Smokebush, Wig Tree,
Venetian Sumach
Spr-Sum; 10 ft/3 m; rounded; deciduous

ANACARDIACEAE

After the Smokebush has flowered
(and you may be forgiven for not
noticing the event) its maximum display appears. These are the tiny
stems left after flower fall which
become enlarged and persist for
months, giving the appearance of
puffs of red smoke or a red wig.

Cotinus coggyria is a tall-growing
bush and completely deciduous,
turning on a dazzling display of
autumn colour in cooler areas. In late
winter, though, it should be pruned
back to growth buds by two-thirds.
Propagate from spring seed, root cuttings, layers or hardwood stem cuttings taken in winter. These should
be dusted with hormone rooting
powder before attempting to strike in
sharp sand. Rooted plantlets should
be grown on in well-drained soil,
with light but regular water.

Cotinus coggyria. Venetian Sumach.
S. Europe, Asia

Cotoneaster microphylla. Rockspray (in flower).
W. China

Cotoneaster

(ko-toh-nee-**ass**-tər)   ☼ C T W
Cotoneaster, Rockspray
*Spr-Sum; 2–15 ft/60 cm–4.5 m; trailing
branches; mostly evergreen*

ROSACEAE

I wouldn't dare criticize my readers'
pronunciation of plant names, but I
must beg, the lovely Rocksprays are
not called 'cotton easter' (as in Easter
eggs). The name is adapted from two
old Greek words, *kotoneon* and *aster*,
meaning 'like a quince'. They are the
same family as quinces and their
flowers, fruit and leaves look exactly
like those of a quince, though on a
smaller scale.

There are perhaps 50 species of
them, all fairly hardy; and they must
be the favourite berry-bearing shrub
in any climate from cold to warm-
temperate. They grow without fuss in
almost any soil from acid to alkaline
(which happens to be their preference). But just grant them a sunny
position in well-drained soil and
they'll turn on a stunning display
that persists for months. Grow from
seed or semi-hardwood cuttings but
let them grow on their own roots,
and do not attempt to graft.

Cotoneasters grow naturally in
Europe, North Africa and northern
Asia, with the heaviest concentration
being found in western China. They
are remarkably drought resistant,
though cropping better when they

Cotoneaster CV 'Cornubius'.
Hybrid Rockspray

Cotoneaster microphyllus. Rockspray
Cotoneaster. W. China

Cotoneaster horizontalis. Fishbone Cotoneaster. W. China

Crassula arborescens (in bloom). S. Africa

are kept moist. According to species and natural height, you can use them for covering ground or banks, for espalier work, dense hedges or screens or (with light pruning) as a large, arching specimen shrub. *C. horizontalis* and *C. microphyllus* are best for low cover. C. CV 'Cornubius', *C. frigidus* and *C. salicifolius* are taller, with weeping branches weighed down by fruit. Most *Cotoneasters* are semi-evergreen but often produce a lesser display of autumn colour.

Cotoneaster salicifolius. Willowleaf Cotoneaster. China

Cotoneaster frigidus. Himalayan Rockspray. Himalayas

Crassula arborescens. Chinese Jade. South Africa

Crassula

(**krass**-yoo-lə)   ☼ Ⓦ Ⓗ
Jade-plant, Silver Dollar,
Chinese Jade
*Winter; 2–3 ft/60 cm–1 m; spreading;
evergreen*

CRASSULACEAE

Looking just like a Chinese ornament fashioned from jade, the South African *Crassula arborescens* makes a stunning rockery or container plant—but not indoors, where they refuse to flower.

Cuttings strike easily in sand and the plants grow best in a sandy, fast-draining soil. Don't worry about pruning except for removing faded flowers: they seem to have great taste in shaping themselves.

They are ideal for arid areas or by the sea, where the fleshy leaves' waxy coating protects them from salt. *Crassula* is hardy down to 28°F/–2°C. Dainty panicles of tiny pink and white flowers appear in winter in the warm-temperate areas *Crassula* prefers.

Crinodendron

(*syn.* TRICUSPIDARIA)

(krai-noh-**den**-drən)   ☼ Ⓣ Ⓦ
Lantern Bush, Red Lantern
*Spr-Sum; 10–15 ft/3–4.5 m; erect;
evergreen*

ELAEOCARPACEAE

Like many Chilean plants closely related to Australian genera, the showy *Crinodendron* has been classified with an Australian genus, in this case, Elaeocarpus.

I have seen it growing happily in the south and west of England, in Italy and in Ireland where it looks just fine with plenty of air moisture. It grows most readily from semi-hardwood cuttings taken with a heel in mid-summer and struck in a sandy mix. Later, it will grow best in a rich, acid soil.

C. hookeranum is evergreen with coarsely toothed, leathery leaves. Their red lantern-like flowers hang from the leaf axils. Generally it grows as a bush with a rounded top but in some conditions may prefer to reach for the sky. In England it seems most often used as a wall shrub.

Crinodendron hookeranum. Red Lantern. Chile

Crossandra

(kros-**san**-drə)   ☼ Ⓦ Ⓗ
Firecracker Flower
Summer; to 3 ft/1 m; bushy; evergreen

ACANTHACEAE

Whether the showy Sri Lankan *Crossandra* is a true shrub or merely a perennial that acts like one is a decision I shall leave to others. Certainly it is woody in most warm to tropical areas, and one of the most colourful plants for the tropical garden, where it may grow to 3 ft/1 m tall. Away from the tropics, they are more usually seen as house or conservatory plants but will do quite well outdoors in frost-free temperate areas, though growing much smaller.

Crossandra infundibuliformis. Firecracker Flower. Sri Lanka, India

Grow them from soft-tip cuttings and plant out in sandy but leaf-rich soil. Keep uniformly moist while temperatures remain above 60°F/15°C, tapering off as winter approaches. The *Crossandra* develops into a neat bush of glossy dark green, topped at intervals during summer with clusters of pleasant salmon to orange-red flowers.

Crossandra infundibuliformis (yellow form). Sri Lanka, India

Crotalaria agatiflora. Canary-bird Bush. Uganda to Rhodesia

the plants' popular names. Seed should be soaked for at least 12 hours. Plant seedlings out in a moderately rich, well-drained soil and prune regularly after flowering to stimulate a further flush of bloom.

C. *agatiflora* has soft-green leaves like the European Laburnum. Before opening, its flowers look exactly like yellow-green birds hanging by their beaks. C. *semperflorens* has simple, heavily ribbed leaves with golden pea-flowers in a terminal spike. Both species produce the bloated seed pods that rattle in the wind.

Crotalaria semperflorens. Indian Rattlebox. India

Crotalaria

(kroh-tə-**leər**-ee-ə)   ☼ ☀ Ⓦ Ⓗ
Rattlebox, Canary-bird Bush, Rattlepod
All year; 6–12 ft/2–4 m; open; evergreen

FABACEAE

Gardeners in cool northern hemisphere areas may well be unaware of the very large genus *Crotalaria*. It includes more than 500 species, many of them great favourites in warmer climates. But they are just *not* frost hardy.

Both illustrated species, one from Kenya, one from India, are happily naturalized in my native Australia, where they join many endemic species. Both can be grown from the hard seeds which rattle round in the mature pods, giving rise to several of

Crowea

(**kroh**-wee-ə)   ☼ Ⓦ Ⓗ
Crowea
Winter; to 2½ ft/75 cm; open; evergreen

RUTACEAE

Perhaps if anyone had ever thought to give these lovely plants a popular name, more Australians could tell them from Boronias. They do look alike, there's no doubt at all, but *Croweas* can't compete when it comes to fragrance. They are showy little shrubs and bloom sporadically throughout the year, though most

Crowea exalata. Crowea. S.E. Australia

heavily when Boronias are not in bloom, as though out of deference.

Grow them from semi-hardwood cuttings struck in a sand/peat mixture from late summer to late autumn. They'll root faster with high humidity, and though they are considered frost hardy in Australia, they are unlikely to stand up to more severe winters. Pinch back as they grow to keep them compact.

Cryptandra

(krip-**tan**-drə) ☼ W H
Spiny Cryptandra
Winter; 1–2 ft/30–60 cm; wiry; evergreen

RHAMNACEAE

If there's one description that strikes me about these curious shrubs it's 'transvestite'. The name *Cryptandra* means 'hidden male parts' and it's true their stamens or anthers are hidden way up under their skirts, or petals. Heaven knows what goes chasing the pollen up there!

The whole genus is endemic to Australia where some of the 40 species are found in all states, generally in heathland surroundings.

Propagation is usually by cuttings, though seed has given good results, too. Most species prefer a semi-shaded location, and well-drained soil is a must, though the plants are not fussy as to whether it is light or heavy. *Cryptandra* look charming in containers, or in rockery pockets where they enjoy the cool root run.

Cuphea ignea. Cigar Flower, Pua Kika. Central America

Cryptandra spinescens. Spiny Cryptandra. N.S.W.

Murray Fagg

Cuphea micropetala. Firecracker Plant. Mexico

Cuphea

(*syn.* PARSONIA)

(**koof**-ee-ə) ☼ W H
Firecracker Plant, Cigar Flower,
False Heather, Elfin Herb
*Sum-Aut; 1–5 ft/30–150 cm; rounded;
evergreen*

LYTHRACEAE

An enormous genus of some 250 species, all endemic to the western hemisphere, the *Cupheas* have become popular in landscape work in all temperate to subtropical areas of the world. Forget about them, though, in colder climates, as they

can be cut back to the ground by frost.

The Cigar Plant, *C. ignea*, is most commonly seen and makes a fine display in warm weather. Though a dainty sub-shrub, it tends to become so untidy in later life that it is often raised as an annual from seed.

The Elfin Herb, pink flowered *C. hyssopifolia*, should not be encouraged in warm climates as it has already become something of a pest in several countries because of its habit of seeding widely. A real problem when you consider it blooms throughout the year.

C. micropetala is the largest of the three illustrated species and should be replaced periodically as mature plants lose vigour. Take cuttings annually All species like moisture.

Cuphea hyssopifolia. Elfin Herb. Mexico, Guatemala

Cuttsia viburnea. False Elderberry. E. Australia

Cuttsia

(**kut**-see-ə)   ☀ W H
Native Elderberry
Summer; 10–33 ft/3–10 m; treelike; evergreen

ROUSSEACEAE   FRAGRANT

Not really common anywhere, in nature or in the garden, the lovely *Cuttsia viburnea* or Native Elderberry is endemic to the deep, moist forests around the Queensland/New South Wales border of Australia. It is the only member of its genus.

Easily propagated from seed or cuttings, *Cuttsia* likes a position with dappled shade and deep, well-drained soil. It can take a light frost and is most often seen in mountain gardens, or in and around Melbourne. It is a tall-growing shrub with dark green, toothed leaves and panicles of ¼ in/

Cyanostegia lanceolata. Tinselflower. Western Australia

Murray Fagg

5 mm snowy white flowers. These have 6 petals and are very showy in a mass. They are sweetly fragrant. A light, annual pruning will keep the shrub compact.

Cyanostegia

(sai-an-oh-**stee**-jə)   ☀ ☀ W H
Tinselflower
Late spring; 3–8 ft/1–2.5 m; dense; evergreen

DICRASTYLIDACEAE

Another charmer from Western Australia's rich flora, the *Cyanostegia* is named for the deep blue colouring of its flowers. In well-drained, even gravelly soil with light water, it grows into a dense bush, simply covered in early spring with loose panicles of 5-petalled flowers and persistent mauve calyxes. Each bloom is ½ in/ 1 cm in diameter and is pale mauve, shading purple towards the outer edge of the petals. The prominent stamens are gold. Leaves are narrow and deep green. The bush is most versatile, flourishing in a dry, even arid climate, yet being also resistant to light frost. *C. lanceolata* (one of 5 species) is becoming quite popular in cultivation.

Cyathodes

(sai-ə-**thoh**-dees)   ☼ ☀ T
Pink Mountain Berry,
Crimson Berry
Autumn; 3–33 ft / 1–10 m; erect; evergreen

ERICACEAE

Limited in their natural range to Tasmania, New Zealand and mountainous Hawaii, the genus *Cyathodes* contains about 15 species, only one of which is in wide cultivation. This is *C. juniperina* var *oxycedrus*, a most variable plant which can range from groundcover to almost tree-like. It grows well along the coast provided it has some protection from salt spray but is also found at higher altitudes.

Cyathodes juniperina var *oxycedrus*.
Crimson Berry. E. Australia

Cyathodes are propagated from cuttings, and like a moist but well-drained soil. Full sun suits them in cool climates, but the hotter it gets, the more shade is needed. *C. juniperina* bears a persistent crop of pink berries in autumn; related species may fruit in tones of white, red, purple or blue.

Cyphanthera albicans ssp *tomentosa*.
Hoary Rayflower. E. Australia

Cyphanthera

(kai-**fan**-thur-ə)   ☼ ☀ W H
Rayflower
*Win-Spr; 6–10 ft / 2–3 m; pendulous;
evergreen*

SOLANACEAE

A useful genus of 9 shrub species, the *Cyphantheras* are found in all Australian states in one species or another. Illustrated *C. albicans* ssp. *tomentosa* is confined to the eastern states where it has proved quite happy in cultivation.

Firm-tip cuttings are easy to strike any time and the plant demands a well-drained, light soil, though heavy clays are tolerated.

C. albicans has a spectacular, silvery appearance, both stems and leaves being covered with white hairs. The 5-petalled flowers are yellow-green, appearing from late winter into early spring. The plants are frost and heat resistant and develop a charming pendulous habit.

Cyrilla

(ki-**rill**-ə)   ☼ ☀ W T H
Leatherwood, Titi,
Myrtle, He-huckleberry
*Summer; 3–6 ft / 1–2 m; treelike; can be
deciduous*

CYRILLACEAE

A most variable plant, the *Cyrilla* covers a wide range from the southern USA to Brazil. In Texas, it is invariably deciduous, with a spectacular display of summer colour as the long flower racemes begin to form. Further south, in the West Indies and Brazil, it is completely evergreen and grows much taller, 33 ft/10 m having been recorded.

Propagation is easy from seed, or from cuttings of short side shoots struck in summer under glass. The best planting time is spring, in an acid mixture of peat and sandy loam. A light pruning in early spring should shorten straggly branches. Bees find the long racemes of white summer blooms irresistible.

The deciduous form is widely grown in southern England and is fairly hardy. The evergreen forms do not grow away from the tropics.

Cyrilla racemiflora. Southern Leatherwood.
S.E. USA, Caribbean

Cytisus scoparia. Scotch Broom. Europe

place. In England, the named varieties are often grafted onto stocks of Laburnum seedlings.

Brooms are generally improved by cutting back several times during the first three summers, but never cut into old wood. When a broom becomes tall and bare-stemmed, it should be replaced by a younger plant. All types are splendid in large rock gardens or at the back of mixed borders. Mature *Cytisus* do not transplant readily, so they should be set in their final position as early as possible.

The colour range includes shades of pink, red, cream, tan and mahogany as well as the pure yellow.

Cyrilla racemiflora. He-huckleberry. S.E. USA, Caribbean

Cytisus racemosus. Canary Island Broom. Canary Islands

Cytisus 'Marie Burkwood'. Burkwood Broom. Hybrid

Cytisus
(*syn.* SAROTHAMNUS, GENISTA)

(**sit**-iss-əs)   ☼ C T W
(but correctly **kit**-iss-əs)
Broom, Atlas Broom,
Scotch Broom
Spring; 3 ft / 1 m; arching; deciduous

FABACEAE   FRAGRANT

Native to the Mediterranean area and Atlantic islands, the 50-odd species of *Cytisus* are among the showiest of pea flowers, taking the place of the warmer growing Crotalarias. Many of the most popular types are sports, and will not come true from seed. They must therefore be grown from cuttings of firm shoots, which are taken in late summer and struck under glass in a shady

Cytisus albus. Portugal Broom. S.E. Europe

Daboecia cantabrica. St Dabeoc's Heath.
Ireland, Spain, Azores

Propagated from semi-hardwood cuttings struck under glass, it likes to grow in a very peaty, well-drained soil that is kept moist all the time. It is not a very fast grower, but blooms most of the year except winter. The leaves are tiny and heathlike, with small racemes of lily-of-the-valley type bells in vivid pink, or sometimes in white or purple. They enjoy full sun in cool areas, midday shade elsewhere. Charming in rockeries or along sandstone paths.

Däis

(**dae**-əs) ☼ ☀ Ⓦ
South African Daphne,
Pompon Bush
Spring; 14 ft/4 m; multi-trunked;
deciduous

THYMELAEACEAE   FRAGRANT

Though I've used it once before as a tree, I make no apologies for including the South African *Däis* a second time, as a shrub. It is one of my favourite plants and can stand the repetition. Anyway, it often tends to adopt a shrubby multiple-trunked habit in the home garden—probably due to a lack of the leaf-eating animals with which it must cope in its native Africa.

It is a handsome, slender plant with reddish bark and blue-green

bad days. It is suspected that while naming this delightful little Irish shrub after Ireland's St Dabeoc, he became mixed up in his Irish spelling (a very easy thing to do!) and the name somehow came out the wrong way, *Daboecia* instead of Dabeocia, which would have made more sense. However, it is still a delightfully dwarfed member of the heath family Ericaceae, and native to Ireland, south-west Europe and the Azores.

Däis cotinifolia. Pompon Bush. South Africa

Daboecia

(*syn.* BORETTA, MENZIESIA)

(dab-oh-**ee**-shə) ☼ ☀ Ⓣ
St Dabeoc's Heath, Irish Heath
Spring; 2 ft/60 cm; dense; evergreen

ERICACEAE

Even famous botanists like Linnaeus, who invented the system of binomial nomenclature, sometimes have their

Daïs cotinifolia. South African Daphne. South Africa

leaves to 3 in/8 cm long, widest at the tips. In South Africa it is supposedly evergreen, but it certainly loses most of its foliage in Australia and California. The tubular pink flowers, which appear in a dense pompon-shaped cluster in late spring, tend to hang on the tree too long after they have faded; they have a fragrance reminiscent of related Daphne. Propagate by cuttings of half-ripened wood.

Dalea spinosa. Indigo Bush. S. California, Mexico

Dalea
(*syn.* PAROSELA)

(**dae**-lee-ə)   ☼ T W
Smokebush, Indigo Bush
Spr-Sum; to 30 ft/9 m; sparse

FABACEAE   FRAGRANT

A feature of the landscape in California, Arizona and New Mexico, *Dalea spinosa* is called Smokebush, and does indeed look like a puff of smoke hovering among the desert rocks. Early in the season, in winter, it develops a sparse crop of ½ in/1 cm slender, linear leaves which fall quite early to make way for the brilliant, purple-blue pea flowers, which are extraordinarily fragrant. These, scattered like tiny jewels among the spiny, silvery stems, make a most exotic effect.

Daleas (there are probably 200 species of them) grow readily from seed, and push ahead best in a gravelly, sandy soil. A very pretty plant for the arid garden.

Danäe
(*syn.* RUSCUS)

(də-**nae**-ee)   ☀ ☀ C T
Alexandrian Laurel
Autumn; 3 ft/1 m; open; evergreen

LILIACEAE

The only plant of its genus, *Danäe* was probably named for Danäe the mother of Perseus, who was her father's only daughter, a fact which cannot have escaped the attention of

Danäe racemosa. Alexandrian Laurel. S.W. Asia

Pamela Harper

some unnamed botanist. At a distance, it greatly resembles Ruscus (which see) except the brilliant red fruit appear in short racemes rather than singly.

Danäe is easily grown from divisions, adores cool, moist soil in a shaded place. It should be pruned annually by cutting a proportion of the oldest canes to the ground in winter. It is quite frost hardy, native to Asia Minor, and seems to fruit best after a hard summer. The stems look wonderful in arrangements, especially when they are in fruit.

Daphne mezereum. Mezereon. Europe, W. Asia

Daphne

(**daf**-nee)   ☼ ☀ C T W
Daphne, Garland-flower, Mezereon
Spring; 1–6 ft/30–180 cm; dense; evergreen

THYMELAEACEAE   FRAGRANT

A long time ago, in far-off Arcadia, there lived a nymph called Daphne. One day, while trying for an allover tan, she caught the eye of Apollo, the sun god. He was beside her in a flash, and Daphne, fearing the worst, began praying to her favourite goddesses for help. Her prayers were answered. Daphne's arms turned into sleek branches with shining leaves, her feet took root and she turned into one of the prettiest flowering shrubs you ever saw.

Daphne burkwoodii. Burkwood's Daphne. Hybrid

Daphne cneorum. Garland-flower. European mountains

That, according to Greek legend, was the origin of the charming European *Daphne laureola*, a species not much grown since the discovery of its more beautiful Asian cousins like fragrant *D. odora*.

We now know there are between 40 and 50 *Daphnes*, fragrant winter and spring flowering shrubs, favourites everywhere except in the subtropics. Most are of hillside, woodland origin and hardy from 21°F/ −8°C. They like dappled shade and well-drained, slightly acid soil— though the Garland-flower, *D. cneorum*, will tolerate a touch of lime, provided there's plenty of leaf mould mixed in. Only light watering is needed, with a meagre ration of complete fertilizer immediately after bloom. Over-watering in summer will lead to collar rot, which will put paid to an apparently healthy plant in no time, by cutting off its circulation. Best grow *Daphnes* in a raised position with the root junction above soil level, and let the surface dry out between summer waterings.

Daphnes are usually evergreen, though the illustrated *D. mezereum* is deciduous, and flowers on bare wood. The berries that follow are quite eyecatching in the spring garden. It is found naturally from Europe to Siberia.

Pale mauve flowered *D. burkwoodii*

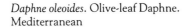

Daphne oleoides. Olive-leaf Daphne. Mediterranean

Daphne odora rubra. Sweet Daphne. China

Daphne collina. Hill Daphne. Sicily, Crete

is also semi-deciduous. The Garland-flower, *D. cneorum*, is a low-growing alpine plant, native from Spain, through Germany, to Russia. It likes a cool position facing away from the sun, with a root-run under rocks. It is hardy to 23°F/−5°C and is a favourite container plant. Propagate it from leafy tips struck in midsummer, and plant in a well-drained, only slightly acid soil. *D. collina* is similar, but from the south of Italy across to the Balkans.

D. *odora* in all its forms is from China and Japan, where it is seen sheared as a dense hedge. It is particularly prone to root rot, but the golden-edged variety *D. o. marginata* seems a little sturdier. Variety *D. o. rubra* is the most striking, with a deep red exterior and white crystalline interior to the flowers. *D. oleoides*, the Olive-leaf Daphne, is found from Spain to Afghanistan.

Daphniphyllum

(daf-nee-**fil**-əm)   ☼ⒸⓉ
Daphne Leaf
Spring; to 30 ft/9 m; tall; evergreen

DAPHNIPHYLLACEAE   PUNGENT

The only real likeness to the true Daphne in these very large plants is in the waxy leaves. The tiny, petal-less flowers are greeny-red and found in the leaf axils. They are not fragrant but pungent, and are followed by small black fruits which are somewhat poisonous, as are many plants in the family Euphorbiaceae, in which it was formerly classified.

Native from Japan and Korea right down to South-east Asia, *Daphniphyllums* are quite frost hardy and easily raised from cuttings or seed. They prefer a neutral soil, but will cope with an alkaline balance. They don't like full sun and make attractive container plants for a sheltered or indoor situation.

Daphniphyllum macropodon. Daphne Leaf. Japan, Korea

Darwinia fascicularis. Scent Myrtle. N.S.W.

Darwinia meeboldii. Cranbrook Bell. Western Australia

Darwinia

(dar-**win**-ee-ə)   ☼ ☀ Ⓦ
Scent Myrtle
Spr-Sum; 8 in–6 ft/20 cm–2 m; compact; evergreen

MYRTACEAE   AROMATIC

Named in the 18th century for the *other* Darwin, noted scientist and physician, *Darwinias* form an endemic Australian genus of perhaps 60 species, mostly from Western Australia, where they are found in tem-

Darwinia procera. N.S.W.

Michael Morcombe

perate zones, in sandy coastal areas. Wherever, they enjoy a well-drained, neutral to acid soil, and appreciate moisture for the greater part of the year. If dryness is a possibility, a light, coarse mulch is beneficial.

Propagation can be from seed or layering in most species. Cuttings are best struck from almost hardened lateral tips, leaving the natural foliage in place. Many species enjoy partial shade, at least in the middle of the day. They thrive with a minimum of water, and only an occasional light dressing of organic fertilizer.

The evergreen leaves are small and aromatic, generally sharply pointed and linear. Flowers appear in terminal and axillary clusters, and their petals are often inconspicuous. Other Western Australian types such as illustrated *D. leiostyla* and *D. meeboldii* feature spectacular bell-flowers of carmine, green and white. All *Darwinias* bloom in this colour scheme.

Darwinia taxifolia. Scent Myrtle. N.S.W.

Darwinia leiostyla. Stirling Bell. Western Australia

Daubentonia
(*syn.* SESBANIA)

(doh-ben-**toh**-nee-ə)   ☼ Ⓦ
Scarlet Wistaria Bush
Spr-Sum; to 6 ft/2 m; treelike; evergreen

FABACEAE

Scarlet Wistaria! What a wonderfully evocative image—and the bush to which it applies certainly lives up to its name. As a member of the vast pea or bean family, Fabaceae, it certainly has the characteristic long pods that contain the hard seeds. You soak these when dry for half a day or overnight, then set them out in pots, lightly covered with soil. Water, and place them in a warm, sheltered place until growth begins. Finally they are grown in a well-drained, sandy soil, rich with leaf mould, until they reach flowering size.

The compound leaves are pinnate (large leaflets) and the gorgeous red flowers appear in drooping racemes. You can extend the flowering period

Daubentonia tripetii. Scarlet Wistaria Bush. N. Argentina, Brazil

Decaisnea

(dee-**kays**-nee-ə) ☼ ❋ C T
Sausage Tree
Autumn; 6–15 ft/2–5 m; upright;
deciduous

LARDIZABALACEAE

The Chinese used to cultivate the native *Decaisnea fargesii* because they ate the curious sausage-shaped fruits which are coloured a sort of violet green. These appear at the ends of branches after the really insignificant flowers have fallen. Just why it should be popular in Western gardens is more difficult to explain, but apparently it is seen a good deal in cool-climate gardens of Europe and North America.

Decaisnea fargesii. Sausage Tree.
W. China

by removing seed pods. A fast grower with a short lifespan, *Daubentonia tripetii* is native to Brazil and northern Argentina and needs ample water through the growing season. Prune hard in earliest spring to stimulate bloom.

Daviesia mimusoides. Blunt-leaf Bitter Pea.
S. & E. Australia

Daviesia

(dae-**vee**-see-ə) ☼ W H
The Bitter Peas
Spring; 3–8 ft/1–2.5 m; bun-shaped;
evergreen

FABACEAE   FRAGRANT

One of the several pea genera referred to collectively as 'Bacon and Eggs' because of their pink and yellow pea flowers, the *Daviesia* nevertheless have one characteristic that sets them apart from all other genera. Their pea pods are triangular in section. There are 75 species of them, largely endemic to Western Australia, though the illustrated species is found only in the eastern states.

Propagate from seed which sprouts rapidly in the warmer months—scarify or soak them before setting out in the usual way. The plants will grow fast in well-drained, light to medium gravelly soil, and full sunlight is essential.

When *Daviesia mimusoides* is in full bloom, it does indeed remind one of Mimosa (Wattle). It suckers strongly, and may give up the ghost at a moment's notice due to infection by the root disease Phytophthera.

It grows from seed, provided you can make a leaf-rich, well-drained soil. It is deciduous, but in early spring produces very large (1 ft/30 cm) odd-pinnate leaves from the ends of its rather gaunt branches. The fruits persist through winter.

Delostoma

(de-lə-**stoh**-mə)   ☼ ☀ W H
Colombian Trumpet
Summer; 10 ft/3 m; shrubby; evergreen

BIGNONIACEAE

If flowers could speak, one suspects this one would deafen us. Its botanical name means 'big mouth', or something very like that. Outside its native South America it seems to be grown only in California, Florida and a few English glasshouses.

It is usually grown from seed, though grafting onto a stock from other members of the Bignonia family seems a possibility. Its leaves are simple and leathery, the trumpet flowers (pink or rose) appear in terminal panicles up to 8 in/20 cm long. They are followed by woody purple seed capsules. *Delostoma roseum* is one of seven species found in Colombia, Ecuador and Peru.

Delostoma roseum. Colombian Trumpet. Colombia, Ecuador

Dendromecon

(den-**drom**-ee-kon)   ☼ ☀ W H
California Tree Poppy
Spr-Sum; 3–5 ft/1–1.5 m; rounded; evergreen

PAPAVERACEAE

The most beautiful variety of the glittering California Tree Poppy is found on the islands of Santa Cruz and Santa Rosa off southern California.

Dendromecon rigida var *Harfordii*. Island Tree Poppy. S. California islands

Dendromecon rigida var *Harfordii* grows almost double the height of the mainland variety, and comes true from seed, which is very slow to germinate.

Grow these lovely shrubs in a well-drained, gravelly soil with light watering, or strike well-ripened summer shoots in sharp sand with some heat. They will turn on a gorgeous display throughout spring and summer. Tip pruning after bloom will extend the flowering season. The blooms have a shining texture and are 2 in/5 cm in diameter, contrasting magnificently with the sharply pointed grey-green foliage which has a leathery texture.

Desfontainea

(dae-fon-**tae**-nee-ə)   ☀ T W
Peruvian Holly
Sum-Aut; 10 ft/3 m; compact; evergreen

COLUMELLIACEAE

For much of the year, in a mild climate, this eye-catching bush really can be mistaken for a holly, and a rather ferocious one at that. But come midsummer, small flower buds elongate and suddenly become long orange-scarlet tubular flowers lined with yellow.

Desfontainea is a slow grower, even in the good peaty soil it adores, and will do no good at all where the soil

Desfontainea spinosa. Peruvian Holly. Andes Mountains

Deutzia scabra 'Candidissima'. Wedding Bells. Japan

is limy. Seed is probably the best method of propagation, but semi-hardwood cuttings of lateral shoots taken with a heel will strike in summer. *Desfontainea* may reach 15 ft/ 5 m in a warm, moist area, but more commonly half of that. It is not really frost hardy.

Deutzia longifolia. Long-leaf Deutzia. W. China

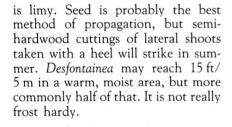

Deutzia X *kalmiifolia.* Kalmia-flowered Deutzia. Hybrid

Deutzia

(**doit**-zee-ə)   ☼ ☀ C T
Wedding Bells, Bridal Wreath
Spring; 5–7 ft/1.5–2 m; erect canes; deciduous

PHILADELPHACEAE

Scrappy for most of the year when not in bloom, most species of the

genus *Deutzia* change into a miracle of loveliness as their buds open in spring profusion. There are some 40 species, all growing into a dense clump of arching canes which produce their pretty but unperfumed flowers from the side buds of the previous year's growth. Mostly from Japan, China and the Himalayas, they are related to Philadelphus

Deutzia gracilis. Slender Deutzia. Japan

(which see), which they closely resemble except in the matter of size and fragrance.

Propagation is by striking soft summer tip cuttings from the new year's growth, or hardwood cuttings in winter. Soil should be rich and well-drained, moisture is needed at all times. A generous ration of complete fertilizer in early spring will boost the flower yield. To force bloom, pruning should be heavy, removing about half of the old canes entirely.

Leaves are spear-shaped and crepe-textured. Flowers appear in erect panicles, may be white, pink or bicolored, according to variety. The lovely *D. scabra* 'Candidissima' is double and snowy white.

Dichroa

(syn. ADAMIA)

(dai-**kroh**-ə) ☼ ❋ Ⓦ Ⓗ
Mountain Hydrangea
Summer; 3–7 ft/1–2 m; evergreen; open

HYDRANGEACEAE

Strongly resembling Hydrangeas, and related to them, the small genus *Dichroa* are found in mountainous

Dichroa versicolor. Mountain Hydrangea. E. Asia

areas of the Asian tropics like Malaysia, China and Japan. The lovely *D. febrifuga* seems to be the only species in cultivation all over Asia, and of course in southern England. As a rule, the more tropical the climate, the larger the leaves.

Easily propagated from cuttings, if you can find a source, they should be cultivated in an open, loamy soil. Leaves are coarsely toothed like those of many Hydrangeas. Flowers appear in branched terminal clusters, and are followed by deep blue fruits. White flower buds generally open to 5-petalled mauve flowers—though white varieties are known.

Diervilla middendorfiana. Bush Honeysuckle. W. China, Japan

Diervilla

(dee-**ur**-vil-lə) ☼ ❋ Ⓒ Ⓣ
Bush Honeysuckle
Spring; 2–4 ft/60–120 cm; suckering; deciduous

CAPRIFOLIACEAE

A division of the honeysuckle family, Caprifoliaceae, and sometimes included in the genus Weigela, depending on which school of botanical

thought you follow, today's *Diervillas* are quite a small group, all from North America, all with yellow flowers. They sucker heavily and are helpful in controlling erosion.

Propagated from division, all *Diervillas* prefer a light soil, enriched with compost, or a heavier loam lightened with sand. Plant out in spring or autumn.

The shrubs are deciduous, with wrinkled ovate-lanceolate leaves and clusters of charming golden bell-flowers in late spring. Hard pruning after bloom improves shape and flower yield.

Dillenia indica. Elephant Apple. India to Java

Dillenia

(dil-**len**-nee-ə) ☼ Ⓦ Ⓗ
Chulta, Elephant Apple
Summer; 20 ft/6 m; treelike; evergreen

DILLENIACEAE

A wonderful plant found from India right down to Java, the Elephant Apple is often seen grown to tree size in older gardens, though the more decorative plan is to trim it back regularly to become a shrubby screen. Treated in this way, one gets to appreciate the wonderful pleated foliage and large, golden-yellow magnolia-like flowers.

Propagated from seed or semi-hardwood cuttings, it grows fast in a tropical climate where the golden flowers are followed by edible, apple-sized fruit that are used in curries and jellies. Where there is a distinct dry season, the *Dillenias* turn deciduous and develop a very different appearance without their 1 ft/30 cm leaves. All in all, a very handsome plant for the tropical garden no matter which size you grow it. There are about 60 species.

Dillwynia retorta. Parrot Pea. E. Australia

Dillwynia

(dil-**win**-ee-ə)   ☼ ☀ W H
Parrot Pea
Spring; mostly to 5 ft/1.5 m; open; evergreen

FABACEAE

Another yellow-flowered genus of the family Fabaceae, to be known as Eggs and Bacon (see Daviesia and Pultenea for others). The 22 species of *Dill-wynia* also bear the more distinctive name of Parrot Pea. Spring and summer flowering *D. retorta* grows 10 ft/ 3 m in height, and usually in an open, spreading shape.

It can be grown from seed soaked at least 24 hours and strikes easily from cuttings. Most soils suit, so long as they're well-drained, and a year-round mulch is appreciated. Dappled shade seems to suit it best, and the flowers retain maximum brightness in the shade of full grown trees. It is not worried by frost, withstands drought, but alas, now for the bad news! It is very prone to the root

disease Phytophthora, and can die suddenly.

The tiny, twisted linear leaves are rarely more than ½ in/1 cm long. The pea-shaped gold and red flowers are little larger. *Dillwynias* are found in eastern Australia and can be raised in containers.

Dipelta

(dai-**pel**-tə)   ☼ ☀ C T
Shield Flower
Spring; to 12 ft/4 m; stiff; tall; deciduous

CAPRIFOLIACEAE   FRAGRANT

Shield Flower? Just look at the pair of greenish bracts protecting each flower in our illustration. *Dipelta* is closely related to both Diervilla and Weigela, and is a member of the honeysuckle family. It is frost hardy, comes from outback China, and is not common in Western gardens.

If you can find a source, it grows easily from seed or summer soft-tip cuttings, and will grow in any soil in a cool-temperate climate. The finely-toothed leaves are pointed and deciduous. The golden flowers are rather like those of a foxglove, but with an orange throat.

Dipelta ventricosa. Shield Flower. China

Dirca

(**dur**-kə)   ☼ T
Leatherwood, Ropebark, Wicopy
Summer; 3–6 ft/1–2 m; many-trunked; deciduous

THYMELAEACEAE

Not very much in fashion these days, the two small shrubs of the Leatherwood genus *Dirca* are found in older gardens of eastern North America, where they were once used for baskets and rope making (the branchlets are tough and flexible, the bark fibrous). They can be grown from layers or seed, enjoy a moist, peaty

Dirca palustris. Wicopy, Moosewood. Canada to Florida

root-run, and are very useful for growing in wet ground. The bush bears insignificant yellow flowers before the foliage in early spring. The alternate leaves (hairy when young) are of oval shape, slightly wider towards the tip. They are pale green in colour and large compared to the shrub's size. All in all a useful plant, if not particularly showy.

Disanthus

(dis-**an**-thəs)   ☀ ⃞C ⃞T
Japanese Witchhazel
Autumn; 10 ft/3 m; treelike; deciduous

HAMAMELIDACEAE   FRAGRANT

Not for hot gardens, the lovely Japanese *Disanthus* is an interesting shrub that is closely related to the Witchhazels, but looks more like a Cercis (which see). It is easy to grow from semi-hardwood cuttings struck in autumn, and should do well in a cool area, needing soil with good drainage. Australians and Californians should find it does well in

Tony Rodd

Disanthus cercidifolius.
Japanese Witchhazel. Japan

mountain gardens or in semi-shaded positions.

Disanthus' round to heart-shaped leaves are handsome all year, but really come into their own in autumn, when they blaze into a glowing orange and red. In autumn, too, small purplish flowers appear in pairs from many leaf axils. Useful in the open garden of cooler climates.

Discaria discolor. Wild Irishman. Argentina

Discaria

(dis-**kair**-ee-ə)   ☀ ⃞T ⃞W
Wild Irishman
Spring; 7 ft/2 m; spiny; evergreen

RHAMNACEAE

At least one species of this small southern hemisphere genus is known as the Wild Irishman—presumably because of its greenish flowers and prickly nature. There are about 15 species—all from South America, Australia and New Zealand.

Strike from semi-hardwood cuttings under glass in summer, and set out the growing plants in well-drained soil. Leaves are small and shining; greenish flowers appear in dense axillary clusters. *Discaria* make a useful shelter for small birds or can be used as an effective traffic barrier where there are no fences.

Dissotis

(dis-**soh**-tis)   ☀ ⃞W ⃞H
Creeping Lasiandra
Winter; to 1½ ft/45 cm; dense cover; evergreen

MELASTOMATACEAE

Small shrub or woody perennial? The principal authorities seem to differ, and you'd need to go at least as far as the subtropics to work it out for yourself. *Dissotis* is a small African plant within the family Melastomataceae (the Lasiandra relatives). *D. plumosa* looks exactly like the dwarf groundcover Heterocentron, or Spanish Shawl, from the same family, but is much larger in every way. The leaves may be 1 in/3 cm, the flowers 2 in/5 cm across, and the 4-angled stems are woody as opposed to wiry.

You can propagate by striking spring cuttings, or by separating layers, which occur naturally. *D. plumosa* is from Sierra Leone and revels in the dappled shade of a subtropical garden. It is a splendid groundcover, and blooms for months on end.

Dissotis plumosa. Creeping Lasiandra. Sierra Leone

Dodonaea

(də-**doh**-nee-ə)   ☀ ☀ ☀ ⃞W ⃞H
Hopbush, Ake Ake
Spring; 3–17 ft/1–5 m; dense; evergreen

SAPINDACEAE

An interesting range of dense foliage plants, mostly from Australia, but also found in New Zealand, tropical Africa and Asia, tropical America and New Guinea. Their principal display is not in the insignificant flowers, but in the showy fruit or pods that follow. These are in the form of a capsule with up to six wings or angles.

Dodonaeas are propagated from cuttings, and provided water is available, will strike in any position from exposed seashore to arid desert. Different strokes for different folks, however! Some *Dodonaeas* prefer dense shade, others tolerate sun. There are species which will tolerate temperatures of 45°F/7°C. While *Dodonaeas* are known for their fast growth, do understand that they are short lived as well. The dark, often purplish foliage has a sticky texture, and is patterned with resinous dots on both surfaces.

Dodonaea lobulata. Lobed-leafed Hopbush. Australia

Dombeya X cayeuxii. Cape Wedding Flower. Hybrid

Dombeya

(*syn.* ASSONIA)

(dom-**bae**-ə) ☼ ☀ W H
Cape Wedding Flower,
Wild Pear
Autumn; to 10 ft/3 m; floriferous; deciduous

MALVACEAE

Grown in many lands and climates, all 100 species of *Dombeya* are originally from eastern Africa, and islands of the Indian Ocean. Some are tree-like, but all are officially classed as evergreen shrubs, often with a stunning flower display.

Propagate them from late spring cuttings struck under glass, and kept moist in a fairly rich, well-drained soil. Faded flowers of all species should be snipped away or they will persist on the bush to a most unat-

Dombeya spectabilis. Wild Pear.
S.E. Africa, Madagascar

tractive stage. Not really hardy, they are susceptible to light frost damage, but make a quick recovery. A sheltered position is best for the very large-leafed species like *D. X cayeuxii* or unsightly leaf damage may result. *D. spectabilis*, the Wild Pear, is inclined to be deciduous. Its pale pink blossoms give a spring display before the new leaves appear.

Dracophyllum

(drak-oh-**fil**-ləm) ☼ T W
Dragon Heath
Spring; 8–60 in/20–150 cm; spreading; evergreen

ERICACEAE

Named for the supposed resemblance of their leaves to those of the Dragon tree (Dracaena draco), the *Dracophyllums* are a genus of some 30 species, mostly from New Zealand, New Caledonia and Tasmania, but with 5 species in Australia. One of these, *D. secundum* is quite popular in cultivation, and said to be a trailer in wet, shaded places. Most often, though, it is seen as a tight, rounded bush with sharp-leaved, curved-toothed foliage.

It is slow growing, but very long

Murray Fagg

Dracophyllum secundum. Dragon Heath.
N.S.W.

lasting, and its spectacular panicles of
pale pink heath flowers catch the
light in early spring. *Dracophyllum* is
difficult to grow from cuttings, even
from seed. It needs a sandy well-
drained soil with moisture most of
the year. Best in a country garden.

Drejerella
(*syn.* BELOPERONE, JUSTICIA)

(drej-ur-**el**-lə)   ☀ W H
Shrimp Plant, Prawn Plant
*Summer; 3 ft/1 m; rounded bush;
evergreen*

ACANTHACEAE

Nature was surely in a mimic mood
when she designed this flower, for a
bush in full bloom really does seem
festooned with crustaceans. The
pinkish-brown petal forms are actually bracts, or modified leaves, with
tiny white flowers almost hidden
among them.

   Drejerella guttata prefers a rich,
well-drained soil, colours best in
semi-shade. A weak, sprawling plant,
it needs regular light pruning to

remove spindly growth and encourage new flowering wood. In tropical
or subtropical climates it is in almost
continuous bloom, but will flower in
coastal areas where the temperatures
don't drop below 45°F/7°C. *Drejerella* can be raised from tip or semi-
hardwood cuttings, and there are two
principal varieties, with pink or the
yellow bracts.

Drejerella guttata aurea.
Yellow Shrimp Plant. Tropical Mexico

Drejerella guttata. Prawn Plant. Tropical Mexico

Dryandra polycephala. Bush Rose.
Western Australia

Dryandra

(drai-**an**-drə)   ☀ T W H
Bush Rose, Dryandra
*Spring; 3–11 ft/1–3.5 m; upright;
evergreen*

PROTEACEAE

Away from their native Western
Australia, the stunning *Dryandras*
(named for the Swedish botanist
Jonas Dryander) are more likely to be

found in Californian gardens or English greenhouses than on their own continent. The problem appears mostly to be their hatred of humidity and the prevalence in Australia of a fatal root-rot, Phytophthera.

Commercially, many *Dryandras* are grown with related Proteas. In the florist trade they are used in long-lasting arrangements, often appearing unchanged for years.

Cultivation (away from the areas mentioned above) is difficult. Full sun and perfectly drained sandy soil over a layer of gravel may give the best results. *D. polycephala* (the Many-headed Dryandra) may be propagated from seed; others are raised from cuttings, or grafted onto related Banksia stock. Plant them out where they can remain completely undisturbed.

Leaves of most types are elongated and saw-toothed. Flowers tend to be some shade of gold, a notable exception being the illustrated Shaggy Dryandra, *D. speciosa*, in which the blooms have a distinctly reddish tone.

The Showy Dryandra (*D. formosa*), grown in England since 1803, has bright, shining terminal flower-heads to 4 in/10 cm across. It is quite adaptable, will grow in part shade or full sun, even in coastal positions. It needs scant water, resists frost well.

Dryandras are usually about as wide as they are high. Annual pruning needs are satisfied by picking the long-stemmed blooms.

Dryandra speciosa. Shaggy Dryandra. Western Australia

Dryandra formosa. Showy Dryandra. Western Australia

Duboisia

(dyoo-**boi**-zee-ə)
Corkwood
Spring; 18 ft/6 m; upright; evergreen

SOLANACEAE

Here's a flower that will open your eyes! It's true! *Duboisia* (or a distillation from it) is used by your friendly eye specialist to dilate your pupils for examination.

D. myoporoides grows naturally throughout Australia's north-east coastal area, even spreading into nearby islands. It is propagated from seed, grows in any well-drained sunny position, and will bloom almost continually with regular pruning and plenty of fertilizer.

Duboisia may grow almost to small tree size, and produces a decorative display of bell-shaped white and purple blooms in many-branched panicles. Small black berries follow. Leaves are shiny, lanceolate and bright green, and the plants are raised commercially for their drug content.

Tony Rodd

Duboisia myoporoides. Corkwood.
N.E. Australia & islands

Duranta

(dyoo-**ran**-tə) ☼ W H
Pigeonberry, Brazilian Skyflower,
Violetina, Golden Dewdrop, Adonis,
Garbancilla, Velo de Viuda
Summer; 12–18 ft/4–6 m; weeping;
evergreen

VERBENACEAE

Among the fastest-growing of shrubs,
Duranta repens suckers heavily without regular pruning, and is frequently
seen as a hedge or windbreak in
warmer climates. The piebald *D.*
repens variegata is particularly attractive for this purpose. In the warmer
months, *D. repens* is sprinkled with
tiny violet-blue flowers that have
earned it the name of Violetina in
parts of Latin America. The charming blooms are followed by a spectacular curtain of orange berries
which may persist through autumn.
Unfortunately, these fruits are
poisonous, so thought must be given
before planting where curious children are free to roam!

Durantas of all types (there is a
white-flowered variety too) grow easily in well-drained soil that doesn't
need to be too rich. Start them in
autumn from hardwood cuttings, or
in spring from softer-tip cuttings, and
begin shaping early for an attractive
multi-trunked effect. The leaves are
shiny, stems are inclined to be
spined, while the flowers are borne in
complex, drooping panicles.

Just remember, it wasn't given the
specific name *repens* for nothing. In a

Duranta repens. Golden Dewdrop. Florida to Brazil

Duranta repens variegata.
Variegated Violetina. Florida to Brazil

Duranta repens variegata (foliage).
Florida to Brazil

subtropical area it can be extremely invasive.

Expect flowers at any time of the year, but most heavily in summer. *Duranta*, named for a 16th century Italian physician, is strictly a subject for warm-temperate to tropical climes.

Duvernoia
(*syn.* ADHATODA)

(doo-ver-**noy**-ə)   ☼ Ⓗ Ⓦ
Acanthus Shrub
Summer; to 10 ft/3 m; bun-shaped; evergreen

ACANTHACEAE   FRAGRANT

A typical member of the Acanthus family, and from tropical Africa, the *Duvernoia* is suitable only for the warm-climate garden. It rather resembles Barleria (which see), but with purple markings on the white flowers.

Striking easily from semi-hardwood or soft-tip cuttings taken in late spring, the illustrated *D. adhatodoides* grows fast in well-drained, fairly rich soil in a bright sunny position. It looks good in rockeries or raised borders.

The simple leaves are shiny and large, the fragrant flowers appearing in a spike during summer and autumn. They have a beautifully marked lower lip and throat, but are spotted badly by tropical rain.

Duvernoia adhatodoides. Acanthus Shrub. Tropical Africa

Echium fastuosum. Pride of Madeira. Canary Islands

Echium wildpretii. Tower of Jewels. Canary Islands

Echium

(**ek**-ee-əm)   ☀ ☼ Ⓒ Ⓣ Ⓦ
Viper's Bugloss,
Tower of Jewels, Snake's Head
Pride of Madeira
Spring; 6–10 ft/2–3 m; upright; evergreen

BORAGINACEAE   FRAGRANT

The Australian rural experience with *Echium vulgare* (known hopefully as Salvation Jane, but more generally as Paterson's Curse) should not blind us to the many uses and charm of the shrubby species of *Echium*, which hail from either the Mediterranean area or the Canary Islands.

Surely among the most spectacular of plants in cool to temperate climates is the stunning Pride of Madeira, *E. fastuosum*, which sends up tall panicles of purple-blue bell-shaped flowers and attracts bees from far and wide. Naturally a salt-resistant, seaside plant, it grows to 6 ft/2 m in well-drained gravelly soil, where it needs water only during severe drought. The Pride of Madeira will

tolerate temperatures down to 28°F/−2°C, to come out battered, but ready for another bout with the elements. Avoid rich soil or constant moisture in case the plant bolts to stem, and don't be too generous with the fertilizer.

Prune to compact shape (especially in windy places where the shrub is inclined to sprawl widely) and to stimulate growth of the handsome, silvery-hairy foliage.

Ruby-flowered *E. wildpretii*, sometimes known as Tower of Jewels, sends up tall stems to a height of 10 ft/3 m.

All shrubby *Echiums* can be grown rather too easily from seed, or can be propagated from layers or cuttings of firm tips. Their close relationship to the herb Borage is easy to spot. All species are lightly honey-fragrant.

Edgeworthia

(ej-**wur**-thee-ə)
Paperbush, Mitsumata,
Yellow Daphne
Early spring; 6 ft/2 m; spreading;
deciduous

THYMELAEACEAE   FRAGRANT

Native to eastern Asia, the Paperbush or *Edgeworthia papyrifera* is

seen in cooler climate gardens, though it is frost hardy only in a sheltered position. It should be grown in well-drained soil that's rich in leaf mould and will slowly reach a height and spread of 6 ft/2 m though it is usually pruned to a lower 'bun' shape.

Propagation is easy from cuttings struck under glass or by layering one of the lower branches. As you might guess from the flowers, *Edgeworthia* is a sweet-scented Daphne relative, differing from those fragrant charmers only in the rich yellow to which the flowers fade.

The branches are tough and fibrous, and were once used for papermaking in Japan. The plant is deciduous, opening its flower display briefly before bursting into leaf in early spring.

A curious point is the flexibility of the branches, which may be knotted without breaking.

Elaeagnus

(el-ae-**ag**-nəs)
Wild Olive,
Oleaster, Silverberry
Spring; 9–15 ft/3–5 m; dense; spreading;
mostly evergreen

ELAEAGNACEAE   FRAGRANT

Popular shrubs found all over the northern hemisphere, 30-odd species of *Elaeagnus* are favourites for hedge and background work.

Spiny *E. pungens* is most common, its leaves usually backed with silver scales and greyish-green on the upper side. Sometimes they are striped or edged with gold, green and pink. The small white blooms appear in autumn, are fragrant and followed by ½ in/1 cm fruit that ripen red. Its hybrid *E. X Ebbingei* grows only half the height, and its red winter berries make a good, tart jelly. The leaves are striped gold-green, and the stems are spineless.

E. umbellata varieties are deciduous in cooler climates, grow to 16 ft/5 m and may spread just as wide. They produce round fruits which birds adore and autumn leaf colours which are quite startling.

All *Elaeagnus* species grow in poor soil, are frost hardy and easy to grow from stratified seed or hardwood cuttings.

Elaeagnus pungens maculata.
Oleaster. China, Japan

Elaeagnus umbellata parvifolia.
Wild Olive. China, Japan

Edgeworthia papyrifera. Yellow Daphne. Japan

Elaeagnus pungens. Silverberry. China, Japan

Embothrium coccineum. Chilean Firebush. Chile

garden, Bodnant, the gorgeous species of Chilean *Embothrium coccineum* bursts into bloom below eye level. And that is the way to see it, for though a multi-trunked, suckering shrub, it tends to shoot up towards the light and flower above head height in an ordinary garden setting. Best keep it pruned back so you can look down on it, but the position is critical.

All 4 species of *Embothrium* dislike

over-cultivated soil, lime or animal manure. Just a loose, peaty, acid soil. Propagate from seed and keep moist always.

Embothriums have glossy, leathery leaves and the tubular flowers, borne both from leaf axils and terminally, are typical of the family Proteaceae to which it belongs. The cultivar *E. lanceolatum* 'Norquinco' is particularly free-flowering.

Elaeagnus X *Ebbingei*. Gilt Edge Elaeagnus.

Embothrium lanceolatum 'Norquinco'. Norquinco Firebush. Chile

Encelia farinosa. Incense Flower. Utah. California

Embothrium

(em-**both**-ree-əm)   ☼ ☀ C T
Chilean Firebush
Spr-Sum; to 40 ft/12 m; stiff; erect; evergreen

PROTEACEAE

Down in shaded valleys of cooler climates, as you find it in its native Chile and in the wonderful Welsh

Encelia

(en-**kee**-lee-ə) ☼ T H
Incense Flower,
Brittlebush, Incienso
Spring; 5 ft/1.5 m; bun-shaped; evergreen

ASTERACEAE AROMATIC

In desert regions of the Americas from Utah right down to Chile, a familiar shrub of the barren places is *Encelia farinosa* or Incense Flower, so called for the fragrant resin obtainable from cut stems, and once used as incense by the missionaries. Its clumps of silver, woolly foliage help it stand out against the red desert landscape, particularly in early spring. Later, its small, purple-centred, golden daisy flowers are quite striking.

Popping up from seed it reaches 5 ft/1.5 m in height over several years, so it's not a fast grower. From the earliest times, *Encelia* was planted in the gardens of the desert missions as Incienso; it is still popular in home gardens of desert regions today.

Enchylaena tomentosa. Ruby Saltbush. Australia

Enkianthus quinqueflorus. Chinese Bellflower. S. China

Enchylaena

(en-kai-**lae**-nə) ☼ W H
Barrier Saltbush,
Ruby Saltbush
All year; 1–3 ft/30 cm–1 m; spreading; evergreen

AMARANTHACEAE

Another valuable denizen of the barren places, *Enchylaena tomentosa* originates in Australia where it is found in the worst areas of all states except Tasmania. Seaside, saline or calcareous soils, it romps through the toughest going—and yet its closest relatives are the leaf vegetables spinach and Good King Henry (Chenopodium).

Readily propagated from seed or cuttings, it spreads into a densely foliaged bun, with stems and slender, succulent 1 in/2.5 cm leaves both covered with silvery, stiff hairs. The leaves form a dramatic background for the tiny flowers which swell into succulent jelly-like fruit. These mature from green through yellow then into a brilliant ruby red, and I rather imagine from its relationships that the entire plant might be edible. *Enchylaena* makes a good container plant or seaside specimen and is stunning in a rock garden.

Enkianthus

(*syn.* ANDROMEDA, MELIDORA)

(en-kee-**an**-thəs) ☼ ✲ T W
Bellflower
Spring; 3–6 ft/1–2 m; treelike; deciduous

ERICACEAE FRAGRANT

Dainty *Enkianthus* species will flower anywhere you grow Azaleas and heaths, to both of which they are closely related. Slow-moving lovers of cool mountain places, they have migrated from Japan and China to beautify our cool-climate gardens wherever the soil is acid and rich in leaf mould. A background of dense foliage helps disguise the open, spreading habit and accents the hanging bellflowers which appear in spring, and again in autumn as the leaves colour brilliantly.

Enkianthus perulatus. Japanese Bellflower. Japan

Enkianthus cernuus 'Rubrus'. Red Bellflower. Japan

Enkianthus species are hardy down to 17°F/−8°C and do best in country gardens because they resent air pollution.

Propagate Enkianthus species from seed or autumn cuttings of lateral shoots taken with a heel. Dip these in hormone powder and strike in a standard sand/peat mix under glass. Flowers may be white, pink, red or green.

Entelea

(en-**tee**-lee-ə)   ☼ ☀ W
Corkwood, Whau
Spr-Sum; 8 ft/3 m; treelike; evergreen
MALVACEAE

The only species in the genus, the New Zealand Corkwood, *Entelea arborescens*, has spread world-wide, more as a botanical curiosity than because of any inherent beauty. Readily raised from seed or cuttings, it grows rapidly and can easily be mistaken in its juvenile stage for the popular house plant Sparmannia africana, to which it is related.

Planted out in loamy soil, it soon grows into a handsome shrub with large heart-shaped leaves, clusters of white and gold, 4-petalled flowers and finally a crop of spiny green fruit. The wood of *Entelea* is one of the lightest known and the plant is often grown as a greenhouse curiosity in Europe and California.

Epacris

(e-**pak**-ris)   ☼ ☀ T W
Australian Fuchsia,
Native Fuchsia, Native Heath
Win-Spr; 3 ft/1 m; loose; open; evergreen
ERICACEAE

Very similar in appearance to the South African Ericas (which see) the 40-odd species of *Epacris* are widespread in Australia, New Zealand

Epacris reclinata. Red Heath. N.S.W.

and New Caledonia. Both genera have the same small, stemless leaves, often spiky to the touch. The flowers of both may be bell-like or tubular.

They are easy to grow from seed but it is not commercially available. Cuttings of young growth succeed when dipped in rooting hormone and set in sharp sand kept constantly moist. *Epacris* are the right size for the rock garden where the fast drainage suits them, and popular in Cali-

Entelea arborescens. New Zealand Corkwood. New Zealand

Epacris microphylla. Native Heath. E. Australia, New Zealand

Epacris impressa. Common Heath.
S.E. Australia, Tasmania

fornia and England where they are generally kept under glass in winter. They bloom well in containers, provided they are grown in a sandy soil and pruned back in spring after bloom. Feed them with dilute liquid manure rather than chemical fertilizer.

Epacris longiflora. Native Fuchsia.
N.S.W., Queensland

Ephedra

(e-**fed**-rə) ☼ ◑ H
Mormon Tea, Joint Fir
All year; 2 ft/60 cm; spreading; leafless
EPHEDRACEAE

Resembling nothing so much as a tangle of grey wire, *Ephedra nevadensis* is an inhabitant of the south-west United States, where it is often found along the roadsides. It is leafless, bears sparse catkins which become dry seed receptacles. No beauty, it is designed for the practicalities of desert life.

There are in fact about 30 species in this curious genus, found mostly in dry mountainous places in South America, north Africa, northern Asia, the Mediterranean and Afghanistan. They are all leafless or have their leaves downgraded to scales. They propagate easily from division but we don't expect you to rush out and grow one. Instead, we're telling you all this in case you ever run across a situation where nothing else will grow.

Ephedra nevadensis. Mormon Tea.
S.W. USA

Epigaea

(epi-**gae**-ə) ◑ C T
Trailing Arbutus,
Mayflower, Ground Laurel
*Late spring; 6 in/15 cm; matlike;
evergreen*

ERICACEAE   FRAGRANT

On either side of the north Pacific, in Japan and the United States respect-

Epigaea repens. Trailing Arbutus.
Newfoundland to Florida

ively, a pair of most unusual prostrate shrubs bursts into fragrant, daphne-like bloom as spring blends into summer. They are the 2 species of *Epigaea*: *E. asiatica*, the Ground Laurel and *E. repens*, the Trailing Arbutus. Both are also known as Mayflower.

They are commonly propagated from seed as soon as it is ripe, though divisions including part of the underground stems are also used. *Epigaeas* prefer a shaded position with moist, acid soil imitating their natural habitat, and a wide pocket in the rock garden would be ideal. Slow, horizontal growers, they spread by underground stems, and become much wider than they are high. Their botanical name is from the Greek *epi* (upon) and *gaea* (the earth).

Eranthemum

(syn. DAEDALACANTHUS)

(ər-**an**-thə-mum) ☼ ◑ W H
Blue Sage, Guerit Petit
*Win-Spr; 2–3 ft/60 cm–1 m; branching;
evergreen*

ACANTHACEAE

Found widely from India, through Malaysia to the Philippines, the lovely *Eranthemum* is valued through

Pamela Harper

all that part of the world both as a thing of beauty and for its many medicinal properties. It is used, for instance, to heal wounds and to treat both earache and rheumatism.

It is, of course, frost tender, and can be grown outdoors only in the south of the United States, South Africa, and most of Australia. In England it is usually confined to the greenhouse. In the tropics, *Eranthemum* self-seeds, but you will probably want to grow it from spring cuttings which strike easily.

Eranthemum pulchellum. Blue Sage. India

It needs a well-drained, leaf-rich soil, regular feeding, heavy watering, and grows much wider than its height. It needs regular shaping and should be pruned continuously in a warm climate to force lots of stems and thus flowers. These are Jacaranda blue, appear terminally and from the leaf axils in late winter and early spring, except in the tropics where flowering is virtually continuous. A very beautiful plant.

Eremaea beaufortioides.
Round-leaf Eremaea. Western Australia

Eremaea

(e-re-**mae**-ə)　　　　☼ Ⓦ Ⓗ
Eremaea
Spring; 5 ft/1.5 m; spreading; evergreen

MYRTACEAE

Hard to see why this lovely little genus within the myrtle family has acquired no real popular name. There are 17 species of them, all endemic to Western Australia and several of them quite popularly grown. *Eremaea beaufortioides* is most commonly seen. Needing a spot with as much sun as possible, low summer humidity and very well-drained, light soil, they are not really frost hardy but propagation is easy from seed or cuttings. *E. beaufortioides* has even been grafted onto plants of the sturdier, related species, Kunzea.

Eremaea leaves are often needle-like, the flowers, like related Callistemon and Melaleuca, consist of bundles of brightly coloured stamens. In the case of *E. beaufortioides* these are a bright orange-red and borne terminally.

Eremocitrus

(e-re-moh-**cit**-rəs)　　　☼ Ⓦ Ⓗ
Limebush, Wild Lime,
Native Kumquat, Desert Lemon
Spring; 6–23 ft/2–7 m; treelike; evergreen

RUTACEAE　　　　　　FRAGRANT

Not common anywhere except the drier areas of Queensland, New South Wales and South Australia, *Eremocitrus* is the only one of its genus, though closely related to the edible Citrus fruits. In nature it suckers and soon forms dense, spiny clumps. In cultivation, it should be grafted onto commercial Citrus stock.

It makes a decorative container plant with its naturally drooping branches, particularly when in fruit. The dainty flowers are greenish-white and very fragrant, somewhat smaller than those of a true kumquat. The fruit (or berry) is about ½ in/1 cm in diameter. Though sour, it makes a pleasant drink or marmalade. *Eremocitrus* would seem to have a good future in Citrus hybridization programmes.

Eremocitrus glauca. Native Kumquat. Central Australia

Eremophila
(*syn.* STENOCHILUS)

(e-re-**mof**-i-lə)   ☼ ☀ W H
Emu-bush, Poverty-bush,
Tarbush
All year; to 5 ft/1.5 m; bun-shaped;
evergreen

SCROPHULARIACEAE

'Lovers of lonely places' translates
into the rather more poetic name
Eremophila, given to this enormous
Australian genus about two centuries

Eremophila 'Silver Emu'. Hybrid Emu-bush. Arid Australia

ago. And lovers of lonely places they
are. About 200 species, found exclusively in outback areas of South Australia, New South Wales and Queensland, they have been brought into
cultivation in many parts of the
world, but never in areas where the
humidity is high.

Apart from that dislike, and
another for really moist soil conditions, they might be grown anywhere, we know so little about them.
Their native haunts are very variable,
but many species naturally put up
with scorching heat, quite a deal of
frost and a complete lack of rain for
several years. The limits of their
tastes in soil conditions are not yet
known but it has been observed that
in nature, a great many of them
occur in limy pockets or where the
principal soil is an alkaline red earth.
So lime and good drainage would
seem to be important.

Eremophila bushes come in all
shapes and sizes, all of them sprinkled

Eremophila maculata. Emu-bush.
Arid Australia

Eremophila glabra. Emu-bush. Arid Australia

Eremophila sturtii. Poverty-bush.
Arid Australia

Eremophila laanii. Laan's Poverty-bush.
Western Australia

most of the year with tubular flowers of many different colours, though red, pink and mauve seem most common. The most attractive species form a low, spreading bush with grey-green, lightly hairy foliage and somewhat heath-like flowers in a vivid scarlet.

Eremophilas grow easily from autumn cuttings taken with a heel and struck in sharp sand. Grow on for a year or two before planting out and water sparingly, if at all.

Erica

(e-rik-ə)   ☼ C T
Heath, Heather
Aut-Win; 1½–12 ft/40 cm–4 m; evergreen

ERICACEAE   FRAGRANT

Though named from *ereike*, the ancient Greek word for a European variety, some 470 of the known *Erica* species are native to South Africa and now grown all over the temperate world, especially in its cooler regions. They are, in fact, the cool-climate gardener's joy, for it is quite possible to have several different species in bloom throughout the year.

Most *Ericas* are grown in raised beds or rock gardens, for good drainage is essential to success. They are a

Erica colorans. Rainbow Heather. South Africa

Erica regia 'Variegata'. Balloon Heather. South Africa

magnificent genus of the botanical family Ericaceae which, of course, includes Azaleas, Rhododendrons and many other sought-after genera of flowering plants. *Ericas* are remarkably floriferous, with a long flowering season which may be at any time of the year, depending on species.

That's the good news. The bad is

Erica ventricosa. Swollen Heather. South Africa

Erica cerinthioides. Hybrid heather, Rooihaartjie. South Africa

that they are among the fussiest of plants and seem to need special attention wherever they are grown. They need porous, acid soil that keeps moist at all times, and a good mix would be two parts of fibrous peat to one part of silver or bush sand. They

Erica vagans 'Lyonesse'. Cornish Heather. Cornwall, S.W. Europe

Erica hybrida. Hybrid Cape Heath. Hybrid

cannot abide lime in any form, or any type of animal manure, and are best kept moist with pure, unpolluted rain water, though if this is not possible, water that has stood in a tank or barrel for some time may be used. They need consistent moisture to simulate the rain and mist of their native home in South Africa's Cape Province. They also need a cool root-run and a year-round mulch of pebbles or other lime-free material.

Most species are increased easily (if very slowly) from seed which is simply spread on the surface of a damp sand/peat mixture and kept moist and sheltered until the young plants appear. These are unlikely to come true to type if you grow more than one species, as Ericas are notoriously promiscuous. The practical gardener will propagate them from 1 in/ 2 cm tip cuttings taken in autumn or early winter and struck in a constantly moist sand/peat mix.

Ericas commonly make light, twiggy growth with small linear leaves borne in whorls (grouped around a stem rather than along it) and tubular, waxy flowers of varying lengths and varying degrees of plumpness. Outside South Africa, they seem not as popular as they once were, perhaps due to the advent of softer-growing greenhouse hybrids

which require a higher temperature range.

Of the illustrated species, E. cinerea and E. vagans are European in origin, the others are South African. In nature, most Ericas have a symbiotic relationship with a fungus and this may have to be introduced into soil where Ericas have not been grown before. A nursery specializing in the Ericaceae can best advise on this.

Erica cinerea. Bell Heather. Europe

Eriocephalus

(e-ree-oh-**kef**-ə-ləs)   ☼ W H
Wool-flower, Wild Rosemary
Win-Spr; to 2 ft/60 cm; branchy; evergreen

ASTERACEAE   FRAGRANT

Scarcely your average daisy, the South African *Eriocephalus* spends much of the year looking like a sheep in need of shearing. The commonly seen *E. africanus* or Wool-flower is a dwarf shrub 2-3 ft/60 cm-1 m high but usually spreading much wider. It likes sandy, acid soil, full sun, and will stand a certain amount of frost in a sheltered location. Useful at the seaside, it is also drought tolerant.

Grow it from cuttings of young shoots and give it room to spread. Its needle-like leaves are silky, the late winter flowers white with gold or purple centres and borne for quite a few weeks in dense terminal umbels. They're quite fragrant and after bloom the seed heads expand into woolly balls that are sometimes dried for indoor decoration. Prune occasionally to restore a neat shape. The *Eriocephalus* is extraordinarily drought tolerant.

Eriocephalus africanus. Wool-flower. S. Africa

Eriogonum giganteum. St Catherine's Lace. S. California & islands

Eriogonum

(air-ee-oh-**goh**-nəm)   ☼ W H
St Catherine's Lace, Buckwheat
Summer; to 8 ft/2.5 m; branching;
evergreen

POLYGONACEAE

Not common away from the Rocky Mountains states of the USA and particularly California and nearby islands, the delicate St Catherine's Lace is reminiscent of the European Queen Anne's Lace, though in no way related. It is a roadside shrub related to the knotweeds and seems to bloom throughout the warm weather in semi-arid areas, sending up tall, branching cymes of small white flowers which are good for cutting, together with their white woolly foliage.

It self-seeds freely or can be raised from seed in any well-drained soil, particularly in seaside or dry areas. It seems seriously to need water only in severe droughts and should be pruned after flowering, cutting right back to the silvery, mounded foliage.

Eriostemon

(air-ee-**oss**-tem-ən)   ☼ ✴ W H
Waxflower, Native Daphne
Win-Spr; 3–8 ft/1–2.5 m; rounded;
evergreen

RUTACEAE   AROMATIC
                            FRAGRANT

Long before growing native plants became the flavour of the month among Australian gardeners, *Eriostemons* were grown all around the country and in many overseas lands as well. There are around 30 species, mostly found in nature as forest understorey shrubs; in cultivation they do best in the dappled shade of your average shrub border. They are usually raised in acid to neutral soils where the drainage is good. They are not happy where lime is present and are thus suited to garden communities of acid-loving plants.

Eriostemon can be grown from seed, soaked for 24 hours before sowing, or from semi-hardwood cuttings taken in autumn. They are all susceptible to root rot so excellent drainage is a must.

Waxflowers are found in all Australian states in various climatic regions from the coast to the mountains. They are relatively frost hardy and can even survive in arid areas. By far the most popular species is *E. myoporoides*. At a distance it does resemble the Asiatic Daphne, but the leaves are much smaller and the flowers not as fragrant though they do have a sharp, citrusy scent.

Eriostemon australasius. Pink Waxflower. N.S.W., Queensland

Eriostemon myoporoides. Native Daphne. E. Australia

First is the Tambookie Thorn, a remarkable plant from well-drained or even arid areas of South Africa. It is grown from seed, which should be soaked for at least 24 hours, but will still take up to 4 years before blooming. It is like a grotesquely dwarfed bonsai plant, growing much broader than its height, and flowers on bare wood in early spring with a dazzling profusion of scarlet, cream and green elongated pea flowers. The leaves when they appear are trifoliate.

Also from South Africa is *E. zeyheri* which sends up twiggy stems annually from an underground rhizome. These sprout large trifoliate leaves and 18 in/50 cm spikes of scarlet pea flowers. In dry weather, the entire plant above ground disappears until the next rain.

Erythrina zeyheri. Creeping Thorn. E. South Africa

Eriostemon 'Stardust'. Hybrid Eriostemon.

Erythrina

(e-rith-**rai**-nə)   ☼ ☀ Ⓦ Ⓗ
Tambookie Thorn,
Creeping Thorn
Spring; 2–7 ft/60 cm–2.5 m; dwarf; deciduous

FABACEAE

The 100-odd species of *Erythrina* include many of the most garish and noticeable of trees in a tropical or hot landscape setting, worldwide. It is a splendid genus, including several very worthwhile shrubby plants for the warm-temperate to subtropical climate.

'Stardust' is its hybrid, with noticeably warty stems. *E. australasius* is a taller, more open shrub with profuse pink flowers from winter into spring.

Eriostemons belong to the same family as the many Citrus species, and there is a strong resemblance when in flower.

Erythrina acanthocarpa. Tambookie Thorn. South Africa

Escallonia bifida. Escallonia. Brazil, Argentina

Escallonia laevis. Escallonia. Brazil

Eucalyptus burdettiana. Burdett Mallee.
S.W. Western Australia

Escallonia 'Peach Blossom'.
Hybrid Escallonia. Hybrid

Escallonia

(ess-ka-**loh**-nee-ə)   ☼ ◑ T
Escallonia
Sum-Aut; to 15 ft/4.5 m; open; evergreen

ESCALLONIACEAE   FRAGRANT

Shrubs and small trees from mountainous areas of South America's Andes region. They are evergreen (with one exception), enjoy a well-drained but compost-rich soil and plenty of summer moisture. They grow superbly in Ireland, the San Francisco area and the eastern United States.

Sturdy, glossy-leafed shrubs, they are hardy down to 15°F/-9°C, and are best propagated from 4 in/10 cm cuttings of half-ripe, unflowered wood taken with a heel in late summer. A light pruning to remove spent flower heads only is advisable, though they can be trimmed more heavily if you risk the sacrifice of more flowering wood. *Escallonias* leaves are glossy, simple, with serrated edges. The flowers may be open, bell-like or tubular. They are all pleasantly fragrant and borne in terminal, often hanging, clusters.

Eucalyptus

(*syn.* SYMPHYOMYRTUS)

(yoo-ka-**lip**-təs)   ☼ T W H
Eucalyptus, Flowering Gum
Win-Spr; to 13 ft/4 m; sprawling; evergreen

MYRTACEAE

Where would Australia be without its omnipresent *Eucalyptus* trees? We may soon know, if a group of local taxonomists have their way and split our largest tree genus into a handful of parts with unspellable names like Symphyomyrtus! No single word has a right to so many ys! Anyway, enough of that relatively unimportant bit of information—what I *should* have been saying is that a few of Australia's Eucalypts are shrubby, and that they seem to grow superbly in California. Those under discussion are from Australia's West, and do well neither in the humidity of our eastern states, nor within 100 miles of the seacoast.

All of these shrubby Eucalypts can be raised from seed, but which colour their flowers will be depends on *both* parents. Propagation from cuttings has been managed in recent years,

Eucalyptus rhodantha. Rose Mallee, Blue Bush. Western Australia

Eucalyptus macrocarpa. Mottlecah, Rose of the West. Western Australia

but the technique is very difficult. These plants enjoy a deep, sandy, very well-drained soil over clay, a little on the acid side. Extra water is needed during drought. Crowded many-trunked old specimens can be pruned selectively back to the ligno-tuber; but do not prune lightly all over.

E. macrocarpa grows ever so slowly, but looks sensational spilling over a bank. Its flowers are stalkless, 3 in/8 cm across and borne singly. *E. rhodantha* is a smaller plant, its buds and rounded foliage a blue-grey. The 3 in/8 cm blooms are borne over a long period. *E. burdettiana*, third of our shrubby trio, has slender leaves, large open yellow flower heads and is an endangered species in the wild. Still, popular in cultivation, it may grow to 13 ft/4 m in height and produce multiple trunks.

Eucalyptus rhodantha. Blue Bush. Western Australia

Eucryphia

(yoo-**krif**-ee-ə)   ☼ ☀ T
Leatherwood
Late spring; 9–23 ft/3–7 m; dense; evergreen

EUCRYPHIACEAE   FRAGRANT

Separated by the vastness of the Pacific Ocean, there are only 4 natural species of the elegant *Eucryphia*:

two in Chile and one each in Tasmania and mainland Australia. These are also the only plants in their family, Eucryphiaceae. You may know the Tasmanian species as the source of delicious Leatherwood honey, but in a cool climate they are worth growing for the beauty of their flowers alone. Hardy down to at least 23°F/−5°C, they enjoy a dappled, sheltered spot in leaf-rich soil. Acid soil seems to suit them best, but they will certainly tolerate lime.

Jean Johnson

Eucryphia lucida. Leatherwood. Tasmania

Eucryphias can be grown from ripe seed or summer cuttings taken with a heel and struck in a sandy compost. In suitably moist places, such as Ireland, and in mountainous gardens, they may grow to 23 ft/7 m, spreading about a third as wide. Flowers are 2 in/5 cm in diameter, white and very fragrant.

All-over pruning is recommended after flowering to keep the plants compact, although their naturally conical shape is most attractive. In the shade of larger trees they make useful screening plants.

Eugenia
(syn. SYZYGIUM)

(yoo-**jee**-nee-ə)   ☼ ◐ W H
Australian Brush Cherry
Spr-Sum; 6 ft/2 m; spreading; evergreen

MYRTACEAE   FRAGRANT

Once upon a time, there was a very large subtropical genus named *Eugenia*, until the taxonomical splitters got to work. Then the genus suddenly acquired such indigestible monikers as Phyllocladyx, Stenocladyx and, Lord help us, Syzygium. Thank heaven, though, for California's nurserymen who don't care who gets a guernsey for inventing the clumsiest name. They stick to Eugenia (after that talented Rambo of the 17th century, Prince Eugene of Savoy, who was also a patron of botany).

The shrubby *E. myrtifolia* from eastern Australia has become one of California's most widely used plants, though which Syzygium it should correctly be is uncertain! Charming evergreens with shining lanceolate leaves and fragrant myrtle-type flowers in terminal and axillary clusters, they are sold by the million for hedges, topiaries and screening plants. In early summer, they are covered in cream blossom that drives the bees to distraction!

In Hawaii, they sell *E. uniflora,* the Surinam Cherry, which is used for the same purposes. It has larger leaves, reflexed petals and curious yellow fruit, grooved longitudinally. *Eugenias* are grown from seed or cuttings, and like rich, moist, well-drained soil.

Eugenia uniflora. Surinam Cherry. Tropical America

Eugenia myrtifolia. Australian Brush Cherry. E. Australia

Euonymus alatus. Winged Spindle Bush. Temperate E. Asia

respect, as is the taller *E. sachalinensis* from further north, which presents a wonderful contrast between carmine foliage and orange seed capsules.

The ubiquitous evergreen *E. japonicus* is more suited to warm-temperate areas, has a myriad leaf varieties in multiple combinations of cream, yellow, green and white. These leaves are lightly serrated and punctuated with greenish-white flower clusters, and later, pink seed capsules.

All species can be grown from ripe seed, sown in moist sphagnum at 41°F/5°C. Semi-hardwood cuttings can be struck in early summer in a mixture of sand and peat. Rich, well-drained, damp soil brings on the best fruit display, and a light winter pruning will shorten too-vigorous leading shoots. Use *E. japonicus* for hedges and screens.

Euonymus
(*syn.* EVONYMUS)

(yoo-**on**-ə-məs) ☼ T W
Spindle Bush
Spr-Sum; 10 ft/3–4 m; variable foliage

CELASTRACEAE

The 120 species of *Euonymus* are mostly shrubs, and from all continents, yet there are a few small tree

Euonymus japonicus aureo-picta.
Japanese Spindle Bush. Japan

Euonymus sachalinensis. Northern Spindle Bush. N.E. Asia

species and even the odd climber, just to spread things around. They are all grown mainly for foliage display, and for the curious spindle-shaped long-stemmed fruits or seed pods.

The deciduous types (strictly for cool-temperate climates) are valued for their stunning display of autumn colour, though it is not very long lasting. *E. alatus* from Japan and China is particularly showy in this

Eupatorium megalophyllum. Mist-flower. S. Mexico

Eupatorium
(*syn.* HEBECLINIUM, OSMIA)

(yoo-pə-**tor**-ee-əm) ☼ ☀ W H
Mist-flower, Shrub Ageratum
Spring; 7 ft/2 m; globose bush; evergreen

ASTERACEAE

Too soft to survive even the lightest frost, the showy Mist-flower flourishes in lightly-shaded places in warm-temperate climates where its superb display of misty mauve flowers appears in stunning contrast to nearby spring blossom.

It is easy to propagate from slim, semi-hardened cuttings with short internodes. These should be cut cleanly and struck in autumn or winter in light, sandy soil. When they are rooted, set them out in rich, well-drained soil and give plenty of water in warm weather.

Eupatorium seeds profusely, and to prevent its taking over your garden it is wise to prune back flowered stems right after blooming. New shoots can be tipped back in summer to maintain shape. *Eupatoriums* (there are about 50 species of them) are just like Ageratums that grew up fast. Their furry, floppy leaves may be 10 in/25 cm across. The panicles of blue blossom are the size of a human head, and can look a sorry sight after heavy rain.

Euphorbia

(yoo-**for**-bee-ə)   ☼ ✹ W H
Poinsettia, Crown of Thorns, Spurge
Win-Sum; 1½–10 ft/45 cm–3 m; variable foliage

EUPHORBIACEAE

Except for the popular Poinsettia (*Euphorbia pulcherrima*) which is used as a houseplant everywhere, cool-climate gardeners' knowledge of the genus *Euphorbia* is largely limited to the many yellow-green flowered annual and perennial types. However

Euphorbia grandicornis. Cow's Horn. South Africa

the 1000-odd species of this very large genus include many spectacular shrubs, often with very little resemblance one to the other. What, then, do they have in common? First, is an unpleasant milky sap, usually quite poisonous. Second, are spectacular flower-like arrangements which are not flowers at all, but a series of highly coloured bracts, or modified leaves.

Of the shrub species, the hollow-stemmed Poinsettia, *E. pulcherrima*, is the showiest, its dwarfed indoor specimens being only a pale shadow of its gorgeous outdoor display.

Curiously enough, all this colour is stimulated by the shortening hours of daylight in winter. From Mexico, it likes well-drained soil, plenty of water, and is usually grown from soft-tip cuttings taken in summer and autumn. Prune heavily after bloom, shortening flowered stems by half. It is not at all frost hardy, blooms in scarlet, pink, cream and green, sometimes in bicolours. Both single and double varieties can be found.

The Crown of Thorns, *E. milii*, is a spiny, succulent plant, deciduous in cooler areas, propagated from spring cuttings, dried off before striking in sharp sand. Drought resistant and hardy down to 50°F/10°C, it likes regular water in summer, tapering off in the winter resting period. The scarlet or cream bracts appear in spring with the foliage, and intermittent blooms are borne throughout the warmer months.

E. cotinifolia, found from Mexico down into South America, is a handsome shrub grown mostly for its foliage appeal, though it does bear masses of yellow flower-like structures during the summer. The copper-coloured leaves are borne in threes at stem nodes, and have an interesting greenish sheen.

Some of the most interesting *Euphorbia* species are often mistaken for Cacti, though all Cacti are from the Americas. These Cactus mimics are South African, like the illustrated Cow's Horn, *E. grandicornis*; its appeal is in its shape and texture, because of course it bears no spectacular flowers. Grow it from stem cuttings.

Euphorbia cotinifolia. Coppertone Plant. Mexico—N. South America

Euphorbia milii. Crown of Thorns. Madagascar

Euphorbia pulcherrima. Poinsettia. Mexico

Eupomatia

(yoo-pom-**ae**-tee-ə) ☼ ☀ W H
Copper Laurel, Native Guava
*Spr-Sum; 1–3 ft/30–100 cm; straggly;
evergreen*

EUPOMATIACEAE   FRAGRANT

Largely of interest to rainforest fans, the two species of *Eupomatia* or Copper Laurel are found in moist areas of open forest near the Queensland/New South Wales border. *E. bennettii* is the smaller of the two, a neat, shrubby plant with rather tuberous roots and long, beautiful coppery young foliage with winged stalks. *E. bennettii* often grows on rocky soils and can be propagated from seed or cuttings. Later on it can be planted out as a striking container plant or set out in rich, well-drained soil in a partly shaded position.

Eupomatias have a most unusual flower structure, and are believed to be a very ancient genus, with no modern botanical affiliates. The fragrant 1 in/2.5 cm blossoms, borne singly, are of a creamy colour. The petals are fused into a deciduous cup which drops, and the male and female parts of the flower are separated by a barrier of red-stained

Eupomatia bennettii. Copper Laurel.
N.S.W., Queensland

Murray Fagg

staminodes which prevent fertilization except by a particular beetle. My difficulty in describing this unusual structure adequately should not detract from appreciation of the plant's beauty. The other species, by the way, is a tree, *E. laurina*.

Euryops

(**yoo**-ree-ops) ☼ W H
Yellow Marguerite, Brighteyes
*Win-Spr; to 3 ft/1 m; rounded bush;
evergreen*

ASTERACEAE

The 60-odd *Euryops* species are shrubby evergreens endemic to South Africa, and are hardy down to 28°F/−2°C. All are similar except in minor botanical details and are grown in most temperate climates. Their habit of growth is rather spreading, with stems reaching out about 3 ft/1 m before sprawling onto the ground. A certain amount of pruning after bloom helps keep them in some semblance of shape.

Euryops pectinatus. Brighteyes.
South Africa

The alternately borne leaves are 2½–3½ in/6–9 cm long and deeply lobed. In some species they're a dark grey-green, in others they're covered with fine silvery hair. The golden daisy flowers appear singly on long stems for many weeks during late winter and spring, and cut well for small bouquets.

A gravelly, well-drained soil suits them best, with ample water during dry weather. Propagate from short semi-hardwood cuttings in late autumn.

Eutaxia

(yoo-**tak**-see-ə)   ☼ ☽ W
Sunshine
Spring; to 3 ft/1 m; twiggy; evergreen

FABACEAE

Eutaxias are light, lacy shrubs and, with one exception, endemic to Western Australia. In spring, they glow in the dappled shade of light forest covering, generally on or near the coast.

It is difficult to give a comprehensive key to soil preferences, for the various species are found in soils of many types. *E. obovata*, however, prefers a well-drained milieu, but is otherwise very adaptable. It was one of the first Australian plants to become popular in England, in 1825, and does well in a wide climatic range. It is not frost hardy, but unlike most Australian plants, responds well to hard pruning. Cuttings strike without problems, but propagation may also be carried out from scarified seed. Do not over-water.

Eutaxia obovata. Sunshine.
Western Australia

Exochorda

(eks-oh-**kor**-də)   ☼ ☽ C T
Pearlbush, String of Pearls
Spring; 4–10 ft/1.5–3.5 m; open; deciduous

ROSACEAE

Although the relatively few species of *Exochorda* are seen in a wide variety of climates, their preference really lies in the cold to cool-temperate range. Some heat they will take, but not the humidity of warm climates.

Exochorda racemosa. String of Pearls. China

Exochordas should be planted in loamy but well-drained soil, and can be propagated from spring-sown seeds kept warm under glass, or from soft-tip cuttings struck with misting in summer or autumn. Watering should be regular and heavy.

Blooms appear from the bare wood and really do look like a string of pearls before they open, at which time they are valued for indoor arrangements. New foliage unfurls before the flowers are done. *Exochordas* are deciduous and produce some leaf colour in a sharp autumn.

Fabiana imbricata. False Heath. Chile

Fabiana

(fab-ee-**ah**-nə)   ☼ T
False Heath, Mock Heath,
Chile Heath
Late spring; 3–6 ft/90 cm–2 m; spreading; evergreen

SOLANACEAE

Not another heath, I hear you say? False, I reply. And indeed the strange False or Chile Heath is not a heath at all, but in the same botanical family as the potato, tomato and eggplant.

Fabiana imbricata (named for the Spanish botanist, Fabiano) is an interesting evergreen shrub that may grow 6 ft/2 m high, but is usually rather prostrate. Its branches are densely covered with scale-like leaves. The flowers are tubular (a little like those of related Cestrum), and white, and each one is at the end of a small extension of the main twig.

Something of a novelty in California and the southern UK, it can't cope with the frost further north. Propagate it in summer from cuttings of the side shoots struck under glass. It thrives in a light, well-drained soil.

Faradaya splendida. Buku. Queensland

X *Fatshedera lizei* 'Aureo-Marmorata'.
Botanical Wonder. Bi-generic hybrid

Fatsia

(**fat**-see-ə)   ☼ ☀ T W
Japanese Aralia
Autumn; 5 ft/1.5 m; suckering; evergreen

ARALIACEAE

One of the world's favourite house
plants and the sedate parent from the
previous entry, *Fatsia japonica* is more
commonly known as Aralia in many
countries. It is a shrubby plant that
produces magnificent leaves in almost
any conditions. It is ideal for shaded
gardens or indoors and grows well in
fast-draining soil.

Fatsia japonica (fruit). Japanese Aralia. Japan

Faradaya

(**fa**-ra-dae-ə)   ☼ ☀ W H
Buku, Pitutu
Spring; 6 ft/2 m; spreading; evergreen

LAMIACEAE   FRAGRANT

One of the glories of Queensland's
fast-vanishing rainforests, the splendid *Faradaya splendida* is most aptly
named. Subtropical in nature, it
reduces in size the further away from
the equator it is grown. I have seen it
in subtropical Brisbane as a spectacular lawn shrub, perhaps 6 ft/2 m high
and at least twice that across. Planted
out in a hot climate in rich soil with
plenty of water it will positively bolt
into growth.

You can raise it from cuttings and
enjoy dense panicles of showy and
very fragrant white flowers in spring.
The roots should be shaded but the
rest of the plant enjoys full sun. Just
keep it away from the trees.

X Fatshedera

(fats-**hed**-ur-ə)   ☼ ☀ T W
Tree Ivy, Botanical Wonder
*Autumn; to 8 ft/2.5 m; branching;
evergreen*

ARALIACEAE

It seems that somebody once locked
up a sedate *Fatsia japonica* with a
randy Irish Ivy (*Hedera hibernica*).

The result was that botanical rarity,
a bi-generic hybrid that might have
been called a climbing Fatsia or an
ivy tree. Instead, botanists sensibly
called it X *Fatshedera*, the X signifying
the problems of its parentage.

Apart from its popularity as a
house plant, its principal use is as a
groundcover in large, shaded, temperate gardens. X *Fatshedera* would
collapse below 15°F/−9°C and its
beautiful leaves burn to a frazzle in
hot-climate sun. You can grow it
from cuttings and pinch back to stop
it falling over when it heads for the
stars. Any ordinary garden soil will
suit.

Fatsia japonica. Japanese Aralia. Japan

Raised from suckers, seed or cuttings, it can be cut back hard if it
becomes too leggy. Give *Fatsia* regular water and liquid fertilizer, but
never let it remain sodden. It produces terminal clusters of greenish-
white flowers in autumn. There are
several variations in leaf shape, with
a variegated type that is particularly
effective in shaded places. It is hardy
down to at least 28°F/−2°C.

Feijoa

(fae-**joh**-ə)   ☼ ☀ ⬚T ⬚W
Pineapple Guava,
Fruit Salad Plant
*Spring; 13–20 ft/4–6 m; globose;
evergreen*

MYRTACEAE

A novelty autumn fruit in cooler climates, the *Feijoa* is borne on a plant
that seems content to remain a
rounded shrub in Australia but is
reported to reach small-tree size in
southern England. It is not a true
guava but certainly related within the
myrtle family, Myrtaceae.

Feijoa sellowiana (one of only 2
species) needs rich, well-drained soil
and ample water in dry summers to
develop the ovoid green fruit, which
have a tangy, guava-like taste when
ripe. The shiny leaves are oval and
have a woolly reverse. The decorative

Felicia amelloides. Kingfisher Daisy. South Africa

Felicia frikartii 'Alba'. Dwarf Marguerite.
South Africa

Feijoa sellowiana. Pineapple Guava.
Argentina

fuchsia-like flowers are borne over a
long period in spring. They appear in
twos at the base of new season's
growth and have white, reflexed
petals and deep red stamens. Propagate from seed or semi-hardwood cuttings in autumn, struck with heat
and humidity.

Felicia

(fə-**lee**-see-ə)   ☼ ⬚W ⬚H
Kingfisher Daisy,
Blue Daisy, Blue Marguerite
Spring; 1½–3 ft/.5–1 m; tidy; evergreen

ASTERACEAE

Finding true blue among flowers is
the gardening equivalent of finding
gold among the dross, and the dainty
Blue Marguerite, *Felicia amelloides*, is
about the truest blue you're likely to
find. Classed as a sub-shrub, it is a
sturdy little plant that grows so fast
in temperate climates it is often
treated as a bedding plant and struck
afresh from soft-tip cuttings at any
time. It can also be raised from seed.

A low, generally tidy plant, it
makes a brilliant warm-weather display in rock gardens, as a path edging
or by the seaside. It is also useful in
hillside gardens and is hardy down to
27°C/–3°C.

F. frikartii 'Alba', the Dwarf Marguerite, is more what you expect of a
shrub. It grows to about 2½ ft/75 cm
in height and is studded in late spring
with typical white daisy flowers,
though there are also pink and
mauve varieties. Both species need
full sun and prefer dryish, very well-
drained, gravelly soil enriched with
organic matter.

Ficus

(**fai**-cəs)   ☼ ☽ ☀ ⬚W ⬚H
Fig, Banyan
All year; 8–10 ft/2–3 m; open; evergreen

MORACEAE

In the last quarter century, many
species of *Ficus*, or Fig, have become
the most popular of indoor plants for
tropical effect or leaf interest. These
are mostly trees in nature, and cannot be grown outdoors where the
winter temperature falls below
55°F/13°C.

In warmer climates, though, it is

Ficus aspera. Clown Fig. South Pacific

Forsythia

(for-**sai**-thee-ə) ☼ C T
Golden Bells
Spring; 6–13 ft/2–4 m; vase-shaped; deciduous

OLEACEAE

You can say one thing about being a Royal Gardener—the pay might be lousy but you get some nice plants named after you. William Forsyth, for instance, was the gardener to George III at Kensington Palace and had some newly discovered, golden-flowered shrubs named after him—*Forsythia*!

Hardy down to 17°F/–8°C, these beautiful plants light up cold-climate gardens at the first breath of spring, the new, slender branches arched with the sheer weight of blossom. Bare stems cut in bud will even open indoors in plain water.

Easy to grow in rich, well-drained soil, they are also easy to propagate either by division or from semi-hardwood tip cuttings taken in summer and struck in a cool, humid place.

F. suspensa is commonly self-layering, and well-rooted layers may be severed and lifted in late winter. The cultivar 'Lynwood Gold' is the

Forsythia 'Lynwood Gold'. Golden Bells. Hybrid

most unwise to plant them in the garden. They have an unerring gift for sending their greedy roots into nearby drains and are adept at destroying foundations. Some even develop into the widest-spreading trees in the world, a feat which they perform by means of aerial roots sent down from the outer branches. These develop into new trunks, and the spreading process starts again. Several *Ficus* are known which cover more than a square mile.

But among the genus are also some delightful plants classed as shrubs. The showiest of these is the Clown Fig, *F. aspera*, a slender, many-branched plant with rough-textured leaves that are beautifully marked in ivory and green. These form a decorative background for the cherry-sized fruit, which are striped in green, cream and pink.

F. deltoidea is epiphytic in nature, and has been grown to 10 ft/3 m in height. It is now popular as a Bonsai subject, with small paddle-shaped leaves and pea-sized scarlet fruits. It does develop miniature aerial roots. *F. ticoya*, the Waipahu Fig, is of unknown origin, but used as an attractive groundcover in Hawaii and other warm climates.

None of these *Ficus* species is particular as to soil, but all do better, grow larger, where it is leaf-rich and provides plenty of moisture.

Ficus deltoidea. Mistletoe Fig. Malaysia

Ficus ticoya. Waipahu Fig. Pan-tropical

Forsythia X intermedia. Hybrid

are becoming more and more popular as colourful residents on the terraces of apartments and home units. They flower and fruit profusely and do look exactly like miniaturized Citrus, to which they are related and with some of which they hybridize. (See X *Citrofortunella*).

One rarely sees them planted out in the open garden, although they certainly would grow that way, at least in South Africa, Australia and the Mediterranean region. Cultivation is exactly the same as for Citrus (which see). The principal differences are that Kumquats are almost

Fortunella japonica 'Variegata'. Variegated Marumi. S. China

most brilliant yellow of all but, like most *Forsythias*, dislikes subtropical or even warm conditions, preferring areas where winters are always at least frosty. There, it forms a dense, many-stemmed bush up to 13 ft/4 m tall. The bell-shaped flowers appear in small clusters from lateral buds of the previous season's wood, so annual pruning should not be undertaken until flowering has finished.

Fortunella

(for-tyoo-**nel**-lə) ☼ T W H
Kumquat
Summer; 3–17 ft/1–5 m; treelike; evergreen

RUTACEAE   FRAGRANT

Much hardier than most other Citrus fruits, the Kumquats (*Fortunella* spp.) are hardy down to 20°F/–7°C and are valued New Year's gifts in many parts of China. In the West, too, they

Forsythia suspensa. Weeping Forsythia. China

Fortunella margarita. Nagami Kumquat. S.E. China

totally spineless and the flowers (and fruit) mostly appear in the leaf axils, singly, rather than in terminal clusters. As well as for their decorative appearance, Kumquats are grown for the table.

There are three species. The Marumi (*F. japonica*) has globose, bitter fruit about 1½ in/4 cm in diameter. It has an attractive variegated cultivar. The fruit is preserved in alcohol and eaten with coffee. The fruit of the Nagami (*F. margarita*) is oval to oblong, 1 in/3 cm in diameter, with sour pulp but sweet rind. It is eaten, skin and all, straight from

Fortunella japonica. Marumi Kumquat. S. China

the tree. The third type of Kumquat is the Meiwa (*F. crassiflora*). The fruit is ellipsoidal and can also be eaten fresh. It is less common in Western countries. All 3, of course, make delicious marmalade.

Fothergilla

(foth-ur-**gil**-lə)   ☼ ✲ C T
Mountain Snow
Spring; 6 ft/2 m; spreading; deciduous

HAMAMELIDACEAE

Treasures for the cool-climate garden, the 4 species of *Fothergilla* are native to the eastern USA, where they are found in remote mountain

Fothergilla monticola. Mountain Snow. S.E. USA

parts. Illustrated *F. major* is the best known kind, its large, elliptic leaves not appearing until after the superb display of snowy-white, puffball flowers in mid-spring. Another display comes in autumn when the foliage turns a rich yellow.

Another popular species is *F. monticola* which is similar but turns scarlet and crimson in the fall. Plant all *Fothergillas* from layers or semi-hardwood cuttings taken with a heel in midsummer. All species need lime-free soil and constant moisture.

Fothergilla major. Mountain Witchhazel. E. USA

Fouquieria

(foo-kee-**eə**-ree-ə)   ☼ W H
Ocotillo, Jacob's Staff, Coachwhip
Summer; 20 ft/6 m; arching; deciduous

FOUQUIERIACEAE

In desert places of the American south-west and all over Mexico, summer brings a brilliant splash of colour as the Ocotillos or *Fouquierias* burst into bloom with panicles of tubular, orange-scarlet flowers borne at the ends of arching stems that are very much like the whips of their popular

Fouquieria splendida. Ocotillo, Coachwhip. Texas to Baja California

name. The Ocotillos are a feature of western gardens in Palm Springs and other places and should be seen more in warm, dry places world-wide.

A well-drained soil is necessary, though beyond that any type will do, providing water is supplied when the plant is actually growing. The simple, 1 in/3 cm leaves appear in early spring but are deciduous in the hotter weather. Propagate it from cuttings and consider it as a hedge plant in arid areas.

Frankenia

(fran-**ken**-ee-ə)   ☼ T W
Sea Heath
Spring; 6 in/15 cm; spreading; evergreen

FRANKENIACEAE

Small, salt-loving sub-shrubs from Europe, South Africa, Australia and the Canary Islands, the 80-odd species of *Frankenia* are useful right by the sea or in inland areas where the soil is brackish or even completely penetrated by salt. They are evergreen and reminiscent of the true heaths. For the most part prostrate, many are branched and wiry.

Frankenia pauciflora. Southern Sea Heath. Australian coast

Propagate from seed, cuttings or division and plant in light, sandy soil, watered occasionally. Australian *F. pauciflora* is a fine carpeting plant for coastal gardens, a charming, grey-foliaged rockery subject almost anywhere, although its principal value is where there is a salt problem. In spring, the plant is dotted with tiny pink flowers.

Franklandia

(frank-**land**-ee-ə)   ☼ ☀ W H
Franklandia
Spring; 1–5 ft/30–150 cm; erect; evergreen

PROTEACEAE   FRAGRANT

Never well enough known to have acquired a popular name, Western Australia's *Franklandia triaristata* has spent so much time hiding its light under a bushel, it has now been gazetted as an endangered species, and its only real hope for survival is to be introduced into cultivation in private gardens.

Franklandia triaristata. Western Australia

Certainly its rarity has nothing at all to do with being inconspicuous. Though a small shrub, it bears dogwood-like flowers 2½ in/6 cm in diameter, white with a pinkish exterior. These have a perfume redolent of a rich chocolate-vanilla, which suffuses the air around.
Franklandia needs well-drained, light to medium soil and, preferably, a full day's sunshine. It is not frost hardy. Propagation can be from seed, but more usually from cuttings struck in a damp sand/peat mixture with misting. Curiously enough, it is a most *un*typical member of the family Proteaceae.

Franklinia alatamaha. Franklin Tree. Georgia USA

Franklinia

(frank-**lin**-ee-ə)   ☼ T W
Franklin Tree
Sum-Aut; 20–30 ft/6–9 m; bushy; deciduous

THEACEAE

A gorgeous North American Camellia relative, the *Franklinia* was never common in its native Georgia at the best of times and is now completely unknown in the wild. A tall-growing, deciduous shrub (sometimes seen to tree height!) it makes slow growth from seed in rich, light, acid to neutral soil with good drainage, and flowers cannot be expected for at least 7 years. It can also be propagated from cuttings. All in all, *Franklinia* likes the same conditions as Rhododendron—grow one and you can grow the other.

It has handsome reddish bark, glossy deciduous leaves that turn scarlet in autumn and showy, velvety-white 3 in/8 cm blooms with spoon-shaped petals and rich gold stamens.

Fremontodendron californica. Tree Poppy. California, Mexico

Fuchsia 'Pink Jade'. Hybrid

Fremontodendron

(free-**mon**-tə-den-drən) ☼ T W
Tree Poppy, Flannelbush
Spring; 6–16 ft/2–5 m; bun-shaped;
part-deciduous

MALVACEAE

How do you cultivate this lovely *Fremontodendron*? Answer: with extreme care! The plant is so beautiful that many people can't resist touching it—and that is where the trouble starts, for it is covered in all its parts with tiny hairs which, to some people, are highly allergenic.

Though native to dry, almost desert areas of California, Arizona and Mexico, the *Fremontodendrons* (there are 2 species) will grow well in a sandy, well-drained soil in almost any area where the humidity is low, and turn on a spectacular display several times a year. Even in southern England they bloom quite well against a south-facing, sunny wall, being hardy down to 26°F/–3°C. Propagate them from seed or softwood cuttings and please, wear gloves!

Fuchsia

(**fyoo**-shə) ☼ ☀ T W
Ladies' Eardrops
Spr-Aut; 2–6 ft/60 cm–2 m; bushy;
evergreen

ONAGRACEAE

Some years ago I wrote an article in which I described the wonderful *Fuchsia* hedges in western County Cork—miles and miles of arching *Fuchsias* meeting above the coastal roads as far as you could see. Alas, I have just returned from another visit to Cork and the arching hedges have gone, cut back to make room for the high-top tourist buses—yet another example of a country destroying the very things that tourists come to see.

The climate of southern Ireland is ideal for *Fuchsias*. It is warmed by the Gulf Stream, has humid summers and frost-free winters. Frequent mists and cloudy skies raise the humidity, soft rains drench the plants at any time of year. All of this creates the

Fuchsia 'Japana'. Hybrid

Fuchsia 'Lisa'. Hybrid Fuchsia

Fuchsia splendens. Shining Fuchsia. Mexico

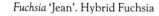

Fuchsia 'Jean'. Hybrid Fuchsia

atmosphere that *Fuchsias* love and are used to in their native South American coastal forests.

They will grow in almost any soil provided it contains plenty of organic matter. They'll even overlook variations in soil pH provided it is not over-acid. If your Azaleas bloom beautifully, better add half a cup of dolomite to the square yard or metre for *Fuchsias* and feed them carefully with bone meal. They have a terrible thirst, so water deeply and often but never while the sun is directly on the plant. They will grow best among other shade-loving plants or in the shelter of deciduous trees. In hot, dry areas, grow them in pots in a shade-house and keep the humidity high.

Varieties with a weeping habit make elegant basket plants in a sheltered position; those with stronger, upright growth can be trained as standards or espaliers. They even make showy, if temporary, indoor plants, but sulk if left too long in the dry indoor atmosphere.

Prune *Fuchsias* while they are dormant in late winter, and begin pinching back new growth in spring for a compact shape and more flowers. New plants are easily raised from soft-tip cuttings of 2–4 nodes taken from

Fuchsia magellanica 'Tricolor'. Hardy Fuchsia. Chile, Argentina

Fuchsia thymifolia. Thyme-leaf Fuchsia. Mexico

Fuchsia triphylla 'Gartenmeister Bonstedt'. Haiti, San Domingo

late spring through autumn. Strike them in a warm, humid place. Most *Fuchsias* are deciduous and bear their hanging flowers at leaf axils, most heavily at the ends of arching branches. Each flower consists of four reflexed sepals and four or more petals, frequently in a contrasting colour.

Galphimia
(*syn.* THRYALLIS)

(gal-**fim**-ee-ə)　　☼ W H
Rain of Gold,
Mexican Gold Bush, Rama de Oro
Summer; 7 ft/2 m; erect; evergreen

MALPIGHIACEAE

So profuse is the summer flowering of the small Central American *Galphimia* that the soil for yards around literally disappears beneath a carpet of golden bloom. On a mature specimen in full flower, the red stems are literally weighed down by terminal spikes of tiny golden blossoms for weeks on end. Strictly a subject for the warm-temperate to tropical climate, it needs rich, well-drained soil and regular water to keep its roots damp.

The opposite leaves are ovate, shining and about 2 in/5 cm in length; they are also evergreen. Propagation can be undertaken from seed or from cuttings of ripe wood, struck in sharp, sandy mix with warmth and humidity. *Galphimia* may be clipped into a hedge.

Galphimia glauca. Rain of Gold. Central America

Galvezia speciosa. Island Bush Snapdragon. S. California islands

Galvezia
(syn. ANTIRRHINUM)

(gal-**vez**-ee-ə)   ☼ ✳ T W H
Island Bush Snapdragon
Spring; 6–7 ft/2 m; spreading; evergreen

PLANTAGINACEAE

Scattered around coastal areas from the southern Californian islands all the way down to Peru is a small genus of shrubs going under the name of *Galvezia*. The 'island' species *G. speciosa* is very much in cultivation on several continents—and not fussy about a wide range of soils so long as they are well-drained. They are very salt and drought resistant, and when established need little water except in the driest of seasons. A sun-lover, *Galvezia* nevertheless appreciates midday shade in hot areas of the warm-temperate to tropical climates it loves.

It is easily propagated from cuttings, is evergreen and inclined to sprawl. The red flowers, 1 in/2.5 cm long, are borne in the leaf axils and look like small Antirrhinums.

Gamolepis
(syn. EURYOPS, PSILOTHONNA, STEIRODISCUS*)*

(**gam**-oh-lae-pəs)   ☼ T W
Paris Daisy
All year; 4–6 ft/1–1.8 m; rounded;
evergreen

ASTERACEAE

This small genus of golden daisy flowers consists mostly of annual or perennial plants. However the species

Gamolepis chrysanthemoides. Paris Daisy. South Africa

Gamolepis chrysanthemoides is a genuine shrub and widely grown in most temperate parts of the world because of its habit of flowering almost continuously, even when there's frost about. It is no problem to propagate, for it self-seeds all over the place, but cuttings can be used.

It thrives in any soil, but does best in leaf-rich, well-drained loam with year-round water. The alternate leaves are bright green, deeply toothed and glossy; the long-stemmed daisy flowers are yellow with a deep gold centre and are 2 in/5 cm in diameter. They pick well for posies and small arrangements. Dead-heading of faded flowers is advisable to promote continuous blooming. *G. chrysanthemoides* is virtually indestructible but needs regular pruning and pinching to maintain any sort of shape at all.

Gardenia augusta 'Magnifica'. Cape Jasmine

Gardenia

(gah-**deen**-yə)   ☼ ✳ T W H
Cape Jasmine
All year; 20 in–10 ft/50 cm–3 m;
hemispherical; evergreen

RUBIACEAE   FRAGRANT

While sympathetic to garden-lovers faced with really cold winters, I am sick of reading about how difficult it is to grow *Gardenias*. '50–60°F [10–15°C] will suffice during the winter' says the Royal Horticultural

Gardenia augusta 'Gold Magic'. Yellow Gardenia. Hybrid

Society's Dictionary of Gardening. 'They require night temperatures of about 65°F/18°C' says Cornell University's *Hortus 3*. Nonsense! I grow them on an open terrace with morning to midday sun, but sheltered from cold winds. Temperatures in the 40's (5–9°C) are not at all unusual here. 'Buds fail to open if humidity is below 50 per cent and if night temperatures are below 60°F/15°C' they say. Nonsense again. My terrace used to be

Gardenia thunbergia. Star Gardenia. South Africa

Gardenia augusta 'Professor Pucci'.
Giant Gardenia. Hybrid

age, water regularly and otherwise forget them!

The most commonly grown type is *Gardenia augusta* (syn. G. *jasminoides*) and its varieties. There is G. augusta with single flowers 2 in/5 cm in diameter; G. *augusta* 'Florida' with 3 in/8 cm double blooms; G. *augusta* 'Magnifica' with 4 in/10 cm doubles; G. *a.* 'Professor Pucci', even bigger; G. *a.* 'Gold Magic' with yellow blooms, and tiny G. *a.* 'Radicans', a spreading dwarf that still manages 1 in/3 cm blooms. Tall-growing G. *thunbergia* from Africa, reaching 11 ft/3.5 m, has single flowers; and there are several other smaller types from the Indo-Malaysian region and Tahiti. All have the same wonderful scent.

Gardenia augusta. 'Radicans'. Dwarf Gardenia. China

dry as a bone during the day and while the night temperatures are frequently below that limit, the *Gardenias* go on flowering twelve months of the year. I now have a drip watering system to reward them for seeing out the 'dry old days' but the only feeding they get is fallen flowers and leaves from nearby plants which I dump around them for convenience.

So try them yourself. Use a rich, peaty compost with sand for drain-

Gardenia augusta. Single Gardenia.
Malay Peninsula

Garrya

(**gar**-ree-yə)   ☼ ☀ T
Silk Tassel, Curtain-bush
Winter; 4–8 ft/ 1–2.5 m; dense; evergreen

GARRYACEAE

Though both male and female bushes of *Garrya* are needed to produce a crop of pleasant, grape-like fruit, the male bush on its own is responsible

Garrya elliptica. Silk Tassel.
West Coast USA

Gardenia augusta 'Florida'. Common Gardenia

for the plant's main display, the theatrical curtain of green and pink catkins up to 8 in/20 cm and more in length. On the strength of this one species, one could be forgiven for noting that, as in much of nature, the male of the species is the showier.

G. elliptica is best propagated from semi-hardwood cuttings taken in summer. The mature plant varies in height according to its position. In good, deep, moist soils it may reach 20–30 ft/6–9 m and take on the appearance of a tree, while in poor soil or exposed sites it is more usually seen as a 6 ft/2 m shrub. Either way, it's a fine foliage plant that thrives in sun or part shade on the coast or inland. It is hardy down to 23°F/−5°C.

They are members of the heath family, Ericaceae, with similar urn-shaped flowers and succulent berries. Somewhat cool-growing, the Waxberry needs semi-shade, a cool root-run and is hardy enough to survive light frosts. They are normally grown from seed or cuttings, prefer a mildly acid, very well-drained soil with a year-round mulch of leaf litter.

Not particularly colourful with its white bell flowers and snowy white berries, *G. hispida* is handsome enough all year with dark green, slightly serrated leaves. A pleasant shrub for cool, hillside gardens.

Cranberries and do best in a shaded location with peat-enriched, sandy soil. *Gaylussacia brachycera* can be propagated in a variety of ways: cuttings of half-ripe wood, seed, layers and even divisions.

It is evergreen, a prostrate, creeping plant with small, elliptical leaves like a Box (see Buxus) but finely toothed. The flowers are typically heath-like bells, pink or white and borne in short racemes. They are followed by small blue fruit, used principally for jams and jellies. The young foliage is quite reddish, turning green later.

Gaultheria hispida. Tasmanian Waxberry. Tasmania

Gaultheria
(*syn.* CHIOGENES)

(gorl-**theer**-ee-ə)   ☼T

Snowberry, Tasmanian Waxberry
Spring; 2–5 ft/60 cm–1.5 m; spreading; evergreen

ERICACEAE

This Tasmanian species of *Gaultheria* is but one of almost 100 species in the genus, others hailing from North and South America and from Asia through Australia to New Zealand.

Gaylussacia
(*syn.* BUXELLA, DECACHAENA, LASIOCOCCUS)

(gae-loo-**satch**-ee-ə)   ☼ ☀ T

Huckleberry, Dangleberry
Spring; 1½–3 ft/50 cm–1 m; heavily branched; mostly deciduous

ERICACEAE

Lime impregnated soil is a complete no-no for these useful members of the heath family, Ericaceae. They are related to the Blueberries and

Gaylussacia brachycera. Box Huckleberry. E. USA, Delaware to Tennessee

Geleznowia verrucosa. Western Australia

Geleznowia

(gel-ez-**noh**-vee-ə)   ☼ ☼ T
Spring; 1½–3 ft/50 cm–1 m; erect; evergreen

RUTACEAE

The popularity of this Boronia-relative as a cut flower has led to its becoming quite rare in the wild, though Australian native plant fanatics are doing their best to reestablish it. Cuttings of firm, new wood can be struck after applying rooting hormone, but it is a long process. Seed is recommended as an alternative, but it must be fresh. Pour boiling water over newly collected *Geleznowia* seed in autumn. Let the water cool, then sow the seed in a light, sandy soil. Germination should occur in about a month and seedlings should be pinched out after a few days.

Choose a hot, sunny position when planting out. With perfect drainage, the young plants should branch heavily, each stem becoming crowded with round, grey-green leaves, and the whole developing into a 2 × 2 ft/60 × 60 cm rounded shrub. Small, yellowish flowers cluster in dense masses at stem tips from early to mid-spring.

Gelsemium

(gel-**see**-mee-əm)   ☼ T W H
Carolina Jasmine,
Evening Trumpet Flower
Win-Sum; stems to 20 ft/6 m; laurel-like leaves; semi-deciduous

GELSEMIACEAE   FRAGRANT

Though the Carolina Jasmine, *Gelsemium sempervirens*, is found in nature all the way from the south-eastern states of the USA down to Central America, it seems to grow quite happily in cooler, even frosty climates, and has much to recommend it for smaller gardens. First and foremost, its shining yellow trumpet flowers, pleasantly scented, bloom over a long period from late winter, or even as early as late autumn in especially mild areas. Secondly, though nominally a climbing shrub, it is not particularly rampant, and will provide a rewarding show on the smallest support. It is also useful as a groundcover, spilling down banks and walls. *Gelsemium* grows quite well with minimum care and water, and can easily be controlled by pinching away soft new shoots in spring. Semi-deciduous and virtually pest free, it is also quite poisonous in all its parts. Propagation is easy from seed or cuttings and, naturally, *Gelsemium* will grow best in a moist, compost-rich soil.

Genista

(*syn.* SPARTIUM)

(jen-**iss**-tə)   ☼ C T
Dyer's Greenweed,
Broom, Genet
Spr-Sum; 1½–10 ft/50 cm–3 m; many-branched; deciduous

FABACEAE   FRAGRANT

Valued in ancient times as the source of a number of colourful dyes, *Genistas* are planted in today's gardens for their fragrance and the sheer

Genista tinctoria. Dyer's Greenweed, Woadwaxen. Europe, W. Asia

Gelsemium sempervirens. Carolina Jasmine. S. USA to Central America

Genista hispanica. Spanish Broom.
E. Pyrenees

Genista aetnensis. Sicilian Broom. Sicily, N. Africa

beauty of their massed flower display.

There are 75 species, mostly blooming in golden yellow, though some are white. All are native to the Mediterranean area of southern Europe, North Africa and Asia Minor. They are very sturdy plants, revelling in hot weather but surprisingly hardy in cold, suffering damage only in a prolonged freeze.

They thrive by the sea, bloom their heads off in dry, drought-stricken areas, rejoice in well-drained soils.

Grow them from spring-sown seed that's been soaked for 24 hours, or propagate from 4 in/10 cm cuttings of semi-hardwood, taken with a heel in summer. Almost all species are deciduous, and should be tip-pruned to encourage bushiness.

Genista pilosa var Prostrata.
Europe

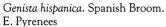
Genista saggittalis. Arrow Broom. Europe, W. Asia

Globularia cordifolia. Globe Daisy. S. Europe

Globularia

(glob-yoo-**lah**-ree-ə)   ☼ Ⓒ Ⓣ
Globe Daisy, Blue Daisy
Spr-Sum; 2–6 in/5–15 cm; prostrate;
evergreen

PLANTAGINACEAE

One of 15 species of *Globularia* found naturally around the Mediterranean and in central Europe, G. *cordifolia* is even more of a sub-shrub than most of its close relatives, often running loosely over the ground at no height at all. It is a perfect plant for a sun-drenched rockery in cool-temperate climates.

Propagate it from cuttings, set out rooted plants in dryish, neutral to alkaline soil and water infrequently. Once established, it will spread gradually, the branches rooting at intervals, and produce solitary heads of pretty mauve stamens from late spring to early summer. The unusual leaves are rather spoon-shaped and distinguish *Globularia* from Mimosa (which see: Mimosa has a similar habit and flowers, but pinnate leaves).

Gmelina

(g-mel-**ee**-nə)   ☼ Ⓦ Ⓗ
Spiny Gmelina
Spr-Aut; to 10 ft/3.5 m; untidy/ arching;
evergreen

LAMIACEAE

Formerly classified in the Verbenaceae, this oddly-flowering plant looks nothing like a Verbena, except in the texture of its leaves. Until recently, I would have said you'd only find *Gmelina asiatica* in the tropics, but rows of them have recently turned up at my local warm-temperate nursery, so I may have to change my mind. Still, ask me again after the winter!

Meanwhile, if you catch it in the tropics, you'll find it flowering almost any month of the year. The inflorescence is most curious, resembling nothing so much as a head of the hop plant until the flowers actually open. Up to that time, there is a reversed cone-shaped mass of red-spotted bracts, tapering down to a point. From beneath each bract in its time there emerges a trumpet-shaped yellow bloom with a long lower lip. These flower-masses develop at the ends of somewhat arching and sometimes spiny branches. These are decked, somewhat sparsely, with simple (or occasionally lobed) leaves up to 4 in/10 cm in length.

Other species of the *Gmelina* genus are large trees found naturally in east Asia or northern Australia, but G. *asiatica* is normally large shrub size (say 10 ft/3.5 m) or much smaller when grown as a container plant.

It needs a well-drained position with regular water and, for preference, rich, fibrous soil. It can be propagated from semi-hardwood cuttings over heat, which is something it needs throughout life. Its minimum winter temperature needs are around 55°F/13°C. Your *Gmelina* will need shelter from full sun in summer, but do keep watch on the arching branches. If they can get a toehold they're likely to scramble through and over anything within reach. Best keep them to themselves.

Gnidia

(**nid**-ee-ə)   ☼ Ⓣ Ⓦ
Spring; 1–6 ft/30 cm–2 m;
heathlike; evergreen

THYMELAEACEAE   FRAGRANT

Not often cultivated away from their native South Africa and Madagascar, some of the 60-odd species of *Gnidia* have proven quite at home in Australia, California and even in the south of England.

Closely related to Daphne, Dais and the Australian Pimelea, *Gnidia* leaves are generally small and heathlike. The tiny tubular flowers are mostly yellow or white and borne terminally in clusters.

They are easy to strike from semi-hardwood cuttings taken while the plants are in active growth. Plants should be set out when young, for they abhor transplanting. Use them in exposed places, even on the coast. All they need for success is a light, porous soil and a careful hand with the water. *Gnidias* are evergreen.

Gmelina asiatica. Spiny Gmelina. India, Sri Lanka

Gnidia squarrosa. South Africa

Goethea

(**gur**-tee-ə) ☼ W H
Goethea
Summer; to 4 ft/1 m; many-stemmed;
leafy; evergreen
MALVACEAE

Though they have no popular name
in English, the two species of *Goethea*
are popular among growers of warm-
climate plants. Both from Brazil, they
are sufficiently adaptable to grow outdoors in the southern United States
or coastal areas of South Africa. Elsewhere they are a popular subject in
the heated greenhouse where they
can be guaranteed a winter minimum
temperature of 55°F/13°C.

Propagate from summer cuttings
struck in sandy soil under glass. Set
out or pot up the following spring in
a moisture-retentive soil mix of two
parts loam, one part peat and plenty
of sand. Both *Goetheas* love semi-
shade and a humid atmosphere, but
air and soil should remain fairly dry
in winter. *Goetheas* have large,
toothed, evergreen leaves. The pink
or yellow flowers appear directly from
leafless stems or in leaf axils.

Goethea strictiflora. Brazil

Gompholobium latifolium. Golden Glory Pea.
E. Australia

Gompholobium

(gom-foh-**loh**-bee-əm) ☼ T W
Golden Glory Pea, Wedge Pea
Spring; to 8 ft/2.5 m; erect; evergreen
FABACEAE

The 26 species of *Gompholobium* bear
the largest pea flowers of any Australian endemic genus—up to 1¼ in/
3 cm across in the species *G. latifol-*
ium. Most (but not all) of them have
bright yellow flowers and nearly all
are low shrubs, their narrow, linear
leaves signalling their origins in the
sandy, coastal heaths where they prefer dappled shade.

Oddly enough, they seem to have
a greater following in countries other
than their own, for they are widely
grown in mild-climate gardens elsewhere. They are fussy, though, and
demand humus-rich, sandy soil,
always just moist yet well-drained.
Grow them from scarified seed and
prune lightly and regularly to preserve compactness.

Goodenia

(goo-**den**-ee-ə) ☼ ☀ T W
Hop Goodenia
Spr-Sum; 3–4 ft/1 m; compact; evergreen
GOODENIACEAE

Common in south-east Australia,
Goodenia ovata is perhaps best known
as a colonizing plant, often appearing
all over the place in the wake of

Goodenia ovata. Hop Goodenia.
S.E. Australia, Tasmania

bushfires. Everyone knows it, few
grow it, though it was at one time
greatly valued in diabetic treatment.
For that reason it was one of the first
Australian plants introduced into
England, in 1793.

Though it sets seed regularly, it is
easiest propagated from cuttings.
Once struck in a mildly acid to neutral soil, it will spread at a great rate
in shaded areas. *Goodenia* should be
pruned from its earliest days to prevent it becoming straggly. The evergreen leaves are toothed, ovate, with
a sticky feel to the new growth. The
flowers, borne in leaf axils, are flat,
yellow but rather like those of a Lobelia. *Goodenia* is a useful plant for the
shaded rock garden or slope, and is
hardy down to 19°F/−7°C.

Goodia

(**good**-ee-ə) ☼ ☀ T W
Clover Tree, Golden-tip
Spring; 7–10 ft/2–3 m; dense; evergreen
FABACEAE   FRAGRANT

One of an endemic Australian genus
with a scant handful of species,
Goodia lotifolia is found in all states,
and grown in many places outside
Australia. Adaptable to most soils, it
is very striking in cultivation. Propagation is easy from seed, cuttings or
suckers, and the young plants grow
fast, often suckering as they go. The
full range of temperate climates seems
to suit them: they will even stand

Goodia lotifolia. Clover Tree.
E. Australia, Tasmania

frost down to 19°F/-7°C.

Beautiful in a mixed border or as a specimen, the Clover Tree can reach 10 ft/3 m, though more commonly only half of that. With regular pruning it can become a handsome specimen or formal hedge. Foliage is blue-green, with small, tri-lobed leaves. The showy golden pea flowers appear in dense racemes, mostly in spring.

Gordonia

(gor-**doh**-nee-ə)   ☼ ☀ T W
Crêpe Camellia
Aut-Win; 16–17 ft/5 m; treelike;
evergreen

THEACEAE   FRAGRANT

In a sunny position in deep, acid soil, the Chinese *Gordonia axillaris* may

Gordonia axillaris. Crêpe Camellia.
Taiwan to Vietnam

reach tree size after many years—say 30 ft/9 m in height. But in normal garden conditions, 6–10 ft/2–3 m is a more usual size range. It is a handsome, glossy-leaved plant, and though evergreen, it produces a limited autumn and winter display as isolated leaves turn rich scarlet or gold.

One of a small genus of mostly evergreen plants, its closest relations are found in North America (see Franklinia). It likes an acid, well-drained spot and is best propagated either from late-summer cuttings with a heel or from layers.

Subtropical in origin, it will resist cold down to 26°F/-3°C, and produces magnificent waxy-white, 5 in/12 cm blooms in the leaf axils. These feature frilled, creamy petals framing a mass of deep orange stamens. Several *Gordonia* species have been hybridized with the related Camellias. Bees go beserk.

Gossypium sturtianum. Sturt Desert Rose.
Arid Australia

Gossypium

(gos-**sip**-ee-əm)   ☼ T W H
Sea Island Cotton,
Sturt Desert Rose
Win-Spr; 3–7 ft/1–2 m; rounded;
evergreen

MALVACEAE

An agricultural crop of great importance, the *Gossypiums* or Cotton Bushes have been cultivated for centuries. Certainly the Greek writer

Gossypium barbadense. Sea Island Cotton.
South America

Herodotus recorded them as being grown in India in 450 B.C. when he referred to 'Wild Trees that bear Fleeces as their Fruit', an apt description of a cotton crop when the ripened seed pods burst to expose a number of seeds covered in cottony lint or down.

One of the many commercial crops is the South American G. *barbadense*, the Sea Island Cotton, a 3–7 ft/1–2 m shrub with yellow flowers followed by 1¾ in/4 cm cotton bean seed capsules. Of less commercial interest is the Australian G. *sturtianum* or Sturt Desert Rose. Found in the arid outback, they grow in gravelly, well-drained soil and bear magnificent 3 in/8 cm mauve flowers in winter. These are purple-centred and give way to 4-celled seed capsules filled with greenish fuzz, not true cotton. This beautiful shrub is the floral emblem of Australia's Northern Territory and, like other Cotton Bushes, is not frost hardy.

Graptophyllum

(grap-toh-**fil**-əm)   ☀ ✹ W H
Letter-leaf, Scarlet Fuchsia,
Caricature Plant
Summer; 10 ft/3 m; erect; evergreen

ACANTHACEAE

A subtropical genus from northern Australia and the Pacific Islands, the *Graptophyllums* have become popular in warm-climate gardens everywhere. The most commonly grown species (from New Guinea) is valued for the novelty of its curious foliage, which is marked with irregular scrawls that resemble ink-blot tests. Leaves may be green and yellow, or pink and red, according to variety. Small heads of magenta flowers form in warm weather.

These tropical *Graptophyllums* strike easily from cuttings and should be replaced regularly before they become too straggly.

Graptophyllum pictum. Caricature Plant. Solomon Islands

Grevillea 'Boongara Spinebill'. Garden Origin

Graptophyllum excelsum. Scarlet Fuchsia. Australia

Grevillea

(grə-**vil**-lee-ə) ☼ ☀ C T W
Spider Flower
All year; 10 in–13 ft/25 cm–4 m; evergreen

PROTEACEAE   MANY FRAGRANT

As if 250 original species were not enough, at least as many again hybrid forms of *Grevillea* have now been developed in Australia, widening the range of available colours to include almost every shade short of blue. All in all, they now constitute the most decorative and most improved of the antipodean shrub gen-

era. They are endemic to Australia and nearby islands including French New Caledonia.

They have now been taken up in a big way by American gardeners and are popular shrubs in South Africa, New Zealand and all round the Mediterranean. In a word, they have caught the imaginations of modern gardeners, just as they once did the early plant hunters of the southern continent.

This remarkable genus is so variable in flower, foliage and habit, it is hardly surprising to learn that it belongs to the family Proteaceae, named for the demi-god Proteus, who

Grevillea 'White Wings'. Snowflake Grevillea. Garden Origin

Grevillea punicea. Red Spider Flower. N.S.W.

Australia has a native species grown just for the beauty of its scarlet blossoms, which are larger than the leaves. This is G. *excelsum*, the Scarlet Fuchsia, which may reach 10 ft/3 m in rich, well-drained soil. It needs a warm-temperate climate, regular water and is improved by light pruning after summer bloom. It is drought resistant, but probably not frost hardy.

could change his appearance at will. He might appear at any time as a tree, a serpent, a lion or even a living fire. It was this gift of unlimited shape-changing which suggested the family name Proteaceae to botanists classifying a newly discovered group of South African plants. With them were included about fifty other closely related genera of plants from warm (and once connected) parts of the southern hemisphere—Leucadendron and Leucospermum from South Africa, Embothrium from Chile and a dazzling array of Australian native plants including Banksia, Dryandra, *Grevillea* and many other plants of bizarre appearance which you will find in this book.

Like most of the others, *Grevilleas* seem to prefer full sun and grow best in a well-drained soil that is rich in leaf mould and somewhat gravelly. It must also be slightly acid and on the dryish side. Species from the inland and Western Australia abhor humidity. *Grevilleas* appreciate a light ration of balanced fertilizer from time to time, but an excess of phosphorus can result in very unhappy plants.

While it is possible to grow *Grevilleas* from absolutely fresh seed, the preferred method of propagation is from firm-tip cuttings taken in late summer. These should be treated with a rooting hormone and set in a fast-draining sand/peat mixture. Warmth and humidity at this stage will promote rooting in no time. *Grevilleas* can also be grafted, and this is the clue to one of our most

Grevillea biternata. Woolly Grevillea. Western Australia

Grevillea brachystylis.

spectacular garden plants—a weeping G. 'Poorinda Royal Mantle' grafted onto a lopped trunk of the tree species G. *robusta*.

Of the illustrated cultivars, G. X 'Robyn Gordon' is the most popular and moderately frost hardy. It is a hybrid of the species G. *banksii*, as is the newer hybrid 'Pink Surprise'. Western Australia's white G. *biternata* is used for groundcover, growing to about 20 in/50 cm high and bearing clouds of perfumed flowers in spring. It is hardy to sev-

Grevillea 'Canberra Gem'. Hybrid

Grevillea pteridifolia. N.E. Australia

eral degrees of frost, lower than most species. Random upright branches should be pruned away. Tropical G. *venusta* blooms in a stunning colour scheme of green, black and yellow.

All *Grevilleas* are attractive to birds, particularly honeyeaters which enjoy a nourishing feast among their flower-laden branches.

Grevillea 'Robyn Gordon'.
Robyn Gordon Grevillea. Hybrid

Grevillea 'Honey Gem'. Garden Origin

Grevillea 'Poorinda Royal Mantle'.
Hybrid

Grevillea venusta. Black Grevillea. Queensland

Grewia

(**groo**-wee-ə) ☼ ◑ T H
Lavender Star, Kruisbessie,
Crossberry
Summer; to 10 ft/3 m; open; evergreen
MALVACEAE

Mostly native to parts of Africa and the Orient, there are about 150 species of *Grewia*, interesting plants of the linden family, Tiliaceae.

Grewia occidentalis. Lavender Star.
Africa

Undoubtedly the most widely grown is *G. occidentalis* from Africa. It is a popular plant in California and other parts of the southern United States. It is also grown in Australia and the Mediterranean area.

The Lavender Star (as it is affectionately known) is raised from seed or cuttings and should be grown in average garden soil that is well-drained. However, for maximum effect, an admixture of leaf mould is desirable. *Grewia* will survive frost down to 22°F/−5°C; it appreciates moisture in warm weather and needs frequent pruning to compact.

Greyia

(**grae**-ee-ə) ☼ T W
Mountain Bottlebrush,
Baakhout, Natal Bottlebrush
*Win-Spr; 6-8 ft/2-2.5 m; sparse;
deciduous*
MELIANTHACEAE

Named for a one-time Governor General of Britain's Cape Colony, Sir George Grey, this small genus of 3 species makes up in appearance what it lacks in numbers.

The semi-deciduous leaves resemble those of the edible fig and cluster at branch tips above the spectacular orange-red inflorescences. These appear any time in winter or

Greyia radlkoferi. Natal Bottlebrush. South Africa

spring. In cooler areas, some leaves may colour in the autumn before falling. All three species need protection where winters are really cold but are hardy to the occasional light frost. They prefer a fast-draining soil and should be watered sparingly except in summer, their main growth season.

Greyia species grow well in containers, flowering at an early age, and are usually hardy down to 22°F/−5°C.

Griselinia littoralis 'Variegata'. Kapuka.
New Zealand

Griselinia

(griz-ə-**lin**-ee-ə) ☼ T
Kapuka
All year; 6-16 ft/2-5 m; dense; evergreen
GRISELINIACEAE

More evidence of a prehistoric connection between Australasia and South America, the small-growing *Griselinia* is endemic to both New Zealand and Chile, growing close to the shore in both countries.

G. littoralis, a New Zealand species, is popular as a seaside plant in Ireland, California and New England, where it is particularly effective in its cultivar 'Variegata'. In cultivation and other aspects, it needs similar care to its fellow countryman, Coprosma. The Kapuka has simple, shining, oval leaves. The minute greenish flowers appear in small panicles from the leaf axils and are followed by small black berries.

Guichenotia

(gee-shə-**noh**-tee-ə) ☼ ☀ ▣ T
Win-Spr; 3–6 ft/1–2 m; loosely branched;
evergreen

MALVACEAE

This small genus of evergreen Western Australian shrubs was named after Antoine Guichenot, a noted French botanist. They are easy to grow, not very spectacular, but useful in arid climates because they are cleverly engineered to do without water. The entire plant, stems, leaves and flowers, is covered with a grey, woolly down. The flowers are up to ¾ in/ 2 cm in length. They are pale purple, sharply ribbed, and the anthers (which are almost completely hidden) are purplish black.

Guichenotia macrantha. Western Australia

Grow them from seed or cuttings, plant in well-drained, gravelly soil and water only during extended droughts. Light pruning after spring bloom will help maintain shape. A useful plant for dry, neglected rockeries.

Gustavia

(goos-**tah**-vee-ə) ☼ ☀ H
Spr-Sum; 10–16 ft/3–5 m; treelike;
evergreen

LECYTHIDACEAE   FRAGRANT

These splendid plants were named for Gustav III of Sweden, the patron of the great botanist, Linnaeus. All native to South America, they are grown from cuttings of ripened shoots which strike freely in sand under glass. A heavy, leaf-rich soil is best for *Gustavia* and a tropical climate essential—our picture was taken in Singapore which is right on the equator.

The 11 species seem equally split between trees and shrubs, though the

Gustavia marcgraviana. South America

tree species are stunted and shrubby. The leaves are large and glossy, the flowers very spectacular and reminiscent of a Magnolia except in the big mass of pollen-rich stamens which are most attractive to insects. Flowers of all species are a fine, rosy-pink.

Hakea sericea. Silky Needle Hakea. S.E. Australia

Hakea

(**hae**-kee-ə) ☼ T W
Pincushion Tree, Needle Bush
Win-Spr; to 13 ft/4 m; bushy; evergreen

PROTEACEAE   FRAGRANT

This decorative genus of the family Proteaceae is so variable from one species to another that they have acquired no general popular name. The *Hakeas* are endemic to Australia, some 140 species of them, with around 50 per cent found only in the south-west corner of the continent. Few of them grow much taller than 13 ft/4 m, many less than half that height and then only in dry, acid gravelly soils with fast drainage. They are widely grown as a decorative shrub in the Mediterranean area, in southern California, South Africa and New Zealand, and often have a strong fragrance.

Hakeas are usually propagated from seed, which is easily collected, or from ripened cuttings. These are struck in sharp, damp sand in a sheltered position, but are not very reliable. Some growers in more humid areas have repeatedly had success in grafting dry-country species onto a shoot of *H. salicifolia.*

The entire genus was named for Baron von Hake, an 18th century

Hakea victoria. Royal Hakea. Western Australia

professor of botany. The most commonly seen species is *H. sericea* which has stiff, needle leaves and silky white or pink flowers. It is regarded as a noxious weed in South Africa. Popular world-wide, the spectacular *H. laurina* or Pincushion Tree has a delightful perfume. It is sometimes seen pruned to a rounded shape as a street planting in Melbourne, but in nature, it is a loose, gangly sort of plant with branches often weeping and densely covered with 4 in/10 cm leathery leaves of an interesting blue-green colour. The eye-catching flower clusters appear during winter to spring and the plant is hardy down to 20°F/−7°C.

A real conversation piece not often grown away from its western home is *H. victoria*, the Royal Hakea, which is a sparsely branched plant less than 3 ft/1 m high. Its small clusters of insignificant green flowers are cupped into brilliantly variegated 5 in/13 cm leaves.

Hakea bucculenta. Western Australia

Michael Morcombe

Hakea laurina. Pincushion Hakea. Western Australia

Hakea purpurea. Crimson Hakea. Queensland

Halgania

(hal-**gan**-ee-ə)　　　☼ T W
Native Borage
All year; 16 in/40 cm; dense; evergreen

BORAGINACEAE

Found in hot dry areas all over mainland Australia (though not in Queensland), the showy *Halgania cyanea* adds a touch of blue to the landscape quite randomly at any time of the year. Usually much less than our suggested 16 in/40 cm in height, it has quite a suckering habit. These can be used for propagation along with cuttings or division. Water is no problem except in prolonged droughts.

Halgania cyanea. Native Borage. Australia

Halgania is not fussy about soil make-up so long as the drainage is good. The dull green leaves are quite small (2 in/5 cm on average) and the violet-blue flowers are barely ½ in/ 1 cm in diameter and may appear at any time. *Halgania* is related to Borage, and looks a bit like Borage, but whether it would make a good Pimms No 1 Cup, I wouldn't like to guess.

Halimium

(*syn.* CISTUS)

(ha-**lim**-ee-əm)   ☼ T W
Great Sunrose
Spr-Sum; 3 ft/1 m; low; spreading;
evergreen

CISTACEAE

Not one of the world's richest areas for native vegetation, the Iberian Peninsula has produced a few plants of great decorative value, among them, the illustrated Great Sunrose, *Halimium lasianthum.* It is obviously closely related to the Cistus and to the sub-shrubby Helianthemum, but grows, in a warm climate, to 3 ft/1 m and more—a dazzling sight in spring or summer when it is decked with 2 in/5 cm red-marked, open, golden flowers.

Halimium grows happily in all temperate areas, including the south-

western counties of England. Where the winters are harsh, as in the northern United States and Canada, it will need frost protection. Grow from seed or soft-tip cuttings and plant in well-drained, alkaline soil. It is evergreen and needs little water except during droughts.

Halimium lasianthum. Great Sunrose.
Spain, Portugal

Hamamelis

(**ham**-ə-mel-əs)   ☼ ☀ C T
Chinese Witchhazel
Winter; 14–17 ft/4–5 m; spreading;
deciduous

HAMAMELIDACEAE   FRAGRANT

A wonderfully cold-resistant shrub from western China, the Witchhazel, *Hamamelis mollis*, is hardy down to at least 17°F/−8°C. Blooming in midwinter, its strap-like golden petals resist icy winds to drape the bare zigzag branches all through the cold months. Branches can be cut for stunning winter flower arrangements, and the blooms offer a delicious fragrance when used indoors.

   Hamamelis should be propagated from 4 in/10 cm heeled cuttings taken in autumn. Seed germination is possible but very slow. *Hamamelis* prefers sun only part of each day and should be grown in well-drained, acid soil, enriched with plenty of leaf mould. Its growth is slow.

Hamamelis mollis. Chinese Witchhazel.
W. China

Hamelia

(ha-**mel**-ee-ə)   ☼ T H
Firebush, Scarlet Bush
Sum-Aut; to 10 ft/3 m; treelike; evergreen

RUBIACEAE

Neither as beautiful nor as fragrant as their close relatives the Bouvardia, Gardenia or Rondeletia, the half-

Hamelia patens. Firebush. Caribbean, South America

Hardenbergia CV 'Happy Wanderer'. False Sarsaparilla. E. Australia

dozen or so species of *Hamelia* make a useful background screen in tropical gardens. In their native territories of Florida and the Caribbean they may grow as high as 25 ft/7.5 m, but in cooler areas less than half that.

Growing best in warm climates, they may be propagated from seed or semi-hardwood cuttings struck over heat. Water regularly, feed occasionally to replace nutrients leached out by tropical rains, and give plenty of sun. Flowers are sparse, tubular and come in various shades of orange and scarlet at branch tips. The evergreen leaves have a grey, pubescent finish.

Hardenbergia

(hah-den-**burg**-ee-ə) ☼ ☀ T W
False Sarsaparilla,
Australian Lilac
Spring; 3 ft/1 m; mat-forming; evergreen

FABACEAE

Greatly improved in recent years, as witness the illustrated CV 'Happy Wanderer', the *Hardenbergias* are dainty Australian groundcovers with little inclination to climb. They are not at all rampant, preferring to wander harmlessly through and over shrubs or up and around verandah posts, wire fences or trellises.

Although native to southern and eastern parts of Australia, they are often found in elevated places where winter temperatures of 19°F/−7°C are quite the rule.

The small, pea-type flowers occur during the warmer months and are almost always purple, though pink or white forms are sometimes seen.

Hardenbergia is not a demanding plant and requires only well-drained

Hauya heydeania. Morning, Noon and Night. Central America

soil to thrive. Water only if rainfall is inadequate and go easy on the fertilizer. The seed coat is hard and must be filed or softened in warm water for 24 hours before sowing.

Hauya

(**hou**-yə) ☼ ☀ W H
Morning, Noon and Night
Spring; to 5 ft/1.5 m; compact; evergreen

ONAGRACEAE

Endemic to Central America, there are around 14 species of *Hauya*, a few of which have made their way north of the border from down Mexico way. They are also found in gardens of Hawaii and other tropical areas. I know little about them but what I do know pleases me greatly.

H. heydeania (one of 3 species I have examined) has glossy, long-stemmed leaves reminiscent of an Oleander (see Nerium). The flowers, which appear in the leaf axils during warm weather, are 4-petalled and have extremely long stamens. They open pure white but on successive days change first to pale rose and then deep pink. This gives rise to a popular name, Morning, Noon and Night. Sepals of older flowers reflex.

Hebe salicifolia. Koromiko. New Zealand

Hebe 'Karl Teschner'. Edging Hebe.
New Zealand

Hebe hulkeana. New Zealand Lilac.
New Zealand

Hebe

(syn. VERONICA)

(hee-bee)   ☼ ☀ ❋ T
Veronica, Shrub Speedwell
Sum-Aut; 12 ft/3.5 m; rounded; evergreen

PLANTAGINACEAE

In mythology, Hebe was a daughter
of Zeus and cup bearer to the gods,
whose chalices she kept filled with
nectar. No wonder her name was
revived for this remarkable genus of
New Zealand shrubs, whose nectar
never ceases to flow—judging by the
clouds of bees that hang about whenever they're in bloom.

Hebes include some 80 natural
species, mostly native to New
Zealand but with a few outliers in
Chile and New Guinea. They are all
evergreen and bear dense spikes of
tiny, 4-petalled flowers, mostly in
shades of purple, white or cerise.
They thrive in the cool, frost-free,
coastal garden, where they are used
as thick groundcovers, in massed
shrubberies or trimmed as dense
hedges. They are completely resistant
to salt and sea winds and favour a
semi-shaded spot. *Hebes* are fast-

growing and will bloom both winter
and summer. They are hardy down
to 23°F/−5°C.

Commonly planted garden types
are mostly cultivars which can only
be propagated by means of cuttings
taken in midsummer. Trim these to
4 in/10 cm and insert in a mixture of
peat and sand, keeping them in a
cool place. Generally rooted by the

Hebe pinguifolia 'Pagei'. Shrub Speedwell.
New Zealand

Hebe 'La Seduisante'. Hybrid

Helianthemum 'Fire King'. Red Sunrose.
Hybrid

following spring, they should be potted up individually, hardened outdoors and finally placed in a permanent position in early autumn.

Hebes are not fussy as to soil, accepting even a little lime, and are remarkably maintenance free, though an occasional shearing in earliest spring will improve their vigour. Take branches back to half their former length, feed over the root area and new growth will break from the cut twigs within days.

Hebes are attractive all year, each alternate pair of glossy leaves being borne at right angles to its neighbour. Some typical varieties are illustrated.

Helianthemum

(syn. CROCANTHEMUM, CISTUS, CHAMAECISTUS)

(hel·ee·**an**·thə·mum)   ☼ T W
Sunrose, Rockrose
Spr–Sum; 1 ft/30 cm; prostrate; evergreen

CISTACEAE

Sun-flowers, the ancient Greeks called them (Helios anthemon) and the name has stuck to the present day because it is so descriptive.

The Sunroses are small relatives of the handsome and shrubby Cistus or

Rockrose and are classed as sub-shrubs. Low, mound-forming, evergreen plants with attractive foliage that varies from deep to greyish-green, they enjoy a sun-baked, well-drained spot with slightly alkaline soil. In spring they become a carpet of dazzling bloom in warm reds, pinks, oranges or yellows. When flowers fade, shear the plants all over to promote a second flush.

Helianthemums survive well in cold-winter areas and temperate climates. Heeled 3 in/8 cm cuttings of lateral shoots taken in summer root rapidly in a sandy mix. Pinch out to develop a bushy habit and set outdoors the following spring.

Watch for powdery mildew in hot weather. From 4–12 in/10–30 cm high, they can spread to 3 ft/1 m across. Not truly frost hardy.

Helianthemum 'Rhodanthe Carneum'. Pink Sunrose. Asia Minor

Helianthemum 'Golden'. Yellow Sunrose.

Heliotropium arborescens 'Aureum'. Turnsole. Peru

Heliotropium

(hel-ee-oh-**troh**-pee-əm)   ☼ ☼ W H
Heliotrope, Cherry Pie, Turnsole
Spr-Sum; to 7 ft/2 m; branching; evergreen

BORAGINACEAE   FRAGRANT

A cottage garden favourite because of its fragrance (Cherry Pie) and quaint habit of turning its flower heads to follow the sun (Turnsole), the old-time Heliotrope is actually an exotic

South American import, tender to frost but fast-growing in mild climates. So fast, many gardeners set out cuttings in early spring and treat them as annuals. In fact, Heliotrope is one of those borderline plants some authorities list as a sub-shrub, others as a shrubby perennial.

Growing in any enriched, well-drained garden soil, in full sun, *Heliotropium arborescens* enjoys humidity. In very hot, dry areas, it is best raised in semi-shade and the foliage sprinkled regularly. Reaching a

Heliotropium 'Lord Roberts'. Cherry Pie. Peru

height of up to 7 ft/2 m, it needs regular, weak, liquid fertilizer while growing and should be cut back by half in very early spring to promote bushiness.

Hemichaena

(hem-i-**kae**-nə)   ☼ W H
Two-lips
Summer; 3–5 ft/1–1.5 m; pyramidal; evergreen

SCROPHULARIACEAE

If you ever happen to be strolling around in Guatemala at an altitude of, say, 10,000 ft/3000 m, you might think you've run across a new, bright yellow-flowered species of foxglove or snapdragon or Penstemon. Yes, there is such a plant, closely related to all

Hemichaena fruticosa. Two-lips. Guatemala

three of the named genera. But botanists have already been there and christened it *Hemichaena fruticosa* or Two-lips, and have adopted it happily to grow in semi-shaded borders at lower altitudes.

Two-lips, so called because of its two-lipped flower, is an evergreen shrub with long, felty leaves, like those of a foxglove. The brilliant golden flowers usually appear in bunches of three. It likes a light, open loam and looks quite wonderful in San Francisco where I photographed it.

Hermannia
(*syn.* MAHERNIA)

(hur-**man**-nee-ə) ☼ T W
Honeybells
Win-Spr; 1 ft/30 cm; straggly; evergreen

BYTTNERIACEAE   FRAGRANT

Not very much seen away from their native South Africa, the 80 or so species of *Hermannia* are really charming shrubs and sub-shrubs for the temperate garden, where they'll add a dash of brilliant yellow to the mixed border. Some species are fully shrubby, others, like the illustrated *H. verticillata*, are sub-shrubby and a bit on the straggly side.

Honeybells, to make use of the popular name, are raised from seed in well-drained soil, where they spread

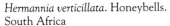

Hermannia verticillata. Honeybells. South Africa

rapidly. They also make a fine hanging basket subject. The alternate leaves are slender, evergreen and noticeably notched. The small bell flowers are borne on slim, arching stems, like golden lilies-of-the-valley. They are quite fragrant if you can get close enough to them.

Heteromeles arbutifolia. Toyon. California

Heteromeles

(het-ur-**om**-el-ees) ☼ T W
Toyon, Christmas Berry, California Holly
All year; to 30 ft/9 m; treelike; evergreen

ROSACEAE

Without California's ubiquitous Toyon, there wouldn't be a Hollywood. For the movie capital was so named for the widely-spreading groves of these colourfully fruited plants which reminded early settlers of the cold-climate, European hollies. Alas, the groves have now disap-

Heteromeles arbutifolia. California Holly. California

peared beneath a landscape of neon and concrete. The Toyon is a close relative of both the rose and the apple, in fact the botanical name *Heteromeles arbutifolia* is a Greek/Latin mixture meaning 'different apple with leaves like the Arbutus'.

They grow to 30 ft/10 m in nature, but in a garden setting a third of that is more likely. They have leathery, elliptical leaves and often need a bit of help from the secateurs to stay shrubby. They can be propagated from seed, cuttings or layers and are hardy in cool, frost-free areas, even coastal parts of the British Isles.

Birds of all types love the berries and come from far around to feast in the colder months.

Hibbertia
(*syn.* CANDOLLEA)

(hib-**bur**-tee-ə) ☼ ✸ C W
Guineaflowers
Spr-Sum; 8 in–8 ft/20 cm–2.5 m; mostly prostrate; evergreen

DILLENIACEAE

Not, as many Australians believe, confined to the island continent, the lovely Guineaflowers or *Hibbertias* are also found out through New

Hibbertia scandens. Guinea Gold. Australia

Caledonia to Fiji, in Madagascar and the Malay Peninsula. Australia, however, has more than 70 species, including the internationally popular ones. These include shrubs, subshrubs and climbers, and *H. scandens* in particular has become popular all over the world.

A shrub with twining stems, it likes sandy, well-drained soil, thrives on sand dunes, covers rocks and will climb a sturdy wall or fence. *H. serpyllifolia* has tiny, thyme-like leaves and pale yellow flowers. *H. stellaris* is a bun-like shrub with wiry stems and

Hibbertia stellaris. Golden Star Flower.
Western Australia

orange flowers but, alas, is not very sturdy. Be sure drainage is good. *H. cuneiformis* is a Western Australian entry, also popular in California. *H. empetrifolia* is a woody, 3 ft/1 m shrub found in all parts of Australia except the west.

Hibbertias grow from cuttings, like enriched, sandy soil and look good in well-drained rockeries. None of them is particularly frost hardy.

Hibbertia obtusifolia. Round-leaf Hibbertia.
E. Australia, Tasmania

Hibbertia cuneiformis. Cut-leaf Hibbertia.
Western Australia

Hibiscus syriacus 'Ardens'. Rose of Sharon.
E. Asia

Hibiscus

(hib-**iss**-kəs, hai-**biss**-kəs)   ☼ C T H
Rose of China, Rose Mallow,
Rose of Sharon, Shrub Althaea
*Sum–Aut; 3–12 ft/1–3.5 m; soft-wooded;
evergreen*

MALVACEAE

It was Karl Linné, or Carolus Linnaeus, as he preferred to be known, who invented our present system of botanical nomenclature. And it was he who first used the name 'Rose of China', in the 18th

Hibiscus clayii. Horace's Hibiscus. Hawaii

Hibiscus brackenridgei. Hawaii

Hibiscus rosa-sinensis. Rose of China.
Tropical Asia

Hibiscus rosa-sinensis. 'Catavki'. Hybrid

century, when he christened these fantastic tropical flowers *Hibiscus rosa-sinensis*. The name *Hibiscus* itself was Greek, and previously used for the related and similar wild European Marsh-mallow, a much smaller flower.

The origin of the word is obscure, but probably an adaptation of 'Ibis' the name of the birds which feed on the young mallow plants in nature. But even Linnaeus could be wrong. He believed *Hibiscus* were from China itself; they were certainly grown there at the time of the earliest European contacts, but modern botanical research suggests the Indian Ocean area as the most likely original home. Species sufficiently compatible to cross are found in East Africa, Madagascar and Malaysia, and also throughout the Pacific Islands. Other species native to the Middle East and China itself do not cross with *H. rosa-sinensis*. At any rate these Roses of China reach their full glory only in warm to tropical gardens. In really tropic zones they flower year round; in cooler areas in summer only, the flowers peaking at about 10 in/25 cm in diameter with the advent of autumn rains.

Hibiscus mutabilis. Confederate Rose. S. China

Hibiscus calyphyllus. Tropical Africa, Madagascar

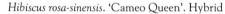

Hibiscus rosa-sinensis. 'Cameo Queen'. Hybrid

Early *Hibiscus* introductions to the West were sometimes known as 'Flower of a Day'—for that was generally their span. But as the result of modern hybridizing, certain varieties may last as long as three days, either on the plant or picked early in the morning. It makes no difference to their lasting qualities whether you place them in water or just leave them lying about the house.

The spiritual, if not the actual, home of the giant ornamental *Hibiscus* is Hawaii, whose floral emblem it has become. The Hawaiian Islands have several native species, and these have been crossed with at least three other species from different tropic areas to produce the stunning hybrids we know today. At one time, there were over 5000 named varieties growing there, but the islanders became bored with them, and now reserve their enthusiasm for other flowers. Though on my last visit to Honolulu, I did notice that the famous rose garden in Kapiolani Park has been replanted with *Hibiscus*— most of them raised in Australia!

Hibiscus species run all the way

from small annuals to trees, but the most popular types, illustrated on these pages, are all shrubs. *H. syriacus* (which really does come from Syria) is a favourite in European and North American gardens. It has single and double varieties in shades of pink, white and mauve, often with a deep red blotch. It is not compatible with any of the others illustrated, but they will rarely be found in gardens with the same climate anyway. *H. caly-phyllus* is native to East Africa, uncommon *H. insularis* has been found only on Norfolk and Phillip Islands in the South Pacific, but grows particularly well in coastal areas.

Hibiscus insularis. Island Hibiscus. Norfolk Island

Hibiscus rosa-sinensis. 'Firedance'. Hybrid

Hibiscus arnottianus. Arnott Hibiscus. Hawaii

All are best propagated from 4 in/10 cm cuttings taken in spring and summer and struck in a peat/sand mixture at a temperature of around 64°F/18°C. If growing them in containers, pot them up from time to time, and if living in a borderline climate, don't hesitate to grow them as a compact pot-shrub that you can bring indoors during the cooler months.

Among the Hibiscus species endemic to Hawaii are the illustrated *H. arnottianus, H. brackenridgei, H. clayii.*

Hippophäe

(**hip**-oh-fae-ee) ☼ C T
Sea Buckthorn, Sallow Thorn
Autumn; 30–37 ft/9–11 m; treelike; deciduous

ELEAGNACEAE

Tall as a tree where the soil and climate suit it, the Sea Buckthorn rarely grows above 10 ft/3 m in garden surroundings. Densely branched and spiny, with dark green linear leaves backed with silver, the *Hippophäe* is resistant to salt air and wind and not the least fussy about soil so long as it is well-drained. This very useful plant is a good soil binder, particularly at the seaside where it roots heavily and suckers into thickets. The big display,

Holmskioldia sanguinea. Chinese Hat Plant. Indian Ocean region

Gillian Beckett

Hippophäe rhamnoides. Sea Buckthorn. Britain to Asia

however, is in the ¼ in/5 mm orange fruit which are edible and persist right through winter. However, these only appear when both male and female plants are together.

Hippophäe is deciduous and is propagated from seed, layers or semi-hardwood cuttings of ripened wood taken in spring. Forget about the yellow flowers, which are insignificant. It's the fruit you want!

Holmskioldia

(hohm-**shohld**-ee-ə) ☼ T W H
Mandarin's Hat,
Chinese Hat Plant, Parasol Flower
Sum-Aut; 12 ft/3.5 m; arching; evergreen

LAMIACEAE

Brightening the summer days around the Indian Ocean area from India to Madagascar, the startling *Holmskioldia* species (there are around 10 of them) catch the eye wherever they grow.

A grown-up relative of the humble Verbena, they adore warm coastal climates or sunny banks where they can arch their branches contentedly. A single plant of *H. sanguinea* may spread far wider than its 12 ft/3.5 m height, and the curious orange-scarlet flowers appear in warm weather, clustered in dense terminal or axillary racemes. Each is small and tubular, backed with a thin, disc-like bract.

Holmskioldias are propagated from semi-hardwood tip cuttings struck over heat in spring or summer, and mature plants should be kept vigorous by pruning away several of the oldest canes entirely. Pink and lime yellow varieties are also in cultivation.

Holodiscus discolor. Ocean Spray. British Columbia to California

Holodiscus

(syn. SPIRAEA)

(hol-oh-**dis**-kəs)   ☼ ◑ C T
Rock Spiraea, Ocean Spray
Spr–Sum; 20 ft/6 m; rounded; deciduous

ROSACEAE

Endemic to the western states of North America, the handful of *Holodiscus* species are woodland favourites from late spring on as they produce great arching panicles of tiny white flowers for all the world like a breaking wave. These are succeeded by a mass of berries which are most attractive to birds.

Holodiscus discolor (which was once included in the genus Spiraea) can be propagated from seed, layers or soft-tip cuttings struck under glass. The growing plants enjoy a rich, well-drained soil and look delightful planted where the sunlight can catch their flower masses. Leaves are roughly triangular and deeply toothed.

Homalocladium

(syn. MUEHLENBECKIA)

(hom-al-oh-**clad**-ee-əm)   ☼ ◑ W H
Centipede Plant,
Tapeworm Plant, Ribbonbush
All year; 2–4 ft/60 cm–1 m; tangled; evergreen

POLYGONACEAE

A great favourite in temperate gardens of Edwardian days, or in English glasshouses, the curious *Homalocladium* is from the Solomon Islands, though it will grow in cli-mates a great deal less tropical. It has quite a woody trunk, but is grown for the flat, twisted, jointed stems which many believe are the leaves. There *are* leaves, which fall immediately after forming, but this unusual plant photosynthesizes by means of its stems and branches.

The plant is propagated from any of the light stems twisted off with a heel and grown fast in a sharp, sandy mix. Mature Tapeworm Plants grow well in a deep, well-drained soil and look quite eye-catching. The tiny green flowers are followed by shiny red fruits which form at the stem joints and persist for months.

Homalocladium platycladium. Tapeworm Plant. Solomon Islands

Homoranthus papillatus. Gold Myrtle. N.S.W., Queensland

Homoranthus

(syn. RYLESTONEA)

(hoh-mor-**an**-thəs)   ☼ ◑ T W
Homoranthus
Spr–Aut; 16–32 in/40–80 cm; spreading; evergreen

MYRTACEAE   ACRID SMELL

A delightful small genus within the myrtle family, Australia's handful of *Homoranthus* species greatly resemble Darwinia and Verticordia (which see). They are low and spreading, and make delightful foliage specimens in a well-drained rock garden.

Raise them from cuttings, grow them on in sandy but compost-rich soil with super drainage. The nectar-rich golden flowers are said to attract honeyeaters, but if so, they have a poor sense of smell, for the various *Homoranthus* species have an acrid odour.

H. papillatus is particularly colourful with tiny, bluish foliage, red buds and bright yellow flowers. *H. darwinioides* has many tubular flowers of greenish yellow. What a pity the *Homoranthus* species have no popular name. May I suggest Gold Myrtle?

Hovea pungens. Prickly Hovea. Western Australia

Hovea

(**hoh**-vee-ə)   ◑ ☀ T W
Purple Pea Bush
Spring; 6–7 ft/2 m; open; evergreen

FABACEAE

Thriving in the dappled shade cast by open trees, or in the shelter of other, taller shrubs, *Hoveas* are themselves lovely and lightly branched and foliaged, decking out in early spring with masses of purple pea flowers. These

Hovea lanceolata. Purple Pea Bush. N.S.W., Queensland

appear along the entire length of every stem but, sadly, are not particularly long-lived. The whole show comes and goes within a month.

Hoveas demand well-drained soil and prefer it on the sandy side as well. And if their roots can be kept cool under large, flat stones, so much the better. Illustrated H. lanceolata is an understorey shrub of the moist eastern Australian forests and is hardy down to 23°F/−5°C. H. pungens grows similarly in Western Australia and perhaps enjoys more sun. Both species are grown from scarified seed and benefit from a light pruning after bloom.

Grown in full sun it becomes woody and almost leafless. But in well-drained, leafy soil and in almost full shade, it develops dark green, woolly-backed foliage and blooms profusely through most of the warm weather—tiny, 1 in/3 cm Hibiscus flowers of a glowing violet. Grow from cuttings set in a mixture of bush sand and leaf mould and keep out of the sun.

Howittia trilocularis. Blue Howittia. N.S.W., Victoria

Howittia

(hau-**witt**-ee-ə)   ☼ ☀ Ⓦ
Blue Howittia
Win-Sum; 10 ft/3 m; erect; evergreen

MALVACEAE

A plant of the moist, deep gullies in New South Wales and Victorian forests, the *Howittia* (there is only one species) is really an adaptation of the Hibiscus for cool, shaded areas—and so it should be treated in the home garden.

Hoya

(**hoi**-yə)   ☼ ☀ Ⓦ Ⓗ
Waxflower, Honey Plant
Summer; to 3 ft/1 m; arching; evergreen

ASCLEPIADACEAE   FRAGRANT

What can one say about *Hoyas* that hasn't been said before? We all know how beautiful they are, and how *sticky*, dropping tacky nectar all over the furniture indoors or on other plants outside. They are all from either Australia or nearby areas such as Java and New Guinea and they are hardy outdoors only down to 50°F/10°C. Most are trailing

Hoya multiflora. Shooting Stars. Malacca

shrubs that flower in summer, but a few, like *H. bella* and *H. multiflora*, confine their growth to arching branches and look great in hanging baskets.

Hoyas strike from spring stem cuttings and grow best in a rich, fast-draining soil, though you must keep them moist in summer. They will be grown in pots, except in the tropics, and flower best when potbound. Do *not* pick *Hoya* flowers. That would cancel out next year's show, as they bloom in the same stem place year after year.

Hoya carnosa 'Crimson Princess'.
Waxflower. Queensland

Hoya purpurea fuscata. Purple Waxflower. Java

Hoya bella. Beautiful Honey Plant. India

Hydrangea
(*syn.* HORTENSIA)

(hai-**draen**-jee-ə)   ☼ ☀ C T W
Hortensia, Hills of Snow,
Lacecap, Pee-Gee, Hydrangea,
Christmas Rose
Sum-Aut; 3–15 ft/1–4.5 m; long display;
fast; mostly deciduous

HYDRANGEACEAE   AROMATIC

Favourite shrub for the large sunless
border or shaded waterside garden,
Hydrangeas produce large, showy
flower heads in midsummer, and are
often used for Christmas decorations
in the southern hemisphere. There
are over 30 deciduous species from
China, Japan and North America,
and only one evergreen species, *H.
integerrima*, which is found naturally
in Chile, and generally develops a
climbing habit.

All species enjoy deep, rich, porous
soil and heavy watering through the
summer months, as they make mass-
ive growth and transpire heavily
from their soft stems and large, serrated leaves. Their terrible thirst is
clearly indicated in their botanical
name, which is a combination of the
Greek words, *Hydor* and *aggeion*,
together meaning 'water vessel'.

Hydrangeas of all types can be

Hydrangea macrophylla. Mixed Hortensias. Japan

Hydrangea arborescens discolor.
Hills of Snow, Sevenbark. E. United States

Hydrangea macrophylla normalis.
Lacecap Hydrangea. Japan

Hydrangea aspera. Star Hydrangea. E. Asia

planted in autumn or in early spring in any soil that is moisture retentive and has been enriched with plenty of old manure or well decayed compost. They need overhead shelter from frost in colder areas and look better in a position where morning sun cannot damage their foliage. All species do best in semi-shade, except in generally cloudy areas, where full sun is readily accepted.

The most commonly grown species is *H. macrophylla* from China and Japan. It has many flower forms which must be propagated from cuttings to come true. One very striking peculiarity is that while they do equally well in acid or alkaline soil, their colour is quite changeable. Generally mauve or blue in acid soils; in alkaline they become pink or red. And it is possible to switch from one colour range to the other by means of chemical additions to the soil. Aluminium sulphate turns them blue, lime turns them pink—it is as simple as that. But there are also white and greenish varieties which rarely tone at all.

All *macrophylla* Hydrangeas have two sorts of flower, one tiny and fertile with minute petals surrounding a cluster of stamens, the other sterile

Hydrangea anomala ssp. *petiolaris*.
Climbing Hydrangea. Himalayas

Hydrangea 'Blue Wave'. Blue Wave Hydrangea. Japan

Hydrangea paniculata. Pee Gee Hydrangea. China, Japan

with large, showy petals and no stamens at all. Varieties consisting almost entirely of the sterile florets are known as 'Hortensias' after Hortense Bonaparte, Queen of Holland; heads with a large proportion of fertile florets are known as 'Lacecaps'.

Both types are pruned back heavily during late winter, cutting each cane to a pair of plump growth buds. The ultimate size of each bush can be controlled in this way.

The second most popular *Hydrangea* species are the Pee-Gee types, *Hydrangea paniculata grandiflora*, which grow taller than the *macrophyllas* (to 16 ft/5 m) and bear terminal panicles of white bloom up to 16 in/45 cm in length. These are greenish at first, gradually fading to pink.

Rarely seen in the southern hemisphere is climbing *H. anomala* ssp. *petiolaris*, which can climb a rough-barked tree or textured wall and produces flat heads of creamy-white bloom in summer.

All Hydrangeas can be propagated from 6 in/15 cm cuttings of unflowered shoots taken in early autumn. These should be struck in a peat/sand mixture, preferably over heat,

Hydrangea macrophylla 'Atlantis'. E. Asia

Hydrangea 'Parsifal'. Hybrid Hydrangea

Hydrangea macrophylla hortensia. Hortensia. Japan

and planted out the following autumn. Keep watch for aphids and red spider mites which can defoliate entire plants where the air is dry. In cold-winter areas, both flowers and foliage of some *Hydrangea* varieties turn gorgeous shades of red, green or rust, and make wonderful indoor displays.

Less commonly, there are fancy-leaf species such as the illustrated *H. quercifolia* or Oak-leaf Hydrangea, and variegated-leaf varieties of several other species. These are striking, but rarely bloom well.

Hydrangea quercifolia. Oak-leaf Hydrangea. S.E. United States

Hymenanthera dentata. Porcupine Bush.
S.E. Australia, New Zealand

Hypericum

(hai-**pe**-rik-əm)   ☼ ❋ T W
St John's Wort, Goldflower,
Aaron's Beard, Rose of Sharon
*Sum/Aut; 1–4 ft/30–120 cm; spreading;
floriferous; evergreen or deciduous*

HYPERICACEAE

Though there are perennial and even annual species of *Hypericum*, this wonderfully showy genus is represented in the wild mostly in the form of shrubs, and on every continent. Sometimes evergreen, sometimes deciduous, they reflect year-round sunshine in a mild-temperate climate and are easy to grow.

Full sun is a must, for at least part of each day, and a well-drained soil will give best results. Set out cuttings in autumn or spring (though preferably the latter) in enriched, deeply-dug soil, and give the roots winter protection with a deep mulch. Small species should be propagated from 2 in/5 cm cuttings taken in late spring. Taller types grow best from 5 in/12 cm summer cuttings of non-

Hypericum X *moseranum* 'Tricolor'.
Goldflower. China

Hymenanthera

(hai-men-**an**-thur-ə)   ☼ T
Porcupine Bush
Spring; to 7 ft/2 m; rigid; evergreen

VIOLACEAE   FRAGRANT

Some taxonomist must have done a bit of fast talking to get these spiny plants included in the same family as the violets. Maybe it's the fragrance. But there they are, 4 or 5 very interesting shrubs to be picked only with great care, and they are found in New Zealand and Australia together with several nearby islands.

They grow from seed, cuttings (which root under glass) or layers, depending on variety, and they are mostly quite frost hardy, at least in Australia and New Zealand.

Hymenantheras flourish in a soil mixture that's mostly peat and sand with just a dash of loam. The small yellowish flowers are no great shakes, but they are followed by berries which are said to be attractive to birds. I'd say those tweeties should be very careful, or they'll finish up like Oscar Wilde's Nightingale, impaled on a thorn.

Hypericum cerastoides. Prostrate Goldflower. S.E. Europe

Hypericum leschenaultii. Sumatra, Australia

Hypericum inodorum. Goldflower. Mediterranean region

flowering shoots. Both types are set out in their final position when well-rooted, about 10 months later.

All species need annual pruning to maintain shape and prevent legginess. It is customary to cut them back to within a few shoots of old wood during the winter. Pests do not seem to be a bother, but leaves are occasionally affected by rust and should be sprayed with a fungicide when this appears.

Some 300–400 *Hypericum* species are recognized, with the most spectacular blooms being found amongst the cultivars. Those of illustrated *H.* 'Rowallane' can be 3 in/7.5 cm in diameter. Smaller flowered *H. inodorum* makes the best mass display, while dwarf *H. cerastoides* (syn. *H. rhodopaeum*) is a showy plant in rock gardens or at the front of the mixed border. *H. leschenaultii* is a more tropical species, found naturally from Sumatra right down into Australia.

Seed pods should be pruned from all species to maintain vigour.

Hypericum chinense. St. John's Wort. China

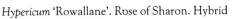

Hypocalymma robustum. Swan River Myrtle.
Western Australia

Hyptis

(hip-tiss) ☼ W H
Desert Lavender
Win-Spr; 3–10 ft/1–3 m; erect; evergreen

LAMIACEAE   AROMATIC

Of some 400 *Hyptis* species scattered through and around tropical America, the only one in wide cultivation seems to be *H. emoryi*, California's Desert Lavender. Curiously attractive in the desert badlands, this highly aromatic member of the mint family forms large clumps in gravelly, well-drained soil. Apparently the poorer the medium, the better *Hyptis* likes it.

The mature shrub branches heavily and is covered from head to toe in woolly grey foliage very like many of the Mediterranean Salvias—and is even more heat resistant! The tiny, Salvia-like flowers are a rich violet but enclosed by grey calyxes to match the foliage. Bees find the *Hyptis* most attractive—I guess there isn't much else they could find out there.

Hypericum 'Rowallane'. Rose of Sharon. Hybrid

Hypocalymma

(hai-poh-kal-**lim**-ə) ☼ T W H
Swan River Myrtle,
White Myrtle
*Win/Spr; 3 ft/1 m; soft; rounded;
evergreen*

MYRTACEAE

A very useful genus of small shrubs for cutting, as well as outdoor decoration, the *Hypocalymmas* are all endemic to Western Australia, but have been grown in the UK, at least as a novelty plant. They *must* have the west's typical well-drained, sandy soil and a dry atmosphere to go ahead.

Cuttings strike readily in summer but seed is more of a problem. Regular moisture is needed and hard pruning is wise after bloom to compact the bush. Regular cutting of the flowering stems is the easy way.

Botanically, *Hypocalymma* is part of the myrtle family. What makes it different is that the tiny white and pink flowers are almost stalkless and borne in pairs at the leaf axils right down each stem. Leaves are like those of the Geraldton Wax.

Hyptis emoryi. Desert Lavender.
California, Arizona, Mexico

Mildred Matthias./Lewis

Hyssopus

(**his**-sop-əss) ☼ ❄ W
Hyssop
Sum-Aut; 1½–2 ft/45–60 cm; many-branched; evergreen

LAMIACEAE   PUNGENT

With renewed Western popularity as an ornamental herb, the ancient Hyssop (*Hyssopus officinalis*) has always been common from the Mediterranean area through to Asia where it grows in dry, rocky, limestone soil. Give it the same conditions and it will reward you with tall stems of bluish-violet flowers from summer almost through to winter. These are highly aromatic and the entire plant is used to make a popular tea in some areas.

Hyssop is a typical, square-stemmed member of the mint family, drought resistant and even capable of putting up with a bit of frost. Grow it from seed, cuttings or divisions and pick regularly to help compact the bush. It can be grown in containers in the kitchen garden or on a terrace.

Iboza riparia. Nutmeg Bush. South Africa

Hyssopus officinalis. Hyssop. Mediterranean to Asia

Iboza

(*syn.* MOSCHOSMA)

(i-**boh**-zə) ☼ T W
Nutmeg Bush, Misty Plume Bush
Winter; to 7 ft/2 m; open; deciduous

LAMIACEAE   AROMATIC

No, it doesn't really smell like nutmeg or ginger, but it certainly is aromatic—something like spice with overtones of mint. South African *Iboza riparia* is one of around a dozen species in a decorative genus of the mint family. This is of particular value in a mild, coastal climate, where the entire bush bursts into bloom in mid-winter!

The shrubs are almost completely deciduous, with toothed, velvety leaves developing as the tiny, silvery-pink blooms fade. These are sprinkled with purple anthers and appear in long terminal panicles.

Hard pruning is needed to maintain shape, and up to three-quarters of the previous season's growth should be removed after bloom.

Cuttings taken in early spring and struck in sandy soil will flower the following winter. *Iboza* is hardy down to 28°F/−2°C.

Ilex aquifolium 'Albo-Marginata'. English Holly. Europe, N. Africa, W. Asia

Ilex

(**ai**-leks) ☼ ☀ C T
Holly
Aut-Win; 10–16 ft/3–5 m; erect;
evergreen

AQUIFOLIACEAE

Many cool-climate gardeners can't get their *Ilex* bushes to fruit at all and wonder why. It is because Hollies are dioecious in nature. That is to say, while all Hollies produce small clusters of rather charming white or greenish blossom with a fruit fragrance, there are two sexes, just like us! And unless you have both—no berries!

Hollies are propagated from semi-hardwood cuttings in early autumn and grow best in a deep, leaf-rich soil that is moist but well-drained. They grow slowly and in the Middle Ages held an almost mystical attraction for the peoples of Europe. When forests were bare of leaves, there were the shining pyramids of Holly, catching the winter sunlight with masses of brilliant scarlet fruit.

There are about 400 species, mostly with typically spiny leaves. However, in China, the young foliage of *I. chinensis* is enjoyed as a salad vegetable. Hollies are planted in early autumn.

Ilex chinensis. Kushi Holly.
Japan, China

Ilex pedunculata. Japanese Holly. Japan, China

Illicium

(il-**liss**-ee-əm) ☼ ☀ T W
Purple Anise
Spring; 10 ft/3 m; multiple-trunked;
evergreen

ILLICIACEAE   FRAGRANT

An interesting genus of 40 shrubs and small trees native to both Asia and the Americas. The largest of them, *Illicium vernum*, produces the star anise of commerce. The smaller *I. floridanum* of our illustration is grown only for its flowers—and what flowers they are! Rich, deep red or purple blossoms around 2 in/5 cm in diameter and with up to 33 narrow, twisted petals. Somehow, in spite of their colour, it is obvious they are related to the Magnolias.

Illiciums grow only in acid soil, which should be sandy with lots of leaf mould or peat. Propagate by layering in autumn, from seeds or from summer cuttings which must be kept under glass until they root. The name comes from the Latin *illicio*, to entice, in reference to the exotic perfume.

Illicium floridanum. Purple Anise.
S. USA

Impatiens

(im-**pae**-shəns) ☀ ☼ T
Oliver's Snapweed,
Poor Man's Rhododendron
Summer; to 8 ft/2.5 m; heavily branched;
evergreen

BALSAMINACEAE

Not truly woody in the same way as a real Rhododendron, Oliver's Snapweed is certainly a very different plant from its smaller, succulent relatives that dissolve at the first touch of frost. In fact, provided it is grown under the shelter of a spreading tree, *Impatiens oliveri* can resist a light frost in any cool-temperate climate.

Grow it from seed or cuttings like other *Impatiens* and plant in a leaf-rich, well-drained soil. The handsome leaves are borne in whorls of 4 to 8, the long-spurred, pale lilac flowers may be 2½ in/7 cm in diameter. It is from the cooler highlands of tropical east Africa.

Indigofera australis. False Indigo. Australia

Impatiens oliveri. Poor Man's Rhododendron. E. Africa

Indigofera incarnata. Summer Wisteria. Japan, China

Indigofera

(in-dig-**off**-ur-ə) ☼ ☀ T W H
False Indigo, Summer Wisteria
Spr-Sum; to 7 ft/2 m; spreading; evergreen

FABACEAE

Well known in most warmer parts of the world, the genus *Indigofera* includes between 700 and 800 species of which the illustrated, mauve-flowered *I. australis* is an Australian representative growing to 4 ft/1.3 m. The pink-flowering *I. incarnata* is from Japan and China, but popular in both the northern and southern hemispheres wherever the winters are not too hard. *I. incarnata* is an untypical species, maintaining a dense, bushy shape. The Australian False Indigo bears the more usual weeping branches with long sprays of Wisteria type blossom in the warmer months.

Indigoferas are frost hardy and drought resistant and very useful in drier gardens where the soil is poor. Propagate from cuttings. Shape annually from an early age.

Iochroma

(*syn.* CHAENESTES)

(ai-oh-**kroh**-mə) ☼ ☀ W H
Tubeflower
Sum-Aut; 3–10 ft/1–3 m; open; evergreen

SOLANACEAE

Tropical relative of the Cestrum, Petunia and Salpiglossis, the 20-odd species of *Iochroma* hail from Central

Iochroma lanceolata. Violet Tubeflower. Colombia

Iochroma coccinea. Scarlet Tubeflower. Central America

over time and can be cut back to keep the plant to a more compact shape.

Its heart-shaped leaves are 6 in/ 15 cm or so in length and hairy on their reverses. The typical Morning Glory flowers, in which the flattened corolla is unbroken, are about 3 in/ 8 cm in diameter, appear in pairs towards stem tips and last for several days. They are succeeded by globular seed pods. The Shrub Morning Glory is propagated from these seeds, though cuttings are also successful.

Iresine

(**ai**-res-een)   ☼ ☀ Ⓦ Ⓗ
Bloodleaf
Summer; 3 ft/1 m; spreading; evergreen

AMARANTHACEAE

Not frost hardy at all and scarcely woody enough to be classified as a shrub, the gorgeous Bloodleaf (*Iresine herbstii*) seems content enough with its sub-shrub classification, at least in a sheltered position.

It grows from soft-tip cuttings and in cooler climates is sometimes set out in spring to be used as an annual bedding plant. However, where the climate is warmer, and the soil well-

and South America and come from a family notorious for its hallucinogenic and poisonous properties. So far as has been discovered *to date*, however, the *Iochromas* are merely decorative. Their long, tubular flowers, mostly in shades of purple and red, hang all summer and autumn among their felt-textured leaves.

Iochromas are easily raised from cuttings and grow best in a warm, sheltered spot with lots of water. As summer heats up, they quickly become untidy and straggly unless kept in shape with a regular trim.

I. grandiflora, *I. lanceolata* and *I. tubulosa* bloom in varying shades of purple; *I. coccinea* is scarlet, while *I. flava* is pale yellow. None is frost hardy.

ical shrub which either stands up to a 6 ft/2 m height or flops horizontally in much the same dimensions, probably dependent on available water. Its fleshy stems become quite woody

Ipomoea fistulosa. Shrub Morning Glory. Tropical America

Ipomoea

(ip-oh-**mee**-ə)   ☼ Ⓦ Ⓗ
Shrub Morning Glory
Summer; to 6 ft/2 m; sprawling; evergreen

CONVOLVULACEAE

Not one of your Morning Glories that twine around the cottage door, *Ipomoea fistulosa* is a spectacular trop-

drained and leaf-rich, it will hang on year after year, with a hard pruning at the end of the cold weather to keep it in its prime. It looks magnificent in semi-shaded areas as a massed planting and though its small lime-green flowers are insignificant, they make a striking contrast to the crimson foliage.

Iresine herbstii. Bloodleaf. South America

Isopogon latifolius. Ruby Coneflower. Western Australia

Isopogon dubius. Rosy Coneflower. Western Australia

Isopogon anethifolius. Drumsticks. E. Australia

Isopogon

(ai-**sop**-ə-gon)   ☼ T W
Coneflower, Drumsticks
Win-Spr; 3–7 ft/1–2 m; spreading; evergreen

PROTEACEAE   FRAGRANT

Less familiar outside their native Australia than other genera of the extraordinary Protea family, the 30-odd species of *Isopogon* have been cultivated successfully in California, the Mediterranean and even England's Scilly Isles. They all have stiff foliage (mostly needle-like) and cone-shaped flowerheads from which elongated florets and stamens appear from late winter. The blooms cut well and are useful for adding bulk to large arrangements.

Propagate *Isopogons* from well-ripened seed sown in winter or from cuttings struck in sharp sand and peat. They are hardy down to 23°F/−5°C.

Itea

(**ai**-tee-ə)   ☼ ☀ C T W
Sweetspire
Summer; to 16 ft/5 m; treelike; evergreen & deciduous

SAXIFRAGACEAE   FRAGRANT

Although America has its own species of *Itea, I. virginiana,* a shrub less than 5 ft/1.5 m high, there is no doubt that the taller, more treelike *I. ilicifolia* from China is the more popular garden subject. Both have slender leaves and long racemes of greenish-white summer flowers that are quite fragrant, but *I. virginiana* has deciduous, willow-like leaves that turn brilliant colours in autumn.

I. ilicifolia has leaves that distinctly resemble those of holly, although

J. H. Willis

Itea ilicifolia. Holly-leaf Sweetspire.
W. China

much narrower. It is most at home in
the deep, rich soil of humid coastal
areas or a sheltered position in the
hills, well protected from frost. A
very handsome, evergreen foliage
plant.

Iteas can be struck from cuttings of
ripe wood taken in summer, when
the flower racemes appear both from
the leaf axils and as terminal clusters.

Ixora

(**ik**-sor-ə) ☀ W H
Jungle Geranium,
Flame of the Woods, Jungle Flame
Summer; 3–7 ft/1–2 m; dense; evergreen

RUBIACEAE

What Geraniums are to the cooler-
climate garden, *Ixoras* are in the
tropics. They are used for mass bedding, container subjects, hedges,
screens. There are some 400 species of
them found all over tropical Asia and
Africa and into the Pacific Islands, so

Ixora chinensis alba. Jungle Ghost. Malaysia

Ixora chinensis. Jungle Geranium. Malaysia, China

Ixora duffii. Jungle Flame.
Caroline Islands

the choice is wide. They are striking
plants for gardens where the humidity is high.

Grow them in a sandy soil, rich
with leaf mould, and give plenty of
moisture throughout the summer.
Cut back to shape in winter when
they may be allowed to dry out a
little. *Ixoras* should be propagated
from summer cuttings struck in sharp
sand.

I. chinensis 'Prince of Orange' is
most often used as a bedding plant in
the tropics, but its flowers bleach
badly. *I. coccinea* and *I. duffii* have
rich scarlet blooms and make a splendid sight. Well known cultivars
include 'Henry Morat', light pink;
'McGees', yellow; 'Williamsii', dark
red; 'Fraseri', salmon-pink. None is
frost hardy.

Jacksonia

(jak-**soh**-nee-ə) ☀ ☀ W H
Dogwood, Native Broom,
Golden Fleece
*Spring; to 12–14 ft/4 m; densely
branched; evergreen*

FABACEAE

Often of a tree-like form, *Jacksonia
scoparia* can be the most noticeable
plant in the eastern Australian landscape from late spring on. In the
outer suburbs of Sydney and all

Jacksonia scoparia. Dogwood.
N.S.W., Queensland

Jacquinia pungens. Braceletwood.
Central America

Jamesia americana. Jamesia.
W. North America

along the great range which divides the coastal plain from the interior, great clouds of orange-yellow pea blossoms appear almost overnight and persist for months.

Propagation is easy from scattered seed, and the resulting plants grow well in any well-drained, hillside soil. They grow fast, live long to display their golden fleece for years to come. Their dense flower heads are made up of very many twigs which bear terminal clusters of 3 to 6 pea flowers, each ¼ in/5 mm. Young plants bear small leaves which disappear in the adult stage.

Jacquinia

(jak-**kin**-ee-ə)　　　☼ ☀ W H
Braceletwood
Spring; 3–12 ft/1–4 m; dense; evergreen

THEOPHRASTACEAE　　FRAGRANT

Grown for their decorative value in many subtropical gardens, the 25-odd species of *Jacquinia* have a more grisly practical use in their native Central America—both leaves and fruit are highly regarded as an effective fish poison to help supply hungry villagers.

J. pungens is an attractive shrub, usually reaching about 3 ft/1 m in a semi-shaded position. Its oblong-elliptic leaves are spine-tipped and the small, 5-petalled, orange-red flowers are often strongly fragrant; the fruits that follow are nearly 1 in/ 3 cm in diameter and spiny. These are sometimes strung as bracelets, hence the popular name. Grow from seed or cuttings in leaf-rich soil.

Jamesia

(**jaem**-zee-ə)　　　☼ ☀ T W
Jamesia
Spring; 6 ft/2 m; stiff, erect; deciduous

HYDRANGEACEAE

This attractive deciduous shrub from western North America is related to the *Deutzia*, from which it is separated only by a few highly technical points. Its soft, serrated leaves have grey reverses; the white or pink 5-petalled flowers, only about ½ in/ 1 cm in diameter, appear in terminal clusters. It has a dwarf variety, 'Californica', which rarely grows above 20 in/50 cm and always blooms in a deep rose-pink.

Jamesia is frost hardy, grows well in leaf-rich, well-drained soil in a sunny location. You can propagate it from seed or cuttings of ripe wood taken in summer. Under glass, these form roots in a matter of weeks. *Jamesia* foliage colours brilliantly in autumn.

Jasminum fruticans. Yellow Jasmine.
North Africa, Mediterranean

Jasminum X *stephanense*. Hybrid Jasmine

Jasminum sambac. Arabian Jasmine. India

Jasminum nudiflorum. Winter Jasmine. China, Japan

Jasminum

(**jas**-min-əm) ☼ ✹ T W H
Jasmine, Jessamine, Pikake
Various; 3–20 ft / 1–6 m; rambling; mostly evergreen

OLEACEAE   FRAGRANT

Ranging from frost hardy to fully tropical in their climatic needs, the 200 species of *Jasminum* spread themselves all over the old world (Asia, Europe, Africa) and also Australia, but the Azores and Madeira are as close as they come to the Americas.

Ranging from bushy shrubs to delicate climbing or leaning plants, they bear dainty starry flowers in yellow, white or pink according to species, and the best of them are native to all the fabled lands of the Arabian Nights.

You can have Jasmine scenting your house and garden the whole year round if you pick the right species from among the 200-odd listed by taxonomists. Just give them a partly shaded or sunny position, reasonable soil, a regular ration of water and watch them take off.

They'll need occasional going over with the secateurs to keep them in bounds, though, for almost all Jasmines love to turn climber if you let

them have their heads. I like to train them onto wires plugged into a brick wall and let them fall forward (see our illustrated *J*. X *stephanense*).

J. nudiflorum is the first to bloom, opening single, ½ in / 1 cm flowers from its bare twigs in the winter sunlight. In its native Japan, they call it 'the flower that welcomes spring'. *J. mesneyi*, the Primrose Jasmine, has much larger, semi-double golden blooms on arching canes and follows

Jasminum polyanthum. Pink Jasmine. W. China

at the first sign of warm weather. It is hardy to 27°F/−3°C.

But you'll know spring has truly arrived when pink-budded, *J. polyanthum* bursts into bloom. It is strictly a climbing shrub and will cover a wall in no time with light support. Many gardeners like to cut it right back to about 20 in/50 cm after bloom as it flowers best on new wood. Golden *J. fruticans* and white *J. angulare* join in the fragrance contest later in spring and are joined by *J. azoricum* and the Italian Jasmine, *J. officinale*, which bloom throughout summer and until the following winter. In warmer climates, *J. rex* and the shrubby *J. sambac* will bloom intermittently throughout the warm weather.

Jatropha. Guatemala Rhubarb. Central America

Jasminum mesneyi. Primrose Jasmine. W. China

Almost all Jasmines are easy to propagate from 3 in/8 cm cuttings of fairly ripe wood in summer, by layers, even from seed when it is produced.

Plant a Jasmine by your bedroom window and wait for the magic carpet to arrive.

Jatropha

(**jat**-roh-fə)   ☼ T W H
Guatemala Rhubarb,
Gout Stalk, Gouty Foot, Tartogo,
Australian Bottle Plant
Summer; to 1½ ft/45 cm; erect; deciduous

EUPHORBIACEAE

Since this remarkable plant comes from Central America, the sobriquet 'Australian Bottle Plant' seems rather careless. So let's settle on the Guatemalan name instead. It is most often seen among landscaped cactus collections, though it's not in any way related.

There are about 125 species, most easily grown from seed or cuttings of firm young branches allowed to dry out before setting them in a damp, sandy mix. They are then grown on in light, sandy soil in a position that's well-drained and sunny. A rock pocket is ideal. They need water during the summer growing season, less during their winter rest.

Young *Jatrophas* soon develop a swollen, knobby stem with heavy scarring, and topped with red-veined, deeply divided leaves that are reminiscent of rhubarb. The small scarlet flowers, which have red stems, appear at the tips of long, terminal cymes.

Jovellana

(joh-vel-**lah**-nə)   ☼ T W
Chilean Figweed
Summer; to 6 ft/2 m; suckering; evergreen

SCROPHULARIACEAE

Closely related to the Calceolaria and once included in that genus, the half-dozen *Jovellana* species have now been separated into a different group and, like quite a few Chilean plants, they are also found in New Zealand. Although not really woody, they are surprisingly resistant to light frosts, and in England have been known to survive for many years. A New Zealand species, the yellow-flowered *J. sinclairii*, is grown on North America's west coast.

Jovellana violacea. Chilean Figweed. Chile

The most common species, Chilean *J. violacea*, is an evergreen, 6 ft/2 m shrub with densely haired branches, coarsely toothed leaves and ½ in/1 cm flowers of pale mauve. These have spotted throats and are borne in branched, terminal corymbs. They grow from seed, like leaf-rich soil and a moist position.

Justicia ghiesbreghtiana. Red Tongue.
Mexico

Justicia pauciflora. Paradise Plant, Libonia. Brazil

Justicia

(*syn.* JACOBINIA, LIBONIA,
CYRTANTHERA, ADHATODA,
BELOPERONE, DREJERELLA,
SERICOGRAPHIS)

(jus-**tis**-ee-ə) ☼ ⚫ ☀ T H
Paradise Plant,
Plume Flower,
Shrimp Plant, Water Willow
*Spr-Aut; 2–10 ft/60 cm–3 m; upright;
evergreen*

ACANTHACEAE

'If at first you don't succeed, try, try
again' would seem to have been the
motto of taxonomists trying to sort
this lot out. According to the botanical dictionaries, there are now over
300 species of *Justicia* left after hiving
off the remainder into as many as 30
other genera! All the remaining
Justicias are remarkably handsome
plants of tropical or subtropical origin. In any cooler climates, you'll
have to try them in a greenhouse,
though I have known them to last a
year or two in a sheltered position in
my warm-temperate garden.

Most of these showy South American Plume Flowers produce tall
spikes of typical Acanthus blooms in
flushes, starting in late spring and
continuing all the way to autumn.
The colour range is wide—pink, red,
orange, yellow and white—but each
flush is short. However, prompt
removal of faded flower heads,
coupled with a well-drained soil and
regular fertilizer, will quickly initiate
the formation of new buds.

Start new plants from cuttings and
prune back hard in earliest spring to
encourage branching and prevent
their growing tall and straggly. Well-
grown specimens can reach 10 ft/
3 m, though half that is more usual.
All species prefer dappled shade, and
should be sprayed with a suitable
insecticide to prevent caterpillars
making a meal of both flowers and
foliage. Lay snail bait regularly or the
dark green leaves will soon be ruined.
In areas with cool winters, grow in
wide pots so you can bring the plants
indoors. Most are hardy down to
29°F/−2°C.

Justicia aurea. King's Crown.
Central America

Justicia carnea. Brazilian Plume Flower.
South America

Kalanchöe beharensis. Felt Bush, Velvet Elephant Ear. Madagascar

Kalanchöe marmorata. Penwiper. Ethiopia, Somalia

Kalanchöe

(syn. KITCHINGIA*)*

(kal-an-**koh**-ee)   ☼ ◑ W H
Felt Plant, Penwiper,
Copperleaf
*All year; 2–10 ft/60 cm–3 m; vase
shaped; evergreen*

CRASSULACEAE

About 25 species of succulent plants
mostly from Africa and Madagascar,
some of them quite woody and
shrubby. The most commonly grown
are spring-flowering perennials such
as Flaming Katy (*Kalanchöe blossfeldiana*) which is a popular house plant
in many countries, and *K. manginii*,
the Basket Kalanchöe, which bursts
into a mass of hanging, waxy bells in
summer. All of the other species
bloom too, of course, but in most of
them, it's the foliage that features.
The spectacular Ethiopian Penwiper
Plant, for instance, has wide-ended,
spoon-shaped leaves up to 10 in/
25 cm long and marked with purple
blotches as well as small white flowers

that are not half so spectacular.

Madagascar's 10 ft/3 m *K. beharensis* has green, felty, triangular leaves
up to 15 in/36 cm long, but the yellow flowers are less than ¼ in/5 mm
long. The Copper Spoon, *K. orgyalis*,
grows 8 ft/2.5 m tall, has coppery
new foliage and again, tiny yellow
flowers.

These spectacular plants grow from
cuttings of leaves or stems which root
readily in a warm, sheltered position.
Just dry them out before planting in
damp sand. A gritty, well-drained
soil is best and regular water should
be tapered off in winter.

Kalanchöe orgyalis. Copper Spoon.
Madagascar

Kalmia CV 'Nancy'. Hybrid Kalmia

R. A. Jaynes

Kalmia latifolia. Mountain Laurel. E. North America

Kalmia

(*syn.* KALMIELLA)

(kal-mee-ə)   ☀☀ⒸⓉ
Mountain Laurel, Calico Bush,
Spoonwood, Wicky, Lambkill
Spr-Sum; 6–10 ft/2–3 m; treelike;
evergreen

ERICACEAE   FRAGRANT

Attractive to humans because of
their charm and fragrance, all *Kal-*
mias are quite poisonous to stock, as
witness names like Lambkill. Garden
treasures away from their native
American mountains, the slow-
growing *Kalmias* enjoy the same conditions as their Rhododendron relatives: part shade, humidity, an acid
soil rich in leaf mould and an assured
supply of water. They detest lime in
any form.

The laurel-like leaves are dark and
glossy, the flowers (white, red or
apple blossom pink according to variety) have a curious sticky feel and are
borne profusely at the ends of last
season's growth, during spring. *Kal-*
mias will survive temperatures well
below 0°F/−18°C. In fact they seem
to need frosty winters to do well and
are not recommended for mild areas.

K. latifolia develops into a broad,
densely foliaged shrub, 6–10 ft/2–3 m

tall and about as wide. Plant out in
late spring or early autumn and don't
prune except to remove faded
flowers. They are best propagated by
layering new wood in summer, but
may also be struck from cuttings,
though this is far less reliable.

Keraudrenia integrifolia. Common Firebush.
N.E. Australia

Keraudrenia

(ke-ror-**dree**-nee-ə)   ☀ⓉⓌ
Common Firebush
Spring; 3 ft/90 cm; neat, compact;
evergreen

MALVACEAE

An interesting genus of small shrubs
from the north and east of Australia,
not particularly well known in cultivation as yet, but with great possibilities. The Common Firebush, *Ker-*
audrenia integrifolia, is raised from
seed which should be sown in a light
mixture of bush sand and peat moss.
It should be planted out in deep,
sandy soil that is particularly well-
drained, but likes a year-round mulch
to preserve moisture.

The Firebush makes a fine rockery
subject with its naturally neat, compact shape and dense foliage. Its
simple leaves are glossy and lanceolate. The crepe-textured flowers, red-
dish-mauve in colour, are borne in
clusters at the leaf axils. I can find no
reference to fragrance.

Kerria

(**ke**-ree-ə)   ☀☀ⒸⓉ
Jew's Mallow, Japanese Rose,
Globe Flower, Bachelor's Button
Spring; 4–6 ft/1–2 m; suckering;
deciduous

ROSACEAE

'Roses, roses everywhere'—but perhaps not *too* many others of this great
family bloom with the rich gold of
the *Kerrias*. There is only one species
in the genus and it is a great favourite
in cooler climate gardens where it
lights up shaded corners with a profusion of golden spring blossom.

Easily grown from cuttings, layers
or divisions, it spreads rapidly and
needs at least a 7 ft/2 m diameter
space to display its graceful, arching
branches. These are festooned with
delicate, doubly-toothed leaves from
early spring and glow later with
autumn colour. The flowers (double
in CV 'Pleniflora') open in spring at
the ends of lateral shoots which cut
well for indoor display.

Kerria needs a rich, well-drained
soil and occasional heavy watering. It
is hardy down to 21°F/−6°C and
does best with a heavy pruning to
stimulate new growth. This should be
done as soon as possible after bloom.

Kerria japonica 'Pleniflora'. Bachelor's Buttons.
China, Japan

Kolkwitzia

(kolk-**wit**-zee-ə)
Beauty Bush
Spring; 7–10 ft/2–3 m; arching; deciduous

CAPRIFOLIACEAE   FRAGRANT

Most splendid of the honeysuckle family (Caprifoliaceae), *Kolkwitzia* is a graceful, arching shrub from the neighbourhood of Hupeh in western China, where it is found at an altitude of 10,000 ft/3000 m and more.

Easy to grow from cuttings, provided your climate is right, best results are had from soft-tips taken in spring or summer or semi-hardwood in late summer. These should be kept warm and moist under glass until they root. A typical mountain soil suits best, well-drained and rich in leaf mould. There, it roots deeply and sends up deciduous, arching branches which are festooned in spring with terminal corymbs of small foxglove-like flowers. These, produced in pairs, are pink with hairy, golden throats and delightfully fragrant. *Kolkwitzia amabilis*, the only species, is hardy down to at least 14°F/−10°C.

Kolkwitzia amabilis. Beauty Bush. W. China

Kopsia

(**kop**-see-ə)
Rosy Dogbane
Spring; 20 ft/6 m; upright; evergreen

APOCYNACEAE   FRAGRANT

Old world equivalents of the new world *Plumeria* (which see), the *Kopsias* have a strong visual resemblance, though their leathery leaves

Kopsia florida. White Kopsia. New Guinea

Kopsia fruticosa. Rosy Dogbane. Malaysia

Murray Fagg

Kunzea pulchella. Scarlet Tickbush. Western Australia

are evergreen. There are 4 species, all Indo-Malaysian in origin, and they are popular in subtropical or warmer gardens worldwide.

K. fruticosa is the best known, with beautiful 3 in/8 cm, periwinkle type flowers coloured like strawberry ice-cream. An erect shrub, fast-growing to around 20 ft/6 m tall, it needs a sunny position, sheltered from strong winds. Leaves are an attractive, glossy, dark green and the flowers have a fragrance reminiscent of Frangipani. Its much smaller cousin, K. florida, has gold-throated white flowers.

All Kopsias are grown from cuttings of young shoots struck under glass. The growing plants need an acid, sandy soil rich in humus—and above all, a warm winter.

Kunzea

(kun-zee-a) ☼ ☼ Ⓦ
Tickbush, Kunzea
Spring; 5–10 ft/1.5–3 m; rounded; evergreen

MYRTACEAE   AROMATIC

One of Australia's most beautiful genera within the myrtle family, the Kunzeas include some 35 exquisite

Kunzea capitata. Tickbush, Pink Buttons. S.E. Australia

shrubs and, as usual, hardly one of them has a popular name to bless itself with. They are closely related to both Callistemon and Leptospermum, have tiny heath-like leaves and produce showy masses of fluffy, long-stamened flowers that can be red, pink, cream, mauve or white.

Kunzeas are raised from firm-tip cuttings which strike easily in moist sand during the warmer months. K. capitata is a small, rounded shrub decked with pinkish flowers most of the spring. K. pulchella can reach 10 ft/3 m and blooms in a stunning mass of red. K. affinis, K. parvifolia and K. pauciflora bloom in various shades of pink. The flowers have a faint honey fragrance but the scent of the aromatic foliage is stronger.

Kunzea parvifolia. S.E. Australia

Kunzea opposita. S.E. Australia

Kunzea affinis. Pink Tickbush.
Western Australia

Lachnostachys

(**lak**-noh-stak-əs) ☼ W H
Lamb's Tails
Spring; 2 ft/60 cm; rounded; evergreen

LAMIACEAE

Hard to propagate, harder to grow, but well worth the challenge, particularly if you happen to live in an arid area, the 10 *Lachnostachys* species are

Lachnostachys verbascifolia. Lamb's Tails.
Western Australia

endemic to the sand plains of Western Australia. All are low shrubs with densely woolly, silvery foliage and plump spikes of tiny purplish or yellow flowers deep within woolly calyces. Illustrated *L. verbascifolia* grows to 2 ft/60 cm and is an appealing plant for a fully sunny spot in sandy, well-drained soil.

Seed is as hard to get as it is to germinate, but enthusiasts should try it in autumn or spring. Cuttings will strike in just-moist sand without mist or high humidity. Water only during drought or when distressed.

Lagerstroemia

(lah-gur-**stroh**-mee-ə) ☼ T W H
Crepe Myrtle, Pride of India, Melindres, Queen Flower, Telinga China, Kahili Flower
Summer; to 16 ft/5 m; vase shaped; deciduous

LYTHRACEAE

These days, when *Lagerstroemia* are available all the way from 2 ft/60 cm annual plants to 60 ft/20 m trees, it's comforting to know that one of the 30 species is available in shrub form

Lagerstroemia indica 'Rubra'. Crepe Myrtle. China

to suit the modern garden, and can be kept that way with judicious pruning.

The Chinese Crepe Myrtle, *L. indica*, is, anyway, the only species you're likely to find, and then only in a warm-temperate climate because any cooler and it's unlikely to flower. It is easily grown from seed or hardwood cuttings, though only cuttings will assure you the colour you want. Young plants positively shoot ahead in rich, well-drained soil.

Bare for much of the winter, Crepe Myrtles come into leaf in late spring and burst into bloom on new wood in summer when panicles of charming, crepey flowers appear terminally. These are mauve, pink, white or deep red according to variety. Each bloom is about the size of a peach blossom and consists of 6 roundish, wrinkled petals, a mass of gold stamens and a glossy green calyx.

Lagerstroemia indica 'Alba'. Crepe Myrtle. China

Lambertia multiflora. Western Lambertia. Western Australia

Murray Fagg

Lambertia formosa. Mountain Devil. N.S.W.

Lambertia

(lam-**bur**-tee-ə)   ☼ ✳ Ⓣ Ⓦ
Mountain Devil, Honeysuckle
Spr-Sum; 7 ft/2 m; open; evergreen

PROTEACEAE

Perhaps the tourist novelties made from the seed pods of this genus are better known than the flowers themselves. For though dainty and charming, they are the least spectacular inflorescences in the Protea family.

There are believed to be 10 species in the genus, all but one endemic to Western Australia. They can all be grown from seed or semi-hardwood cuttings taken in late autumn. All need a rich, well-drained soil—acid in the case of *Lambertia formosa*, slightly alkaline for the Western Australian species. *L. formosa*, the plant of rocky hillsides, is hardy down to 21°F/ −6°C and has a particularly long flowering season.

Lambertias need regular tip prun-

ing from an early age to give them any sort of recognizable shape. They are evergreen with stiff, dark green foliage borne in whorls, with clusters of nectar-rich flowers appearing at branch tips. In summer, regular moisture is essential.

Lantana camara 'Nivea'. Shrub Verbena. Tropical America

Lantana

(lan-**tah**-nə)   ☼ Ⓣ Ⓦ Ⓗ
Shrub Verbena,
Polecat Geranium
Spr-Aut; to 6½ ft/2 m; broadly prostrate; evergreen

VERBENACEAE   AROMATIC

The relationship to the annual Verbenas is easy to spot in these splashily-blooming shrubs, which seem to be sprinkled with posies. Native mostly to the Americas, they have become a great favourite in mild-winter areas, but many species can quickly become unwelcome guests.

Mauve-flowered *L. montevidensis* and its hybrid *L. X callowiana* are the exceptions. Their dainty arched stems make a wonderful groundcover or small hedge and never become troublesome.

Lantana CV 'Chelsea Gem'. Hybrid Lantana

The more robust *L. camara* is a different story. It has been proclaimed a noxious weed in many countries where it has been spread by birds, which excrete seeds from the juicy black fruit. But while the species is a hated weed, there are many sterile hybrids of *L. camara* which are among the most useful of hedging shrubs in the warm-climate garden. These must be propagated from 3 in/ 8 cm cuttings, taken in summer and struck in sharp sand and peat.

Larrea
(*syn.* COVILLEA)

(**lah**-ree-ə)   ☼ W H
Creosote Bush
Spring; to 10 ft/3 m; thin; hairy; evergreen
ZYGOPHYLLACEAE

Practical but not pretty, might be an apt description of the homely Creosote Bush which has many medicinal uses, particularly in tribal North American Indian medicine, probably because of its high resin content.

Larrea tridentata is widespread from California through to Texas and down into Mexico, growing in conditions which any sensible plant would reject out of hand. It is evergreen (ever olive green might be a more accurate description). It has tiny pinnate leaves, small, 5-petalled yellow flowers followed by hairy, globose fruit which splits to reveal a mass of silky threads surrounding 5 seeds. The flower buds are often pickled and eaten like capers. Grow from semi-hardwood cuttings in summer, plant out in dry, fast-draining soil.

Larrea tridentata. Creosote Bush. California, Texas, Mexico

Lantana X *callowiana*. Yellow Sage. Hybrid

Lantana montevidensis. Polecat Geranium. South America

Lasiopetalum
(lass-ee-oh-**pet**-ə-ləm)   ☼ ☼ C W
Shrubby Velvet Bush
Spring; to 7 ft/2 m; erect; evergreen
MALVACEAE

Endemic to most of Australia (though principally the eastern states) the 30-odd *Lasiopetalum* species are closely related to (and easily mistaken for) plants of the genera Guichenotia and Thomasia (which see). They are spring-flowering shrubs, not very

Murray Fagg

Lasiopetalum dasyphyllum. Shrubby Velvet Bush. S.E. Australia

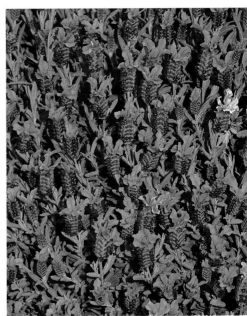

Lavandula stoechas. Spanish Lavender.
Mediterranean

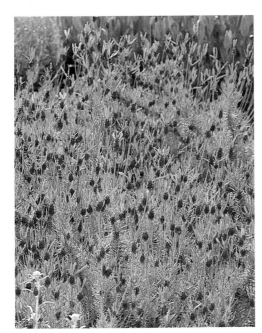

Lavandula stoechas pedunculata.
Portuguese Lavender. N.E. Portugal

Lavandula

(la-**van**-dyoo-lə) ☼ C T W
Lavender
Spr-Sum; 4 ft / 1 m; compact; evergreen

LAMIACEAE   FRAGRANT

Most fragrant of the mint family and raised by the square mile in southern Europe for the perfume industry, Lavenders include about 20 species, all with grey-green foliage and 'lavender' coloured flowers almost hidden beneath a series of bracts. They like a cool-temperate climate and are hardy down to at least 23°F/−5°C. In warmer areas they do not bloom well, though this would seem to be related to a lack of limestone in the soil.

All should be propagated from autumn cuttings of ripened shoots with a heel and set out the following spring. Grow on the dryish side in light, gravelly soil. Deadhead regularly, and shear new growth fre-

Lavandula angustifolia. English Lavender. Mediterranean

showy except when viewed from below, and they are great survivors, growing in any soil and needing little water except during droughts.

Grow them from semi-hardwood cuttings struck in damp sand and when rooted, plant out in a position with light, dappled shade.

The brown stems of *Lasiopetalum* are spotted, the 4 in/10 cm lanceolate leaves hairy on their reverses. The small flowers are most unusual, rosy-petalled but surrounded by a white calyx which is rusty-furry on its reverse.

quently to keep compact, but don't cut into the old, woody stems.

Lavandula angustifolia is the mounded, silver-leafed type with long-stemmed heads of flowers that are so easy to strip for sachets. *L. dentata* is the French Lavender with woolly foliage and shorter flower stems. Italian Lavender, *L. stoechas*, has many sub-species including the illustrated *L. s. pedunculata* in which several of the bracts elongate into a colourful petal form.

Lavatera olbia. Tree Lavatera.
Portugal, Sicily

Lavatera

(la-va-**teer**-ə)   ☼ C T
Tree Lavatera
Spr-Sum; 3–6 ft/1–2 m; open; evergreen

MALVACEAE

Mediterranean look-alike cousins to the Hibiscus of the southern hemisphere, the *Lavateras* are mostly annuals or perennials. But in the several shrub species, the likeness to Hibiscus is startling.

L. olbia is a particularly showy plant, native to the western Mediterranean from Portugal to Sicily. It is grown from seed or cuttings and grows fast, although its lifespan is not very long.

The lobed, elongated leaves are softly hairy, the mauve flowers have notched tips and a striped effect on the petals. They are borne singly in the leaf axils. Plants prefer full sun and are ideal for seaside gardens if protected from strong winds.

Lawsonia

(lor-**soh**-nee-ə)   ☼ T W H
Henna, Mignonette Tree
All year; to 13 ft/4 m; loose; evergreen

LYTHRACEAE   FRAGRANT

Cultivated commercially in Asia for the long-lasting orange dye extracted from its crushed leaves, the Henna plant will always be associated with the popular 'flaming twenties' hair tint. Actually it is more commonly used in India to stain the palms and soles of Hindu women.

A most variable shrub, Henna (known botanically as *Lawsonia*

Lawsonia inermis. Henna, Mignonette Tree.
Africa, Asia, Australia

inermis) may range in height from the usual 13 ft/4 m to double that, and is native to a wide tropical range from northern Africa right through southern Asia. It grows readily from seed or cuttings and seems not particularly fussy about soil.

The habit of growth is loose with frequently-branching grey twigs covered in fine grey-green foliage. The stems are spiny and the tiny rose-pink flowers appear in terminal panicles. In the cultivars 'Alba' and 'Rubra' they are white and red respectively. Not the most exciting of shrubs horticulturally, but its silver foliage makes a nice contrast in a mixed planting of shrubs, and the flowers produce a delicious, pervasive perfume.

Lechenaultia CV 'Sunrise'.
Hybrid Lechenaultia.

Lechenaultia

(lesh-en-**orl**-tee-ə)   ☼ ✸ C T W
Lechenaultia
Spring; 1–3 ft/30–90 cm; prostrate; evergreen

GOODENIACEAE

Generally so low-growing they can scarcely be thought of as shrubs at all, West Australia's gorgeous *Lechenaultias* are more accurately described as sub-shrubby and turn on a dazzling spring display wherever con-

Lechenaultia formosa. Beautiful Lechenaultia. Western Australia

Of around a dozen species, the most popular include *L. formosa*, ranging from 2–12 in/5–30 cm in height, generally with open scarlet blooms, though there are cultivars in orange, yellow and rose-pink as well. Illustrated CV 'Sunrise' is very popular. *L. biloba* may vary from 6–20 in/ 15–50 cm in height, often with a straggling habit, and has open flowers in many shades of blue, including some of the most intense colours known.

In cultivation, *Lechenaultias* are not long-lived, and regular replacement from cuttings is advised. Though found in naturally sunbaked positions, they will cope with a little light shade.

Lechenaultia formosa 'Orange'.
Orange Lechenaultia. Western Australia

ditions suit them. They'll accept most climatic variations from cool to warm temperate, but demand drainage that's top quality. This is best achieved by planting in a raised rockery bed (or even a container) of soil that is sandy or gravelly with a degree of acidity.

They may be propagated from firm-tip cuttings or divisions at any time in mild-winter areas; English enthusiasts confine their propagation to the warmer months, using a sand-peat mixture.

Though American garden books make no mention of them, *Lechenaultias* would seem to be ideal subjects in California, where the climate brings out the best in so many West Australian natives.

Lechenaultia biloba. Blue Lechenaultia. Western Australia

Lechenaultia floribunda. White Lechenaultia. Western Australia

X *Ledendron*

(lee-**den**-dron)   ☼ ☼ C T
Ledendron
Spring; 3 ft/1 m; open; evergreen

ERICACEAE   FRAGRANT

The genus Ledum (see next entry) is sufficiently closely related to the Rhododendrons to have allowed hybridists the possibility of creating a bigeneric cross of great beauty—and one that can be grown through a much wider climate range than either of its parents. Using cold-loving Ledum groenlandicum as the pollen parent,

X *Ledendron* 'Arctic Tern'. Bigeneric Hybrid

and Rhododendron trichostomum from Yunnan as the female parent, we now have a charming shrub that nature never intended.

It is called X *Ledendron* 'Arctic Tern', and growing a little taller than the male parent, it has tiny, narrow leaves, and 1 in/2 cm rose to white spring flowers. Acid soil is necessary, preferably a mixture of sand and peat, but with good drainage. Propagation of course must be from cuttings or layers, since the plant is sterile. It has not been around long enough to acquire a popular name.

Ledum

(**lee**-dəm)   ☼ C T
Labrador Tea, Hudson's Bay Tea
Spring; 3 ft/1 m; dense; evergreen
ERICACEAE

Not widely seen in nature or cultivation, the *Ledums* are a small genus of evergreen shrubs native to Arctic areas of Eurasia and North America. The illustrated *L. groenlandicum* may even be the only plant from Greenland that is grown elsewhere in the

world. Rarely reaching 3 ft/1 m in height, and commonly half that, it is a small-leafed evergreen shrub that thrives in moist, peaty soil of cold climates, and is propagated from seed, layers or division.

The dainty late spring flowers are snowy white, appear in terminal clusters on rusty stems. Though the plant prefers an open site, shade from morning sun will prevent discoloration of the blooms. The leaves were brewed into a mild-tasting tea during America's revolutionary days.

Ledum groenlandicum. Labrador Tea. Arctic

Leea coccinea. West Indian Holly. Burma

Leea

(**lee**-ə)   ☼ ● T W H
West Indian Holly,
Hawaiian Holly
All year; 8 ft/2.5 m; open; evergreen
LEEACEAE

Popular as indoor plant novelties the last few years, several species of *Leea* give splendid displays where the garden is subtropical or warmer. There, as their popular name suggests, they take the place of cold-

Leea sambucina. Tropical Holly.
Tropical Asia, Western Australia

climate hollies (see Ilex) with shining foliage and clusters of red berries in the cooler weather. The leaves in most species are compound, each leaf-stem branching into a number of leaflets.

Most common and popular is *L. coccinea*, often called West Indian or Hawaiian Holly (though it is in fact from Burma!). It may grow to almost 10 ft/3 m but will begin to flower when only a fraction of that size. In the tropics it grows fast in dappled shade, though morning sun is acceptable. Leaflets are to 4 in/10 cm long, the small flowers rose red to pink in a flat-topped cyme, followed by dark red berries. A purple-foliaged cultivar is sometimes seen.

Related *L. amabilis* from Borneo has leaflets striped white, or, in its CV 'Splendens', with red.

Leea is easily propagated from seed or cuttings, grows best in rich loam, with regular water in warm weather.

Leiophyllum
(*syn.* LEDUM, DENDRIUM)

(**lae**-oh-fil-ləm)   ☼ T
Sand Myrtle, Box Sand Myrtle
Spring; 1½ ft/45 cm; compact; evergreen

ERICACEAE   FRAGRANT

Leaves like a Buxus, flowers like a small Rhododendron, could easily be a myrtle . . . what shall we call it? said one botanist. Let's make up a new name, said another. And so this dainty plant finished up as *Leio-*

Leiophyllum buxifolium. Sand Myrtle.
E. North America

phyllum—the only species in a very small genus, though at one time it looked as if there'd be others. But the new species from Kentucky, North and South Carolina, Georgia and Tennessee turned out to be only localized varieties of the original.

All the varieties of *Leiophyllum* grow well in a sandy, acid loam and can be raised from seed, cuttings or layers. Growing into neat, compact, bun-shapes, *Leiophyllums* make ideal rockery subjects. Individual glossy leaves are ¼ in/5 mm long, individual flowers the same in diameter. They are 5-petalled, white shading to pink at petal tips, and borne in terminal clusters about 1 in/3 cm in diameter. They are only mildly fragrant and enjoy constant moisture.

Leonotis
(*syn.* PHLOMIS)

(lee-on-**oh**-tis)   ☼ T W
Lion's Ear, Lion's Tail,
Dagga
All year; 7 ft/2 m; erect; can be deciduous

LAMIACEAE

Leonotis, a small genus from Africa, consists mainly of annuals and perennials, but one shrub species, *L. leonurus*, is popular throughout the temperate world due to its spectacu-

Leonotis leonurus 'Albiflora' White Dagga. S. Africa

lar appearance. Tall and striking (if kept well groomed) it sends up 7 ft/ 2 m flowering stems decked with regularly-spaced whorls (or layers) of velvety orange or white flowers. This process will continue throughout the warm months.

Plant *Leonotis* in a warm, sunny, well-drained position with good quality soil, and do not overwater. It is fairly drought resistant except in very hot weather. Growing tips may be damaged by prolonged frosts, but the plant will generally recover quickly, for it is quite hardy down to 29°F/ −2°C. You can grow it from seed, divisions or semi-hardwood tip cuttings struck under glass in winter.

Lepechinia
(*syn.* SPHACELE)

(lep-e-**shin**-ee-yə)   ☼ T W
Pitcher Sage
Spring; 4 ft/1 m; upright; evergreen

LAMIACEAE

All very similar in appearance, differing in minor details of interest to a taxonomist, the 40 species of *Lepechinia* are native to limited areas from California to Argentina and also in parts of Hawaii.

So far as their leaves and stems are

Leonotis leonurus. Lion's Ear. S. Africa

Lepechinia hastata. Pitcher Sage. Mexico

concerned, they are typical members of the mint family, with oblong-lanceolate leaves and stems rather squarish in section. The flowers are another matter, quite showy in the mass though arranged in tall racemes enclosed in a pair of leaf-like bracts. The individual flowers of *L. hastata* are a deep crimson-pink with striped throat and prominent white-tipped stamens. The whole is set in a 5-lobed, trumpet-shaped calyx.

Grow them from seed or cuttings. They do best in an open, sunny position in light, well-drained, leaf-rich soil. Other species bloom in white or pale pink.

Leptodactylon
(*syn.* LINANTHUS)

(lep-toh-**dak**-til-ən)   ☼Ⓦ
Prickly Phlox
Win-Sum; 3–4 ft/1 m; stiff; evergreen

POLEMONIACEAE

I guess I must have gone looking for Prickly Phlox in late summer, but there was certainly no sign of life. Now, of course, I know that the shrub takes an annual rest about that time, turning very brown and shabby. Otherwise, it is most floriferous, producing handsome, silky 1½ in/4 cm blooms from late winter till early summer.

Leptodactylon californicum is grown

from seed or spring cuttings, turning on a magnificent display in poor, gravelly soil or where water drains. It needs moisture just before bloom and more attention with the hose during drought.

It is a stiff, dense plant with woody stems and spine-tipped, prickly leaves. The lovely blooms are mauve-pink or rarely white; other species bloom in yellow, pink and cream.

Leptodactylon californicum. Prickly Phlox. California

Leptospermum lanigera X *macrocarpum*. Woolly Tea Tree. S.E. Australia, Tasmania

Leptospermum petersonii. Lemon-scented Tea Tree. E. Australia

Mildred Matthias/Wittman

Leptospermum

(lep-toh-**spur**-məm)   ☼ⓉⓌⒽ
Tea Tree, Manuka, Moonah
All year; 5–10 ft/1.5–3 m; arching; evergreen

MYRTACEAE   FRAGRANT

Because so many showy species of *Leptospermum* hail from south-eastern Australia, Tasmania and New Zealand, they are very suited to the cool-temperate gardens of Europe and America. Some species are better known there than in their home countries and many hybrids and cultivars were first developed in the northern hemisphere. The whole genus has been blessed internationally with the popular name of Tea Tree since Captain James Cook brewed a beverage from the tiny leaves of one New Zealand species to protect his crew from scurvy. *Leptospermum*, then, are now deservedly treasured all over the temperate world for their graceful habit and soft, casual appearance that makes

Leptospermum laevigatum. Moonah, Coastal Tea Tree. S.E. Australia

Leptospermum flavescens 'Pacific Beauty'. Tantoon Tea Tree. N.E. Australia

them ideal subjects for the informal landscape garden.

Grown in full sun, they resist drought, wind and even salt spray. In spring, all make a profuse display of small white, pink or red flowers, quite like peach blossom.

Propagate them from half-ripe cut-tings struck in summer in a moist sandy mix. None of the species like root disturbance, so they should be planted out when small. L. flavescens is a more tropical species and its cultivar 'Pacific Beauty' is successful in subtropical gardens.

Leptospermum nitidum. Glossy Tea Tree Tasmania, Victoria

Leptospermum scoparium 'Red Damask'. Manuka. Hybrid

Lespedeza

(less-pə-**dez**-ə)   ☼ ☀ T W
Bush Clover
Sum-Aut; 10 ft/3 m; erect; evergreen

FABACEAE

Mainly frost-hardy plants from Japan, China and Korea, the 100-odd species of *Lespedeza* have become popular garden subjects all over the cool-temperate world where their arching branches of mauve and purple pea flowers make a gorgeous display in the summer sunlight.

Easily grown from seed or divisions, they should be kept moist throughout the growing period but not when they are dormant in winter, for it is then the entire bush will die back almost to the roots, at least in cold climates. Where winters are mild, a certain amount of growth will remain.

Lespedezas bear their leaves alternately, each consisting of three leaflets, paler on their reverses, and just like the clover from which they inherit a popular name. Where *Lespedezas* do die back, they never attain the size for which they are noted in temperate climates.

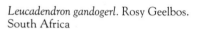

Pamela Harper

Lespedeza bicolor. Bush Clover.
China, Japan

Leucadendron argenteum. Silverbush.
South Africa

The actual flowers are unspectacular, male and female being borne on separate plants. Male flowers are a mass of stamens; the female ones are woody cones. Both are surrounded by modified leaves called bracts which persist for many months and can be attractively coloured, especially in winter and spring. Propagate from seed in autumn or late winter and replace plants after about five years when they become woody and unsightly. Though normally evergreen, a proportion of leaves will turn gold or crimson in late winter.

Leucadendron gandogerl. Rosy Geelbos.
South Africa

Leucadendron

(loo-kə-**den**-drən) ☼ T W
Gold-tips, Geelbos,
Silwerboom
Winter; 3–13 ft/1–4 m; decorative foliage; evergreen

PROTEACEAE

South Africa's 70-odd species of *Leucadendron* are remarkably decorative shrubs, but suffer by comparison to their more spectacularly floriferous

cousins, the Proteas. In Protea, the flower is all-important. In the case of *Leucadendron*, the foliage is decorative as well—stiff, upward-pointing leaves which may be smooth or silky and are sometimes coloured silver, gold or pink as well as green.

They demand acid, well-drained, leaf-rich soil, a sunny, hillside position and a thick layer of mulch that does not contain manure. Humidity keeps the plants thriving and they'll happily accept ocean breezes.

Leucadendron sessile. Geelbos.
South Africa

Leucophyllum

(**loo**-koh-fil-ləm) ☼ T W H
Barometer Bush, Ceniza,
Texas Ranger, Purple Sage
Summer; 3–7 ft/1–2 m; compact; can be semi-deciduous

SCROPHULARIACEAE

This really exquisite genus of three species is tied to the weather in many areas. Native to Texas and Mexico, they will survive down to 10°F/

Leucophyllum minus. Barometer Bush.
Texas, Mexico

−12°C but need high heat to bloom well. The more humid it is (after rain for instance) the more it flowers—hence the name Barometer Bush. It is a magnificent sight in Thailand—now that's humidity for you!

Grow them from seed, grow them from cuttings, they will push ahead in any soil, even alkaline if it is well-drained. The silvery stems and foliage are very heat resistant and contrast magnificently with the vivid, fox-glove-like flowers with spotted throats. Low-growing *L. minus* blooms in a rich violet, *L. frutescens* (a larger plant) produces rosy-purple flowers.

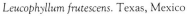

Leucophyllum frutescens. Texas, Mexico

Leucospermum

(loo-koh-**spur**-mom)   ☼ Ⓣ Ⓦ
Pincushion, Speldekussing,
Flamespike
Spring; 5–13 ft/1.5–4 m; spreading; evergreen

PROTEACEAE

Many of South Africa's 30-odd species of *Leucospermum* have been raised successfully in the open air of

Leucospermum cordifolium. Speldekussing.
S.W. South Africa

Leucospermum reflexum. Rocket Pincushion.
South Africa

Leucospermum tottum. Firewheel Pincushion. South Africa

Leucospermum nutans. Nodding Pincushion. South Africa

the western United States, Australia, Britain's Scilly Isles and other warm-temperate areas. They are strikingly handsome in both flower and foliage and enjoy a soil that is light and fast-draining, enriched with leafmould but not animal manure. 22°F/–5°C is a safe low temperature for mature shrubs but young plants will need frost protection.

L. reflexum, the Rocket Pin-cushion, has unusual soft-grey leaves which make a stunning contrast to the dazzling red flowers. It blooms from mid-winter into spring but needs an area of at least 10 × 10 ft/ 3 × 3 m. The Firewheel Pincushion, *L. tottum,* flowers from mid-spring to late summer. It is much more com-pact, being just 3 ft/1 m tall and about the same across. The Nodding Pincushion, *L. nutans,* has dark green leaves with silver reverses, and flowers that are almost crimson. *L. cordifolium* makes a neat, symmetrical mass up to 5 ft/1.5 m in height and twice that across. For months it is almost hidden beneath a mass of globular, pincushion flowers up to 4 in/10 cm across.

Leucothöe
(*syn.* ANDROMEDA)

(loo-koh-**thoh**-ee)   ☼ C T
Dog-hobble, Fetterbush,
Switch Ivy
Spring; 7 ft/2 m; arching; evergreen

ERICACEAE   FRAGRANT

A close relationship with the god Apollo was likely to have a hazard-ous outcome. The nymph Daphne took root and became a shrub; while Leucothöe, daughter of the King of Babylonia, was buried alive by her father, whereupon that same Apollo metamorphosed her into a growing perfume factory.

There are some 50 species, mostly from North American woodlands, but others are native to Asia, South America and Madagascar. Most are evergreen with strongly reflexed leaves and showy racemes of lily-of-the-valley type flowers suspended on arching stems. These look sensational in large arrangements.

Grow them from semi-hardwood tip cuttings taken in late spring and struck over heat, or from spring-sown seeds.

Leucothöe likes a moist, humus-rich, acid soil, regular summer water and part-shade; even the evergreen types colour well in autumn. Hardy down to 18°F/ − 8°C, *L. fontanesiana* from Georgia and Tennessee grows into a rounded shrub about 7 ft/2 m tall but slightly wider. Flowers appear during late spring.

Leucothöe fontanesiana. Dog-hobble. Virginia, Tennessee

Leycesteria

(less-(ess)-**tear**-ee-ə) ☼ ☀ C T
Himalaya Honeysuckle
Sum-Aut; 7–10 ft/2–3 m; erect; deciduous

CAPRIFOLIACEAE FRAGRANT

Not very much like a real honeysuckle (Lonicera spp.), the two species of *Leycesteria* are nevertheless closely related, and above all, fragrant.

They enjoy a moderately rich, well-drained soil with high humidity and are hardy down to 23°F/ − 5°C in a sheltered position. In appropriate, woodsy locations, they send up closely packed, arching stems, rather like bamboo, but decked with hanging spikes of claret-bracted white flowers. These are lightly perfumed and followed by purplish, many-seeded fruits that are attractive to birds. The lightly toothed leaves, covered with fine hairs when young, colour well in the autumn.

Leycesteria should be propagated from 8 in/20 cm hardwood cuttings which are grown on for 12 months before autumn planting. Cut out some of the flowered canes in early spring.

Leycesteria formosa.
Himalayan Honeysuckle. Himalayas

Lhotzkya

(**lotz**-kee-ə) ☼ ☀ T W
Mountain Heather
Spring; 1½–2 ft/50–60 cm; dense; evergreen

MYRTACEAE

Closely resembling Calytrix (which see), the Australian genus *Lhotzkya* includes some 8 species of heath-like plants, all found in Western Australia, some in other states as well.

Typical *L. acutifolia* sends up hairy, slender, erect shoots crowded with

Lhotzkya alpestris. Mountain Heath. Victoria, Western Australia

Murray Fagg

heath-like needle leaves less than ½ in/1 cm in length. These are borne almost parallel to the stem, and between them, in spring, appear slender white flower buds which open rapidly to form a cylindrical cluster of starry white 5-petalled flowers.

Lhotzkya is propagated from cuttings struck in damp sand. The growing plants enjoy a compost of loam, peat and sand.

Ligustrum lucidum 'Excelsum Superbum'. Variegated Chinese Privet. China, Korea

Ligustrum

(li-**gus**-trəm) ☼ ☀ C T W
Privet
Summer; 10–20 ft/3–6 m; rounded; evergreen or deciduous

OLEACEAE ACRID

After publishing several earlier books, I received plaintive queries from readers who wondered why I had omitted to include the Privets. Now whether this was seriously a favourite plant or whether they were just interested in the name, I cannot imagine. But I had a reason for my omission. I do not greatly care for Privets myself, having once spent a year or so hauling them out of a neglected garden to which I had moved. The trunks were like cast iron, the roots like a struggling boa-constrictor with a grip on everything

Ligustrum japonicum. Wax-leaf Privet. Japan, Korea

in sight. And for years afterwards, my every gardening effort was thwarted by a crop of tiny new plants from long-discarded berries.

There are small and large-leafed Privets but their flowers are much the same whatever the species—small, creamy-white, in dense clusters, with a rather sickly smell. Pictured *L. japonicum* is popular in California as a fast-growing hedge plant under the unlikely name of *L. texanum*. It may reach 7 ft/2 m in a few years. I will concede that several variegated leaf cultivars are acceptable screening

Ligustrum ovalifolium CV 'Aureum'. Golden California Privet. Japan

plants. But please, prune away any green shoots promptly and chop off those berries and dispose of them before the birds begin to eat (and thus spread) them.

Lindera
(*syn.* BENZOIN)

(**lin**-dur-ə)   ☼ Ⓒ Ⓣ Ⓦ
Spice-bush, Benjamin Bush
Spring; 6–15 ft/2–4.5 m; bun-shaped; deciduous

LAURACEAE   AROMATIC

An inhabitant of damp, woodland areas right down the east coast of North America from Ontario and Maine to Florida and Texas, the Benjamin Bush has many hidden charms. From a bare tangle of winter branches appear, first, 6-petalled yellow-green flowers, then pleasantly aromatic, obovate leaves, rich with balsam. Showy ½ in/1 cm scarlet or yellow berries come in summer and, finally, gorgeous autumn colour. *L. benzoin* is only one of 100 species, the others native mainly to south and east Asia.

Propagate from cuttings, layers or ripe seeds and grow in leaf-rich, acid soil that is both moist and well-drained.

But why Benjamin Bush, you ask? Apparently a misspelling of Benzoin, which was the name of all the early Asiatic *Linderas*, or in Javanese, Banjawi.

Lindera benzoin. Benjamin Bush. USA, Maine to Texas

Linum arboreum. Shrub Flax. Crete

Linum

(**lai**-nəm)   ☼ Ⓣ Ⓦ
Flax, Shrub Flax
Spring; 12 in/30 cm; compact; evergreen

LINACEAE

A delightful dwarf shrub for rock garden work, *Linum arboreum* is from Crete, where it grows on well-drained, rocky hillsides. Seed should be sown in early spring or cuttings taken at the same time for propagation.

The dwarf Shrub Flax grows fast but is relatively short-lived. Forming a compact mound, it develops small, alternate leaves, almost triangular in shape, and in late spring is literally covered with pale yellow flowers in the typical flax shape. These are 1½ in/3 cm in diameter in few-flowered cymes. It is not a plant for cold climates and not at all frost hardy.

Lithodora
(*syn.* LITHOSPERMUM, BATSCHIA)

(lith-oh-**dor**-ə)   ☼ ☀ Ⓣ Ⓦ
Heavenly Blue, Puccoon, Gromwell
Spr-Sum; 6–12 in/15–30 cm; prostrate; evergreen

BORAGINACEAE

Like the related herbal Borage, *Lithodora diffusa* blooms in blue—but what a blue! No more intense colour

Lithodora diffusa. Heavenly Blue, Gromwell. Morocco, S.W. Europe

large ones, too, I believe, though I've only seen pictures of them. They grow high on the slopes of Mt Kilimanjaro (right on the equator) and on the mountain tops of the big island of Hawaii.

The principal shrub variety is illustrated *L. laxiflora* or Torch Lobelia. It is a woody plant growing around 3 ft/1 m high and more, that tends to act like a herbaceous perennial in cool climates, where it dies back, to be replaced by suckers the following spring. In the warmer areas in which it feels at home, it remains woody, sending up stunning spikes of tubular red and yellow flowers on arching canes. In warm-temperate and subtropical climates, it will form dense clumps. Propagate from seed or divisions, grow in deep, rich soil with plenty of water.

Chilean *Lomatia ferruginea* has its young shoots covered with a rust-coloured down; its leaves are doubly and trebly divided and it bears axillary racemes of deep rose and golden flowers. It is grown in England. Australian *L. silaifolia* bears similar leaves, tripinnately divided, but the white flowers are more recognizably those of the Protea family. They are borne in loose racemes.

Lomatias are easy to propagate from seed or cuttings; they like sandy but leaf-rich soil in a well-drained position.

Lomatia silaifolia. Crinkle-bush. S.E. Australia

is found in nature than the flowers of many *Lithodora* species, though there are white and yellow varieties as well in these attractive rock plants. Some species are perennial, some subshrubs, but the illustrated *L. diffusa* is a true shrub, if a dwarf one and, like most of the other *Lithodoras*, can't abide lime in any form.

L. diffusa is a 6–12 in/15–30 cm, spindly sort of plant and in cool-temperate, mountain gardens, it makes a stunning ground or rock cover in contrast with white Arabis and golden Aurinia. Seeming to reflect the intense blue of mountain skies, it likes full sun except in hot areas, demands fast drainage and light watering, even in summer.

Grow from cuttings of last year's growth struck in shade in a mix of peat and sand. Shear after bloom to keep compact and promote a dense display the following year.

Lobelia laxiflora. Torch Lobelia. Argentina to Colombia

Lobelia

(loh-**beel**-yə)   ☼ T W
Torch Lobelia
Summer; 3 ft/1 m; shrubby; evergreen

LOBELIACEAE

Those gardeners familiar only with the dainty, blue Edging Lobelia are about to receive a bit of a shock, for this remarkable family goes all the way from annuals, through perennials and shrubs to trees—and very

Lomatia

(loh-**mae**-tee-ə)   ☼ ☀ T W
Crinkle-bush
Summer; 5–8 ft/1.5–2.5 m; stiff, erect; evergreen

PROTEACEAE

Here's another of those plant genera that point to an ancient, trans-Pacific continent. The *Lomatias* (12 of them) are almost equally divided between Australia and Chile. One day, some fossil remains will be discovered in Antarctica and the whole question will be simply answered.

Lomatia ferruginea. Rust-bush. Chile

Lonicera

(lon-**iss**-ur-ə)   ☼ ◑ T W
Honeysuckle, Woodbine
*Spring; 6–14 ft/2–4.5 m; many-trunked;
deciduous*

CAPRIFOLIACEAE   FRAGRANT

Gardeners in warm-temperate climates or even hotter, think of Honeysuckles as climbing plants with scented, honey-rich flowers, twining evergreen stems and leaves which make useful cover for sheds and pergolas. We grow them from cuttings or layers taken in late summer. They are rampant plants and should be used only where there's plenty of room. This applies particularly to *L. hildebrandiana*, the Burmese Honeysuckle, a giant shrub for frost-free gardens only, with stems as thick as your arm and 6 in/15 cm tubular flowers of rich cream changing to orange. Its perfume is almost overpowering. Of more manageable size are yellow and red *L. japonica* 'Halliana', pink and cream *L. periclymenum*, the Woodbine, and scarlet *L. sempervirens*, the Coral Honeysuckle.

But in gardens of Europe and North America, you are just as likely to see a group of shrubby Honeysuckles that don't climb at all. These include the Tartar Honeysuckle, with flowers in various shades of pink followed by scarlet fruit. American Twinberry has pinkish-yellow flowers and twin purple-black berries. It is found from Alaska to Quebec and down to Mexico. The most fragrant species of all is the Chinese *L. fragrantissima* or Wintersweet, with

Lonicera hildebrandiana. Giant Burmese Honeysuckle. Burma

Lonicera involucrata. Twinberry. Alaska to Mexico

Lonicera sempervirens. Coral Honeysuckle. USA, Connecticut to Texas

Lonicera periclymenum serotina. Woodbine. Europe, N. Africa, W. Asia

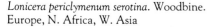

Lonicera fragrantissima. Wintersweet. China

Lonicera tatarica. Tartar Honeysuckle (fruit). Russia

Lonicera tatarica 'Arnold Red'. Tartar Honeysuckle. Russia, Turkestan.

arching stems flowering on the bare wood.

These shrubby Honeysuckles should be grown from summer or autumn cuttings struck in sharp sand. They call for a rich but well-drained soil and should be pruned annually, taking back half the new season's growth.

Species with a caning habit, such as *L. fragrantissima*, will be improved by the complete removal of some canes each year. Interestingly, the shrubby Honeysuckles are almost exclusively deciduous.

Finally, there is the small-foliaged Box-leaf Honeysuckle, *L. nitida*. This is evergreen but with a display of bronze to plum coloured foliage in winter. Its cream flowers are small and scentless, the fruit amethyst.

Loropetalum

(lor-oh-**pet**-ə-lum) ☼ C T W
Fringe-flower, Strap-flower, Chinese Witchhazel
Spring; 7 ft/2 m; many-branched; evergreen

HAMAMELIDACEAE   FRAGRANT

On a visit to Japan some years ago, I was almost shocked to see a *Loropetalum* growing to at least 23 ft/7 m tall in Tokyo Botanic Gardens. Shocked, because for years I'd been advising people to use it as the dwarf rockery shrub I believed it to be. Now we understand one another and it looks most elegant in my garden as a series of dark, woody trunks topped with clouds of dainty foliage and, in spring, masses of fragrant cream blooms with strap-like petals. These resemble the flowers of Hamamelis with which it is often confused.

Loropetalum is best grown from semi-hardwood cuttings taken in winter or summer and struck with bottom heat. Plant in a moderately rich soil and keep the roots moist. Hardy down to at least 27°F/–3°C, it needs little pruning except to remove twiggy growth. Keep its natural shape in mind when pruning.

Loropetalum chinense. Fringe-flower. E. Asia

Luculia gratissima. Luculi Swa. Himalayas

Luculia grandifolia. Bhutan Luculia. Bhutan

most common and can be grown from seed or tip cuttings struck in spring or summer in individual pots. Cut it back heavily after bloom and tip prune the new growth to shape.

L. grandiflora from Bhutan grows a little larger with leaves up to 15 in/40 cm long, often with a reddish tone. The flowers are white with a cylindrical tube up to 3 in/8 cm long.

Both these *Luculias* (and presumably their three cousins) are among the most beautiful and fragrant of flowers. It seems only fair they go to so much trouble choosing the lucky gardeners.

Lupinus

(loo-**pee**-nəs or loo-**pai**-nəs)   ☼ Ⓦ
Bush Lupine
Spring; 4 ft/1 m; bun-shaped; evergreen

FABACEAE

Lupines are one of the most widespread of plant genera in the world. Some 300 species, they are found in both the west and east of North America, in South America and the Mediterranean. The most commonly grown are annual and perennial species, several of which were known by their present name to the ancient Romans, who called them after *lupus*, the wolf, as they were believed to ravage the garden soil. Now we know the opposite is true and crops of

Lupinus albifrons. Bush Lupine. California

Luculia

(loo-**kool**-ee-ə)   ☼ ☀ Ⓣ Ⓦ
Luculia, Luculi Swa
Autumn; 10–13 ft/3–4 m; tree-like; semi-deciduous

RUBIACEAE   FRAGRANT

I am never likely to see a forest of *Luculia*, but I am told they grow that way in the far west of China and the Himalayas. What a wonderful sight it must be in autumn, particularly as so

many of us have trouble in getting them to grow at all. There are a million reasons, a million excuses. It likes morning sun—or is it afternoon sun? It likes warmth and humidity, but its roots must be cool at all times and left undisturbed. The colder the winter, the drier it should stay. It may be hardy down to 27°F/–3°C, but should be protected from frost with a root cover of deep, organic mulch.

L. gratissima (one of 5 species) is the

annual Lupines are often grown to be dug in so they can enrich the soil with precious nitrogen.

One of the most interesting species, from the California region, is a shrub, *Lupinus albifrons*, which occurs in sandy or rocky locales. It can be cultivated from seed or division and, even when planted in full sun in a poor soil, it needs little water. It grows into a bun-shaped shrub, heavily branched and massed with silky grey, palmately compound leaves. The typical pea flowers, a striking mauve-blue, appear in terminal racemes. They can be cut for arrangements.

Lycium

(**lai**-see-əm)   ☼ ☀ T W H
Box Thorn
Spring; 8 ft/2.5 m; rambling; deciduous
SOLANACEAE

A most interesting genus of rambling shrubs, rather like a blackberry in habit, the Box Thorns or *Lyciums* are sometimes known as Matrimony Vines, though they sprawl rather than climb. Many of them are good seaside plants, originating in coastal areas of North and South Africa, the Mediterranean, Asia, Chile, Argentina and the United States. Most species are fairly hardy and train well on walls or trellises in a sunny position.

Propagation is from seed or suckers and most *Lycium* species seem to enjoy any soil so long as it is well drained. *L. halimifolium*, most commonly seen, originated in the Balkans and western Asia. Its deciduous branches may arch 10 ft/3 m in any direction. The ½ in/1 cm flowers, similar to those of related Solanum, appear 1–4 to a node and are followed by ¾ in/2 cm scarlet fruit hanging on long stems. The grey-green leaves are deciduous.

Lyonia lucida. Tetterbush. Florida, Louisiana

Lycium halimifolium. Box Thorn. S.E. Europe, W. Asia

Lyonia

(*syn.* PIERIS, ANDROMEDA, DESMOTHAMNUS)

(lai-**oh**-nee-ə)   ☼ ☀ T W H
Tetterbush, Fetterbush
Spring; 6 ft/2 m; compact; evergreen
ERICACEAE

'Cultivate as for Leucothoë' says one of the great horticultural dictionaries. Well, let's give it a try, say I; it looks so like a Leucothoë it may as well be treated like one. Indeed, there is apparently some confusion, as other authorities have named it Pieris or Andromeda as well as half a dozen other generic names which are not included in this book.

You can grow it from cuttings or

divisions and it does best in a porous, sandy loam, a little on the acid side, something like its natural surroundings in low, warm-climate woodlands of the southern United States. It is not really hardy and requires constant moisture.

Lyonia lucida is evergreen with leathery, oblong leaves, borne alternately. Charming, lily-of-the-valley type flowers appear in axillary clusters in spring. They may be pink or white.

I wondered why it was known as a Tetterbush but my dictionary says a tetter is any one of a number of skin diseases such as eczema. So perhaps *Lyonia* has medicinal value as a palliative.

Lysiphyllum

(*syn.* BAUHINIA)

(**lai**-si-fil-ləm)   ☼ W H
Pegunny
Summer; 10–15 ft/3–4.5 m; treelike; deciduous
CAESALPINIACEAE

Lysiphyllum hookeri is catching the eye of more and more tourists who visit its native Queensland, where it blooms most heavily in late spring. In the tropical north of Australia, it is a showy, tree-size plant, reaching 33 ft/10 m in the wild—but the further away from the equator it is planted, the smaller it grows, often reaching only shrub size. Under those circum-

Lysiphyllum hookeri. Pegunny. N.E. Australia

stances, it also blooms later and turns from deciduous to evergreen.

The Pegunny enjoys full sun and heavy, moist soil. Very frost tender, it must be grown from scarified seed. New foliage is copper coloured, the white blossoms have showy, scarlet bracts.

Macaranga

(ma-ka-**ran**-gə)   ☼ ☀ W H
Macaranga
Spring; 6–20 ft/2–6 m; open; evergreen
EUPHORBIACEAE

Sometimes found to small tree size (20 ft/6 m), in South-east Asia, *Macaranga tanarius* is more usually found as a shrub in Australia, where it is regarded as one of the most handsome foliage plants in frost-free areas.

Only one of a genus of about 80 species in tropical Asia, it attracts with rather magnificent, heart-shaped leaves to 12 in/30 cm in diameter and with radiating veins. Individual flowers are insignificant but they make a stunning show with their long, twisting panicles.

Propagate *Macaranga* from seed or cuttings and always plant in leaf-rich soil with good drainage. It is not at all hardy, but makes a good shade plant given regular water.

The botanical name, *Macaranga*, is also a native popular name in parts of Malaysia.

Macaranga tanarius. Macaranga
S.E. Asia to N. Australia

Mackaya bella. Asystasia. South Africa

Mackaya

(*syn.* ASYSTASIA)

(ma-**kai**-ə)   ☼ ☼ ☀ W H
Asystasia
Summer; 7–10 ft/2–3 m; erect; evergreen
ACANTHACEAE

Sometimes seen in coastal or water-side gardens where there is reasonable humidity, *Mackaya bella* does best in the tropical garden where climatic conditions are really to its liking. It enjoys light though leaf-rich soil, and while it will take full sun in milder areas, the hotter the climate, the more shade it needs to maintain a rich blue-mauve colour in its flowers. Where light frosts might be expected, tree shelter is essential.

Propagate from semi-hardwood cuttings taken in summer and keep moist after the rooted plants are set out. Its growth is not fast, but ultimately *Mackaya* may reach 10 ft/ 3 m, though usually only half that at the limit of its range. The open bell flowers are quite spectacular against the shiny wavy-edged leaves. *Mackaya* needs protection from strong winds and is frost hardy down to 28°F/–2°C.

Magnolia

(mag-**nohl**-ee-ə)   ☼ ☼ C T W
Star Magnolia
Spring; 8 ft/2.5 m; densely branched; deciduous
MAGNOLIACEAE   FRAGRANT

Cultivated in Chinese gardens since time immemorial, *Magnolias* have been traced back in fossils for many thousands of years. Today, the tree species are the ultimate spring-flowering treasures in cool-climate gardens everywhere, while evergreen American species are seen in warmer areas like Italy and California.

Magnolia stellata 'Rosea'.
Pink Star Magnolia. Hybrid

In the shrub garden, options are fewer, limited to the dainty white Star Magnolia (M. *stellata*) and its hybrids in various shades of pink. Flowering on bare wood, M. *stellata* produces a profuse display of 3 in/ 8 cm blooms with strap-like petals. It is a lovely shrub by the front door, or in woodland gardens, rarely surpassing 8 ft/2.5 m in height, and that only after many years. Propagation is by grafting, and the shrub *Magnolias* are hardy down to 23°F/–5°C.

Magnolia stellata. Star Magnolia. Japan

Mahonia
(syn. BERBERIS)

(mah-**hoh**-nee-ə)   ☼ ❋ C T
Oregon Grape, Holly Grape,
Mountain Grape
*Spr-Sum; 5–13 ft/1.5–4 m; suckering;
evergreen*

BERBERIDACEAE   FRAGRANT

More than 100 different *Mahonia* species are found in North America and east Asia. Leaves of most are leathery and holly-like and in some the new foliage is highly coloured. The flowers, which sometimes open in late winter, are almost invariably yellow, and though tiny, make quite a display as they are borne in dense racemes or panicles.

Mahonias are useful plants in harsh conditions where they are often seen as dense hedges or windbreaks. Frosty or hot, moist or dry, sunny or shaded, any position seems to suit them; and the flowers are generally followed by blue-black berries that look like miniature grapes and make a good jelly.

Mahonias should be grown in full sun in cold areas, and in semi-shade

Mahonia lomariifolia. Fern-leaf Mahonia. China

Mahonia aquifolium. Holly Mahonia.
N.W. North America

Mahonia piperana. Oregon Grape. Oregon

Mahonia japonica. Japanese Barberry.
China, Japan

Mahonia nevinii. Long-leaf Mahonia.
S. California

Mahonia amplectans. Spine-leaf Grape.
N.W. America

where the temperatures are high. They enjoy rich, well-drained soil where they can sucker to their hearts' content. Most are propagated from rooted divisions, but they can also be struck from autumn cuttings in a cool, moist place. Old bushes may be rejuvenated by cutting selected shoots back to the ground. Species M. *nevinii* and M. *lomariifolia* are taller growing, to 13 ft/4 m. Other illustrated species rarely pass 7 ft/ 2 m. Californian M. *pumila* is a useful groundcover, rarely reaching 1 ft/ 25 cm.

The majority of *Mahonia* species are only faintly fragrant, and are hardy down to 14°F/–10°C.

Malacothamnus
(syn. MALVASTRUM, SPHAERALCEA)

(ma-lac-oh-**tham**-nəs)   ☼ ✳ T W
Chaparral Mallow
Spring; 6–7 ft/2 m; slender; erect; evergreen

MALVACEAE

This small genus of the mallow family, found in the coastal valleys of California and Mexico, greatly resembles its close relatives Malvastrum and Sphaeralcea and was classified with them at various times.

Malacothamnus fasciculatus. Chaparral Mallow. California, Mexico

While not hardy to severe winters, they manage to resist the average Californian frost with a minimum of leaf damage.

Propagate them from seed or cuttings with bottom heat, and plant out in dry, well-drained soil.

Malacothamnus leaves are multi-lobed and extraordinarily handsome. The 1¾ in/4 cm flowers are a rich red-mauve, elegantly shaped.

Malpighia coccigera. Singapore Holly. West Indies

Malpighia

(mal-**pidg**-ee-ə)   ☼ ✳ W H
Singapore Holly,
Miniature Holly
Summer; 3–6 ft/1–2 m; many-stemmed; evergreen

MALPIGHIACEAE

This fine example of botanical misnomenclature is a very worthwhile plant for the warm-climate garden. It is not a holly, nor from Singapore either, but it can be clipped into shape as a neat hedge or low mound. The leaves are small, sharp and spiny, the feathery flowers (which appear for most of the summer) are white to pink with a blur of golden stamens, and sometimes there are tiny red fruits to follow.

Malpighia coccigera (one of about 30 species) prefers well-drained, moderately rich soil that is kept continuously moist. It is a slow growing plant but regular feeding will speed it along into a dense mass of cane-like trunklets, 6 ft/2 m tall at most. These should be pruned to different heights if a good foliage cover is desired. Propagate from cuttings of almost-ripe shoots struck over heat.

Malus X *purpurea* 'Eleyi'. Eley's Purple Crab. Hybrid

Malus
(syn. PYRUS)

(**mal**-əs)   ☼ C T W
Crabapple, Apple
Spring; 10–20 ft/3–6 m; dense; deciduous

ROSACEAE   FRAGRANT

With all the problems facing the fruit grower these days, it's a lot easier to plant one of the many lovely varieties of flowering Crabapple, feed our souls on the beautiful spring blossom and pop out to the fruit shop later. Many of these Crabs have the advantage of being classed as shrubs and are of a handy size for the home garden.

One of the most elegant is the Sargent Crabapple, *Malus sargentii*, a many-trunked plant rarely 10 ft/3 m in height and with attractive zig-zag growth. It becomes quite bushy and is loaded down in spring with white

Malus sargentii. Sargent Crabapple. Japan

Pamela Harper

1 in/3 cm flowers and later, tiny ¼ in/5 mm fruits that are attractive to birds. Favourite Eley's Purple Crab can also be grown as a shrub with a little care; it has a short, single trunk and pendulous branches, resulting in a fountain effect. Leaves are bronzy in colour and the flowers of deep purple-pink appear in summer. *Malus,* the botanical name of both Apples and Crabs, is the original Roman name of a wild European species. The illustrated species are hardy down to 14°F/−10°C and are propagated from cuttings or seed.

Malvaviscus

(*syn.* ACHANIA)

(mal-va-**viss**-kəs)   ☼ ◐ W H
Turk's Cap, Cardinal's Hat,
Fire Dart Bush, Wax Mallow
Sum-Win; 7–10 ft/2–3 m; broad, bun-shaped; evergreen

MALVACEAE

If your Hibiscus bush seems to have lost the energy to open properly, make sure it's not a *Malvaviscus*

before you throw it out. These extra-ordinary South American plants bloom from early summer right through to winter in frost-free or sub-tropical climates. They are particularly showy where the humidity stays

Malvaviscus arboreus. Turk's Cap. Mexico to Brazil

high and the sun is lightly filtered. Then, they really do look like a red Hibiscus waiting for a green light.

Propagate them from semi-hardwood cuttings struck in winter or early spring in a warm, moist place, or layer from naturally low-growing branches tied down in winter and severed from the main plant when roots have formed, usually over a year later.

Enriched, sandy soil is best, so long as it can be kept well-drained, but *Malvaviscus* can also be raised in large containers. Flowers are not always scarlet—there is a pale pink variety.

Manihot

(**man**-i-hot)   ☼ ◐ H
Cassava, Manioc,
Tapioca, Yuca
Summer; 10 ft/3 m; erect; evergreen

EUPHORBIACEAE

Like many spectacular foliage plants, *Manihot* is tropical and, unless you

Manihot utilitissima 'Variegata'. Cassava, Yuca. South America

live in a very warm climate, must be raised in a glasshouse. The beautifully marked green and cream leaves with scarlet stems have made it popular but it is also an important crop. The poisonous sap becomes a useful antiseptic and the tuberous, edible roots are the basis of tapioca, cassava and starch. They do not keep well however, and should not be dug until immediately before use.

Propagate *Manihot* from 6 in/ 15 cm cuttings struck in sharp sand. Grow in a sandy, rich but well-drained soil. Continued moisture is the rule. Needless to say, it is not frost hardy and red spider mites seem to find it irresistible.

Medinilla

(med-in-**ill**-ə) ☀ Ⓦ Ⓗ
Javanese Rhododendron
Summer; 3 ft/1 m; epiphyte, evergreen

MELASTOMATACEAE

This superb shrub is said to live as an epiphyte in the jungles of the Philippines, but unless you live there or can afford a heated conservatory, you're unlikely to enjoy the showy blooms of this most gorgeous of tropical plants. For *Medinillas* are fussy growers and in winter demand a night temperature of at least 70°F/21°C if they're to do well. And as any one with a recent central heating bill can testify, winter temperatures like that don't come cheap.

M. *magnifica* is propagated from cuttings of half-ripened wood in spring. These are potted up in a mixture of sifted peat, sand and fine charcoal and kept in a heated glasshouse until they strike. *Medinilla* may be kept permanently in containers of moderate size but must be repotted regularly to freshen up the soil. Fertilize from time to time, water well, prune to shape after bloom and syringe with miticide to discourage red spider mite.

The fantastic pendent flower clusters appear in late spring and continue throughout summer. They combine strawberry-pink flowers and mauve-pink bracts with purple and yellow stamens.

Medinilla magnifica. Javanese Rhododendron. Philippines

Megaskepasma erythrochlamys. Megas, Brazilian Red-cloak. Venezuela

Megaskepasma

(meg-ə-skee-**paz**-mə)   ☼ ☀ Ⓦ Ⓗ
Brazilian Red-cloak, Megas
Autumn; to 10 ft/3 m; spreading;
evergreen

ACANTHACEAE

In the semi-shade of tropical gardens grow many different species of the Acanthus family, such as Aphelandra, Jacobinia, Pachystachys and Sanchezia—all popular house plants in recent years. But all of them together are not as spectacular as their tongue-twisting relative, *Megaskepasma erythrochlamys* (gasp!), sometimes known as the Brazilian Red-cloak, though in fact it comes from Venezuela.

Megaskepasma is without equal for mass display in the warm-climate garden. It enjoys a light, leaf-rich soil with regular water and fertilizer, and the showy panicles of crimson blooms appear in autumn in warm-temperate gardens, though much earlier in the tropics. Plants form spreading clumps of erect stems, each topped with crimson bracts. Snails seem particularly attracted to the leaves and quickly render them unsightly. *Megaskepasma* are easily increased from cuttings rooted in a warm, humid spot.

Melaleuca lateritia. Robin Redbreast.
Western Australia

Melaleuca

(mel-ə-**loo**-kə)   ☼ Ⓣ Ⓦ
Honeymyrtle, Bottlebrush,
Cajeput, Paperbark
Spring; 5–13 ft/1.5–4 m; woody;
evergreen

MYRTACEAE

One of Australia's most colourful genera, the Honeymyrtles or *Melaleucas* do, in fact, spread to New Guinea and Indo-Malaysia. They are also very well known in other countries, though not necessarily well thought of. A tree species, M. *quinquenervia*, is a proclaimed pest in Florida where it seems likely to clog up the famed Everglades, but in Hong Kong the same plant is regarded as the saviour of the New Territories' swamplands.

Melaleuca ericifolia. Swamp Paperbark.
E. Australia

The shrub species are simply magnificent, noted for their showy blossoms and decorative, peeling bark. All species are evergreen and provide a dense foliage cover or windbreak. They make do with only occasional water in dry times, need little or no fertilizer, and are not at all particular about soil, provided the drainage is reasonable—and even that isn't always essential.

Melaleuca bracteata. 'Revolution Gold'.
Hybrid

Melaleuca can be grown from seed sown in spring in light, peaty soil or from 2 in/5 cm semi-hardwood cuttings struck over heat from summer to mid-winter. The shown species have a sweet, honey scent and attract birds from far and near. They grow well by the coast where they often develop picturesque shapes, but probably their most proper use is sheared to a compact shape for a windbreak. In this form, their profusion of bloom is greatly stimulated.

M. *lateritia*, or Robin Redbreast,

Melaleuca violacea. Mauve Honeymyrtle.
Western Australia

Melaleuca incana. Silvery Bottlebrush.
Western Australia

Melaleuca hypericifolia.
Hedge Honeymyrtle. N.S.W.

usually grows to an open bush less than 10 ft/3 m tall. Its flowers are vivid. M. incana has grey foliage and yellow-green brushes of bloom. M. hypericifolia has leaves like Hypericum and feathery, brick-coloured flowers. M. fulgens has needle leaves and gold-tipped, cerise bottlebrushes. 'Revolution Gold' is a cultivar of white-flowered M. bracteata which is grown as a screen plant for its red-stemmed, golden foliage. M. ericifolia is a dainty, cream-flowered binder of swampy soil. Many other species have mauve, claw-like flowers.

Melastoma

(mel-a-**stoh**-mə)   ☼ ☀ W H
Pink Lasiandra, Blue-tongue,
Indian Rhododendron
Summer; 6 ft/2 m; large-leafed; evergreen

MELASTOMATACEAE

Found in most tropical areas except the Americas, where the Tibouchina genus does the same job better, the 40-odd species of *Melastoma* have a blooming season centring on summer in temperate climates. From this, the hotter it gets, the longer the period of bloom, and tropical gardeners can expect flowers most of the year.

The leaves are spear-shaped and leathery with strongly delineated, parallel veins. Open, 5-petalled flowers cluster at the ends of branches and may be pink, purple or (rarely) white. They are followed by edible blue-black berries that stain the mouth and have led to one of the plant's popular names.

Propagate all species from semi-hardwood cuttings struck in winter under warm, humid conditions. *Melastoma* grow quickly and should be pruned lightly to shape. Mature plants will reach 6 ft/2 m in height with a slightly smaller spread. They are not hardy at all.

Melastoma polyanthemum.
Blue-tongue, Pink Lasiandra. S.E. Asia

Menziesia

(men-**zees**-ee-ə)   ☀ C T
Mock Azalea, Mimic Bush
*Spr-Sum; 1½–2½ ft/40–70 cm; sparse;
hairy-leafed; deciduous*

ERICACEAE

Found naturally in Japan and nearby islands, *Menziesia* species are also known to occur in North America, from Alaska down into California. They are delightful small-size shrubs for the semi-shaded, woodsy, lime-

Melaleuca fulgens. Fiery Bottlebrush. Western Australia

Menziesia purpurea. Mock Azalea. Japan

Metrosideros carmineus. Akakura.
New Zealand

free garden. When not in bloom could be mistaken for related small Azaleas. But when the terminal flower clusters open in spring, the likeness disappears immediately, for the flowers are distinctly urn or bell-shaped.

Easily propagated from winter-sown seed, layers or 3 in/8 cm cuttings taken with a heel in summer, they have only two needs: humidity and perfect drainage. They are almost completely hardy, at least when planted under trees. Keep their roots continuously moist in warm weather and shop around for flower colours which include red, pink, cream and greenish-white according to species. Delightful in the sheltered rock garden.

Metrosideros kermadecensis. Variegated Pohutukawa. Kermadec Islands (Pacific)

Metrosideros

(met-roh-**sid**-ər-os) ☼ ❋ T W
Ironwood, Pohutukawa,
Rata, Ohi'a Lehua, Akakura
Sum-Aut; 6 ft/2 m; sprawling; evergreen

MYRTACEAE

The most splendid of the Pacific islands' myrtaceous genera, *Metrosid-*

eros excelsa (syn. M. *tomentosa*) is aptly called by the Maori people, Pohutukawa or 'sprinkled with spray' for its habit of clinging to sea-washed cliffs. In such a position it becomes a gnarled and picturesque shrub, but in deep soil or garden conditions it reveals its true nature as a tree. Other species, however, have the shrub habit.

Among these, M. *kermadecensis*,

the Kermadec Islands Pohutukawa, sold in a number of variegated leaf forms, makes an eye-catching specimen in full sun or against a background of darker foliage. It is, unfortunately, frost tender. The smaller Akakura, M. *carmineus*, makes a showy groundcover and seems to need to trail. It is sometimes seen as a climber in its native habitat but can be kept to a horizontal shrub with judicious pruning. It is hardy down to 21°F/−6°C. Less useful in coastal

Metrosideros collina. Ohi'a Lehua.
Hawaii, Tahiti

areas but at home in humid mountain districts is M. *collina*, the Ohi'a Lehua, found naturally high on the slopes of Tahiti and the Hawaiian Islands. Its olive green foliage is an effective foil for the vivid orange flowers. All *Metrosideros* grow from cuttings and like well-drained soil.

Michelia sp. Banana Shrub. S.W. China

cuttings taken in summer and autumn. Prune lightly all over after bloom to keep the plant dense and compact. This M. *figo* just loves a moderately rich soil that has good drainage, and it does well in containers. It needs heavy watering in summer and is hardy down to freezing point in winter.

Michelia figo. Port-wine Magnolia. S.W. China

Michelia

(mi-**shel**-ee-ə) ☼ ☀ T W
Banana Shrub,
Port-wine Magnolia
Spring; 10 ft/3 m; treelike; evergreen

MAGNOLIACEAE

There's a mystery at the bottom of our gardens, masquerading under the name of *Michelia figo* but at one time known as M. *fuscata*. Northern hemisphere books call it Banana Shrub, say it has small, flat, creamy yellow flowers smelling like ripe bananas. True! But in the southern hemisphere, we call it the Port-wine Magnolia. Its flowers never open wide, are the colour of a rich port wine on the outsides of the petals, and it does smell like port, not bananas! I believe they are two different species and that botanists have for once become confused in the matter of synonymy. M. *fuscata* and M. *figo*—but which is which?

Grow either from semi-hardwood

Microcitrus australasicus. Finger Lime. E. Australia

Microcitrus

(mai-kroh-**sit**-rəs) ☼ ☀ ☀ W H
Finger Lime,
Australian Wild Lime
Spring; to 16 ft/5 m; dense; evergreen

RUTACEAE   FRAGRANT

A novelty for home Citrus growers (of which I am proud to be one) is the Australian native Finger Lime, *Microcitrus australasicus*, a forest plant which is happy enough to be trained to life in a container. It is a dense, rather spiny plant which can be grown from seed or cuttings, or best of all, grafted onto exotic Citrus stock. It needs a leaf-rich, well-drained soil to be really happy and prefers to be treated like any other Citrus.

The stiff stems are sharply spiny, the 2 in/5 cm leaves obovate, the tiny flowers are fragrant and look like 3-petalled orange blossom. The fruits are most curious; thick skinned, elongated, lime coloured but up to 4 in/10 cm long and 1 in/3 cm wide.

Micromyrtus

(mai-kroh-**mur**-təs) ☼ T W
Hairy Myrtle
Spr-Sum; 2½ ft/70 cm; prostrate; evergreen

MYRTACEAE

Until the small shrub from Southeast Australia bursts into spring blossom, you might imagine it to be some sort of miniature conifer, judg-

Micromyrtus ciliatus. Hairy Myrtle. S.E. Australia

ing by its scale-like foliage. Mostly it is prostrate and up to 3 ft/1 m in diameter, but can be very variable and at times may spill over rock shelves or down banks, adopting a pendulous habit. The tiny flowers appear in unbelievable profusion from spring right through summer. They are like minute red-centred white bells, but gradually fade to red.

Propagation is from cuttings. Soil should be light but well-drained. *Micromyrtus* does not seem to be generally in cultivation, but should make a sensational rockery plant.

Mimosa pudica. Sensitive Plant. S. America

Mimosa uruguayensis. Mimosa. Uruguay

Mimosa

(mi-**moh**-sə)   ☼ Ⓦ Ⓗ
Sensitive Plant, Touch-Me-Not,
Action Plant
*Summer; 10 ft/3 m; many-branched;
evergreen*

FABACEAE

Only a novelty away from the tropics, the famous Sensitive Plant, *Mimosa pudica*, has been the subject of more scientific research than any other plant. A short-lived sub-shrub, it is usually grown as an annual away from the tropics. Decorative, sprawling, with leaves like a Jacaranda and clusters of dainty pink puffball flowers in summer, it has the remarkable habit, when touched, of snapping its leaves shut like a fan, and drooping its stalks. Then, when your

back is turned, it springs back again. But does it have feelings?

Taller *M. uruguayensis* has larger flowers, similar leaves and habits. Both plants have spiny stems, enjoy a peaty, sandy loam and are propagated from seed or cuttings. Neither is frost hardy.

Mimulus
(*syn.* DIPLACUS)

(**mim**-yoo-ləs)   ☼ ☀ Ⓣ Ⓦ
Monkey-flower
*Spr-Sum; 3 ft/1 m; much branched;
evergreen*

PHRYMACEAE

The majority of *Mimulus* species seen in the gardens of the world are annual or perennial. But North America, particularly the western

Mimulus longiflorus. Southern Monkey-flower. S. California, Mexico

Mimulus puniceus. Monkey-flower. S. California, Mexico

part, is home to a number of shrubby species, formerly classified as Diplacus. These include *M. aridis*, *M. aurantiacus* and illustrated *M. longiflorus* and *M. puniceus*. The latter is a many-branched shrub growing to 5 ft/1.5 m with a clammy, even sticky, feel to all its parts. Fast growing, it produces single copper to cerise flowers for much of spring and summer. In frosty areas, cut it right back to the ground in late autumn and protect the roots with a thick layer of mulch.

M. longiflorus is perhaps more profuse in its flowering which is in shades of cream to salmon yellow. But to produce the bloom year after year, it needs an annual rest. This is naturally induced by the winter in colder areas. Where the climate is warmer, withhold all water during late summer and prune to shape. Both plants like a dry, well-drained position, are propagated from seed (scarcely covered) or division.

Mirbelia dilatata. Holly Pea. Western Australia

Mirbelia

(mur-**bee**-lee-yǝ) ☼ ✴ Ⓦ
Holly Pea
Spr-Sum; 10 ft/3 m; columnar; evergreen

FABACEAE

This showy pea flower from Western Australia looks like some exotic cross between a Sweet Pea and a Holly bush. It is not much in cultivation but not difficult to grow if you are in a natural winter rainfall area.

It is best propagated from scarified seed, which may then take three years to bloom, so it is not a plant for the impatient! Plant it in well-drained soil and lay a deep mulch year round.

Mirbelia dilatata is a stiff, columnar sort of shrub, with prickly leaves reminiscent of Holly. Its large pea flowers are a brilliant red-violet and last longest in semi-shade. Related *M. oxyloboides* from south-east Australia flowers in a brilliant orange-yellow.

Moltkia

(syn. LITHOSPERMUM)

(**molt**-kee-ǝ) ☼ ✴ Ⓣ Ⓦ
Moltkia
Summer; 2 ft/60 cm; rounded; evergreen

BORAGINACEAE

Native to Balkan crags and harsh mountains of Asia Minor, the vividly coloured sub-shrub *Moltkia* X *intermedia* is believed to be a natural hybrid between two other *Moltkia* species. There are 8 of these altogether, found in various parts of southern Europe and the Near East. They are related to the herb Borage and flower in shades of blue, purple and yellow.

Moltkia X *intermedia*. Moltkia. Balkans, Asia Minor

They can be propagated from seed, cuttings or layers and grow best in sunny rock crevices. The ideal compost is a well-drained, humus-rich loam.

M. X *intermedia* grows almost 2 ft/60 cm tall, has dark, slender, grasslike leaves and roughly tubular flowers drooping in terminal clusters. A spectacular specimen for the rock garden.

Montanoa hibiscifolia. Tree Daisy. Mexico to Costa Rica

Montanoa

(mon-ta-**noh**-ǝ) ☼ Ⓦ Ⓗ
Tree Daisy
Winter; to 20 ft/6 m; tall; evergreen

ASTERACEAE

These giant bushes are to the English Lawn Daisy what Jack's Beanstalk is to a Scarlet Runner! There are some 50 species found from Mexico down through Central America to Venezuela. Where there's plenty of heat and water, they may reach 20 ft/6 m in height and make a sensational background planting in the subtropical garden, with their winter-long display of gold-centred, snowy daisy flowers on long branching stems. Don't even attempt them in cold-winter areas though, for the brittle, silky stems collapse at the least touch of frost.

Montanoa species can be grown from seed and from stem or root cuttings, struck with heat. Being such large shrubs, they need heavy, well-enriched soil and plenty of water. Deadhead regularly to maintain appearance. The palmately lobed leaves are magnificent.

Murraya
(syn. CHALCAS*)*

(mur-**rae**-yə)   ☼ ☀ W H
Mock Orange, Cosmetic Bark,
Orange Jessamine, Chinese Box
Spr-Aut; 10 ft/3 m; globose; evergreen

RUTACEAE   FRAGRANT

Continuous bloom is something that many shrubs promise but few deliver. One that does is the illustrated *Murraya paniculata* whose jasmine fragrance and clustered flowers like orange blossom earn it a place in any frost-free garden. And if all that were not already enough, in any one year *Murraya* will repeat the display several times, following each blooming with a sprinkling of orange-scarlet fruits like tiny Citrus.

Full sun brings on the best flowering except in really hot areas where semi-shade is best. M. *paniculata* (syn. M. *exotica*) likes well-drained soil rich in leaf-mould and consistent summer water. It should be sheared after the last autumn flowering to encourage heavy flowering the following year.

Murraya is easily struck over heat from heeled cuttings taken in winter and grows into a densely foliaged bush, 10 ft/3 m tall. Fruit may not be set out of the subtropics.

Murraya paniculata. Orange Jessamine.
S.E. Asia

Murraya paniculata (fruit). S.E. Asia

Mussaenda

(mus-sae-**en**-də)   ☼ ☀ W H
Buddha's Lamp, Flagbush,
Ashanti Blood, Paper-chase Tree
*Sum-Aut; 6–10 ft/2–3 m; broad;
evergreen*

RUBIACEAE

The wonderful summer display of these stunning shrubs expands to cover more of the year the further into the tropics one travels. On close

Mussaenda 'Doña Trining'. Philippine Hybrid

Mussaenda 'Queen Sirikit'. Royal Flagbush. Hybrid

Mussaenda erythrophylla. Ashanti Blood.
Congo

inspection, though, the colour is supplied by occasional over-sized sepals, the flowers being quite insignificant and usually white or yellow. *Mussaenda* are of particular interest in the Philippines (to which several are native) because of a series of beautiful cultivars named for the wives of

Mussaenda 'Doña Luz'. Hybrid Flagbush

Mussaenda philippica. Buddha's Lamp. Asia

regional rulers, e.g. 'Queen Sirikit' and 'Gining Imelda'.

In the right climate, all species can be propagated from thin hardwood cuttings taken in mid-winter and kept both warm and humid. A light, fibrous soil with ample summer water produces a spreading shrub to 10 ft/ 3 m in tropical gardens, but much less elsewhere. Prune heavily after bloom to force further flowers. African type M. *erythrophylla* is quite drought resistant.

Mussaenda 'Gining Imelda'.
Flagbush. Hybrid

Myoporum

(mai-oh-**por**-əm)   ☼ ☀ Ⓦ Ⓗ
Ngaio, Boobialla,
Water-bush
Spring; 10–16 ft/3–5 m; dense; evergreen
SCROPHULARIACEAE

More than 120 species of *Myoporum* are scattered from Asia through Australia and New Zealand and out into the Pacific islands.

New Zealand's Ngaio (M. *laetum*) may reach 16 ft/5 m, with 4 in/10 cm lanceolate leaves and masses of purple-spotted white ¾ in/2 cm flowers, rather like those of the Pittosporum. It is hardy down to 25°F/−4°C and is curiously fire

Myoporum montanum. Water-bush. Inland Australia

Myrica californica. California Bayberry. American West Coast

Myoporum laetum. Ngaio. New Zealand

Myoporum insulare. Boobialla. Australia

retardant. The Boobialla (M. *insulare*) is a popular coastal plant on both sides of the Pacific, usually grown for its many 3 in/8 cm leaves and purplish globular fruits which are displayed for weeks.

Most useful and decorative of all *Myoporum* species, perhaps, is the showy Water-bush (M. *montanum*), a drought resistant shrub from inland Australia and valued for hedges and screens in dry gardens. Its daphne-like flowers are white with purple spots; these are followed by purple fruits so brilliant they might have been lacquered. *Myoporum* are propagated from cuttings.

Myrica
(syn. CEROTHAMNUS, MORELLA)

(**mi**-rik-ə)   ☼ T W
Californian Bayberry,
Pacific Wax Myrtle, Candleberry,
Waterberry
Spring; to 30 ft/9 m; treelike; evergreen
MYRICACEAE

A most variable plant in the western states of North America, *Myrica californica* may appear as a low, sprawling mass along the coast, yet grow to a 30 ft/9 m shrub with many

upright branches in inland valleys.

It is a handsome evergreen plant for screening work or informal hedges and has been valued since colonial times because of the wax coating on its purple fruit. This is still used for candle-making by modern crafts-people.

The handsome foliage of *Myrica* exudes a resinous fragrance when crushed. The small, unisexual flowers appear on short catkins and are without petals. The wax-bearing berries that follow are less than ¼ in/5 mm in diameter and appeal greatly to birds.

Bayberries may be propagated from seed, layers or suckers. In nature, they grow in a sterile, sandy soil.

Myriocarpa

(mi-ree-oh-**kah**-pə)   ☼ ☀ W
Chichicaste
Spring; 10 ft/3 m; crepy-leafed; evergreen
URTICACEAE

Curious plants from Central America right down into Brazil, the *Myriocarpa* are, of course, named for their thread-like chains of berries or, as the Greeks would have it, *myrios karpos*, 'myriad fruit'.

Myriocarpa longipes. Chichicaste. Mexico

Propagated from cuttings of young wood, *M. longipes* likes to grow in well-drained loam, rich in leaf-mould. Its large, lightly toothed leaves are borne alternately and from the axils appear the long thread-like stems of almost invisible flowers, the males densely clustered, the females hanging loose. Minute fruits follow but are very hard to see.

Myrtus

(**mur**-təs)   ☼ ☀ ❋ T W
Myrtle, Greek Myrtle
Sum-Aut; 6 ft/2 m; dense; evergreen

MYRTACEAE

This is the plant for which the Myrtle family, Myrtaceae, was named, and all the typical Myrtle features are to be found in it: simple lanceolate leaves that exude a strong scent when crushed, long-stamened, 5-petalled flowers with a pleasant fragrance, and handsome berries to follow. It is a favourite plant for neatly clipped hedges or densely grown screens, for it will grow as tall as 15 ft/4.5 m in old age.

Myrtus is propagated from seed or semi-hardwood cuttings taken in late spring or early winter. It grows slowly in rich, well-drained soil and can

make a handsome, formally trained container plant. In drier areas it is handily drought resistant and it will survive winter temperatures down to 17°F/−8°C. A showy, variegated cultivar, as well as several other varieties, differ mostly in height or leaf size. Altogether, the Myrtle genus has 16 species, mostly from the Caribbean, one from Africa and a second from Europe.

Myrtus communis. Myrtle. Mediterranean

Nandina

(nan-**dee**-nə)   ☼ ☀ ❋ T W
Sacred Bamboo,
Heavenly Bamboo
All year; 6–8 ft/2–2.5 m; suckering; evergreen

BERBERIDACEAE

From its appearance, anything less likely to be a *Berberis* relative would be hard to visualize. In fact, the many erect, cane-like stems of clump-forming *Nandina domestica* have earned it the common names of Sacred and Heavenly Bamboo, though it is not even distantly related to those giant grasses.

In rich, well-watered soil, the evergreen stems can grow to nearly 10 ft/3 m, and *Nandina* is very popular in modern landscaping for the airy, vertical nature of its growth. It thrives equally well in sun or shade, al-

Nandina domestica 'Nana'. Dwarf Bamboo. China

Nandina domestica. Sacred Bamboo (fruit). India, China

Nandina domestica. Sacred Bamboo. India, China

though the handsome reddish foliage, which is a feature of the plant in autumn and winter, does not develop without full sunlight. *Nandina* is hardy down to about 14°F/–10°C. Sprays of small and unremarkable yellow-centred white flowers are produced in summer and autumn, followed by shining, persistent, bright red berries.

The dwarf variety *N. d.* 'Nana' is even more popular and seems to colour more strongly. It is sensational in a rockery or mixed border, and should be propagated from ripe seed or winter division.

Neillia thibetica. Mountain Spiraea. China

Neillia

(*syn.* **PHYSOCARPUS**)

(**neel**-ee-ə)
Mountain Spiraea
Spr-Sum; 7 ft/2 m; arching; deciduous

ROSACEAE

A charming genus of 10 deciduous shrubs from the Himalayas and outback China, the *Neillias* seem some sort of bridge between the rose and the Spiraea. The young foliage on the gracefully arching branches opens a beautiful greenish-gold before darkening. The flowers are very small, but spectacular in the mass as they appear in arching panicles. They are pink with 5 petals, 5 sepals and 10–30 stamens; more than anything else, they resemble the blooms of Tamarisk.

The *Neillias* are generally propagated by autumn division or from cuttings taken in midsummer. They do well in acid soils, better if it happens also to be well-drained and leafrich. Moisture is necessary all year and a hard pruning after bloom should thin out the canes by cutting a proportion of them back to the ground. The leaves vary in shape considerably, from ovate and lightly toothed to strongly lobed.

Nematolepis

(ne-**mat**-oh-lae-pəs)
Western Correa
Spring; 3 ft/1 m; low; spreading; evergreen

RUTACEAE

One of the loveliest of Australian plants, the monotypic *Nematolepis phebalioides* seems to be a Western Australian adaptation of the look-alike Correas which are endemic to the eastern states.

A low, spreading shrub, rarely above 3 ft/1 m in height and mostly less, it grows in acid soil but does best in a position with dappled shade. Leaves are small and shiny green, the spring flowers look just like those of a Correa, scarlet bells with yellow tips, hanging from every twig. They are about 1 in/3 cm in length.

Nematolepis grows well from either seed or cuttings but is not easy to grow in the garden. Perfect drainage is so important that it may do best in a container with year-round mulch. And not, of course, where the humidity is high.

Nematolepis phebalioides. Western Correa. Western Australia

Nerium oleander (mixed); as hedge. Mediterranean

Nerium

(**nee**-ree-əm)   ☼ Ⓦ
Oleander, Rose Bay, Pink Laurel
Most year; 7–10 ft/2–3 m; suckering; evergreen

APOCYNACEAE   FRAGRANT

Oleanders (*Nerium* spp.) have a reputation for being poisonous in all their parts and a danger to human life, so I was surprised to see them as a prominent feature of the landscaping at Disneyland. In conversation with the senior garden staff, I learned that the reputation is largely undeserved. With the exception of hungry stock, Oleanders present little danger to anybody. The fact is, a tremendous number of garden plants have a minimal poison content, particularly

Nerium oleander 'Petite Salmon'. Modern Cultivar

those with milky sap, like Oleanders. But these gorgeously flowering shrubs have such a disagreeable flavour and odour that the possibility of any human being chewing and then swallowing even one leaf, let alone taking a second bite, is quite remote. The trouble may have started with the movie 'Dragonwyck' in which Vincent Price supposedly poisoned his

Nerium oleander 'Sister Agnes'. In California (cultivar)

Nerium oleander 'Punctatum'. Rose Bay.
Mediterranean

wife with some favourite cookies in
which ground Oleander replaced the
herbs. Even allowing for the number
she ate, she could not possibly have
died. More likely she'd have thrown
up after the first biscuit. So, may we
return to our story?

Oleanders are most useful shrubs
wherever the winter temperature
remains above 23°F/−5°C. They are
astonishingly resistant to neglect and
thrive in the toughest of conditions,

Nerium oleander 'Yellow'. Gold Oleander.
Hybrid

Nerium oleander 'Album Plenum'.
Double White Oleander. Mediterranean

blooming away for months even in
heavily polluted industrial areas
where they are sometimes used for
street plantings.

They are the perfect choice in seaside gardens, where they seem un-
worried by salt air; equally spectacular in dry, semi-desert places or in
soils with poor drainage or high sal-
inity. Where the going is good, they
are unmatched in the profusion of
their bloom.

Oleanders are somewhat bulky
plants, sending up many erect
suckers. But with regular pruning,
they can be trained to a single trunk
or forced into an almost two di-
mensional hedge. If space is short,
new dwarf cultivars such as illustrated 'Petite Salmon' are now available. These rarely grow more than
3 ft/1 m tall, being perfect miniatures
of their full-sized brothers.

Oleander's evergreen leaves are
dark, glossy, spear-shaped and up to
6 in/15 cm long; the flowers, 3 in/
8 cm in diameter, are clustered
densely at branch ends and come in
a variety of colours—white, pink,
apricot, red, and pale yellow. They

may be single or double, and improve
in both size and colour as the
weather warms up.

All colour varieties are easily
propagated from 4 in/10 cm semi-
hardwood cuttings taken in autumn
and set in containers of standard
sand/peat mixture with warmth and
humidity. Heavy pruning of old
flowered wood is done in early
spring. Watch for and spray aphids.

Nerium oleander 'Scarlet Beauty'. Oleander.
Mediterranean

Neviusia

(nev-ee-**yoo**-see-ə)   ☀ Ⓣ Ⓦ
Snow Wreath
Spring; 6–7 ft/2 m; arching; deciduous
ROSACEAE

Neviusia is a genus of which the sole
species was discovered in Alabama
only in the mid-19th century. It is
closely related to the Japanese Kerria
(but without petals) and claims your
attention with the incredibly delicate
display of a mass of fine white
stamens, gathered with their sepals in
short, open cymes.

Neviusia is deciduous, with arching
canes furnished with doubly serrated

Neviusia alabamensis. Snow Wreath. Alabama

leaves. It is quite hardy, but grows best in a sheltered position.

Propagate it from seed or soft-tip cuttings in a heated place. A very eye-catching shrub for a sheltered spot in the warm-temperate garden.

Nicodemia
(*syn.* BUDDLEIA)

(nik-oh-**deem**-ee-yə) ☼ ☀ Ⓣ Ⓦ
Indoor Oak
All year; 20 in/50 cm; arching; evergreen

SCROPHULARIACEAE

A favourite indoor plant, in the northern hemisphere at least, *Nicodemia diversifolia* hails from Madagascar and nearby islands and is often found in glasshouse collections of the USA and the UK. In milder climates, like the American southern states, South Africa and Australia, however, it is a decorative, open air foliage plant or dense groundcover.

Nicodemia pushes ahead in any well-drained soil of moderate fertility and consistent moisture. Its ideal temperature is around 60°F/16°C. It seems to grow most of the year and a regular pinching back will keep it dense and bushy. I dare say it does bear flowers, but when your foliage is so beautiful, does it really matter?

At any rate, we grow it because its lovely foliage resembles that of an oak, surprisingly transported indoors.

Nicodemia diversifolia. Indoor Oak. Madagascar

Nitraria billardieri. Nitre-bush. Australia, N. Africa, Asia

Murray Fagg

Nitraria

(nait-**rear**-ee-ə) ☼ Ⓣ Ⓦ Ⓗ
Nitre-bush
Summer; 2–6 ft/60 cm–2 m; spreading; evergreen

NITRARIACEAE

The Nitre-bush is a pandemic shrub, though some Australian botanists prefer to think that its Australian version is distinct and call it *N. billardieri* as opposed to the generally accepted *N. scholeri*. It is fast growing in dry, saline areas of three continents—Australia, North Africa and Asia. While they say 'beggars can't be choosers', many people far better off than your average beggar have reason to be grateful to this rather attractive shrub which has other good points as well.

It makes a dense, tough, soil binder for hot inland areas. Its spines discourage the predatory attempts of stock and other animals. It grows very fast, has thick, fleshy 1¾ in/ 4 cm leaves and clusters of small creamy flowers. But its chief display is when in fruit, for then the entire bush is decked with purple, red or golden berries each ½ in/1 cm in diameter. Grows easily from seed or cuttings.

Norantea guianensis. Red-hot Poker. Guiana

Norantea

(nor-**an**-tee-ə) ☼ ✺ W H
Red-hot Poker
Winter; 6 ft/2 m; climbing; evergreen
MARCGRAVIACEAE

A wonderfully spectacular lawn specimen in the tropical garden, *Norantea guianensis* makes a stunning show with its long, poker-shaped stems of scarlet blossom in winter and early spring. It is easily propagated from semi-hardwood cuttings and grows rapidly in a rich, moist soil, developing large, shiny, oblong leaves and reddish stems as a background to the spectacular floral display.

The shrub must be watched for signs of extreme horizontal growth, and continuously cut back short of any possible support which it could cannibalize. Let it but reach a tree, any tree, and it turns into a parasitic climber, grabbing everything in sight with its tropical roots. A most spectacular plant if you've the patience to play cat-and-mouse.

Nylandtia spinosa. Dunebush.
South Africa

Nylandtia

(nai-**lan**-tee-ə) ☼ T H
Skilpad, Bessie, Bok Bessie, Dunebush
Win-Sum; 3 ft/1 m; erect; evergreen
POLYGALACEAE

Endemic to the Cape of Good Hope, where it is found over many miles of exposed sand dunes, the Duin Bessie or Dunebush, *Nylandtia spinosa*, forms a spectacular display for most of the year. In winter, tubular purple flowers with frilly tips open along the stiff, spiny branches, and as spring begins these are followed by a series of pink sepals which puff up to quite a size. By summer, a crop of succulent red berries forms the main display. These are edible and adored by children today just as they were in centuries past when they formed a valuable part of the diet.

Nylandtia, named for a 17th century Dutch physician, can be propagated from seed or cuttings. It grows well in poor sandy soil with occasional water, and is a good plant for exposed coastal conditions. It is closely related to the showy Polygala.

Ochna

(*syn.* DIPORIDIUM)

(**ok**-nə) ☼ ✺ W H
Carnival Bush,
Birds-eye Bush, Mickey Mouse Plant
Spring; 3–7 ft/1–2 m; globose; evergreen
OCHNACEAE

Some 90 species of *Ochna* are scattered around Africa, India and Indian Ocean islands. They vary from tree to small shrub size, but the most common is *O. serrulata*, a 3–7 ft/1–2 m bush from coastal South Africa.

No worry about propagating this one—any friend who has *Ochna* will soon find seedlings everywhere, though that is only likely to happen in a warm climate. Elsewhere, they can be grown from cuttings of half-ripe wood taken in summer or autumn.

Ochna will grow fast in full sun in almost any soil, so long as it is well-drained, but a slightly acid pH is desirable. It positively thrives in seaside salt air with regular water, and will tolerate one or two degrees of

Ochna serrulata. Carnival Bush.
South Africa

Ochna serrulata. Mickey Mouse Plant (fruit).
South Africa

frost. Bronzy new spring foliage is followed by yellow buttercup flowers which soon fall, leaving the persistent sepals to turn bright scarlet. Within these appear shining black berries, just like a mouse's eyes. Prune just before fruit fall to induce more compact growth and to prevent a carpet of unwanted seedlings which become deep rooted and hard to pull out.

Odontonema

(*syn.* THYRSACANTHUS, JUSTICIA)

(oh-dont-oh-**nee**-mə) ☼ Ⓦ Ⓗ
Red Justicia
Sum-Aut; 5 ft/1.5 m; erect but spreading;
evergreen

ACANTHACEAE

Where winter temperatures drop to
near freezing, *Odontonema strictum*
tends to look somewhat tatty by the
time spring comes around, but hard
pruning will soon encourage fresh
new growth, revitalizing the plant for
its role in the summer garden.
Though tropical in origin, *Odontonema* will adapt to life in frost-free
temperate areas, forming spreading
masses in either sun or shade. There
are some 40 species, but *O. strictum* is
the only one you are likely to see. Its
shiny, elliptical leaves are borne in
opposite pairs all the way up the dark
red stems. The warm-weather flower
display is spectacular but useless for
cutting, as the narrow tubular flowers
open irregularly and drop all over the
place.

Odontonema enjoy moderately rich
soil with good drainage and can be
grown from soft-tip cuttings at any
time in the warm weather. A sheltered spot is essential though, as the
brittle stems are easily damaged by
winds. Tip prune young plants to
promote a bushy habit and cut back
half of the annual growth in winter.

Olearia moschata. Tree Aster. Australia

Olearia macrodonta. Large-toothed Tree Aster.
New Zealand

Odontonema strictum. Red Justicia.
Central America

Olearia

(*syn.* EURYBIA)

(ohl-ee-**ear**-ee-ə) ☼ Ⓣ Ⓗ
Daisy Bush, Tree Aster
Spring; 3–5 ft/1–1.5 m; dense; evergreen

ASTERACEAE   SOME FRAGRANT

Olearias or Daisy Bushes have won a
northern hemisphere following out of
all proportion to their beauty, for
they can scarcely be numbered
among the more spectacular plants of
the Australasian flora. True, they
mostly hail from the cooler parts of
Australia and New Zealand, and
might be expected to be climatically
suited to the UK and parts of the
USA, but even cold parts of Australasia are positively mild by northern
standards.

Olearia gunniana. Mauve Daisy Bush.
Tasmania

Olearia phlogopappa. Daisy Bush.
S.E. Australia, Tasmania.

Olearia tomentosa. Daisy Bush. Australia

Olearias are evergreen and bloom profusely from early spring till late in the season. They enjoy a well-drained loam in full sun and are quite useful in seaside gardens. Of over 100 species, the majority have white daisy flowers, with a few in washed-out mauve. Some have no petals around the central disc at all.

Olearias do better without cultivation of the root area, but need annual pruning and regular deadheading to prevent their becoming woody and straggly.

Olearia megalophylla. Big-leaf Daisy Bush.
S.E. Australia

Omalanthus populifolius. Bleeding Heart.
E. Australia

Omalanthus
(*syn.* HOMALANTHUS)

(homa-**lan**-thəs)   ☼ ☀ T W
Bleeding Heart,
Queensland Native Poplar
Summer; to 17 ft/5 m; tree-like; evergreen

EUPHORBIACEAE

A fascinating plant of the coastal forests in Queensland and New South Wales, the *Omalanthus* (or Homalanthus as it is called with equal frequency) is one of about 40 species in its genus, the others being scattered about South-east Asia. It is always found growing in a shaded position, where it prefers well-drained, leaf-rich soil. It has velvety heart-shaped leaves on red stems, and though it is technically evergreen it does like to turn the odd leaf a vivid scarlet—hence the popular name, Bleeding Heart. It likes plenty of water, needs pruning only to shape and is not frost hardy.

Both male and female flowers appear separately, though often on the same plant. They are arranged in arching racemes up to 5 in/12 cm in length. *Omalanthus* self-seeds readily.

Ononis

(on-**oh**-nis)   ☼ T
Restharrow
*Spring; 1–2½ ft/30–75 cm; spreading;
deciduous*

FABACEAE

Not very well known in the southern hemisphere, the Restharrows are all too often seen in Europe, northern Africa and some Atlantic islands—some 70 species of them, ranging from annuals to shrubs, with the for-

Ononis spinosa. Spiny Restharrow. Europe

mer often treated as weeds. Of the shrubby species, *Ononis aragonensis* is found sporadically in poor soil from the Pyrenees through Spain to Algeria. It has typical pea flowers, faintly fragrant. Its main attraction is the fact that it is tough, survives in poor soil where not much else will grow and needs water only in droughts.

Its cousin, the illustrated *O. spinosa* (syn. *O. procurrens*), has the typical pea foliage of three leaflets, rosy pink flowers and, frankly, it stinks. It spreads rapidly from underground runners, binds soil, and is inclined to be spiny, particularly in dry soils.

Ononis species are easy to grow from seed but inclined to become rampant. Prune back the runners with a sharp spade.

species *Orixa japonica* travels by means of its weeping branches which take root wherever they touch ground. It is then easy to propagate from layers or division, though seeds are always a possibility as well.

It is deciduous, not fussy about soil so long as it is well-drained, and has a number of interesting colour roles. Young spring foliage tends to be pink in tone and aromatic; the leaves are simple and somewhat oblong in shape, but turn white or lemon in autumn, making a nice contrast to surrounding foliage in scarlet and gold. Yes, it does flower: the blooms are green, less than ¼ in/5 mm in diameter and borne in short racemes on the previous year's wood.

pink-tipped stamens largely protected by a colourful brush.

Illustrated *O. zeyheri*, the Silver-leaf Bottlebrush, is covered with silvery hairs on all its parts. Like other *Orothamnus*, it needs an acid soil, enriched with vegetable compost but not animal manure. Drainage should be fast but the soil must never dry out. Given those conditions, the plant will grow into a bush perhaps 8 ft/2.5 m tall. In nature, though, it often does not form a bush at all, remaining just a stem or two. Hardy down to 17°F/−8°C. Propagation is by grafting onto stock of other Proteaceae genera.

Orixa japonica. Oriksa. Japan, China

Orixa

(o-**rik**-sə)   ☼ T
Oriksa
Spring; 10 ft/3 m; arching; deciduous

RUTACEAE   AROMATIC

A charming foliage plant from Japan, where its popular native name has always been Oriksa, the monotypic

Orothamnus

(*syn.* MIMETES)

(or-roh-**tham**-nəs)   ☼ T
Marsh Rose, Soldaat, Vleiroos, Silver-leaf Bottlebrush
Spr-Sum; 6–8 ft/2–2.5 m; erect; evergreen

PROTEACEAE

One of the rarest South African Proteaceae in cultivation, *Orothamnus* is rarely seen outside its native land. There are 16 species altogether, with stem-clasping, leathery leaves over-lapping like fish scales. Those toward branch tips colour purple or rosy pink in winter and early spring and part slightly to reveal a mass of red or

Orothamnus zeyheri. Silver-leaf Bottlebrush. South Africa

Orphium frutescens. Sticky Flower. Cape of Good Hope

Orphium

(**or**-fee-əm)   ☼ ☀ W H
Sticky Flower
Summer; 2 ft/60 cm; erect; evergreen

GENTIANACEAE

A monotypic genus, the gorgeously coloured *Orphium frutescens* is one of the glories of Africa's Cape of Good Hope flora. It is evergreen, and generally quite dwarf in habit, so that it is most effective planted in its final position from seed. Young seedlings, however, can be transplanted. A leaf-rich, well-drained soil is advisable and the plants should be kept moist at all times. They are particularly suited to rockeries or to seaside plantings; they are quite used to salt spray.

Orphium (named of course, for the god of music) has slightly furry foliage and glistening red-violet flowers that open terminally in summer.

Osbeckia X *kewensis*. Cat's Tongue. India

Osbeckia

(*syn.* LASIANDRA, MELASTOMA, TIBOUCHINA)

(oz-**beck**-ee-ə)   ☼ Ⓦ Ⓗ
Cat's Tongue, Rough-leaf Osbeckia
All seasons; 3–5 ft/1–1.5 m; loose, thin; evergreen

MELASTOMACEAE

Look-alikes for Tibouchina and Melastoma, *Osbeckias* are generally smaller plants and bear their showy flowers from early spring right through to winter. They are naturally rather sparse and thin plants, and should be pruned all over lightly and regularly to keep them dense and floriferous.

Propagate them from soft-tip cuttings taken in spring and kept in warm, humid conditions under glass.

They like a light, friable loam, with good drainage an absolute necessity.

The shrub is evergreen, although some leaves turn orange or scarlet and fall from time to time. The leaves are small (¾–1½ in/2–4 cm) and rough to the touch, like a cat's tongue. They are grooved in the same parallel fashion as Melastoma (which see). The 5-petalled flowers appear terminally throughout the season. A showy rockery plant.

Osmanthus

(oz-**man**-thəs)   ☼ ☼ Ⓣ Ⓦ
Fragrant Olive, Kwai Fa
Aut-Spr; 8–18 ft/2.5–6 m; irregular; evergreen

OLEACEAE   FRAGRANT

A rather sparse shrub with glossy, toothed leaves, *Osmanthus* produces almost invisible flowers that exude the most delicious fragrance of all. To many people it's a blend of Jasmine, Gardenia and ripe apricots—and the Chinese certainly think so, for they

Osmanthus fragrans. Kwai Fa, Fragrant Olive. E. Asia

use them to flavour their most precious teas.

O. fragrans is difficult to train and branches at all sorts of odd angles, but it can be hacked into a rough sort of hedge. I have several and I keep them in large pots just outside doors

Osmanthus americanus. Devilwood, American Olive. S.E. United States

Osmanthus delavayi. Siphonosmanthus. W. China

Pamela Harper

where the fragrance is a joy from autumn right through to spring.

O. *delavayi* is altogether smaller with dark, serrated leaves and white flowers, less fragrant than the Kwai Fa. O. *heterophyllus* bears a sparse crown of white blooms, but is grown principally for its ornamental, holly-like foliage. O. *americanus*, not much known outside its native USA, has perfectly smooth edged leaves and greenish-cream flowers that are quite fragrant.

All *Osmanthus* species should be propagated in late summer from cuttings of half-ripe wood. Seeds do not germinate until the second year.

Osmanthus X *fortunei*. White Osmanthus. Hybrid

Gillian Beckett

Osteomeles

(oss-tee-**om**-el-ees) ☼ Ⓣ Ⓦ
Osteomeles
Spring; 10 ft/3 m; pendulous; deciduous

ROSACEAE   ACRID

A relatively unknown genus of the rose family, the few species of *Osteomeles* are found variously in South America, China, Hawaii and New Zealand. They develop arching, pendulous branches decked with elegant

Osteomeles schweriniae. W. China

pinnate leaves, and bear small terminal clusters of summer flowers that look and smell like hawthorn blossom. They are followed by tiny blue-black fruits.

Osteomeles schweriniae is most commonly seen. It is from western China and can be propagated from cuttings or grafted onto related Cotoneaster (which see). Seed is also a possibility, but very slow to germinate.

This graceful plant likes rich, well-drained soil, is hardy down to 23°F/−5°C and can be trained as a very decorative espalier. Where winters are mild it remains evergreen.

Osteospermum 'Burgundy Mound'. Freeway Daisy. South Africa

Osteospermum
(*syn.* DIMORPHOTHECA, TRIPTERIS)

(oss-tee-oh-**spur**-məm) ☼ Ⓣ Ⓦ
African Daisy, Sailor-boy Daisy, Rankmargriet
Spring; 3 ft/1 m; spreading; evergreen

ASTERACEAE

Shrubby plants related to the annual Dimorphotheca and often sold under that name, *Osteospermums* are classed as shrubs, sub-shrubs or shrubby perennials, according to which book you read. I'm honestly not sure which is which and believe the hardiness of growth depends on the climate: the less humidity, the tougher the plant. Whatever, they make a wonderful display in almost any position. They prefer a warm-temperate climate like that of their native South Africa and will produce a carpet of colour for many weeks in spring.

Osteospermum 'Whirlygig'. Whirlygig Daisy. Hybrid

Osteospermums are easy to grow from seed sown *in situ* early spring, or indoors in winter if you can maintain a temperature of 60–70°F/14–21°C.

While all species are seen at their best in good, rich soil with regular

Osteospermum barberae. Sunshine Daisy.
South Africa

water, they are really drought resistant and will continue to reward with a dazzling display of blue-centred daisy flowers throughout the driest season. Dead-heading will ensure repeat blooming, as will cutting back old spindly branches to thicker wood.

Osteospermum ecklonis. Sailor-boy Daisy.
South Africa

Oxalis

(**oks**-ə-lis, oks-**ah**-lis)   ☼ ☀ T W
Shrub Sorrel
Summer; 6–7 ft/2 m; erect; evergreen

OXALIDACEAE

Probably you have enough trouble with various *Oxalis* species as garden weeds, without having to cope with there being a shrub in the family. But indeed there are several, fortunately without the unsociable habits of the other 800-odd species.

O. *gigantea* is a somewhat succulent shrub from desert areas of Chile, the mature plant consisting of a cluster of virtually leafless stems (well they are during the warm weather). Leaves, when it has them, are tiny ¼ in/5 mm leaflets in groups of three. The summer flowers are yellow, the same size and shape as those of the related Soursob. They appear along the entire growth of the new season's stems, opening a few at a time in a display that lasts for months.

Oxalis gigantea. Shrub Sorrel. Chile

Pachypodium

(pak-ee-**poh**-dee-əm)   ☼ W H
Halfmens
Summer; 3–5 ft/1–1.5 m; rarely branched; part deciduous

APOCYNACEAE   FRAGRANT

'Something like a cross between a cactus, a palm tree and a Frangipani' would describe the remarkable *Pachy-*

Pachypodium lamerii. Halfmens.
South Africa

podium. The genus is endemic to dry parts of Madagascar and South Africa where several species are known as Halfmens because, when seen in silhouette at sunset, they look like refugees from 'Day of the Triffids'.

Pachypodiums are indeed closely related to the Frangipani and the Adenium (which see). The precisely circular trunk section offers least resistance to heat and drying winds,

Pachypodium baronii windsorii. South Africa

as does the plants' habit of rarely branching. The palm-like topknot of leaves appears during the winter growing season and later disappears to make way for long spines and a terminal cluster of exquisite flowers which vary according to species.

A mixture of limy rubble, sand and loam grows them best. Cuttings strike well in sand. Grow under glass except in arid zones.

Pachystachys lutea. Lollipop Plant. Peru

Pachystachys

(**pak**-ee-stak-əs) ☼ ☀ Ⓦ Ⓗ
Golden Candles,
Lollipop Plant
*Spr-Sum; 3–6 ft / 1–2 m; vertical;
evergreen*

ACANTHACEAE

I believe the popular Golden Candles is very sensitive to climate. I have complained before that I found it disappointing in its flowering performance, even though I give it the warm shade and humidity it requires. Now, though, I have seen it as a hedge in front of a friend's house, only blocks from the seaside. My main objection was that the admittedly handsome golden bracts and white flowers lasted such a short time before dropping off completely. But my friend's plants seem never out of bloom. The year-round warmth of the seaside climate produces many stems up to 3 ft/1 m high, each crowned with a spike of golden bracts.

Pachystachys is easy to grow from semi-hardwood cuttings taken in winter and likes a well-drained, compost-rich soil. My friend tells me his plants 'go off' when winter temperatures fall below 41°F/5°C but quickly recover in spring.

Paeonia

(pee-**oh**-nee-ə) ☼ ☀ Ⓒ Ⓣ
Tree Peony, Moutan
Spring; 3–7 ft / 1–2 m; rounded; deciduous

PAEONIACEAE   FRAGRANT

Two thousand years ago, the Chinese called these satiny-flowered, perfumed beauties 'the king of flowers'. They are not hard to grow, given the deep rich soil they need, but a cold winter is the real key to success, for they originate in the hard-winter areas of Tibet, western China and Bhutan. They grow to perfection in Britain, Canada and the colder parts of the USA and in mountainous parts of other countries. Peonies can be divided into two main classes: the herbaceous perennials with which we are not concerned in this book, and the shrubby or tree species with which we are.

The so-called Tree Peonies are a

Paeonia lutea 'Ludlowii'. Golden Peony. China, Tibet

handful of species of sparse, woody, deciduous shrubs that grow 6 ft/2 m tall. They are best planted among other shrubs for protection from morning sun which damages the dew-wet blooms. Most species bear very large flowers (up to 9 in/22 cm across) with fewer petals than the perennial types. They also have a wider

Paeonia suffruticosa 'Duchess of Kent'. Moutan. Hybrid

Paeonia delavayii. Tree Peony .
China

range of colours—every shade from darkest red to white, with some in tones of purple, orange and yellow. The shown cultivars of *P. suffruticosa* and *P. lutea* are examples.

Tree Peonies are usually bought as grafted plants but can be grown from 8 in/20 cm hardwood cuttings taken in autumn. They are slow-growing plants but long lived. Little care is needed except to prune out any dead wood in spring.

The dwarf variety *P. suffruticosa* var *spontanea* from China's Shensi province is not, to my knowledge, available outside China. I photographed it in Macau.

Paeonia suffruticosa 'Inspector Lavergne'.
China

Paeonia suffruticosa 'Yacryo Tsusaki'. Tree Peony. Japanese hybrid

Paeonia suffruticosa X *spontanea.*
Dwarf Moutan. Shensi, China

Paeonia suffruticosa 'Suzakuman'.
Hybrid Tree Peony

Pandanus

(pan-**dan**-əs) ☼ ✳ T
Screw Pine, Walking Palm
*All year; 7 ft/2 m; many branched;
evergreen*

PANDANACEAE

A common sight on or near beaches
all around the Pacific, *Pandanus* make
useful house plants when young but
will not survive outdoors below a
winter minimum of 55°F/13°C.

Originally believed to be palms
(because of their foliage) or conifers
(because of their large 'cones'), they
are neither, but a genus all of their
own. They have two distinctive features: first, they produce razor-edged
leaves in a spiral arrangement around
the branches; second, as they mature,
they develop stilt-like aerial roots
with which they can actually travel
some distance.

Pandanus veitchii. Veitch's Screw Pine.
Polynesia

Propagation is from suckers that
arise around the base, and can be
separated and planted in pots over
bottom heat, or from fresh seeds
which should be soaked for 24 hours
before sowing.

Of more than 650 species, *P.
veitchii* is the most decorative for
garden use, being less leggy than the
others. Do not plant close to paths as
the leaves can inflict a nasty wound
while lashing around in the wind.

Parahebe

(*syn.* VERONICA, HEBE)

(par-a-**hee**-bee) ☼ ✳ T
Veronica
Spring; 2 ft/60 cm; dense; evergreen

SCROPHULARIACEAE

About 12 species of shrubby plants
mostly from New Zealand (but some
found in Australia), *Parahebe* resemble Hebe (which see); they differ
mainly in their habit of growth,
which tends to be prostrate or de-
cumbent. They are extensively grown
outdoors in mild climates, particularly as rockery plants or border
edgings. Propagate them from seed or
cuttings, which should be planted
in autumn to bloom the following
summer.

P. cattaractae, one of the most decorative species, spreads rapidly while
lying prone, then turns its branches
to grow upwards. The leaves at
ground level may be 3½ in/9 cm long
and lanceolate in shape. The beautifully marked tiny blooms appear in
many-flowered racemes, though the
flowers drop quickly. They are white
and marked with pink or purple.

Parahebe cattaractae. Dwarf Veronica.
New Zealand

Parkinsonia aculeata. Jerusalem Thorn.
Tropical America

Parkinsonia

(pah-kin-**soh**-nee-ə) ☼ W H
Jerusalem Thorn,
Mexican Palo Verde
Spring; to 20 ft/6 m; sparse; deciduous

CAESALPINIACEAE

The more water it receives, the less
the lovely *Parkinsonia* will flower.
This apparent anomaly is the plant's
great joy. It is so drought resistant
that it is keyed to bloom in drought
conditions: plant a lawn nearby and
water it, and the *Parkinsonia* closes
shop. However, when conditions are
dry, it loses its small leaves—so it
seems like a case of 'you pays your
money and you takes your choice'.

A stunning plant, whose yellow
flowers make a wonderful contrast to
the blue skies of desert areas in the
American south-west, India, North
Africa and the Mediterranean. It
grows *so* well in areas of northern
Australia that it has been declared a
prohibited plant there.

Propagated from scarified seed, it
will grow like nothing else in poor,
alkaline soil of hot dry areas. *Parkinsonia's* stems are spiny, the leaves
(when it has them) pinnate, the yellow flowers 5-petalled and followed
by slender brown seed pods.

Pavetta lanceolata. Forest Bride's Bush.
South Africa

Pavetta

(pa-**vet**-tə)   ☼ ◑ Ⓦ Ⓗ
Forest Bride's Bush,
Bosbruidsbos
Spring; 20 ft/6 m; dense; evergreen

RUBIACEAE   FRAGRANT

How do I love thee? Shall I count the ways? Well, it seems a lot of people have been counting up the beautiful species of *Pavetta* but few of them seem to agree. South African reference books say about 40 (but that's in Africa). The English plantsman's bible says around 100, the Americans guess at 400; but one thing's for sure, Australia has only one species.

Pavetta are small trees or handsome shrubs native to tropical areas of Asia and Africa. They are grown for their showy masses of tubular white flowers, which are often deliciously perfumed and followed by black berries.

Good, rich soil gives the best results, with lavish supplies of water. Propagate from seeds or spring cuttings with several joints.

Pedilanthus

(ped-ə-**lan**-thəs)   ☼ ◑ Ⓦ Ⓗ
Zig-zag Plant, Redbird,
Slipper Flower, Devil's Backbone,
Jewbush
Spring; to 3 ft/1 m; upright; evergreen

EUPHORBIACEAE

Redbird, Devil's Backbone, Jewbush, Japanese Poinsettia, Ribbon Cactus,

Slipper Spurge, Zig-zag Plant—there must be something about this unusual shrub that stirs the imagination, and stirs it in so many different ways! Its real name is *Pedilanthus tithymaloides*, and the strain *variegatus* is most decorative with its pale, waxy green leaves marked in pink and white.

Pedilanthus is easy to grow from cuttings and should be seen in any warm-climate garden or collection of indoor or terrace plants. Besides the variegated leaves, the zig-zag stems are often striped, and the flower consists of scarlet bracts exactly like tiny slippers.

The Redbird enjoys a compost of normal loam and gritty sand over good drainage material. To survive, it needs a temperature about 50°F/10°C—not difficult to provide, for it likes the dry air of heated rooms.

Pedilanthus tithymaloides. Redbird.
Caribbean

Pelargonium X hortorum 'Sleuring Robin'.
Zonal Geranium. Hybrid

Pelargonium

(pel-ah-**goh**-nee-əm)   ☼ Ⓣ Ⓦ
Geranium, Pelargonium
Summer; to 4 ft/1 m; woody-based; evergreen

GERANIACEAE

Few if any of the popular *Pelargoniums* (which we all know as Geraniums) are true shrubs. The farthest anyone is prepared to go is 'shrubby'. Their woody trunks and lower branches remain as a permanent framework in warm-temperate climates, but the closer they get to frost level the more likely they are to collapse, and cuttings of favourite varieties should be over-wintered under glass just in case.

Pelargonium peltatum 'Ville de Paris'.
Strassburg Geranium. Hybrid

But in summertime, is there a garden anywhere without at least one of these free-flowering plants? Blazing away in pots, trailing from baskets, spilling over the ground, even climbing up panels of wire mesh, their garden uses are without number.

Pelargoniums are so easy to grow that even the most purple-thumbed

Pelargonium fulgidum. Robin Redbreast. Hybrid

Pelargonium tomentosum.
Peppermint Geranium. Hybrid

of gardeners is usually rewarded with success. Water regularly in summer; treat them to a weak dose of liquid fertilizer in the growing season—that's all there is to it! And they're so easy to propagate! Just tidy up older plants in early spring and insert the cuttings firmly in pots of sand kept moist. Pinch out growing tips as the plants begin to move, allow a few weeks, then plant them out or pot them up.

Pelargoniums fall into two basic groups: those grown for their fancy, scented foliage and those for their flowers. The former are mostly original species, the latter all hybrids of species brought from South Africa about 150 years ago. Of these, three types are especially popular.

1. The bushy Zonal Geraniums classed as *P. X hortorum* hybrids have velvety, round or kidney-shaped leaves, usually marked with a band or zone of contrasting colour.

2. The Ivy-leafed Geraniums, *P. peltatum* hybrids, have glossy, fragrant, waxy leaves of ivy shape and often a trailing habit.

3. The true *Pelargonium* or Martha

Pelargonium X *domesticum* 'Mrs G. Morf'.
Martha Washington Geranium. Hybrid

Washington Geranium (*P. X domesticum* hybrids) have a bushy habit, sharply lobed leaves that are fragrant when crushed. The flat heads of larger blooms are often beautifully marked.

All *Pelargoniums* should be dead-headed to prolong bloom. Generally, whole flower stems just snap away. The principal pest is budworm, small caterpillars that drill holes into unopened flower buds. Spray with a recommended chemical for caterpillar control. Rust is a common fungus disease of leaves. Pull away rust-marked foliage, spray with fungicide.

Pelargonium crispum. Lemon Geranium. Hybrid

Pelargonium quercifolium.
Oak-leaf Geranium. Hybrid

Pentachondra

(penta-**kon**-drə)   ☼ ☀ C T
Carpet Heath,
Little Mountain Heath
*Summer; 6 in/15 cm; prostrate mat;
evergreen*

ERICACEAE

A veritable flowering, fruiting, carpet is the dainty *Pentachondra pumila*, a mossy plant from alpine areas of south-east Australia and New

Zealand—and a delight in mountain gardens or moist rockeries, where it clings to flat areas of stone.

Pentachondra can be grown from seed or divisions of the growing plant. Cuttings can be tried if stock for division is not available, for they are slow to grow, even in the leafy, well-drained soil the plant loves. Except in cold areas, Carpet Heath should be grown in part-shade, where its many-branched habit turns it quickly into a groundcover.

The tiny 5-petalled heath flowers pop up singly in summer from among the ¼ in/5 mm leaves, and later in the season colourful red berries appear to join them, so flowers and fruit are seen at once. A plant for cool-summer climates only.

Pentas

(**pen**-təs)   ☼ ☀ W H
Star Cluster
*Summer; 2–3 ft/60 cm–1 m; rounded;
evergreen*

RUBIACEAE

Somewhat resembling Bouvardia and easily grown from soft-tip cuttings at any time except winter, *Pentas* is a colourful genus of compact shrubs from Africa. In spite of its tropical origins, *Pentas* will grow in any frost-free climate, but prefers a wet summer and a warm winter.

Well-drained, sandy soil is best (ideally, rich with leaf-mould) and

Pentas lanceolata 'Coccinea'. Red Star Cluster. Tropical Africa to S. Arabia

regular pinching back will encourage a neat, bushy habit and many more clusters of flowers. Be sure to dead-head regularly and shorten flowered stems lightly in early spring.

Pentas species are very much at home by the sea, in rock gardens or as a massed bedding plant. Well-grown specimens can be expected to bloom from spring to autumn. Illustrated *P. lanceolata* commonly blooms in a rosy-mauve shade but has white and scarlet varieties. Its cultivar

Pentachondra pumila. Carpet Heath.
New Zealand, S.E. Australia

Pentas lanceolata. Egyptian Star Cluster. Tropical Africa to S. Arabia

J. H. Willis

'Coccinea' is a larger plant with brilliant carmine flowers. All species grow fast, reaching full-size in a couple of seasons at most. They grow well in pots.

The name *Pentas* signifies all parts of the flower are arranged in fives.

Pereskia

(pə-**res**-kee-ə) ☼ W H
Lemon Vine, Barbados Gooseberry
Spring; to 13 ft/4 m; semi-climbing; can be deciduous

CACTACEAE

What a surprise, when these woody, leafy plants turn out to belong to the Cactus family—at least till cold weather (44°F/7°C) causes the leaves

Pereskia aculeata. Barbados Gooseberry. Tropical America

Pereskia sacharosa. Wax Rose. Paraguay, Ecuador

to drop and reveal the hidden spines.

Pereskia is easily grown from cuttings. It enjoys well-drained soil enriched with rotted organic matter. In pots, crushed charcoal chips help sweeten the soil. *Pereskias* are useful plants to grow on fences for discouraging intruders. Give them plenty of water in summer, just sufficient in winter to stop the leaves from wilting, and, of course, full sun.

P. aculeata, the Barbados Gooseberry, is most commonly seen, its beautiful satiny green blossoms welcoming autumn in profusion. The ¾ in/2 cm fruit are considered most edible in the tropics. A golden leaf variety, *P. a.* var *godseffiana*, has cerise reverses, but I have not known it to bloom. The related *P. sacharosa* from Paraguay and Ecuador is more of a shrub than a climber and produces terminal clusters of rose-pink flowers in summer. These are 3½ in/9 cm in diameter and followed by 1 in/3 cm edible fruit.

Pernettya mucronata 'Rosea'. Pink Pernettya. Straits of Magellan

Pernettya

(per-**nett**-yə) ☼ C T
Pernettya
Spring; 3 ft/1 m; suckering; evergreen

ERICACEAE

Cuttings or suckers are the only way to be sure of berry colour with the idiosyncratic *Pernettya mucronata*. Any batch of seeds may produce plants with white, pink, red or purple

berries—all lovely, but all different. Another snag is that you may not get any berries at all unless you have both a male and female plant.

There are about 25 species of *Pernettya*, mostly native to New Zealand, Tasmania and the southern tip of South America. They need a cool climate, moist peaty soil and full sun to be seen at their best.

P. mucronata is the most popular—quite an invasive plant, suckering in all directions. It is densely branched when young but becomes leggy with age and should then be pruned back hard. Evergreen, it has the typical small, pointed leaves of the heath family though some of these will turn red in winter's cold. Flowers, too, are typical of the heath family, white and urn-shaped and appearing in the leaf axils. The berries often persist right through winter.

Persoonia

(per-**soon**-ee-ə) ☼ ☀ T W
Geebung
Summer; 6–13 ft/2–4 m; upright; evergreen

PROTEACEAE

Endemic to the eastern states of Australia, the highly variable genus *Persoonia* includes some 45 species ranging from small trees all the way down to prostrate groundcovers. All bear 4-petalled yellow flowers which are followed by edible but rather acid

Persoonia laevis. Broad-leaf Geebung. S.E. Australia

Persoonia pinifolia. Pine-leaf Geebung.
S.E. Australia

fruits which were once popular with
the Koori people. These are coloured
green but with a reddish cheek when
ripe.

The two most popular species are
P. laevis and *P. pinifolia*. The first
bears broad lanceolate leaves up to
8 in/20 cm in length, the second,
pine-like needles to 2 in/5 cm. Both
have a flaky, distinctly red bark and
both are found naturally in the semi-
shaded margins of rainforest country
in Victoria and New South Wales
where they enjoy the well-drained,
sandy soils. Neither is easy to propagate but seed is probably the best
way. Taken ripe, it should be soaked
for 24 hours in warm water before
sowing.

Petalostylis

(pet-a-loh-**stai**-lis)   ☼ ☀ W H
Butterfly Bush
*Spring; 6–10 ft/2–3 m; rounded;
evergreen*

CAESALPINIACEAE

A handsome rounded shrub found in
all warm, dry parts of Australia,
Petalostylis labicheoides is easily mistaken for a related Cassia, but the

horseshoe-shaped, red mark on one
petal is the giveaway.

In very dry parts of the continent,
the Butterfly Bush self-seeds and
tends to become an annual. But
where soil is better and water available, it is a true shrub and can be
raised from scarified seed to reach
flowering size in 3 years or less. In
nature, the shrub is wider than it is
high and branches grow horizontally
until their ends almost touch the
ground. In the home garden, it needs
a regular light pruning to compact
the shape.

The yellow 1 in/3 cm flowers are
not very profuse but quite decorative.
The pinnate leaves are made up of
tiny lanceolate flowers.

Petalostylis labicheoides. Butterfly Bush.
Arid Australia

Murray Fagg

Petrophile

(*syn.* PETROPHILA)

(pet-**rof**-il-ə)   ☼ ☀ T W
Drumsticks, Conesticks
*Spring; 1½–10 ft/50 cm-3 m; sparse;
evergreen*

PROTEACEAE

Almost exclusively from Western
Australia, *Petrophile* ('rock lover' in
Greek) huddles in dry, perfectly
drained, rocky places and makes up
in texture what it lacks in colour.

Illustrated *P. linearis* both looks
and feels like a mass of pink pipe
cleaners. The leaves are thick, sickle-

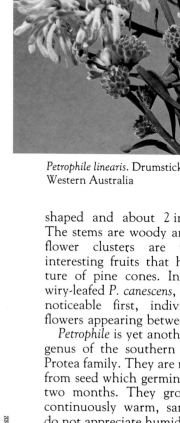

Petrophile linearis. Drumsticks.
Western Australia

shaped and about 2 in/5 cm long.
The stems are woody and the spring
flower clusters are followed by
interesting fruits that have the texture of pine cones. In the case of
wiry-leafed *P. canescens*, the cones are
noticeable first, individual yellow
flowers appearing between the scales.

Petrophile is yet another interesting
genus of the southern hemisphere's
Protea family. They are mostly grown
from seed which germinates in about
two months. They grow best in a
continuously warm, sandy soil and
do not appreciate humidity. Prune by
picking the flower heads.

Petrophile canescens. Conesticks.
Western Australia

Phebalium whitei. Gold Myrtle.
N.E. Australia

Phebalium

(fee-**bae**-lee-əm) ☼ ☀ W H
Gold Myrtle
Spring; 20 in/50 cm; erect; evergreen

RUTACEAE

A showy Australian relative of the Citrus and Correa, *Phebalium whitei* is native to well-drained, sandy areas of the Queensland bush. It may be raised from seed sown in late spring or struck from soft-tip cuttings set out later with humidity. Slow to reach maturity (and then not very tall), these dainty shrubs burst into a mass of 5-petalled, golden spring flowers in warm to subtropical climates. They look best in dappled shade and benefit from a light shaping after bloom to keep them compact. Though from Queensland, *Phebalium* is hardy down to 28°F/−2°C.

Some 45 species of *Phebalium* have been identified, mostly with very limited distribution. Most species have proved difficult to establish, though good drainage and a cool root-run seem to help.

Philadelphus

(fil-ə-**del**-fəs) ☼ ☀ C T
Mockorange, Syringa
Late spring; 3–13 ft/1–4 m; suckering; deciduous

PHILADELPHACEAE   FRAGRANT

In gardens of both northern and southern hemispheres, in climates from cold to warm-temperate, the

Philadelphus mexicanus. Mexican Mockorange.
Mexico, Guatemala

Philadelphus microphyllus. Small-leaf Mockorange.
S.E. USA to Central America

favourite shrub for late spring is a Mockorange, one of 65 *Philadelphus* species, originally from Europe, Asia or the Americas. Their overpowering orange-blossom fragrance should be reason enough for their presence in any summer garden plan, but when you add masses of golden-centred, snowy flowers on tall, arching canes, the effect is irresistible.

They are easy shrubs to grow, will flourish in almost any soil, even turning on a good display where the pH is alkaline. Dependent on the height of individual species, they can be used in open borders, as wall shrubs, or along pathways, where the tall, arching canes will bring heads of bloom close to passers-by.

Individual plants should be thinned out after bloom, cutting

Philadelphus X purpureus-maculata
'Belle Étoile'. Blushing Mockorange. Hybrid

Philadelphus coronarius 'Aureus'.
Golden Mockorange. Europe, S.W. Asia

Philadelphus X *virginalis*. Double Mockorange. Hybrid

away the oldest wood altogether. New plants strike from 2½ in/6 cm soft-tip cuttings or 6 in/15 cm pieces of semi-hardwood in summer and autumn. They must be kept warm and humid until new roots are established.

Most species are deciduous, though *P. mexicanus*, for one, stays evergreen in warmer climates. Leaves vary from 2–3¼ in/5–9 cm long according to variety, except in the more compact *P. microphyllus*, where they rarely pass ¾ in/2 cm. Flowers appear terminally, sometimes singly, sometimes in large clusters. They are snowy white and 4-petalled except in the cultivar 'Virginalis' which generally presents a number of double blooms. Species *P. coulteri*, sometimes called the Rose Syringa, has petals stained with purple-red. This effect is more commonly seen in its hybrid 'Belle Étoile'.

Flowering well after many other spring shrubs have finished, most species are drought and frost hardy.

Philotheca

(fil-o-**thee**-kə)   ☼ ☀ T W
Philotheca
Spring; 3 ft/1 m; erect; evergreen

RUTACEAE

One of only two species of this delightful, heath-like genus, *Philotheca salsolifolia* has no common name that I can track down—certainly none that is really popular.

Philotheca salsolifolia. N.S.W.

Philadelphus X *lemoinei* 'Erectus'. Hairy Mockorange. Hybrid

It belongs to a genus of the rue family, Rutaceae, along with Boronia, Citrus, Correa and Rue itself. It is endemic to subtropical New South Wales where it blooms in spring, opening ¾ in/2 cm star-like mauve-pink flowers that catch the light in semi-shaded positions. It needs a well-drained spot with a cool root-run, so a place in the rockery is ideal. Propagation is normally from cuttings, but the success rate is not good.

Phlomis

(**floh**-məs) ☼ T W
Jerusalem Sage
Summer; 2–7 ft/60 cm –2 m; grey foliage; evergreen

LAMIACEAE

A popular genus of 60 or so species from Europe, Asia and North Africa, *Phlomis* is still known by the name used in ancient Greece. All species look somewhat alike, whether they are perennial, shrubby or subshrubby. Each has tall stems of greyish, wrinkled, felty leaves topped with many-flowered whorls of curled, tubular blooms in yellow, mauve or white. They look a little like, and are related to, the genus Leonotis (which see).

Phlomis cheiranthifolium. Jerusalem Sage. Mediterranean

Phlomis spectabilis. Afghan Sage. Baluchistan

These old-fashioned plants deserve greater popularity, for they do particularly well under adverse conditions, including poor soil, salt-laden coastal winds and prolonged drought. All species can be cut for indoors. That, and pruning back by about half in autumn, results in a neater plant. Staking keeps them tidy in windy places. Propagate by division.

Photinia

(foh-**tin**-ee-ə) ☼ C T W
Japanese Photinia
Spring; 6–10 ft/2–3 m; dense; semi-deciduous

ROSACEAE ACRID

A popular hedging shrub, especially in cooler areas, *Photinia glabra* is most often seen in its two cultivars, 'Rubens', which has brilliant red new foliage, and 'Robusta' which has large leaves of a somewhat bronzier red. In all types, the colourful spring foliage is followed by large flat panicles of tiny white acrid-smelling flowers. These are followed by blue-black berries and finally, in frosty areas, brilliant autumn colouring, for *Photinia* is semi-deciduous, losing a proportion of its leaves each year.

Foliage is shiny and toothed, and the plants may be increased from seed or semi-hardwood tip cuttings taken with a heel during the cold months. *Photinia* is customarily pruned regularly to keep it dense and

Photinia Glabra. Photinia hedge

covered with bright red new growth.

Hardy down to 14°F/−10°C, there are some 40 *Photinia* species, many of tree size. Propagate good varieties by layering, or by grafting onto hawthorn stock.

Photinia glabra 'Rubens'. Japanese Photinia. Japan

Phygelius CV 'African Queen'. Cape Fuchsia. South Africa

Phygelius

(fai-**jee**-lee-əs)   ☼ ✳ T W
Cape Fuchsia, Cape Figwort, River Bells
Spr-Sum; 2–6 ft/60 cm–2 m; erect undershrub; evergreen
SCROPHULARIACEAE

In spite of its most popular name, *Phygelius capensis* is related not to the Fuchsia, but to the Penstemon and Snapdragon. Though truly a shrub in warmer climates, it can act as a perennial where winters are cold.

Plant out in spring (preferably in a sunny position) in light, well-drained soil. Space at 2 ft/60 cm intervals to allow room for rapid, weedy growth. When well fed and watered, the sparsely-branched flowering stems will begin to rise in late spring and bloom throughout summer and autumn.

Phygelius grows to about 6 ft/2 m but needs no staking in sheltered positions. Seed may be sown in spring, germinating in a few days, but the plants are most easily multiplied from divisions taken in the same season. A splendid subject for the large rock garden, as in our picture.

Phylica

(**fai**-lik-ə)   ☼ T W
Flannelbush, Featherhead, Veerkoppie
Winter; 2 ft/60 cm; downy; evergreen
RHAMNACEAE

Carry your magnifying glass with you if you hope to get a close-up look at the actual flowers of this extraordinary plant. A South African, but not a member of the Proteaceae (though you might think so), the Featherhead is, in fact, related to the American Ceanothus, and its almost invisible flowers are surrounded by a circular mass of silken subtending bracts which help each flowerhead to remain quite eyecatching.

P. pubescens is a small, erect shrub, rarely passing 2 ft/60 cm in height. Its flowering, which can begin in late autumn, continues right through the cold months, and although the tiny flowers don't last the bracts are extremely long-lived.

Phylica is evergreen, with downy new growth, narrow, heath-like leaves. Thriving close to the sea, they must have fairly high humidity and well-drained acid soil. Propagate them from seed or from autumn cuttings of half-ripened shoots. If enough flowering stems are picked, no other pruning is necessary.

Phylica pubescens. Featherhead. South Africa

Phyllanthus

(*syn.* CICCA, XYLOPHYLLA)

(fil-**lan**-thəs) ☼ ☀ W H
Ceylon Myrtle
Spring; 3 ft/1 m; wide, arching; evergreen
PHYLLANTHACEAE

A large genus of perhaps over 1000 species, the *Phyllanthus* are almost never seen away from the subtropics or tropics. Many are trees, bearing some notable tropic fruits such as Myrobalan and Otaheite Gooseberry, but one shrubby type, *P. myrtifolius*, is an outstanding plant even in warm-temperate gardens.

Easily propagated from seed and soft-tip cuttings, it grows slowly into a mass of long, arching stems which is far wider than its height of 3 ft/ 1 m. These stems are clothed in ⅓ in/1 cm narrow leaves which are almost stemless. In spring, tiny long-stemmed pink flowers appear, and these are followed by seed capsules about the size of a pea. But all in all, the Ceylon Myrtle is grown for the mossy effect of its foliage.

Plant in a mixture of sand and fibrous peat perked up with charcoal chunks and dried cow manure.

Phyllanthus myrtifolius. Ceylon Myrtle. Sri Lanka

Phyllodoce breweri. Red Mountain Heather. California

Phyllodoce

(fil-loh-**doh**-chee) ☼ C T
Mountain Heather, Red Heather
Summer; 2 ft/60 cm; heath-like; evergreen
ERICACEAE

Transatlantic relatives of the European and African heathers, the 8 species of *Phyllodoce* are native to polar areas of the northern hemisphere, mostly in western North America and Japan.

Named for a nymph in Greek mythology, they are all charming, heath-like plants, very low-growing, with dense branches clothed with ⅓ in/1 cm, heath-like leaves. The summer flowers, appearing in umbel-like clusters, are open bells of cerise-red with long purple stamens.

Phyllodoce breweri, an ideal rockery plant for cool to cold climates (it grows naturally around the 6000 ft/ 1800 m mark), can be grown from seed, cuttings or layers in any peaty, well-drained soil. It is a botanical feature of California's Sierra Nevada mountains and loves moist, rocky places.

Phymatocarpus

(fai-**mat**-oh-kah-pəs) ☀ ☀ T W
Phymatocarpus
Spring; 5 ft/1.5 m; erect; straggly; evergreen
MYRTACEAE

Mostly mistaken for Melaleuca, the small Western Australian genus Phy-

matocarpus includes only two species, which differ from their more numerous cousins in a matter of their sexual parts.

The most popular is *P. maxwellii*. It can be grown from seed cuttings, should be planted in moist but well-drained soil. It is relatively cold hardy, enjoys even a light frost, and grows well in full shade. Leaves are narrow and heath-like. The largely staminate flowers are pinky-mauve and arranged in pompon heads.

Its look-alike, *P. porphyrocephalus*, prefers full sun and is highly resistant to salt spray, making it a useful seaside subject.

Phymatocarpus maxwellii. Western Australia

Phymosia

(*syn.* SPHAERALCEA)

(fai-**moh**-see-ə) ☼ W H
Desert Mallow
Spr-Sum; to 20 ft/6 m; erect; branching; evergreen
MALVACEAE

A small genus of the mallow family, Malvaceae, from Mexico and the Caribbean, the 7 species of *Phymosia* grow very decoratively in light, well-drained soil and a warm-temperate climate. Often seen in California, *P. umbellata* rather resembles a Hibiscus bush both in and out of flower.

The dark leaves are shallowly palmate with 3, 5, or 7 lobes. Blooms appear in a cyme, the deep rose-red flowers emerging from mealy green 1 in/3 cm calyxes. Grow this evergreen shrub from cuttings taken in summer and rooted in a warm, humid place.

Phymosia umbellata. Desert Mallow. Mexico

Physocarpus monogynus. Mountain Ninebark. Central & S.W. USA

Physocarpus
(*syn.* OPULASTER)

(**fai**-soh-kah-pəs)   ☼ ☀ ✹ C T W
Ninebark
Spring; 3–4 ft/90 cm–1.2 m; arching stems; deciduous

ROSACEAE   FRAGRANT

Rarely seen away from its native Rocky Mountains, this mildly fragrant member of the rose family is easy to grow in a sheltered position in average soil with good drainage.

Raise it from seed or strike 4–6 in/ 10–15 cm hardwood cuttings in winter. These can be taken when the shrub is tidied up by removing a full third of the arching canes. This is preferable to shortening the branches, which would interfere with the graceful habit.

Physocarpus monogynus is deciduous, with foliage turning a good colour in autumn. It blooms in spring, doing better in full sun. The 3–5 lobed leaves resemble those of a currant, the flower heads remind one of Spiraea. Water well during droughts.

Pieris
(*syn.* ANDROMEDA, AMPELOTHAMNUS, ARCTERICA)

(**pee**-eə-ris)   ✹ C W
Andromeda, Pearl Flower, Lily-of-the-Valley Bush
Spring; 3–13 ft/1–4 m; dense; bushy; evergreen

ERICACEAE   FRAGRANT

From the colder parts of Asia and North America, *Pieris* are hardy down to 23°F/−6°C and are a relatively small genus of Azalea relatives. Preferring a mildly acid soil that is both well-drained and rich with leaf mould, they grow fairly slowly. A humid atmosphere keeps the evergreen foliage fresh and colourful.

In the case of *P. forrestii*, the leaves change from scarlet in early spring through cream to a deep, lustrous green in midsummer. Along the way, they are joined by panicles of faintly fragrant, cream flowers like lily-of-the-valley. These hang from the tips of every stem for many weeks in spring. This species grows to about 13 ft/4 m.

Pieris japonica variegata. Variegated Andromeda. Hybrid

P. japonica is more common and more compact, with leaves margined creamy-white in its strain *variegata*. Flowers are tipped a delicate pink in P. 'Christmas Cheer'.

Pieris species may be propagated from seed collected in autumn for spring sowing, or from 4 in/10 cm semi-hardwood cuttings in summer. Cultivars, of course, only from cuttings.

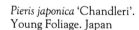

Pieris japonica 'Chandleri'. Young Foliage. Japan

Pileanthus filifolius. Copper-cups.
Western Australia

Pieris japonica. Lily-of-the-Valley Bush. Japan

Pieris 'Christmas Cheer'.
Pink Pearl Flower. Hybrid

Pieris forrestii 'Wakehurst'.
Wakehurst Andromeda. Cultivar

Pileanthus

(pil-ee-**an**-thəs)   ☼ C W
Copper-cups
*Spr-Sum; 3–5 ft/1–1.5 m; heath-like;
evergreen*

MYRTACEAE

This small genus of the myrtle family includes 5 species, all endemic to Western Australia. One, *Pileanthus peduncularis*, really does have flowers of a coppery red, but the name has come to be applied to all species, though, as our picture shows, none of the other flowers is copper coloured. The *P. filifolius* of our illustration is quite magenta.

P. filifolius is a slender, lightweight shrub with tiny heath-like leaves. The flowers, borne in leaf axils for most of the warm weather, are 5-petalled and at least ¾ in/2 cm in diameter.

Pileanthus has been raised from seed and late summer cuttings in dry surroundings, but grafting may be a better possibility in more humid areas. At any rate, in a sandy but leaf-rich, well-drained soil. This spectacular shrub really should be tried if you can supply the drainage and the full sun it needs.

Pimelea

(pai-**mee**-lee-ə)   ☼ ☀ T W H
Riceflower, Banjine
Spring; 2–6 ft/60 cm–2 m; variable;
evergreen

THYMELAEACEAE   FRAGRANT

An important shrubby part of the
Australian flora, the 80-odd species
of *Pimelea* are related to European
and Asiatic Daphnes. Lightly
fragrant, they are scattered right
around the south of Australia and
over to New Zealand. The majority
are hardy down to 23°F/−5°C.

Pimelea spectabilis. Bunjong.
Western Australia

Pimelea physodes. Qualup Bell.
Western Australia

Pimelea rosea. Pink Riceflower. Western Australia

Pimeleas are easy to strike from
semi-hardwood cuttings taken while
the plant is in active growth. They
must be set out while young, for they
will not transplant later.

Many species develop into naturally compact, rounded, bun-shaped
plants, typically 2 ft/60 cm or so tall
but much wider. Use them by the
coast or in open, windy places, in the
front of shrub borders or in the light,
dappled shade cast by tall, open
trees—a position which seems to suit
many species admirably. All they
need for success is a light, porous soil
and plenty of leaf mould to flower
profusely in spring and summer.
Unfortunately, they are mostly short-
lived.

Pimelea linifolia. Slender Riceflower.
E. Australia

Pimelea suaveolens. Scented Banjine.
Western Australia

H. A. Morrison

Pimelea ferruginea 'Selected Red'.
Red Riceflower. Western Australia

Piptanthus

(pip-**tan**-thəs) ☼ ☀ T W
Nepal Laburnum
Spring; 10 ft/3 m; treelike; deciduous

FABACEAE

A short life but a gay one, seems the credo of the 8 or so species of *Piptanthus*, all native to China, India and central Asia. They are, of course, members of the pea family, and very widely grown in England and the southern states of the USA. Their botanical name tells us that their spring flowers fall rather too readily.

All *Piptanthus* species grow from ripe seed in late summer, or from semi-hardwood cuttings taken in the same season. They grow quickly while young but are not very hardy and may be short-lived.

Plant in a dryish, reasonably rich soil that is very well-drained. *Piptanthus* leaves are compound, with 3 grey-backed, dark-green leaflets. Young growth is silky and the bright yellow pea flowers appear in dense racemes at branch ends. Water is important only during droughts.

Pittosporum

(pit-toh-**spor**-əm,   ☼ ☀ ☀ T W H
pit-**tos**-por-əm)
Mockorange, Pittosporum
Spr-Sum; 10 ft/3 m; rounded; evergreen

PITTOSPORACEAE   FRAGRANT

A search for the most fragrant flowers or the world's *tackiest* scent would certainly lead you up the same track and through the door marked *Pittosporum*. There are around 100 species of them—some trees, some shrubs—and they are found in China, Japan, South Africa, Hawaii, New Zealand and all parts of Australia and the Pacific. To pronounce

Pittosporum tobira variegata. Variegated Japanese Mockorange. Japan, China

Pittosporum phillyraeoides.
Willow Pittosporum. Australia

which of them might be the most attractive would be taking a great risk, for national feelings run high in such matters. Let us merely say all *Pittosporum* are handsome evergreen species with interchangeable flowers, fragrant as orange blossoms.

Though many of the tree *Pittosporum* are striking, it is the shrubs

Piptanthus laburnifolius. Nepal Laburnum. Himalayas

Gillian Beckett

Reg. Morrison

Pittosporum revolutum. Shrub Pittosporum. Australia

Pittosporum tobira. Japanese Mockorange. Japan

that concern us here. Best known is probably the Japanese Mockorange, *P. tobira*, particularly in its form *variegata*. A low, rounded plant, it is used world-wide as hedges, container plants, fragrant groundcovers. Taiwan's *P. daphniphylloides* is about the same size, with shiny, much larger leaves, and bright yellow flowers in loose terminal panicles. South African *P. viridiflorum* has tiny yellow-green flowers in profuse panicles and is a fairly low, spreading plant. Australia has two entries in the shrubby *Pittosporum* stakes. One is *P. revolutum* with rusty, woody branches, yellow flowers and leaves with turned-down margins. The other, *P. phillyraeoides*, has weeping branches densely covered with creamy yellow flowers.

All have fruit with sticky seeds from which they grow, but they can also be propagated from cuttings. They like a leaf-rich, well-drained soil and regular moisture.

Pittyrodia

(pit-tai-**roh**-dee-ə) ☼ T W
Foxglove, Native Foxglove
Spring; to 3 ft/1 m; many-branched; evergreen

LAMIACEAE

Endemic to Western Australia, the 20-odd species of *Pittyrodia* are not in any way related to Foxgloves, but the resemblance is so strong, it's easy to see how the popular name arrived. Although they are widely seen in Western Australia, their cultivation

Pittosporum daphniphylloides. Chinese Pittosporum. Taiwan

Pittyrodia terminalis. Native Foxglove. Western Australia

Tony Rodd

is more by accident than design and we don't know too much about their likes and dislikes.

They have been propagated from seed and cuttings and seem to grow best in a well-drained position—a rockery pocket would be ideal. From a woody base, they send up soft-foliaged stems with tubular flowers opening in the upper leaf axils. Orange, white, pink and mauve are among the flower colours, with the illustrated *P. terminalis* blooming in a vivid magenta.

Platytheca verticillata. Western Australia

Platytheca

(pla-tee-**thee**-kə) ☼ T W
Platytheca
(Spr-Sum; 2 ft/50 cm; compact; evergreen

ELAEOCARPACEAE

Not that Western Australia has a monopoly on blue-flowering plants, but sometimes it seems that way. Now on top of Dampiera and Lechenaultia comes *Platytheca*, a monotypic genus from the west which is very similar to the pink-flowered Tetratheca of the eastern states.

P. verticillata is a dwarf shrub. It

loves moist, well-drained soil with a mulch of flat stones to keep its roots cool. Grow it from cuttings, kept lightly moist at all times. The ½ in/1 cm linear leaves appear in whorls at intervals up the stems. The spectacular, deep blue, 5-petalled flowers appear from the leaf axils. They are not known to be long-lived.

Plumbago

(plum-**bae**-goh) ☼ W H
Leadwort
Summer; 4–10 ft/1–3 m; suckering; evergreen

PLUMBAGINACEAE

The ancient Romans are said to have believed that the *Plumbago* plant was a cure for lead poisoning. But the story seems doubtful, for all species known to us are endemic to South Africa, which just wasn't known to the Romans, great travellers though they were.

They are beautiful plants, all 10 species of them, and only one factor prevents more of us from growing them—an acute lack of space. *Plumbago* sucker heavily and quickly become untidy unless cut back to the ground in late winter. Flowers are only produced on new growth, so heavy pruning not only controls size,

Plumbago auriculata alba. White Leadwort. South Africa

Plumbago zeylanica. Ceylon Leadwort. East Indies

Plumbago auriculata. Cape Leadwort. South Africa

but improves flower yield as well.

You can use *Plumbago* as an informal hedge or to disguise ugly walls and fences, for it will climb a little way. Propagate from divisions or soft-tip cuttings taken in the warmer months and struck in moist sand. Good drainage is essential and the plants are hardy down to 27°F/−3°C. *Plumbago* is one of those plants with a curious sticky feel about it.

Podalyria calyptrata. Sweetpea Bush.
South Africa

Podalyria

(pod-ə-**lir**-ee-ə)   ☼ T W
Sweetpea Bush, Keurtjie
*Win-Spr; 7–10 ft/2–3 m; rounded;
evergreen*

FABACEAE   FRAGRANT

We must assume that in earlier days one or more of the 20 species of *Podalyria* was used in medicine—for in legend, Podalyrius was the son of Aesculapius, the Greek god of medicine. However, these days we love *P. calyptrata* for its fragrance and the soft pastel colours of its pinkish-mauve pea flowers and grey-green leaves. It seems not particularly common away from Australia and its native South Africa, but is a most useful shrub for exposed positions. Always decorative, *Podalyria* is ever-green, or to be more accurate, ever-grey, for its leaves are covered in silvery hairs which shine in the sunlight. It is a slow-growing bush of open, rounded shape, made more compact by light annual pruning immediately after bloom.

Grow *Podalyria* from seed which must be soaked for hours in hot

water, or from soft-tip cuttings taken in warm weather and struck in a moist, sandy mix. Gravelly, well-drained soil is best, with heavy, regular water over the winter months, but less in summer. *P. calyptrata* is hardy down to 27°F/−3°C.

Polygala

(pol-**lig**-ə-lə)   ☼ ☀ W H
Milkwort, Langelier,
Bluecaps, Septemberbossie
*Some all year; 5–8 ft/1.5–2.5 m; dense;
evergreen*

POLYGALACEAE

I have in the past suggested that the colour of *Polygala* seems to clash with everything else in the garden, but I won't say it again because the mails ran hot in favour of this spectacular South African shrub.

Usually less than 8 ft/2.5 m in height, it is well-branched and densely foliaged above, but soon grows somewhat bare and leggy below. Its flowers are generously produced from about the end of winter right through summer, with a few hanging around in autumn as well. It is often used as a background plant-

Polygala myrtifolia. Milkwort. South Africa

ing or as a temporary filler behind other, slower plants.

Polygala myrtifolia can be grown from spring or early summer seed, or from soft-tip cuttings struck in autumn with bottom heat. Hardy down to 23°F/−5°C, *Polygala* is not too fussy about soil, doing best in light, well-drained soil in sun or dappled shade.

Polyscias balfouriana. Balfour Aralia.
New Caledonia

Polyscias

(*syn.* NOTHOPANAX, ARALIA, PANAX)

(pol-ee-**skai**-əs)   ☀ ☀ W H
Aralia, Wild Coffee
*All year; 3–25 ft/1–7.5 m; dense;
evergreen*

ARALIACEAE

Since all species of *Polyscias* are endemic to the Pacific, it's not surprising to find them featured in Hawaii's gardens. What *is* surprising is to find them absent from Australian gardens—arguably an equally important area in the Pacific basin.

There are about 70 species of these beautiful foliage plants, sometimes trees, but mostly shrubs with decorative pinnate leaves. These are often deeply cut and wildly variegated. Flowers are small, almost invisible and, in fact, virtually unknown in cultivation.

Polyscias 'Golden Prince'.
Golden Aralia. Cultivar

Polyscias guilfoylei 'Victoriae'.
Victoria Aralia. Polynesia

Portulacaria afra. Elephant's Food.
South Africa

Propagation is from cuttings which, in the tropics, are struck directly in the ground and grow at once in leaf-rich, moist soil. When the growing stems become leggy, prune back to induce lower growth. As well as container plantings, *Polyscias* make marvellous hedges and privacy screens.

The botanical name is from the Greek *polys skias*, meaning much shade, and that's the light condition they adore.

Polyscias scutellaria. Shield-leaf.
Pacific Islands

Portulacaria

(por-tyoo-la-**kea**-ree-ə)   ☼ Ⓦ
Elephant's Food, Spekboom,
Elephant Bush
All year; 12 ft/3.5 m; horizontally branched; evergreen
PORTULACACEAE

Elephants presumably get the credit for eating this succulent shrub merely because they're the largest of its admirers. In fact it is eaten and enjoyed by a whole range of herbivorous animals, both wild and domestic. But it just wouldn't sound exciting to call a plant 'cow food', however spectacular it might be.

Portulacaria afra is a densely branched, red-stemmed shrub clothed in obovate, succulent ½ in/ 1 cm leaves. The tiny pink flowers, ¼ in/5 mm in diameter and forming in clusters of three, are rarely seen in cultivation—nor of course are the seed capsules.

Easily grown from cuttings, this decorative South African shrub can be trained to all sorts of Bonsai shapes, or clipped as hedges and topiaries. It does best in a sandy, well-drained soil with water in dry seasons but not otherwise lest the plant become too leggy.

Posoqueria

(po-zo-**keer**-ee-ə)   ☀ ☀ Ⓦ Ⓗ
Needle Flower
Spring; 6–20 ft/2–6 m; crowded; treelike; evergreen

RUBIACEAE   FRAGRANT

In tropical gardens, the perfume of the Frangipani is rivalled only by that of the exotic Needle Flower whose white blossoms open throughout spring.

Posoqueria latifolia. Needle Flower. Guiana

Though it reaches small tree size in the tropics (20 ft/6 m) it keeps to a tidier shrub size in warm climates, with brilliantly glossy 8 in/20 cm evergreen leaves putting on a show at all times. The flowers are really extraordinary—6 in/15 cm long tubes tipped with small pointed petals that spring open as dainty white reflexed flowers, sometimes with projecting anthers. These flowers appear in densely crowded clusters at branch ends and continue to open for months. The occasional yellow fruits are edible but rarely appetizing.

Posoqueria is normally propagated from cuttings and grows rapidly in the deep, rich soil it likes. It is hardy down to about 27°F/−3°C. Grow from semi-hardwood cuttings taken in the cooler months and plant out in light-textured soil with good drainage.

Potentilla fruticosa 'Tangerine'. Golden Hard Hack. Hybrid

Potentilla

(poh-ten-**til**-lə)   ☼ ☀ C T
Cinquefoil, Widdy, Five-finger, Hard Hack
Summer; 2–4 ft/60 cm–1.2 m; compact; deciduous

ROSACEAE

Omnipresent in cool northern hemisphere gardens, the *Potentilla* genus of the rose family is perhaps most commonly seen in its annual or perennial forms which include many mat-forming alpines. Around 500 species are recorded, as well as many varieties of *P. fruticosa*, a shrub that is found right around the world in the northern polar band.

All *Potentillas* have the telltale 5-lobed leaves and flowers, with petals and sepals also in multiples of five. The flowers may be single or double, can be pink, scarlet, maroon, orange, white or yellow. Shrubby Cinquefoils are raised from seed, divisions or cuttings and are delightful plants for the pathside or low border. Flowers do not last well when picked.

Potentilla fruticosa. Shrubby Cinquefoil. N. Temperate Zone

Prosopis

(proh-**soh**-pis)   ☼ W H
Honey Mesquite, Algarrobo
Spr-Sum; 10–35 ft/3–12 m; many-trunked; deciduous

FABACEAE   FRAGRANT

Native to the American deserts from California to Argentina, the showy *Prosopis* or Mesquite is closely related to the world's Acacias. Though sometimes growing to tree height when its long taproot strikes underground water, it is more usually a large shrub with many trunks. Though largely deciduous, the species *P. glandulosa* (one of 25) is for much of the year a welcome shade tree in the desert, its spiny branches decked through spring and summer with long staminate spikes of dull yellow bloom.

Prosopis glandulosa torreyana. Algarrobo. California to Argentina

Easily propagated from firm young shoots struck in damp sand, the Mesquite grows fast in sandy soil with very little water. The elongated bean pods that follow the flower display are a valuable source of food, the seeds being ground into flour. Cattle eat the pods, shoots and all, bees feed hungrily on the pollen.

Some of the *Prosopis* species are found in tropical Africa and Asia, but none in Australia, where *P. glandulosa* is in fact a prohibited plant.

Prostanthera

(pros-**tan**-thur-ə)   ☼ ☀ T
Mintbush
Spring; 1–10 ft/30 cm–3 m; erect;
spreading; evergreen

LAMIACEAE   AROMATIC

Short-lived but splashy-flowering members of the mint family, Australia's endemic Mintbushes (*Prostanthera* spp.) bloom briefly but with incredible profusion, mostly in shades of mauve, and harmonize perfectly with Prunus, Cornus, and other treasures of the cool-climate spring garden.

Prostanthera ovalifolia. Purple Mintbush. E. Australia

Prostanthera sp. aff. *ovalifolia.* E. Australia

Grow them in a sheltered position anywhere the soil is gravelly, well-drained and rich in leaf mould. They can be propagated from firm-tip cuttings taken in summer or autumn and struck in moist, gritty sand. Longer-lived plants can be produced by grafting *Prostanthera* scions onto stock from the Australian West-

ringia, which is more resistant to root rot. All species can be compacted by lightly trimming new season's growth after blooming is done.

P. ovalifolia is the most common species, but there are about 40 others including silvery *P. baxteri* (shown). Though mauve and white species are most often seen, yellow, green and red *Prostanthera* have also been found.

Protea

(**proh**-tee-ə)   ☼ ☀ T
Sugarbush, Honey Flower
Aut or Spr; 3–10 ft/1–3 m; sparse;
evergreen

PROTEACEAE   LIGHTLY FRAGRANT

Of the many remarkable personalities in Greek mythology, none was more remarkable than Proteus. He had the power to assume any shape and it was this gift that suggested the name *Protea* to 18th century botanists classifying a highly variable group of South African plants. They believed them unique but we now know there are close relatives in South America and Australia. The true Protea genus, however, will always be associated with South Africa.

There are about 100 species, mostly from the sea-girt Cape Province, and they are not too difficult to grow once their needs are under-

Prostanthera magnifica. Splendid Mintbush. Western Australia

Prostanthera baxteri. Silver Mintbush. S. and W. Australia

Protea neriifolia. Oleander-leaf Protea. South Africa

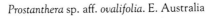

Protea repens. Sugarbush.
South Africa

Proteas last well when cut, and retain shape after fading, so are often saved for dried arrangements. Flower size is not necessarily related to shrub size, by the way. The startling King Protea (*P. cynaroides*) produces 10 in/ 25 cm blooms on a bush only 3 ft/ 1 m tall and must be staked to prevent overbalancing.

Proteas can be raised from autumn- or spring-sown seed, but germination is erratic and the resultant seedlings often untrue to type. Better to use cuttings of well-ripened shoots taken in summer. These should be half-

Protea grandiceps. Peach Protea (buds). South Africa

Protea obtusifolia. Silver Protea. South Africa

stood. Sandy soil is the first rule (preferably acid, though some species will make do with an alkaline pH). Next come perfect drainage and full sun. They are slow growers and relatively short-lived, but the beauty of the often gigantic blooms makes every effort worthwhile.

stripped of leaves, inserted firmly in finely sifted compost, and covered nightly with a bell-jar or upturned bottle, which should be lifted and dried internally each morning.

As a generalization, *Proteas* bear concave, silky leaves clasping tough, woody stems. The blooms consist of a number of tubular flowers surrounded by several rows of coloured bracts. All attract honeyeating birds. Most species are hardy down to 17°F/−8°C. Water regularly through the year, but don't overdo it.

Protea cynaroides. King Protea. South Africa

Protea latifolia. Open Protea. South Africa

Protea eximia. Brilliant Protea.
South Africa

Prunus virginiana. Chokeberry.
Newfoundland to Kansas

Prunus munsonia. Wild Goose Plum.
Ohio to Texas

Prunus

(**proo**-nəs)   ☼ Ⓒ Ⓣ Ⓦ
Bush Cherry, Chokeberry,
Flowering Almond Cherry
*Spring; 2–5 ft/60–150 cm; multiple
trunked; evergreen*

ROSACEAE   FRAGRANT

Impossible to describe the hundreds of *Prunus* species in a single sentence. Beyond their passing resemblance to the true roses, it really takes a creative imagination to spot the relationship between, say, a Japanese Flowering Cherry (*P. serrulata*) and an evergreen Portugal Laurel (*P. lusitanica*). In this book, though, we're only concerned with the shrub-sized members of the genus, which automatically rules out all the popular fruiting trees (Peach, Apricot, Cherry, Plum, etc) and the graceful Flowering Cherry cultivars from Japan. We are still left with some charming ornamental plants, mainly from North America.

The most popular flowering types are the many cultivars of *P. glandulosa* from China and Japan, a sweet touch of spring where space is limited. These are dainty, suckering shrubs less than 3 ft/1 m tall, producing many erect stems packed from top to bottom with single, double, white or pink flowers.

P. lusitanica, from Iberia and nearby islands, is an evergreen which must be kept to shrub size by pruning. It has tiny cream flowers in long racemes and produces ½ in/1 cm purple fruit.

The American natives include *P. munsonia*, the Wild Goose Plum from the midwest; completely cold resistant, it bears ½ in/1 cm single white flowers, quite fragrant, and red to yellow ¾ in/2 cm plum fruit. *P. virginiana* is found from Newfoundland down to Kansas and North Carolina. Its white flowers appear in tightly packed racemes, followed by acid, purple fruit less than ¼ in/5 mm in diameter.

Prunus lusitanica. Portugal Laurel.
Spain, Canary Islands

Prunus glandulosa.
Flowering Almond Cherry. Japan, China

Prunus glandulosa 'Sinensis Alba'.
White Almond Cherry. Japan, China

Pseudanthus

(syoo-**dan**-thəs)   ☼ ✸ W H
Pseudanthus
Win-Spr; 2 ft/60 cm; compact; evergreen

PICRODENDRACEAE

A dainty, compact shrub about which I can find very little. It grows in sparsely timbered forests of north Queensland mountain ranges west of Cairns. The soil is mostly clay with a deal of stone rubble on the surface, and stone outcrops seem to provide a protected site for these delicate plants which need shelter but enjoy full sun.

Pseudanthus seem to have no popular name; they look like Ericaceae but are in fact part of the Euphorbia group. Leaves are narrow and thread-like, about ½ in/1 cm in length; the flowers are tiny, white, multi-pointed stars.

Pseudanthus pimelioides. N. Queensland

Pseuderanthemum atropurpureum.
Purple Netbush. Pacific Islands

Pseuderanthemum

(*syn.* ERANTHEMUM)

(syoo-dur-**an**-thə-mum)   ☼ ✸ W H
Netbush, Eldorado
All year; 3–6 ft/1–2 m; straggly; evergreen

ACANTHACEAE

Seen only in glasshouses outside the true tropics, *Pseuderanthemums* don't take to cold or even cool weather, becoming decidedly unhappy when temperatures drop below 50°F/10°C.

Only one of 60-odd species is seen much in cultivation: *P. reticulatum,* the Golden Netbush or Eldorado, from the Pacific nation of Vanuatu (formerly the New Hebrides). It has golden stems and bright yellow leaves with a network of green lines that could be mistaken for symptoms of a nutrient deficiency. In partly shaded positions it tends to settle for a greener tone.

The Netbush is grown from warm-weather cuttings, is generally erect and bushy. Where the climate is warm enough, bloom is continuous. This consists of dainty, carmine-spotted white flowers, borne in panicles at both leaf axils and branch tips. Rich, well-drained soil is necessary, with regular water and fertilizer. Species *P. atropurpureum* has deep purple leaves marked with pink or green. Fijian *P. laxiflorum* has light green leaves, profuse mauve flowers.

Pseuderanthemum reticulatum.
Golden Netbush. Vanuatu

Pseuderanthemum laxiflorum.
Drooping Netbush. Fiji

Psidium

(**sid**-ee-əm)   ☼ T H
Cherry Guava
*Summer; to 25 ft/7.5 m; fairly open;
evergreen*

MYRTACEAE

Though native only to the warmer parts of Central and South America, the many Guava species have spread around the globe to become perhaps the most widely grown of tropical fruits outside the banana and mango. They are no trouble to propagate

Psidium littorale. Cherry Guava. Brazil

from cuttings and naturalize readily once established.

Over 100 species have been listed, though only three are commonly seen away from their original homes. Foremost among them is *P. littorale* (syn *P. cattleyanum*) the Purple or Cherry Guava, which is often seen as a red-barked, glossy evergreen shrub of no more than 10 ft/3 m. The flowers are white, solitary, rather like Eucalyptus blossom. The summer fruit is purple-red and cherry-sized. They are eaten raw or, more often, made into jams and jellies. The Cherry Guava has a wider climatic range than other species, especially close to the sea. It will grow where oranges do.

Psychotria

(sai-**kot**-ree-ə) ☼ W H
Wild Coffee
Spring; 3–10 ft/1–3 m; compact; evergreen

RUBIACEAE   FRAGRANT

Psychotrias have been relegated to the status of also-rans in the company of other beautiful warm-climate shrubs such as Bouvardia, Gardenia, Ixora and Luculia. Yet they have many good features; glossy evergreen foliage, a long display of dense terminal clusters of pink, white or yellow flowers (small, it's true, but very

Psychotria maingayi. Coffee Berry. Malaysia

Psychotria capensis. Wild Coffee. South Africa

fragrant) and a colourful crop of berries to follow. But that's just not enough when it comes to the fierce competition for space in the warm-climate garden. So most of them remain local favourites in their home territories, which could be South or Central America, Africa, the Caribbean, even Fiji. They can be grown from the seed of dried berries or from cuttings struck under heat.

Illustrated *P. capensis* (Wild Coffee), from Africa, is occasionally seen in foreign areas with similar climates. It grows into a naturally rounded, compact bush no more than 3 ft/1 m tall. The bright yellow flower heads appear through spring. Its fruits are black and, in spite of the name, not edible. Related *P. maingayi* is grown for its clusters of scarlet fruit on arching stems. The flowers are white.

Ptelea

(te-**lee**-ə) ☀ T
Hop Tree, Wafer Ash,
Stinking Ash, Shrubby Trefoil
Spr-Sum; to 13 ft/4 m; spreading; deciduous

RUTACEAE   AROMATIC

'Pleasantly aromatic' in one plant dictionary has been modified to 'ill smelling' in another: one suspects scent is not why the *Ptelea* is grown.

It is a slow-moving deciduous shrub (sometimes even a small tree) which is easily propagated from layers and is not fussy about soil so long as it is well-drained.

The trifoliate, ash-like leaves are joined by fragrant, greenish flowers in large spring clusters. These develop into winged fruits in late summer when the leaves colour an intense gold. All parts of the shrub have tonic properties. Several leaf varieties and 5 other species of *Ptelea* exist, all endemic to North America.

Ptelea trifoliata aurea. Hop Bush. E. North America

Pamela Harper

Pterostyrax

(ter-ro-**stai**-raks) ☼ ☀ T W
Epaulette Bush
Summer; 12 ft/4 m; treelike; twiggy; deciduous

STYRACACEAE

To understand the logic of this graceful plant's nomenclature, one must flash back to the 19th century when officers' epaulettes were all dangling fringes of golden thread—the specific name *psilophyllus* means fringe-leaf.

Pterostyrax is a small genus of deciduous shrubs or small trees

Pterostyrax psilophyllus. Epaulette Bush. China, Japan

which become radiantly beautiful in early summer when decked with golden fringes. Propagation is easy from seed, cuttings or layers, and the Epaulette Bush prefers a sunny position in well-drained but moist, loamy soil. It is hardy in the southern states of Australia, the UK and the USA as far north as New England.

Pultenaea

(pul-ten-**ae**-ə)   ☼ ☀ T W
Bush Pea, Bacon-and-eggs
Spring; 3 in-7 ft/8 cm-2 m; dense; evergreen

FABACEAE

This book has included many genera of endemic Australian pea flowers because of their beauty and because they have been grown with great success in other temperate gardening areas. But the genus *Pultenaea* is the largest pea genus from the southern continent, including more than 100 species, varying from tall, flower-draped shrubs to prostrate matting plants. A fine example of the taller types is illustrated *P. altissima* from New South Wales and Queensland. Its leaves are obovate and about ½ in/1 cm in length. The flowers cover the bush in golden profusion.

P. pedunculata is quite the opposite—a low, matting plant only an inch or so high. It has sharp, stemless leaves only 1¾ in/4 cm in length and bears its red and yellow flowers singly on comparatively long stems.

Propagate all species from scarified seed and grow in light soil, rich in leaf mould. Full sun or part shade are equally advantageous.

Pultenea altissima. Bush Pea. E. Australia

Pultenea pedunculata. Bacon-and-eggs. S.E. Australia, Tasmania

Punica

(**pyoo**-nik-ə)   ☼ ☀ C T W
Pomegranate
Summer; 3-13 ft/1-4 m; dense; deciduous or evergreen

LYTHRACEAE

The tall-growing *Punica granatum* or Pomegranate is rarely seen now, outside the Middle East, for with the smaller scale of modern gardens every plant has to earn its keep. And we have found more fragrant flowers and much more tasty fruit to take the place of the once popular Pomegranate.

Contrariwise, the Dwarf Pomegranate, *P. granatum nana*, is more

Punica granatum 'Flore Pleno'. Pomegranate. Mid East to India

widely seen every day. Its harvest may be of little use, but it has other advantages. Rarely more than 3 ft/ 1 m high or wide, it produces dainty miniatures of the larger Pomegranate flowers and fruit throughout the warmer weather.

Grow it in full sun, in coarse, gravelly soil enriched with a proportion of well-rotted manure or compost. During prolonged droughts, an occasional deep soaking should keep it going, otherwise rainfall will meet its water needs. Light pruning at the end of each winter will preserve the plant's neat, compact shape. *Punicas* will resist heat and drought to a great degree and are also hardy down to 17°F/−8°C.

Punica granatum nana. Dwarf Pomegranate. Asia

Putterlickia

(put-ter-**lik**-ee-ə) ☼ Ⓣ Ⓦ
Firethorn, Pink Nutbush
Summer; 2–6 ft/60 cm–2 m; spiny; deciduous

CELASTRACEAE

There are only two species of *Putterlickia*, both of them endemic to South Africa, where they grow sparsely on the west coast. *P. pyracantha* is the more decorative of the two and quite popular in cultivation along the coast and in hot, dry areas.

Putterlickia pyracantha. Firethorn. South Africa

Commonly grown from seed, *Putterlickia* grows slowly into a spiny, rigid bush with horizontal branches. The shiny obovate leaves often appear alternately and are joined in summer by starry 4- or 5-petalled creamy-white flowers. These appear in axillary panicles and, after fertilization, give way to decorative orange fruit. The shrub is deciduous and very spiny, the fruits long lasting.

Pyracantha

(pai-rə-**kan**-thə) ☼ ☀ Ⓣ Ⓦ
Firethorn
Autumn; 5–16 ft/1.5–5 m; arching; evergreen

ROSACEAE

Though grown exclusively for their superb display of autumn berry colour, *Pyracanthas* are a useful genus of sturdy evergreen shrubs at any time of year. Even their display of tiny spring flowers is heartening in its profusion.

Pyracantha CV 'Waterii'. Spring blossom

Pyracantha coccinea 'Lalandei'. Scarlet Firethorn. S. Europe

Pyracantha rodgersiana 'Flava'. Yellow Firethorn. China

The Firethorns are dense, spiny shrubs and grow well as hedges, espaliers or even groundcovers. The berries, of course, colour better in cooler districts, and dry weather seems only to improve the yield. The berries come in many colours, ripening from summer to winter according to variety.

P. coccinea 'Lalandei' is the most

Pyracantha crenulata. Himalaya Firethorn. China (Yunnan)

brilliant red, P. rodgersiana the best orange-yellow, and flat-fruited P. angustifolia probably the most commonly grown.

All half-dozen species and their many, many varieties may be grown from semi-hardwood cuttings taken in autumn or winter and struck with heat or misting. A rich, well-drained compost gives the best berries, but beyond that they're tolerant of all soils. Pruning is scarcely necessary if you cut branches for decoration.

Quercus

(**kwur**-kəs)   ☼ T
Kermes Oak
Spring; 8–20 ft/2.5–6 m; shrubby; evergreen

FAGACEAE

The old saying that 'tall oaks from little acorns grow' is not universally so. One species at least has adapted itself to life in arid areas around the Mediterranean basin (south of France, North Africa and Asia Minor) by turning itself into a small evergreen shrub.

Quercus coccifera. Kermes Oak. Mediterranean

Propagated from acorns, of course, it grows very slowly in any poor but well-drained soil to all of 8 ft/2.5 m— a good size to adorn a large rockery. In classical times it was valued as the home of the Kermes insect which was processed into a crimson dye. The smallish leaves are most variable and may be flat and smooth or prickly as any holly.

Raphiolepis indica. Indian Hawthorn. South China

Raphiolepis

(raf-ee-oh-**lae**-pəs)   ☼ C T W
Indian Hawthorn,
Yeddo Hawthorn
Spring; 4–10 ft/1.5–3 m; dense; evergreen

ROSACEAE   FRAGRANT

Raphiolepis can be relied on for spring display in climates from cold to warm-temperate. Hardy down to 15°F/ −9°C, they also thrive close to

Raphiolepis umbellata. Yeddo Hawthorn. Japan

Raphiolepis X 'Springtime'. Hybrid Hawthorn

the sea in sandy soil, and are a problem only in very dry areas, where they need semi-shade.

Although *Raphiolepis* may be started from seed, they usually save you the trouble by producing seedlings freely. However, these may not be true to type, and a more reliable method is to take cuttings of half-ripened tips during autumn and winter.

Sweet-scented *R. indica* has lightly toothed leaves and sprays of delicate pink blossoms, followed by black berries. More commonly seen Yeddo Hawthorn (*R. umbellata*) has leathery, simple leaves and red-centred white flowers in packed clusters. *R. indica* 'Springtime' is a low-growing cultivar that forms an absolute blanket of fragrant blossom, very popular for landscaping in southern California.

Rauvolfia

(rou-**vool**-fee-ə)   ☼ ❊ W H
Rauvolfia
Summer; 5 ft/1.5 m; deciduous

APOCYNACEAE

Related to the Vincas and the Plumerias, some 70 species of *Rauvolfia* are found in many tropical areas of the world, though principally

in South-east Asia and South America. Several species have medicinal value and are the source of sophisticated tranquillizers. They are propagated from seed, stem and root cuttings and grow happily in deep, leaf-rich soil with plenty of water.

Most popular in cultivation is *R. verticillata*, a 5 ft/1.5 m deciduous shrub bearing whorls of 5 in/12 cm glossy leaves that resemble those of Frangipani, and long-stemmed terminal clusters of 2 in/5 cm white blooms. Other species have greenish flowers. All species have the poisonous white sap of the Dogbane family.

Rauvolfia verticillata. S. China

Regelia

(rə-**gel**-ee-ə)   ☼ T H
Barrens Regelia
Spring; to 10 ft/3 m; pyramidal; evergreen

MYRTACEAE

Five known species of *Regelia* are endemic to Western Australia, and have a most distinctive appearance, their foliage being arranged in two pairs of opposite rows. The flowers, borne in terminal clusters, may be mauve or, as in our illustrated species, bright red.

Propagation via seed requires great patience as it may be 8 years before blossoming begins, so cuttings provide the easy way out. A light, acid soil is essential, with good drainage, but even so, growth is not fast. Though the leaf structure of *R. velutina* looks hard and geometrical, it is in fact quite soft, with a greyish finish. The plant has a pyramidal shape.

Regelia velutina. Barrens Regelia. Western Australia

Murray Fagg

Reinwardtia

(*syn.* LINUM)

(rain-**wort**-ee-ə)   ☼ ❊ T W
Yellow Flax
Winter; 3 ft/1 m; suckering; evergreen

LINACEAE

Low growing, golden flowering plants that light up the cold weather, *Reinwardtias* are grown from winter divisions or from soft-tip cuttings taken in spring. A light, well drained soil is best, and *Reinwardtias* should be attempted in warm winter climates only, for they are not in the least frost hardy. They look well in semi-shade, but the flowers, which appear for about six weeks in early winter, show up best in full sun, provided ample water can be laid on.

Mature plants grow leggy and should be pinched out regularly to force branching and more flowers. Encourage the formation of a dense clump by chopping the whole plant back to half height in late winter. Yellow Flax is evergreen, though sparsely foliaged, producing many erect 3 ft/1 m stems from a suckering rootstock. Its leaves are simple and rather soft. If grown in a pot it can be hidden among other shrubs when not in bloom.

Reinwardtia indica. Yellow Flax. India, China

Retama monosperma. Mt Etna Broom. Spain, N. Africa

Tony Rodd

Rhagodia baccata. Seaberry Saltbush. S. Australia, Tasmania

Retama

(*syn.* GENISTA, SPARTIUM)

(rə-**tah**-mə)   ☼ T
Mt Etna Broom,
White Weeping Broom
Win-Spr; 7–10 ft/2–3 m; many-stemmed; deciduous

FABACEAE   FRAGRANT

We love *Retama* for its white pea flowers borne profusely along the grey-green stems in spring. They have

a sweet, almost cloying fragrance, but so far as their leaves are concerned, it's here today, gone tomorrow. In any case, the leaves are not important.

R. monosperma is a short-trunked plant with weeping, slender stems, found all about the Mediterranean. Able to withstand heat, it also thrives down to 27°F/−3°C and seems to do well anywhere.

Retama is propagated almost exclusively from seed. Just collect it in autumn, store in a cool, dry place and sow in pots of sandy mix the following spring after a 24-hour soak in warm water. Set the seedlings out in well-drained, gravelly soil, water lightly and just watch the action. Prune all over lightly after bloom.

Rhagodia

(rə-**goh**-dee-ə)   ☼ ☀ T W H
Seaberry Saltbush,
Coast Saltbush
All year; 5 ft/1.5 m; scrambling; evergreen

CHENOPODIACEAE

A very useful plant for the seaside garden, and also for dry inland areas, monotypic *Rhagodia baccata* is a much-branched, scrambling shrub noted for its profuse crop of red ber-

ries borne most of the year. The broadly spear-shaped leaves are up to 1¼ in/3 cm in length. They are semi-succulent, whitish on the reverse, distracting the eye completely from the insignificant whitish flowers that precede the berries.

Propagate from cuttings and set out in light, well-drained soil—in nature they grow in coastal sand dunes. A very useful plant in windy positions where salt air is a problem.

Rhamnus frangula. Alder Buckthorn. Europe, N. Africa, Asia

Rhamnus

(**ram**-nəs)   ☼ ☀ C T
Alder Buckthorn
Spring; 12 ft/3.5 m; dense; deciduous

RHAMNACEAE

Grown principally for its form and its screening capacity, the Alder Buckthorn is considered a useful plant in European coastal gardens. *Rhamnus frangula* is deciduous, with attractively margined leaves; it is but one of some 150 species, mostly from the temperate northern hemisphere.

Propagated from autumn seed or cuttings, it is not fussy about soil and grows fast almost anywhere in sun or partial shade. The leaves colour gold in autumn; insignificant green flowers appear in early spring umbels and tiny reddish fruit turn black when ripe. Eating them is not recommended as they are a secondary source for medicinal cascara. *R. frangula* is resistant to drought, wind and heat. Its wood has traditionally been used to produce charcoal for gunpowder.

Rhododendron 'Avocet'. Hybrid

Rhododendron ponticum. Common Rhododendron. Spain, Asia Minor

Rhododendron

(roh-doh-**den**-drən)   ☀ C T
Tree Rose
Spring; 2½–40 ft/80 cm–12 m; treelike; evergreen

ERICACEAE   SOME FRAGRANT

How curious that the largest of all shrubs (the gigantic tree *Rhododendrons* of the Himalayas), and the tiny heathers of the Scottish moorlands should be close relatives within the same botanical family, Ericaceae. Not much over a century ago, gardeners of Europe and North America were limited to only a few *Rhododendron* species from mountain areas of their own countries. Perhaps 15 were known in all, as opposed to the 800 and more known and grown today. And that is only the species—the modern cultivars would number several thousand at least. Assuming such a visit to be possible, a garden fancier from the mid-19th century might well be struck dumb with amazement on visiting a modern *Rhododendron* nursery. Almost every plant he saw would be quite unfamiliar. There would be new flower

Rhododendron 'Pink Delight'.
Vireya Rhododendron. Hybrid

Rhododendron CV 'Fragrantissimum'. Fragrant Rhododendron. Hybrid

ers to explore and bring back new species from all over the globe. One of the great success stories of that era was the *Rhododendron*, whose species were discovered by the hundred in China, Tibet and Assam.

Today, among all flowering shrub genera, majestic *Rhododendron* surely reign supreme, for the sheer size, brilliance and profusion of their flowers. Most types produce great trusses of bloom in a colour range no other plant genus can rival. Even out of bloom they are attractive, densely clothed with large evergreen leaves.

But there's a catch. *Rhododendrons* won't grow just anywhere. They are native to and do best in places where winters are cool to cold, springs cool

creating their private pleasure domes surrounded by park-like gardens. They engaged designers and landscaping teams who in turn sought out more spectacular plants to furnish their demesnes. There was such big money to be made that many larger nurseries commissioned plant hunt-

Rhododendron lineariifolium.
Spider Flower. Japan

Rhododendron yakusimanum. Dwarf Japanese Rhododendron. Japan

forms, new colours, new habits of growth, new fragrances. Many of them might not be recognizable to him as *Rhododendrons* at all, so great has the change been in this beautiful genus of plants.

The *Rhododendron* is a perfect example of supply and demand as applied to horticulture. The late 19th century saw the rise of the great private estate, as newly rich captains of industry vied with the aristocracy in

and moist, summers warm and humid. They grow perfectly in many parts of Britain and Ireland, in the western United States, in New Zealand and in the mountain tablelands of eastern Australia. *Rhododendrons* do best when protected from hot afternoon sun and strong winds —especially hot *drying* winds. They stay fresh in the rising humidity below tall trees. Generally speaking, the cooler the climate, the more sun is tolerated, especially in winter. Full shade all day results in disappointing flowers, but in warm areas such as the east coasts of Australia and South Africa and the coast of southern California, shade is beneficial, even necessary, during much

Rhododendron X 'Loderi'. (*R. fortunei* X *R. griffithianum*). Loder's White Rhododendron. Hybrid

of the summer. There, light year-round shade may be the only way of growing these desirable shrubs.

Wherever they're planted, soil should be water-retentive, yet porous enough to allow excess water to drain freely. A light, sandy loam enriched with well-rotted compost or leaf mould is suitable. *Rhododendrons* detest lime, and must have an acid soil and a pH of between 5 and 6. Keep the plants consistently moist year round (but never sodden) and mulch annually with compost or old manure to conserve water and feed the surface roots.

Rhododendron 'Earl of Athlone'. Hybrid

Rhododendron macgregoriae X *lochae*. New Guinea hybrid

Rhododendron augustinii. Blue Rhododendron. Sichuan, China

Rhododendron 'Princess Anne'. Hybrid

Rhododendrons hybridize easily, so do not come true from seed. Propagate them vegetatively from spring layers lifted in autumn or from 5 in/ 12 cm semi-hardwood cuttings. These should be taken from early summer to mid-autumn and struck in a gritty mix with warmth and humidity.

Because of their mountain origins, many *Rhododendrons* are perfectly hardy and will withstand temperatures below freezing. Others, from more tropical regions, can stand only the odd light frost. The new Malesian hybrids from New Guinea are some of these. Your local nurseryman will advise you on the best species for your area.

The name *Rhododendron*, most appropriately, means Tree Rose.

Rhodomyrtus tomentosa. Rose Myrtle. India to Philippines

Rhodomyrtus

(roh-doh-**mur**-təs) ☼ W H
Rose Myrtle, Hill Guava,
Hill Gooseberry, Downy Myrtle
Summer; 5 ft/1.5 m; densely foliaged; greyish; evergreen

MYRTACEAE   AROMATIC

A small genus of 20 or 30 species, the Rose Myrtles are found from India to the Philippines, and down to Australia and New Caledonia. Any of several species is useful in the warm-climate garden or heated glasshouse, where their gay, hot-pink myrtle flowers appear all summer. Downy grey-green leaves and purple fruits help keep the bushes attractive all year, but regular summer water is a must, as is a mulch to keep the root system damp.

Satisfactory propagation is obtained by sowing seed in flats. *Rhodomyrtus tomentosa* is not particular as to soil, and will withstand several degrees of frost. The attractive fruit are quite edible, with a sweet, aromatic pulp. Eat them raw or make into a delicious jam.

Rhodotypos

(roh-doh-**tai**-pəs) ☼ ☀ T
White Kerria, Jetbead
Spr-Sum; 3–6 ft/1–2 m; erect; deciduous

ROSACEAE

A most handsome species of the rose family, *Rhodotypos* is monotypic, and greatly resembles the other plant which lends it a popular name— Kerria. It has the same arching stems and good-looking pleated leaves as those of a raspberry. Its flowers, however, are white instead of yellow.

The leaves are simple and have silky reverses, the flowers are borne singly at branch ends. Quite hardy in England, and in coastal areas of the United States, it would need considerable frost protection and a heavy mulch in central areas of North America.

Propagation is by seed or cuttings, and the Jetbead is not fussy about soil provided it is well drained. Around 6 ft/2 m is a good height for this plant in the garden, though in the wild it may reach as much as 15 ft/ 4.5 m.

Pamla Toler

Rhodotypos scandens. White Kerria. Japan

Rhus

(*syn.* MALOSMA, TOXICODENDRON, SCHMALTZIA)

(**roos**) ☼ T W
Sumach, Sugarbush
Sum-Aut; 2½ ft–10 ft/75 cm–3 m; spreading; mostly deciduous

ANACARDIACEAE

Though many of the 150-odd species of *Rhus* are grown as ornamental plants, others have a commercial usage as the source of lacquers and tannin. Useful plants indeed—but for many people, impossible to touch without causing repetitive dermatitis. Still, if you're not allergic to them, and if they're not prohibited where you live, several *Rhus* are attractive

Rhus ovata. Sugarbush. S. California, Arizona

Rhus typhina 'Laciniata'. Stag's Horn Sumach.
E. North America

look good enough to eat. They are mostly endemic to North America, on both sides of the border. A few are native to other parts of the northern hemisphere, particularly Europe. The illustrated flowering species *R. sanguineum* and *R. aureum* are favourite shrubs for the cooler-climate garden, producing masses of spicily fragrant bloom mostly on spiny stems. These appear for quite a few weeks towards the end of winter and into spring. Where autumns are frosty, most species will colour well. *R. aureum* defoliates unless watering is continued into summer. *R. sanguineum* prefers a cool, moist climate, is hardy down to 14°F/−10°C.

R. grossularium, R. sativum and *R. nigrum* are respectively the gooseberry, red and black currants of the cooler kitchen garden, and all native to Europe and Asia.

Ribes aureum. Golden Currant.
N. America, West Coast

garden subjects, particularly the deciduous types.

The Sugarbush, *Rhus ovata*, is not deciduous, but a semi-arid-climate plant from dry inland areas of California and Arizona, tolerant of both heat and drought. It is propagated from seed, planted in autumn, and needs very little water. Its light yellow flowers are succeeded by reddish, hairy seed capsules.

Rhus typhina, on the other hand, is both deciduous and an important source of tannin. Also propagated from seed, it has elegant compound greenish-gold leaves that colour well before falling. The branches are velvety like real stag's horn, and taper to crimson, hairy seed capsules that persist all winter. It is both heat and cold resistant.

Both species grow anywhere except where the soil is alkaline.

Ribes sativum. Red Currant. W. Europe

Like the flowering currants, they can be grown from hardwood cuttings taken as soon as the leaves fall in autumn. Cuttings should be 12 in/30 cm in length, and potted so that only the tips appear above the soil. Where winters are frosty, bury the cuttings outdoors until spring, then pot up.

Ribes are deciduous, have lobed leaves, grow best in well-drained soils with an annual spring top-dressing. Well-grown plants can reach 10 ft/3 m.

Berries of the fruiting types are as attractive to birds as they are to humans, and it is recommended they be covered with fine nets until picking time.

Ribes

(*syn.* GROSSULARIA)

(**rai**-beez)   ☼ ✳ C T
Currants, Gooseberries
Spr-Sum; 4½–12 ft/1.5–4 m; bushy; deciduous

GROSSULARIACEAE   FRAGRANT

Whether or not they are the fruiting currants and gooseberries of the kitchen garden, all 150 *Ribes* species

Ribes sanguineum. Flowering Currant.
N. America, West Coast

Ribes uva-crispa. European Gooseberry.
Europe

Ribes aureum var *gracillimum*.
Buffalo Currant. S. California

Richea

(rich-ee-ə) ☼ ◐ Ⓒ Ⓣ
Richea
Summer; 3 ft / 1 m; erect; sparse; evergreen
ERICACEAE

Nine species from Tasmania, one from mainland Australia, and a handful from Madagascar are the limitations on this curious genus of

Richea procera. Golden Richea. Tasmania

the Australian heath family (Epacridaceae). They are stiff, spiky shrubs, some particularly large for heath plants: Tasmanian *Richea pandanifolia* has been known to reach 50 ft/ 15 m in height with 3 ft/1 m leaves. But the species we illustrate, *R. procera*, is much more what we expect a heath to look like, with straight stems, spiky, stem-clasping leaves and terminal spikes of small flowers, in this case, yellow.

Richea can be grown from seed or cuttings, but the percentage of survival is low. Young seedlings must be handled with care and their fine roots should never be allowed to dry out. Give them a light soil mix that is moist and rich in leaf mould, keep in semi-shade until the plants are really growing. Other species bloom in white, red or pink.

Ricinocarpus pinifolius. Wedding Bush. Queensland to Tasmania

Ricinocarpus

(rai-**see**-noh-kah-pəs) ☼ ◐ Ⓦ Ⓗ
Wedding Bush
Spring; 3 ft / 1 m; bun-shaped; evergreen
EUPHORBIACEAE   FRAGRANT

The 15 species of Australia's endemic genus *Ricinocarpus* are rarely seen in cultivation—one suspects because

they are so common in nature and also not very reliable away from their natural sandy coastal soil. The popular Wedding Bush (*R. pinifolius*) is typical and found right down the east of Australia and Tasmania. It is a low, bun-shaped evergreen with narrow, linear leaves up to 1½ in/4 cm in length. In spring, the entire bush almost disappears under a profusion of 5-petalled white blooms that have an elusive fragrance.

The plants seed naturally, but planned propagation normally takes place from cuttings—though striking them is easier said than done. Give them a compost of moist, leaf-rich sand with regular water, and do try them in your coastal garden if plants should become available.

Ricinus

(rai-**see**-nəs) ☼ Ⓣ Ⓦ Ⓗ
Castor-oil Plant,
Castor Bean, Palma Christi
Summer; 6–15 ft/2.4–5 m; fast-growing; evergreen
EUPHORBIACEAE

The merest *threat* of a dose of castor oil used to send a spasm of terror through the house when I was a child. Though still included in the formulas of many paints and soaps, it rarely finds its way into the medicine cupboard any more, for which we

Ricinus communis. Castor Bean.
Tropical Africa

Murray Fagg

should all be grateful. Even the handsome plant from which it is extracted is somewhat passé. Once known as Palma Christi, it is now banned in some countries because of its poisonous seeds.

But what a variable plant! In cool or cold climates it may be seen as an annual; in warm temperate areas a shrub, but growing several yards or metres in a season; in the tropics a full-sized tree with palmate leaves up to 3 ft/1 m in diameter. The flowers appear in panicles at branch ends. They are petal-less, a mass of red-brown stamens.

If you still yearn for those 'good oil days', grow *Ricinus* in any well-drained soil by sowing seed in spring. The plant gives a lush tropical effect where its growing is legal, and will grow anywhere the soil is not too wet. It is originally from tropical Africa but is now naturalized in many warm regions with a constant proliferation of cultivars, mostly varying in leaf and flower colour. Both foliage and seeds cause an allergenic reaction on the skin of some sensitive souls. Seed pods should be pruned away and burned as soon as their colour begins to fade.

Robinia

(roh-**bin**-ee-ə)   ☼ T W
Rose Acacia,
Allegheny Moss, Locust
Summer; 6–10 ft/2–3 m; suckering; deciduous

FABACEAE   FRAGRANT

Endemic to the mainland United States, all 20 species of the lacy *Robinia* are considered as American as apple pie. The most commonly seen, both at home and abroad, is the tree-sized *Robinia pseudoacacia*, a deciduous, spiny plant which bears hanging racemes of fragrant cream pea flowers in spring, exactly like cream Wisteria if you could imagine such a thing!

But in fact there are many suckering shrub varieties of *Robinia* which are even more beautiful. The spineless *R. boyntonii*, dwarf *R. elliottii*, pale purple flowering *R. hispida* and the illustrated *R. kelseyi* are all less than 10 ft/3 m in height, while one pink flowering species, *R. nana*, grows only to 1 ft/30 cm.

Robinia kelseyi. Allegheny Moss. North Carolina

Most of these species are propagated from seed or suckers, but really fancy varieties should be grafted onto stock of *R. pseudoacacia*. All are very hardy but best grown in poor soil, lest they sucker in all directions. When they do this, however, they are very helpful in erosion control. *Robinias* are unfortunately mostly very spiny plants. Their deciduous foliage turns colour in autumn, mostly to a bright golden yellow.

Rondeletia

(ron-də-**lee**-shə)   ☼ ☀ T W
Rondeletia
Spring; 10 ft/3 m; dense; evergreen

RUBIACEAE   FRAGRANT

In the Caribbean and Central America, the native *Rondeletias* are fragrant and colourful for much of the year, and give a continuous display. However, as none of them is

Rondeletia strigosa. Hairy Rondeletia. Central America

Rondeletia amoena. Rondeletia. Central America

frost hardy, their flowering period grows shorter the further they are away from the tropics. In cooler temperate areas they are raised under glass with winter heat, but they can be grown outdoors anywhere temperatures never drop below freezing. In such climates, the clusters of tiny fragrant flowers appear briefly in early spring, with a few scattered throughout the season.

Rosa 'Penelope'. Hybrid Musk

Rosa 'Madame Meilland'. Hybrid Tea Rose

Rondeletia odorata. Sweet-scented Rondeletia. Cuba, Panama

Rondeletias do best in soil that is barely acid and well-drained; they need uniform moisture throughout the warmer months. Most often seen 10 ft/3 m *R. amoena* and much lower-growing *R. odorata* can be raised from 4 in/10 cm cuttings taken in spring and struck indoors under warm, humid conditions. *R. strigosa*, which has hairy leaves and a suckering habit, is best raised from divisions. It will flower more or less continuously in a warm-temperate climate. All three species are evergreen and improve with an annual pruning, taking flowered shoots back to within a few nodes of last year's growth.

Rosa

(roh-zə) ☼ Ⓒ Ⓣ Ⓦ
Rose
Spr–Aut; 2–29 ft/60 cm–9 m; spiny; deciduous

ROSACEAE

Judging from the literature of the ancient world, roses of one sort or another have been cultivated for at least 5000 years, making them the best-loved flower in history. The Chinese, we know from books, grew them around 3000 B.C. Several millennia later, the Greeks had a word for them, *Rhodos*, and gave that name to the Mediterranean island of Rhodes where they grew to perfection. Greek poets Sappho and Anacreon hailed the rose as queen of flowers.

Later still, the Romans prized these flowers for their fragrance, enjoying them at banquets, both as a delicacy and as a dedication to Venus, their goddess of love. Cleopatra spent 60 pounds weight of gold to buy rose petals for the famous banquet where she seduced Mark Antony. They carpeted the decks of her galley 20 inches thick beneath a golden net.

Roman historian Pliny describes 12 varieties of rose that were cultivated in Rome. Some are still grown, but now take second place to the beauties raised by modern hybridists. New rose species introduced from Persia and India, from China and North America, brought with them yellow, pink, bronze and cerise colourings, and the continuous blooming habit we now take for granted. The ancients knew roses as either red or white, and could look forward to their blooming only at the height of summer.

Roses are now grown all around the world, though wild species occur only north of the equator, and mainly in the temperate zone of all

Rosa 'Old Blush'. (The Last Rose of Summer)

continents. Some indeed have adapted to life almost on the edge of the tropics. Such a one is the Burmese *Rosa gigantea*, a parent of 'Nancy Hayward' (shown). This is one of a limited number of roses suited to really warm climates.

Generally speaking, roses are at their best in areas with mildly alkaline soil of clay texture, though many patient growers have succeeded in raising prize-winning blooms in acid soil and have even adapted sand to a suitable tilth. Over 250 wild species have been identified, and almost all of them have been used by hybridists to produce the rainbow of blooms available today. An entire book could be written on cultural directions for varying climates, and your local nurseryman is your best adviser.

In warm-temperate areas, roses are planted in mid-winter and normally pruned at the same time, except for winter flowering types. Where winters are harder, they are planted in autumn, given a heavy mulch over the roots and pruned when signs of new growth appear in spring.

Roses enjoy full sun, especially in the morning, and do best in a bed of their own, well away from marauding tree roots and without competition from other plants. They need regular feeding, and can exhaust the soil so completely that they leave it in a condition called 'rose sick'. A new rose should never be planted where one has been grown before without complete replacement of the soil over an area 3 ft/1 m square and as deep as the root system.

Regular watering is essential, and a deep surface mulch around the root areas will help produce top quality blooms. While 9 out of 10 rose plants bought today are of the 'hybrid tea' or 'floribunda' types (and even those have been back-crossed so often that they are now listed as a single type) many of the original species are coming back into fashion. They do not flower as continuously as the modern hybrids, but have a beauty and

Rosa X 'Nancy Hayward'. *R. gigantea* hybrid

Rosa 'Greensleeves'. 1980 Floribunda hybrid

Rosa laevigata. Cherokee Rose. China

Rosa banksiae lutea.
Lady Banks' Rose.

fragrance all their own.

Roses are no more prone to attack by pests and diseases than any other group of plants, but their blooms are normally so perfect that any sign of damage stands out. Aphids are the most obvious of pests, though probably the least serious. They crowd new growth of foliage and flower buds, sucking tasty juices and often leaving distortion in their wake. Blast them away with the hose or check with any spray formulated for sucking pests.

Grasshoppers of various kinds chew at foliage, and flower buds may

Rosa 'Broadway'. Hybrid Tea Rose

be holed by caterpillars of several kinds. A systemic insecticide is more effective here. Prune away damaged foliage or buds.

A variety of fungus diseases may become apparent, particularly in humid weather. Most serious is powdery mildew, deposited as a thin white coating on new foliage, causing it to distort. Spraying with a recommended fungicide will usually wipe it out, but the damaged leaves should be pruned away and burned.

Black spot is a fungus clearly described by its popular name. Mature leaves become spotted with black or dark brown blotches which soon increase in size. Leaves finally turn yellow and drop. All diseased foliage must be cut and burned, and the affected plant sprayed with a reliable fungicide. Difficult to cure completely, but in the long run the plant does not seem to be unduly damaged provided regular hygiene is practised.

Rosa luteo-puniceus. 1596

Finally, a fungus known as die-back may enter the plant's sap system through pruning cuts. All dead wood should be cut away with sterilized secateurs, and large cuts sealed with a bitumen pruning compound.

Roses are such good value that hardly anyone bothers to propagate their own. However, they can be raised from cuttings taken in mid-summer. An elderly cousin of mine did this for many years, and acquired a fine collection of roses as a result.

Rosa 'Sophie's Perpetual'. Old Climber

Rosa bourboniana 'Mme Isaac Pereire'

Rosa X *rugosa* 'Pink Grootendorst'. Hybrid Rugosa

Hybrid Tea Roses. Modern assortment

Rosmarinus

(roz-mah-**ree**-nəs) ☼ T W
Rosemary
Spring; 5 ft/1.5–2 m; dense; evergreen

LAMIACEAE   AROMATIC

'Rosemary is for remembrance' so Shakespeare reminds us, and the pale lavender flower spikes appear in autumn, winter and spring and bring bees from far and wide.

Rosemary is a tough, picturesque Mediterranean shrub that puts up with a great deal of heat and poor soil to reward us in many ways. Its flower heads are used fresh to distil an essential oil for perfume; dry as a seasoning for many favourite dishes, especially roasted lamb.

Rosmarinus officinalis. Rosemary.
Mediterranean

The densely foliaged branches prune well to shape hedge or topiary. The plant is frost hardy down to 23°F/−5°C, and is unaffected by the salt-laden winds that sweep seaside gardens. True, it has a tendency to woodiness, and should be pruned lightly all over and regularly to spark new foliage. You can grow it from seed or cuttings, and its trailing variety *R. prostratus* is a useful wall plant.

Rothmannia

(roth-**man**-ee-ə) ☼ ☀ W H
Tree Gardenia,
September Bells (southern hemisphere),
Isi-qoba; Umsugusu; Wildekatjiepiering
Spring; 10–13 ft/3–4 m; multi-stemmed; evergreen

RUBIACEAE   FRAGRANT

Still sometimes sold as Gardenia globosa, *Rothmannia globosa* (together with several other Gardenias) has been switched to a new generic name, but is, for all that, no less fragrant or desirable a specimen for the home garden.

The *Rothmannias* are slender tree-like shrubs with almost black branches and shining Gardenia-type leaves to 6 in/15 cm in length. Like true Gardenias, they enjoy acid soil, plenty of water and regular feeding with an acid-based fertilizer or manure. The spring blooms are quite different from those of the Gardenia, being bell-shaped. In the popular *R. globosa* they are creamy-white in colour, borne in clusters at branch-ends and leaf axils. Each bloom is broadly tubular and about 2 in/5 cm long with round-pointed petals flaring outward to reveal a series of pink lines decorating the open throat.

The shrub is often partly deciduous at flowering time, and blooms are

Rothmannia globosa. Bell-flowered Gardenia.
South Africa

followed by woody, dark-brown seed capsules ¾ in/2 cm wide. *R. globosa* is hardy down to 28°F/−2°C, can be propagated from late summer seed or semi-hardwood cuttings taken in spring. The flowers have a fascinating fragrance.

Rubus idaeus. Raspberry.
Europe, N. Asia

Rubus

(**roo**-bəs) ☼ ☀ C T W
Bramble, Raspberry
Summer; 4–6 ft/1–2 m; arching canes; deciduous

ROSACEAE   FRAGRANT

For those, like myself, who find raspberries the most delectable of fruits, it is somewhat of a surprise to find that there are more than 250 species in the genus, some of them the most ill-favoured of plants that do not bear fruit at all. Still, for every one that is grown for its flowers (like the illustrated *Rubus tridel* X *odoratus*) there is another grown for its fruits (like *R. idaeus*, the Raspberry). The genus consists almost exclusively of clumping plants which are somewhat spiny and spread from canes; it is widely distributed in nature over Europe, Asia and North America. It includes such uncommon fruits as Dewberries, Wineberries, Loganberries, Thimbleberries, Salmonberries, Himalaya berries and the common brambles or blackberries.

All species of *Rubus* are propagated

Rubus tridel X *odoratus*. Flowering Raspberry. N. America

Ruellia dipteracantha. Velvet Plant. Mexico

Rubus micans. Wild Raspberry. N. Asia

Ruellia

(roo-**el**-lee-ə) ☼ ◑ W H
Christmas Pride,
Brazil Torch
Spring; 5–7 ft/1.5–2 m; tender; bushy; evergreen

ACANTHACEAE

Ruellias are so lovely, they are often kept as winter-flowering greenhouse plants in the northern hemisphere,

Ruellia formosa. Brazil Torch. Brazil

Ruellia macrantha. Christmas Pride. Colombia to Argentina

from division of the root system any time during the winter dormancy, setting out the canes or divisions in well-drained ordinary soil. They grow fast, generally to about 3 ft/1 m, but spread much wider. The flowers open in late spring, the fruits ripen in summer. Annual pruning is carried out by removing a third of the oldest canes entirely. Do not shorten other canes.

but where winter temperatures remain above 50°F/10°C they can remain outdoors in a sheltered spot. In mild or warm climates, they are grown from spring cuttings, continually pinched back to ensure bushy growth. Give them semi-shade through the hottest weather, plenty of water and a periodic application of liquid fertilizer to hurry growth along.

R. *macrantha* (one of about 200 species) needs as much winter sun as it can get to force production of the violet-pink flowers—in truth, the best display comes from newly struck autumn cuttings. R. *dipteracantha* is a ground-hugging plant with velvety leaves and vivid purple blooms. R. *formosa* is a stunning 2 ft/60 cm shrub with clusters of 2 or 3 vivid scarlet blooms from the leaf axils. In the tropics, it flowers for much of the year. A fibrous, well-drained soil is best for all.

found all over the continent, not just in the west. *Rulingia hermannifolia* is a useful mat-forming shrub for the Australian native garden, rarely passing 1 ft/30 cm in height, but spreading to 5 ft/1.5 m in width. It has narrow, much wrinkled, shiny leaves with starry white flowers borne in terminal clusters. Soft-tip cuttings are the usual means of propagation, but seed is also a possibility.

The Kerrawang has not proven fussy as to soil, provided drainage is good; it is both drought and frost resistant. The flowers are followed by brown seed capsules which are often used in dried arrangements of native Australian flowers.

they demand gravelly, perfectly drained soil, and rain in summer, not winter.

The species vary from prostrate to erect, but the illustrated *Ruschia granitica* is quite typical, a shrubby plant with woody stems, often bearing the dried remains of older leaves; the newer leaves are opposite, stem-clasping and very succulent. The short display of flowers is almost unbelievably profuse; they may be pink, violet, white or red. Best propagated from cuttings.

Rulingia hermannifolia. Dwarf Kerrawang. New South Wales

Rulingia
(syn. LASIOPETALUM)

(roo-**ling**-ee-ə) ☼ T W
Kerrawang
Spring; 1 ft/30 cm; mat-forming; evergreen

MALVACEAE

Yet another Australian genus which surprises by having one of its species found in distant Madagascar. But in this case, the Australian species are

Ruschia
(syn. MESEMBRYANTHEMUM)

(**roos**-kee-ə) ☼ W
Ruschia
Spring; 1½ ft/45 cm dense; evergreen

AIZOACEAE

Some 350 species of succulent shrubs endemic to South Africa—but you are unlikely to see more than a handful of them elsewhere except in specialist collections. The problem is

Ruschia granitica. South Africa

Ruscus aculeatus. Box Holly (fruit). Azores to Iran

Ruscus aculeatus. Jew's Myrtle. Azores to Iran

Ruscus

(**rus**-kəs) ☼ ❉ C T H
Butcher's Broom,
Box Holly, Jew's Myrtle
Spring; 2–3 ft/60–90 cm; multiple stems;
evergreen

ASPARAGACEAE

Appearance can be deceptive. This densely foliaged shrub bears no leaves at all: what you see are cladodes or stems adapted to *look* like leaves. If you examine them carefully, you'll find that many of them bear a spine or a small mauve and green flower right in the centre. Watch, and some of these will develop into brilliant scarlet berries, though only on female plants. These berries carry the seeds from which the plant may be propagated, though early spring divisions are perhaps more usual. Just remember — divisions from male plants will always be male and never bear berries.

Ruscus adores an alkaline soil and prefers it to be heavy and moist. It grows anywhere from cold to warm-temperate climates and looks better in shade.

Why Butcher's Broom? Well, it seems at one time butchers tied the spiky stems together to brush down their chopping blocks.

Ruspolia

(*syn.* PSEUDERANTHEMUM)

(rus-**pohl**-ee-ə) ☼ H
Rose Eranthemum
All year; to 3 ft/1 m; loose; evergreen

ACANTHACEAE

You're not likely to see this rather floppy plant away from tropical gardens, for it's native to central

Ruspolia seticalyx. Rose Eranthemum.
Tropical Africa

Africa. But in these days of international travel it's likely to turn up anywhere from Singapore across to Honolulu, in your hotel garden.

Known for many years as a Pseuderanthemum, it was one of a group of four red-flowered species that underwent a name change to *Ruspolia*—in this case *R. seticalyx*. It has rather floppy, ornate leaves that are a little hairy viewed in close-up, and the pale red flowers appear terminally in a loose spike. *Ruspolia* may be pruned hard annually, at which time you can take cuttings for propagation, provided you live in a tropical climate.

Russelia equisetiformis. Fountain Flower.
Mexico

Russelia

(rus-**sell**-ee-ə) ☼ W H
Coral-blow,
Fountain Flower
Spr–Aut; 4 ft/1 m; weeping; evergreen

SCROPHULARIACEAE

Wouldn't you know from the lush warm-weather growth and profusion of firecracker-red flowers that this was a true Central American beauty? *Russelia* is a real horticultural celebration, turning from a tangled mess of leafless cold weather growth to a glowing fountain of coral scarlet. Bloom begins in late spring, reaches a peak of profusion in summer, and

slowly fades away like hot coals as the weather turns cool in autumn.

Russelia equisetiformis likes moderately rich, well-drained soil and is not hard to grow from cuttings. It grows fast, spreads rapidly into a stand of arching, sucker-like stems on which the foliage has been modified to long scales. The Fountain Flower is a great seaside specimen, or effective spilling over a wall. Best results are stimulated by a light pruning of the spent flower heads in winter, at which time some old stems can be taken right back to the base. Hardy down to 28°F/–2°C.

Ruta

(**roo**-tə) ☼ T
Herb of Grace, Rue
Summer; 2–3 ft/60 cm–1 m; bun-shaped;
evergreen

RUTACEAE   AROMATIC

'Here's rue for you', offered poor mad Ophelia, with some suggestion of its popularity in the 16th century, if not before. And we might do far worse than to take up her offer for the mixed border or herb garden.

Rue is a sub-shrub in the Rutaceae family, native to southern Europe. It is easily grown from seed sown outdoors in early spring in lightly cultivated soil. It can also be propagated from 4 in/10 cm cuttings of lateral shoots in late summer.

Ruta graveolens forms a dense mat

Ruta graveolens. Herb of Grace.
S. Europe

Ruta graveolens CV 'Variegata'.
Variegated Rue. S. Europe

of bluish, finely divided foliage from which many-branched stems of golden, buttercup type flowers emerge in the warmer months. Rue should be cut back to old wood in early spring to keep the 3 ft/1 m bush compact. Rue is also valued in the herb garden, for its finely chopped leaves add a tangy flavour to salads. For cooking, fresh sprigs are snipped and dried.

Ruttya fruticosa. Jammy Mouth.
E. Africa

Ruttya

(**rut**-tee-yə)   ☼ Ⓦ
Jammy Mouth, Red Ruttya
Sum–Aut; 12 ft/3.5 m; dense; evergreen

ACANTHACEAE

What a wow of a popular name! The shiny black patch on the bright red lips of *Ruttya* flowers looks exactly like somebody who got stuck into the blackberry conserve! *Ruttya* is a small genus of 3 species of African shrubs — 2 from South Africa, 1 (illustrated *R. fruticosa*) from east Africa.

Propagation is from cuttings which, after striking, should be set out in leaf-rich, well-drained soil and kept moist, especially in summer. The ovate leaves are about 2¼ in/6 cm in length and the flowers appear in clusters from short lateral shoots. They vary from yellow through orange to scarlet.

Salix

(**sal**-iks)   ☼ Ⓒ Ⓣ
Willow
Spring; 6–10 ft/2–3 m; upright; deciduous

SALICACEAE

The world is full of willow species (over 250 of them, mostly in the cooler northern hemisphere) and all share the love of water. They are invaluable for preventing erosion of river banks, or soaking up the brackish moisture of low meadows. They are also adept at seeking out and filling water pipes and blocking drains (and do not have very civilized manners in the home garden).

But this is often because they are such very large trees. If only there were smaller, shrub-sized willows so that their more useful habits could be kept within bounds.

There are, in fact, several dozen of them, of which illustrated *Salix gracilistyla* is a decorative example. Growing generally 6 ft/2 m in height, it is easily propagated from leafless cuttings in late winter. In a deep, heavy soil they'll race ahead, producing grey-green foliage shoots in early spring. Young branches can be cut for indoor use to limit its size. They will open their opulent catkins in water. Outdoors, they need plenty of water and can be cut right back to

Salix gracilistyla.
Rose Gold Pussy-willow. Japan, Korea

stubs every three years. *S. gracilistyla* is seen at its best only in cool climates.

Salvia

(**sal**-vee-ə)   ☼ ✵ Ⓣ Ⓦ Ⓗ
Sage, Bush Sage, Ramona
Any time; 2–4 ft/60 cm–1 m; bushy; evergreen

LAMIACEAE   AROMATIC

Blue, purple, pink, yellow, red and white are included in the flower colour range of the *Salvia* or Sage group, an enormously varied genus of the mint family, with which most of them share highly aromatic, spear-shaped foliage and square-sectioned stems. There are annual, perennial and shrub species and they are scattered in nature all over the warmer parts of the world.

All the shrubby sages have tubular, lipped flowers, produced along a spike that rises above the foliage. The individual blooms can be quite large,

Sub-shrubby S. *elegans*, the Pineapple Scented Sage, is also from Mexico. It has green, ovate, 4 in/10 cm leaves, small panicles of scarlet flowers. Foliage of South African S. *aurea* tends to be woolly white with wide-tipped leaves. The flowers are quite long, 2 in/5 cm or more, and appear in the upper leaf axils. They open yellow, turn to a rusty orange.

The flowers of the Common Sage, S. *officinalis*, may be pink, violet or white and there are many leaf variations, such as the illustrated 'Tricolor'. It is, of course, the fragrant pot-herb, grown on many a kitchen windowsill.

Salvias do best in sun but tolerate part shade. Well-drained soil enriched with rotted manure gives best results. Propagate all shrubby sages from 3 in/8 cm cuttings taken in spring.

Salvia aurea. Golden Sage. South Africa

Salvia elegans.
Pineapple-scented Sage. Mexico

Salvia leucantha. Mexican Bush Sage. Mexico

as in illustrated S. *aurea*, or tiny but densely packed, as in the Mexican Bush Sage, S. *leucantha*. The latter grows to around 3 ft/1 m in height but usually somewhat wider. Its stems are woolly with grey-green leaves to 6 in/15 cm long. Velvety purple flowers cover the top of the plant for many weeks from the end of summer. It is drought resistant and should be cut back hard in winter.

Salvia officinalis 'Tricolor'.
Variegated Garden Sage. S. Europe

Sambucus canadensis aurea. Golden Elder.
Nova Scotia to Texas

Sambucus

(sam-**buk**-əs) ☼ C T
Elder, Elderberry
*Summer; 6–10 ft/2–3 m; suckering;
deciduous*

ADOXACEAE

Something of a joke among foreign visitors to England is the local home-brew, elderberry wine. The plant from which it is made, *Sambucus nigra*, is in fact found all around the Mediterranean and has many spectacular leaf varieties which make it a popular foliage plant in cooler-climate gardens. Even more showy, though, are the foliage variations of *S. canadensis*, the American Sweet Elder.

There are in fact 20 and more species of these rather spectacular shrubs, on which a splendid crop of red or black berries follows the leaves and insignificant flowers. And here great care must be exercised: while many of the fruit are quite edible, others are equally not. Best check with your local herbarium before deciding to brew a wine or cook a jam.

All species can be grown from suckers or 10 in/25 cm cuttings taken in late autumn. A rich, well-drained, woodsy soil serves *Sambucus* best. *S. canadensis* is very fast-growing.

But in flowering country (between the tropics) there is no way it can be seen as anything but itself, for the scarlet-bracted, tubular yellow flowers open for weeks at a time.

Sanchezia grows best from cuttings and should be planted in rich, well-drained soil. It makes a wonderful hedge or screen in the tropical garden, just don't let it grow too big. Prune back hard when it becomes leggy—it will soon spring up again.

Santolina chamaecyparissus. Lavender Cotton (foliage). Spain, North Africa

Santolina chamaecyparissus. Lavender Cotton (flowers). Spain, North Africa

Sanchezia speciosa. Brilliant-flowered Sanchezia. Ecuador, Peru

Sanchezia

(san-**chez**-ee-ə) ☼ ☀ T
Brilliant-flowered Sanchezia
Winter; 5 ft/1.5 m; billowing; evergreen

ACANTHACEAE

The gold and white veined leaves of the showy *Sanchezia speciosa* have often caused it to be mistaken for a Croton (see Codiaeum) in cooler areas where the plant rarely blooms.

Santolina

(san-toh-**lee**-nə) ☼ C T W
Lavender Cotton
Summer; 2 ft/60 cm; dense mound; evergreen

ASTERACEAE   AROMATIC

Delicate foliage like feather dusters has brought *Santolina chamaecyparissus* a special place in the mixed border or rockery. It is usually clipped back into a neat mound in early spring, but decorative foliage is only half the story. Left alone, it will produce masses of button-sized blossoms, like small, yellow pompoms, over several weeks in summer.

Santolina of any species (there are 8), while tough and tolerant of neglect, are not frost hardy, being native to mild, coastal parts of the Mediterranean. But, as gardeners have discovered, they will grow any

place there is sun and water. Grow from seed, cuttings or layers and tip prune often to retain a compact, rounded bush around 2 ft/60 cm tall. Try them in light, sandy soil with occasional but regular water. Deadhead continually.

Sarcococca

(**sah**-koh-kok-kə) ☼ ☀ T
Sweet Box
Spring; 2 ft/60 cm; spreading; evergreen

BUXACEAE   FRAGRANT

A wonderful groundcover for the cool-climate garden, the elegant *Sarcococca* species (about a dozen of them) feature shining ovate leaves, fragrant milky flowers in axillary clusters, and bunches of brilliant berries—most often black but in the illustrated *S. ruscifolia*, bright lacquer red. Slow growing, they can be propagated by seed, cuttings or division, so can be encouraged to cover a large area in just a few years, spreading via underground runners.

Sarcococca enjoy a leaf-rich soil and should be kept moist at all times. Though they can take full sun in cooler climates, they really do best in dappled shade.

Sarcococca ruscifolia. Sweet Box. China

Sarcostemma

(sah-koh-stem-mə) ☼ W H
Spring; 1 ft/30 cm; basically leafless

ASCLEPIADACEAE

Basically leafless, *Sarcostemma* are closely related to the Carrion Flower, *Stapelia* spp, and, with rare exceptions, are found in east Africa.

For most of the year, a plant of *S. stipitata* looks stone dead, or like a bird's nest, depending on your point of view. Closer inspection reveals

that it is a mass of slender, succulent, branched stems, greyish in tone, but exuding a milky sap when damaged. Being tropical in origin, they like their rain in summer, with a dry winter to follow. Small greenish-white flowers appear in spring in some of the upper joints of the trailing stems. Small leaves may also appear at this time.

Scaevola

(skae-vol-ə) ☼ W
Round-leaf Fanflower
Warm months; 3 ft/1 m; succulent; evergreen

GOODENIACEAE

Mostly native to Australia, where some 50 species are found, *Scaevola* are also known among the coastal flora of several other countries. By far the majority of species have blue fan-shaped flowers, and the entire genus was named for the Roman hero Mucius Scaevola, who incinerated his right hand in a sacrificial fire and was known thereafter as Scaevola or left-handed.

Shrubby *Scaevolas* like the illustrated *S. crassifolia* are propagated from cuttings struck in sandy compost. They should then be planted out in sandy, well-drained soil. A light hand is needed with the water and they want no fertilizer at any time. *S. crassifolia* enjoys limy soil and is quite resistant to salt spray, so is suited to a seaside garden.

Scaevola crassifolia. Round-leaf Fanflower. Western Australia

Schefflera

(syn. HEPTAPLEURUM)

(shef-ler-ə) ☼ W H
Dwarf Umbrella Tree
All year; 6 ft/2 m; unbranching; evergreen

ARALIACEAE

A splendid novelty for the tropical garden or bright greenhouse, this variegated species of the Dwarf Umbrella Tree seems only to have appeared in the last few years, and there is certainly some difference of

Schefflera arboricola 'Aureo-Maculata'. Dwarf Umbrella Tree. Subtropics

Sarcostemma stipitata. E. Africa

opinion as to its true botanical name—not surprising when you realize that over 150 green-leafed species have been classified! But if you can get hold of a specimen, that's not going to worry you.

Propagated from 4 in/10 cm pieces of hardened stem, the *Schefflera* is struck in a pot of sandy, leaf-rich loam. After growth begins, it should be set out in a sheltered position and gradually moved into the light to retain the variegations. Small spikes of insignificant greenish flowers appear from time to time. The leaves are truly magnificent: palmate, up to 6 in/15 cm in diameter, with as many as 10 leaflets. Makes a most decorative container plant.

Schisandra sphenandra. Magnolia Vine. China

Schisandra

(ski-**zan**-drə)   ☼ C T
Magnolia Vine
Spring; to 16 ft/5 m; climbing; deciduous

SCHISANDRACEAE

As this uncommon climbing shrub was once classified in the family Magnoliaceae, its popular name is presumably a hangover—but the resemblance is certainly hard to pick.

There are about 20 *Schisandra* species, found both in North America and in the eastern provinces of China. Illustrated *S. sphenandra* is

fairly typical. Deciduous, twining around any strong support, it is frost hardy in the English climate when espaliered against a wall. Like all of the genus, it is dioecious, needing plants of both sexes to produce the showy coral-red berries.

Propagate from short cuttings of half-ripe wood taken in summer. Deep, rich soil is best, with moisture in the active season.

Schotia

(**shot**-ee-ə)   ☼ ☀ W H
Tree Fuchsia,
Parrot Tree, Weeping Boer-bean
Spring; 13–38 ft/4–12 m; horizontal to weeping; deciduous

CAESALPINIACEAE

Once again I plead innocent at the classification of this wonderful plant. I would have given it a tree guernsey, but several of the world's most important botanical dictionaries say it is a large shrub—so I don't dare leave it out. Certainly where I have seen it in Rockhampton in Australia it seems tree size. At any rate, it is a slow-growing plant from subtropical Africa which seems to hold a great attraction for the local parrots. In spring they flock to the bright red flowers to gorge upon the intoxicating nectar. Their noisy binge lasts from dawn to dusk, by which time the hapless birds are literally flat on their backs.

Schotia brachypetala is easily propagated from the large bean-like seeds, which should be soaked for 24 hours in warm water before sowing. Transplant seedlings with care. *Schotia* is hardy to occasional frosts but grows faster in a hot climate. Any soil will do.

Selago

(sel-**ah**-goh)   ☼ ☀ W
Blue Haze,
Thunberg's Selago
Spr–Sum; 2 ft/60 cm; heath-like; evergreen

SCROPHULARIACEAE

Few of the 140 species of *Selago* are grown outside South Africa, to which the genus is endemic. One that is seen elsewhere, in my Australian garden for instance, is the Blue Haze Bush, *S. thunbergii*, a charming heath-like shrub or sub-shrub with a long blooming season from spring into summer in warm-temperate climates.

It can be propagated from seed or cuttings and enjoys a sunny position with midday shade and well-drained, leaf-rich soil. With regular water during the growing season, its panicles of tiny mauve-blue flowers develop in such profusion that the branches are literally bowed down. The shrub is evergreen with light grey-green leaves with the linear form of many of the heath family, though in fact it is closely related to the Penstemons.

Schotia brachypetala. Tree Fuchsia, Parrot Tree. Zimbabwe

Selago thunbergii. Blue Haze. South Africa

Senecio

(*syn.* CINERARIA, LIGULARIA, KLEINIA)

(sen-**ess**-ee-oh)   ☼ C T
Groundsel, Ragwort
All year; 1½–11 ft/50 cm–3.5 m; rounded; evergreen

ASTERACEAE   PUNGENT

Tough to start life in old age, but the vast genus *Senecio*, over 3000 species world-wide, take their name from the Latin *senex* (an old man) in reference to the grey or white hairy pappus which replaces the calyx in many of the daisy family.

Senecio forms one of the largest of plant genera; members are found on every continent, though the best species originate in Africa and both the Americas. All categories of plants are represented among them, but of the shrubby types, the most popular include Mexico's enormous *S. grandifolius* with dark 20 in/50 cm leaves and trusses of bright yellow daisy flowers in cold weather. New Zealand's *S. laxifolius* has small, simple, greyish leaves and a floppy

Senecio laxifolius. Dusty Miller.
New Zealand

habit, while the California Geranium, *S. petasitis*, has handsome lobed foliage and sparsely petalled flowers in great panicles.

All grow from cuttings and need annual pruning to keep them compact. *S. cineraria* is the old-fashioned Sea Ragwort or Dusty Miller, so widely used in seaside gardens and for formal park display. It grows so

Senecio grandifolius. Big-leaf Groundsel.
S. Mexico

Senecio petasitis. California Geranium. Mexico

Senecio cineraria. Sea Ragwort. Mediterranean

Serissa foetida 'Flore Pleno'.
Stinking Serissa. S.E. Asia

easily from cuttings it is often planted as an annual, but it is in fact a sub-shrub.

The Spearhead, *S. kleiniiformis*, is least common of the illustrated shrubby species. It is a succulent sub-shrub with prostrate branches and heads of 20–30 flowers borne terminally. Broken stems give off a strongly pungent odour. All species are most easily raised from cuttings.

Senecio kleiniiformis. Spearhead.
South Africa

Serissa
(*syn.* LYCIUM)

(sur-**riss**-ə)   ☼ ☀ Ⓦ Ⓗ
Stinking Serissa,
Hakuchoge, Kaotawk
All year; 2 ft/60 cm; low, spreading;
evergreen

RUBIACEAE

There's a great gap between the perfume of a Gardenia and the odour of closely related *Serissa*. Quite frankly, the latter stinks, especially when the foliage is bruised. So long as you keep your distance, however, it is quite delightful—a low spreading shrub with shiny ovate leaves less than 1/3 in/1 cm in length and with dainty mauve and white terminal flowers about the same size. In the case of the illustrated double species, there is even a visual resemblance to the Gardenia.

Serissa is best grown from cuttings and prefers rich, well-drained soil. The plant is naturally quite a good size for bonsai treatment or for planting in small rock pockets. It is slow-growing so is not going to outgrow its allotted space in a hurry.

Serruria

(se-**roo**-ree-ə)   ☼ Ⓒ Ⓣ
Blushing Bride,
Berg Bruidjie
Winter; 5 ft/1.5 m; slender; evergreen

PROTEACEAE

Not particularly long lasting, the plants of South African *Serruria florida* would be treasured if they

Serruria florida. Blushing Bride.
South Africa

lasted only a single season. For even that would give them an opportunity to produce at least one of their exquisite flowers or 'Little Mountain Brides' as the Cape Dutch call them.

Their genus of the Proteaceae family includes about 50 species, but nobody's going to think beyond *S. florida* because of its large, showy inflorescences, each containing two or three heads of papery, pale pink bracts which last well when cut.

S. florida can be grown from seed which will germinate in three weeks and flower the second year. It needs well-drained but compost-rich soil, and should be pruned from an early age to keep compact. *Serruria* plants should be replaced every 3 years; they look well in rock pockets which will keep them at eye level. Foliage is greyish, and divided into needle-like segments.

Sida fallax. 'Ilima. Polynesia

Sida
(*syn.* ABUTILON)

(**sai**-də) ☼ ☀ W H
'Ilima
Summer; 4 ft/1 m; open; large-leafed, profusely flowering; evergreen

MALVACEAE

Named from a Greek word for waterlily (which, it must be confessed, they do *not* much resemble),

the 120-odd species of *Sida* form an interesting genus of the mallow family, *Malvaceae*. They are found in many parts of the world, though mostly in the vicinity of the Americas, yet rarely seen in cultivation except for the 'Ilima, *S. fallax*, one of the relatively few plants endemic to Polynesia, and as such a desirable flower for Hawaiian gardens, where its flowers are picked for threading into leis.

Grown from seed or cuttings, the 'Ilima does best in well-drained, rich soil. It grows fast, in a warm climate at least, bearing simple, heart-shaped furry leaves and masses of creamy-yellow flowers like miniature Hibiscus.

Simmondsia

(sim-**mond**-zee-ə) ☼ W H
Goat–nut, Jojoba
Summer; 3–6 ft/1–2 m; dense; evergreen

SIMMONDSIACEAE

One of the most desirable plants of the yuppie world, the Jojoba is trying hard to outdo Aloe vera as the essential plant ingredient for—well, you name it. Cuttings are being planted by the plantation load all over the warm-temperate world and raised

Simmondsia chinensis. Jojoba. S.W. USA, Mexico

Pamela Harper

into bushes of *Simmondsia chinensis*, a rather grey-looking shrub with small, nothing-coloured flowers and shimmering, edible green fruit that are the source of Jojoba oil which is a substitute for sperm oil at least, and, as some would have it, for petroleum.

Grow from seed or cuttings in gravelly, well-drained soil. If we could only be sure what it *is* good for, it would certainly make a good cash crop for arid, hot areas. As it is, it is useful for hedging and stock feed.

Sinojackia rehderana. S. China

Sinojackia

(sai-noh-**jak**-ee-ə) ☼ ☀ C T
Sinojackia
Spr–Sum; 15 ft/4.5 m; slender; glossy-leafed; deciduous

STYRACACEAE

Three species of graceful shrubs or small trees from the south of China, *Sinojackia* are grown all over the world in the gardens of dedicated plantsmen for their small, lateral racemes of delicate, frosty white flowers.

They are grown from seed, and flourish in a rich, open, acid loam. The leaves are simple, finely toothed and deciduous, but without spectacular autumn colour. The flowers are followed by 1 in/3 cm spindle-shaped fruit which contain seeds for the future. *S. rehderana* is hardy down to 10°F/ −12°C.

Skimmia

(**skim**-mee-ə) ☼ ☀ C T
Skimmia
Spr–Sum; 3–5 ft/1–1.5 m; dense mound; evergreen

RUTACEAE   FRAGRANT

Just a handful of species from chillier parts of Asia, *Skimmia* are related to Citrus and to the fragrant Murraya which they replace in gardens of cooler climates.

S. *japonica* is most commonly seen in town gardens and parks, for it is remarkably resistant to polluted city air. Clusters of tiny but exquisitely fragrant creamy flowers join the shining evergreen foliage in early spring, and if you've the right planting combination (you'll need at least one male plant to every four or five females), you'll get a crop of bright red berries in summer. These hang on the plant till well into autumn.

A well-drained, acid soil is best, with generous moisture in dry weather. As the bushes remain compact and tidy and never exceed 4 ft/ 1.2 m in height, little pruning is needed, but cuttings may be taken in summer.

Skimmia japonica (fruit)

Skimmia japonica. Skimmia. Japan

Solanum brownii. Spiny Nightshade. S.E. Australia

Solanum mammosum. Cow's Udder Plant. Tropical America

Solanum

(so-**lah**-nəm) ☼ W H
Potato-bush, Flor de Volcan
Variable; 4 ft/1 m; erect; branching; evergreen

SOLANACEAE

Almost 200 species of *Solanum* are scattered throughout the world, with a heavy concentration in Central America. S. *melongena* and S. *tuberosa* are probably the best known of the genus as the eggplant or aubergine from Asia and the potato from South America's Andes. The *Solanum* genus includes climbers, annuals and a tree or two as well as many shrubby types. Most are grown purely for the beauty of their floral display though, it must be confessed, fragrance is something of a rarity among them.

Illustrated S. *rantonettii* or Blue Potato-bush is most variable, seen sometimes as a medium-sized shrub, barely 6 ft/2 m tall, sometimes as a sprawling groundcover. It is from South America, not frost hardy and is best struck from soft-tip cuttings in warm weather. Heavy pruning is needed to keep it shapely—but just look at the result! These yellow-

Solanum capsicastrum. False Jerusalem Cherry. Brazil

Solanum crispum 'Glasnevin'.
Chilean Nightshade. Chile

centred purple flowers, though only small, are produced as generously as this from spring well into summer.

The Cow's Udder Plant, S. mammosum, is a colourful novelty for the tropical garden. The fascinating fruit are not edible and it is recommended you keep your distance from the spiny, lobed leaves.

S. crispum, a cool-climate sub-shrub from Chile, can be trained as a dec-

Solanum rantonettii. Blue Potato-bush. Paraguay

orative wall plant, particularly in its cultivar 'Glasnevin'.

S. capsicastrum, the False Jerusalem Cherry, is popular as a container plant or rock garden specimen and is very ornamental in fruit.

Australia contributes about 80 species to the world's stock of *Solanums*, of which S. *brownii* is one of the best. It is a useful boundary or screening plant, being lightly spined and densely foliaged. It grows about 10 ft/3 m tall with a similar spread. Like all the Australian *Solanums*, S. *brownii* prefers dryish, well-drained soil; it does best in full sun, although it will tolerate light shade for part of the day.

Sollya heterophylla. Austral Bluebell. Western Australia

Sollya

(**sol**-lee-yə) ☼ ✳ ☀ Ⓦ Ⓗ
Bluebell Creeper,
Austral Bluebell
Spr–Sum; 2–3 ft/60 cm–1 m; spreading; evergreen

PITTOSPORACEAE

Often sold as a climber, the lightweight Austral Bluebell needs a great deal of training to be anything of the sort. It is better described as a sort of loose shrub, growing 2–3 ft/ 60 cm–1 m in height. Where it *does* look good is spilling down a retaining

wall from an elevated bed.

Sollya may be grown from semi-hardwood cuttings struck in late summer. It does best in well-drained though moist soil. It is not frost hardy, nor does it like drought-prone positions. Set it in dappled shade and it will romp away in any climate from cool-temperate to tropical. The 5-petalled blue bell flowers hang on long stems, generally beneath the foliage.

Sophora

(*syn.* EDWARDSIA)

(**sof**-or-ə) ☼ Ⓣ Ⓦ
Sophora, Kowhai, Silverbush
Spr–Sum; 8–10 ft/2.5–3 m; multiple-trunked; deciduous

FABACEAE

True *Sophora* are found only in Africa, Japan, Korea, China, New Zealand, Chile, Hawaii and the south-western United States. They are fairly typical members of the pea family, generally frost hardy and with a capacity for display rivalling the European Laburnum. Most popular are the tree species S. *japonica* and S. *tetraptera* from China and New Zealand respectively. But there are a number of shrubby types which look good in mixed borders.

S. *davidii*, also from China, produces terminal racemes of pea flowers in distinctly bluish-white tones. African S. *velutina* produces a spectacular display of pods, especially in its variety *zimbabweensis*. These appear after the creamy pea flowers which are rather unexciting. The

Sophora davidii. Chinese Sophora. China

Sophora tomentosa. Silverbush.
Old World Tropics

Sophora velutina var zimbabweensis.
Velvet Sophora. Zimbabwe

Silverbush, *S. tomentosa*, is found all around the old-world seashores, its golden blooms in fascinating contrast to the velvety grey foliage.

As members of the pea family, all species of *Sophora* can be grown from seed which should first be soaked in warm water. Try 3 in/8 cm soft-wood cuttings or layers as alternatives if seed proves a problem. Deep, sandy loam is the most suitable soil and planting is done in late winter. Light, all-over pruning should be done after flowers have faded.

Sophora toromiro. Dwarf Kowhai. New Zealand

Sorbaria aitchisonii. False Spiraea. Kashmir, Afghanistan

Sorbaria
(syn. SPIRAEA)

sor-**bear**-ee-ə)   ☼ C T
False Spiraea
Sum–Aut; 10 ft/3 m; spreading; deciduous
ROSACEAE

There's only one word to describe the handful of *Sorbaria* species—big! About 10 ft/3 m is average, 23 ft/7 m not unusual. They are deciduous members of the rose family with pithy stems and long pinnate leaves of a delightful bright green. They really are shrubs for large, cool gardens since they sucker riotously.

Propagation is easy from seed, cuttings or suckers, and the soil should be rich and moist. Popular *S. aitchisonii* is an attractive plant with reddish shoots of young foliage, leaves with up to 33 toothed leaflets. Tiny cream flowers appear in profusion in dense panicles over 1½ ft/ 50 cm long. These are followed by tiny red berries. *Sorbaria* species were once included among Spiraea.

Sparmannia

(spah-**man**-nee-ə)   ☼ ☀ T W
African Hemp,
Indoor Linden, Wild Hollyhock
Win–Spr; 10–20 ft/3–6 m; multi-trunked; evergreen
MALVACEAE

Another link to the voyages of Captain Cook is in the naming of the attractive *Sparmannia africana* after

Gillian Beckett

Sparmannia africana. African Hemp.
S. Africa

the Swedish Dr. Andes Sparmann who was a naturalist on the second voyage. *Sparmannia* is commonly seen in the northern hemisphere as an indoor plant. It is not frost hardy, and in the open garden of a warm-temperate climate will grow to 10 ft/ 3 m in height.

The hairy leaves may be heart-shaped or heavily lobed (as in our picture) and trusses of 4-petalled white flowers are produced in winter and spring. These have spectacular bosses of gold and crimson stamens which open flat when touched.

Propagate from cuttings, plant in well-drained, leaf-rich soil. Keep up the moisture level and prune hard every third year to control size.

Spartium

(**spah**-tee-əm) ☼ Ⓣ Ⓦ
Spanish Broom
Spr–Sum; 10 ft/3 m; sparse; twiggy; evergreen

FABACEAE   FRAGRANT

Sad that so lovely a plant should be so poisonous — the mere sight and fragrance of it along Mediterranean highways is quite unforgettable. I remember it in the south of France, rolled out like a yellow carpet, wel-

coming the well-heeled to the Côte d'Azur.

It is an easy plant to grow anywhere the sun is mildly warm. Don't worry about the type of soil, it seems to be happy even in fast-draining, coastal sand. If it has a preference, it is for a little lime to sweeten its growth along.

Spartium junceum is almost leafless, a mass of hollow, straw-like green twigs springing from a crowded base. And if you want it to do anything but sprawl, you must prune heavily after flowering, right into the old wood. That way, you get a bush 10 ft/3 m tall and about as wide. You can use it as a hedge or deep groundcover, particularly for seaside plantings. In windy places, though, give it some shelter, for it is inclined to be shallow-rooted and may topple.

Both drought and cold resistant (hardy down to 14°F/−10°C), it's a gardener's delight, easily increased from cuttings or from seed after a 24-hour soaking. Flowers appear in long terminal sprays, are spicily fragrant and make good arrangements. Keep moist in winter, dryish in summer—oh, and do plant by a Jacaranda, the colour contrast is unforgettable. In warm climates, the Spanish Broom may well give a second flush of flowers in autumn.

Spartium junceum. Spanish Broom. Canary Islands

Spiraea japonica 'Golden Princess'. Japan

Spiraea

(spai-**ree**-ə) ☼ Ⓣ
Spirea, Maybush,
Garland Flower, Bridal Wreath
Spr–Sum; 1½–7 ft/50 cm–2 m; thicket; deciduous

ROSACEAE

The popular Maybushes take their principal popular name from their month of blooming in the northern

Spiraea betulifolia. Birch-leaf Spiraea. N.E. Asia

Spiraea X *bumalda*. Red May. Japan

Spiraea cantoniensis. Reeves' Spiraea. China, Japan

hemisphere, to which they are native. A thicket of erect, often arching stems, they are not particularly eye-catching or elegant for much of the year, but come into their own in springtime, when they are almost smothered under the weight of bloom, pink, white or crimson.

All species are cold hardy down to at least 23°F/−5°C, and like other members of the rose family, do best in a cold-winter climate. They flower in sun or part shade and even in slightly alkaline soil, so long as it is rich and well drained. An occasional top-dressing of manure (say in autumn and very early spring) will help produce displays of top quality, and bloom will be prolonged by reg-ular shearing of faded flower heads. Early-blooming species should be pruned immediately after flowering by thinning out and cutting away spindly stems. Later-blooming species may be pruned at any time during winter. Stems that have flowered can be shortened back to old wood. Most *Spiraea* species can be propagated from layers (peg down in spring, lift and cut back the following autumn). Ripe seed is another possibility, as are firm-tip cuttings taken in summer and struck in warm, humid sur-roundings in a mixture of damp sand and peat.

Of the illustrated species, *S. cantoniensis* from Japan and China produces clusters of small white blossom at leaf axils and resembles Lantana. It can be pruned to a neat hedge. *S. prunifolia* 'Plena' has double white flowers the whole length of its arching branches. Both of these white flowering species, together with *S. betulifolia*, produce a worthwhile display of autumn colour in cold dis-tricts. Of the pink flowering subjects, *S. japonica* 'Golden Princess' presents a brilliant contrast between flowers and foliage. *S. bumalda* is a lower-growing hybrid between *S. japonica* and *S. albiflora* and its cultivar X *bumalda* 'Goldflame' has brilliant red new foliage in contrast with its usual gold leaves.

Spiraea prunifolia 'Plena'. Bridal-wreath May. Japan

Sprengelia

(spren-**gel**-ee-ə) ☼ ❋ W
Star Heath, Swamp Heath
*Spr–Sum; to 3 ft/1 m; erect; sparse;
evergreen*

ERICACEAE

Herr Sprengel of Brandenburg was a celebrated botanical author of the late 18th century and was well remembered by his fellows in the naming of a small but charming heath genus in faraway Australia. It is doubtful if he ever saw the live plant, which is found in wet and swampy heath lands all over southeast Australia and Tasmania. It is propagated from cuttings, although striking them is not easy. Seed sown in early summer is likely to be more successful.

Sprengelia incarnata. Swamp Heath.
S.E. Australia, Tasmania

Sprengelia incarnata is an erect, sparsely branched plant suitable for damp, temperate places. Its rigid, pointed leaves are stem-clasping and the pale pink flowers apparently 10-petalled. On closer examination, the corolla consists of 5 petals alternating with 5 sepals. The small ⅓ in/ 1 cm blooms are crowded into branched heads through spring and summer.

Stachyurus

(stak-ee-**yoo**-rəs) ☼ ❋ C T
Stachyurus
*Win–Spr; 3–10 ft/1–3 m; loose; open;
deciduous*

STACHYURACEAE

Not cultivated in the West long enough to have attracted any sort of popular name, *Stachyurus* are found naturally in Asia but seem at home in any sort of temperate climate, being hardy to around 0°F/−18°C in sheltered places.

Most commonly seen *S. praecox* is attractive at any time of the year. Variable in size, it may grow 3–10 ft/ 1–3 m tall, its branches asymmetrical and weeping, sparsely clothed with simple, medium-sized deciduous leaves. In cool climates, these take on fiery autumn tints. In the same season, long chains of unopened yellow and brown blossoms appear, looking like sections of a beaded curtain. From late winter on, these gradually elongate and open, peaking just as the spring foliage appears.

Grow *Stachyurus* from autumn seed or from tip cuttings taken in late summer and struck with mist and heat. Soil should be rich and well-drained with a generous summer water supply.

Stachyurus praecox. Stachyurus. Japan

Staphylea colchica. Bladdernut. Caucasus

Staphylea

(staf-**fil**-ee-ə) ☼ ❋ T
Bladdernut
*Win–Spr; to 12 ft/3.5 m; treelike;
deciduous*

STAPHYLEACEAE

Scattered about the northern temperate zone is a small genus of shrubs and trees known as Bladdernuts or *Staphylea*. Though they have been named for their inflated, membranous seed capsules, the worthwhile display is actually from the flowers, which appear in late winter in milder climates such as Australia or late spring in the United Kingdom and USA.

Caucasian *S. colchica* is the best known, as a 12 ft/3.5 m deciduous shrub with trifoliate, toothed leaves. It is propagated from seed, cuttings or suckers, does best in a leaf-rich soil with partial shade in hotter areas.

The flowers, which appear in more or less erect panicles 5 in/13 cm long and wide, are rather daffodil-shaped, with the petals standing erect in the form of a trumpet and the larger sepals spreading or even reflexed. *S. colchica* is hardy anywhere in the UK, the southern hemisphere, or in milder parts of the USA.

Stephanandra tanakae. Crown Spiraea.
Japan

Stewartia ovata. Mountain Camellia. E. United States

Stephanandra

(stef-an-**and**-ra)   ☼ ☀ C T
Crown Spiraea
Summer; 6 ft–2 m; arching; deciduous

ROSACEAE

Wonderfully hardy in a cold climate, (not at all upset by temperatures down to −20°F/−29°C), the four species of *Stephanandra* are decorative foliage shrubs from earliest spring to late autumn when they disappear in a blaze of orange and red. Individual leaves are roughly triangular in shape with 3 to 7 lobes and appear alternately along the slender stems, each emerging from a stipule or leaf appendage. In summer, the entire plant is frosted with tiny white flowers which are borne in lax terminal panicles.

S. *tanakae* is propagated from seed, division or cuttings and does best in well-drained loam, kept consistently moist during the plant's period of active growth. The plant can be shaped and thinned in winter to prevent it becoming rampant. Closely planted, it makes quite a good screen or informal hedge.

Stewartia

(*syn.* MALACODENDRON)

(styoo-**wah**-tee-ə)   ☼ ☀ C T
False Camellia,
Mountain Camellia
Summer; to 15 ft/4.5 m; slender; treelike; deciduous

THEACEAE

Some of the most beautiful flowers in the world are those of the *Stewartia* group, a small genus of deciduous Camellia relatives divided almost equally between Japan and the eastern USA. The Asiatic *Stewartia* are trees, the American, largely shrubs.

S. *ovata*, which we illustrate, bears magnificent, 4 in/10 cm blooms of frilly white with purple stamens. It is propagated from seed, layering of lower branches or cuttings which have a poor striking rate. They are fussy as to soil, preferring a well-drained loam. If too sandy, decayed manure and compost must be mixed in. If on the clayey side, add sand with peat-moss or compost.

Stewartias are slow-growing but improve with part-shade in hot areas and regular moisture everywhere. They are acid lovers and, being mountain plants, have need of good drainage. In a cold climate, their purple autumn colour may be seen to advantage.

Stirlingia simplex. Western Australia

Stirlingia

(stur-**ling**-gee-ə) ☼ W
Stirlingia
Spring; 1 ft/30 cm; small; dense; evergreen

PROTEACEAE

I must admit to disappointment that my namesake shrub does not have a more exciting appearance. But at least it's a nice shade of yellow. *Stirlingia simplex* is an unusual undershrub of the Protea family and endemic to Western Australia. It has cylindrical segments, grey-green, deeply divided foliage and heads of pale yellow bloom on 1 ft/30 cm stems.

It loves a sandy soil with first-class drainage and is best propagated from a cutting taken near the base of the plant. It is appearing in cultivation, so who knows, perhaps I'll plant one. Some day.

Stranvaesia

(stran-**vae**-see-ə) ☼ T W
Stranvaesia
Spr–Sum; 20 ft/6 m; spreading; evergreen

ROSACEAE

Poor Mr Fox-Strangways—such a nice fellow, such a famous botanist, and yet when it came to naming a genus of shrubs for him, nobody knew how to spell his name. So *Stranvaesia* is the way it turned out, and a lovely group of plants to be remembered by it is indeed!

Stranvaesias are part of the rose family and grown not so much for the rather insignificant flowers as for the spectacular crop of berries, less than ⅓ in/1 cm in diameter and hanging in long-stemmed clusters. At a distance, *Stranvaesia* can be mistaken for a large Cotoneaster, but its new leaves are reddish and it is happy in hot dry areas and hardy down to 5°F/−15°C. Its lanceolate leaves are quite long (5 in/13 cm) and rather dark in colour, and, surprisingly enough, it is evergreen. Propagate from seed or cuttings and grow in a peaty soil that's not too rich.

Streptosolen

(strep-toh-**soh**-lən) ☼ T H
Marmalade Bush,
Browallia, Firebush
Win–Spr; 7 ft/2 m; crowded, weeping; evergreen

SOLANACEAE

The sole plant in its genus, *Streptosolen* was at one time sold as Browallia, and some still refer to it by that name. Useful in the frost-free garden, it may turn climber or even groundcover as the fancy strikes. It

Streptosolen jamesonii. Marmalade Bush. Colombia, Ecuador

has many minor variations in colour and habit but, as a rule, arching shoots emerge from the base and need regular tip-pruning when young to help the plant develop a shape. It is an ideal plant for a large hanging basket or shrub border and should be grown in light, fibrous, well-drained soil, kept moist.

Flowering begins in spring with clusters of the brightly coloured flowers so profuse, they weigh down the new growth. Easy to grow from semi-hardwood cuttings, struck in either autumn or winter with bottom heat, *S. jamesonii* is not frost hardy. It has a pure yellow form and, in Australia, the dwarf hybrid 'Ginger Meggs' is sold.

Streptosolen jamesonii (yellow form). Yellow Heliotrope. Colombia

Stranvaesia davidiana. China

Pamela Harper

Strobilanthes anisophyllus. Goldfussia. India

Strobilanthes

(*syn.* GOLDFUSSIA)

(stroh-bi-**lan**-thəs) ☼ ☼ ☀ W H
Goldfussia, Persian Shield,
Mexican Petunia
*Spring; 1½–5 ft/50 cm–1.5 m; globose;
evergreen*

ACANTHACEAE

To get the best out of *Strobilanthes*, it
is absolutely essential that they be
blessed with a winter minimum temperature of 55°F/13°C if the leaves
are not to discolour and drop. Originally from South-east Asia, they are
mostly grown as house or greenhouse plants away from the tropics
and raised fresh each year from
heeled cuttings struck in early spring
over bottom heat. Even where plants

Strobilanthes dyerianus. Persian Shield.
Malaysia

can be successfully over-wintered,
they should be pruned back hard in
spring to encourage new, bushy
growth, or they become weedy and
unattractive.

The illustrated *S. anisophyllus* or
Goldfussia is a small, shrubby perennial, usually less than 3 ft/1 m tall. Its
leaves are a glossy purple-red, the perfect foil for clusters of light mauve-
blue flowers that dot the plant during
warm weather.

Flashy *S. dyerianus* is known as the
Persian Shield, perhaps from its
smart purple and green foliage. It is
best propagated annually as the leaf
colour is brighter on young plants. Its
spikes of tubular, pale blue flowers
are rarely seen away from the tropics.

Grow *Strobilanthes* in very well-
drained soil enriched with rotted
manure. Keep well watered and fed
during the growing season, but only
just moist in winter at the cooler end
of its range.

Strophanthus

(stroh-**fan**-thəs) ☼ W H
Corkscrew Flower,
Spider Tresses
*Summer; 12 ft/3.6 m; low; spreading;
evergreen*

APOCYNACEAE

The 30 or so curious species of *Strophanthus* are rarely seen outside
warm-climate gardens. Like so many

Strophanthus preussii. Spider Tresses.
W. Africa

members of the dogbane family
(Allamanda, Cerbera, Mandevilla,
Plumeria), they grow best in sandy
soil enriched with peat, need plenty
of summer water and full sun, and
are definitely not frost hardy.

Illustrated *S. preussii* is naturally a
scrambler, growing to about 10 ft/
3 m, but more often seen draped over
a tree stump or wall. It is evergreen
with simple, shiny leaves that sprout
from reddish stems. The 5-petalled,
late spring flowers are basically
cream, shaded to orange and marked
with purple. The petals develop
thread-like extensions up to 1 ft/
30 cm in length.

Strophanthus gratus. Climbing Oleander. Tropical W. Africa

Strophanthus speciosus. Corkscrew Flower.
South Africa

More common *S. speciosus* is a more erect shrub, bears its leaves in whorls, its yellow flowers spotted red and without the extreme petal extensions. *S. gratus* is a climbing shrub that may reach 25 ft/7.5 m in the tropics. For a long time in spring and summer it's decked with flared tubular white flowers that are flushed pink. Its leaves are leathery, bright glossy green and up to 6 in/15 cm long.

Strophanthus species are propagated from cuttings struck under glass in moist sand. Several species are cultivated commercially for their seeds, a valuable source of cardiac drugs.

Styphelia adscendans. Green Five-corners.
S.E. Australia

Murray Fagg

Styphelia

(stai-**feel**-yə)   ☀T
Five-corners
Spring; to 3 ft/1 m; rigid; prickly; evergreen

ERICACEAE

Spikier and more spectacular than most members of the Australian heath family (Epacridaceae), the dozen or so species of *Styphelia* (Greek for hard, as in their leaf texture) are found all over the southern continent, extending into Tasmania and New Guinea.

Styphelia triflora. Pink Five-corners.
New South Wales

Difficult of propagation, they may be raised from fresh seed with a deal of patience. Germination is slow and erratic; viability of cuttings, not much better. All species of *Styphelia* prefer damp, well-drained, acid soil with filtered sunlight.

Illustrated Pink Five-corners (*S. triflora*) is a sparsely foliaged shrub to about 3 ft/1 m. It is limited to New South Wales. The Green Five-corners (*S. adscendans*) is even lower growing and found over New South Wales, Victoria, Tasmania and South Australia. Its upward-pointing flowers are yellow and green, tubular in shape and appear in winter.

The curious popular name is due to the shape created by five sharply reflexed petals. These roll back to reveal five stamens protruding from the bearded interior.

Styrax

(*syn.* STORAX)

(stai-raks)   ☼ ☀T W
Snowbell, Storax,
Snowdrop Bush
Summer; 20 ft/6 m; treelike; deciduous

STYRACACEAE   FRAGRANT

There are over 100 species of *Styrax* found through all continents of the northern hemisphere, but the species we illustrate is found down through the Balkans and across to Israel. For uncounted ages it has been the source of a medicinal resin called benzoin, the basis of the universal remedy friar's balsam, which was so greatly valued among the Arab people that the greatest sign of beauty was considered to be a navel that could hold an ounce of benzoic ointment!

Styrax species vary in height from 3 ft/1 m shrubs to slender 33 ft/10 m trees. All are deciduous, all bear clusters of delicate, fragrant, hanging bell flowers in summer. These vary from snow white to cream according to species.

Most *Styrax* can be propagated only by seed, layers or grafting onto lookalike Halesia. They prefer acid soil, regular water and, generally speaking, are not frost hardy. All species look best with midday shade in warm-temperate climates.

Styrax officinalis. Snowdrop Bush.
Balkans to Israel

Sutera

(*syn.* CHAENESTOMA)

(**soo**-ter-ə)   ☼ Ⓦ Ⓗ
Purple Glory, Wild Phlox
Sum–Aut; 4 ft/1.2 m; open; evergreen

SCROPHULARIACEAE   AROMATIC

One of Africa's most widespread native flower genera, there are around 150 species of *Sutera*, ranging from annuals to full shrubs. The shown Wild Phlox, *S. grandiflora*, is probably most widely seen in its native area, but is also grown in Australia and the southern United States.

It is easily grown from seed, and charges ahead in ordinary garden soil, with ample water in the growing season. It is, in fact, a rather Phlox-like plant, though belonging to an entirely different botanical family. Its grey-green leaves are wedge-shaped and aromatic and the whole plant has a rather sticky feel. The 5-petalled flowers are vivid purple and borne in racemes up to 1 ft/ 30 cm long. They open in summer and autumn.

Sutera grandiflora. Purple Glory. Swaziland

Sutherlandia

(suth-ur-**lan**-dee-ə)   ☼ Ⓦ Ⓗ
Balloon Pea, Gansies,
Kankerbossie, Cancer Bush
*Win–Spr; 2–3 ft/60 cm–1 m; erect;
evergreen*

FABACEAE

Probably a monotypic genus, though there are some variations in the foliage, the spectacular *Sutherlandia*

Sutherlandia frutescens. Cancer Bush.
S. Africa

frutescens presents a brilliant contrast in orange and green. Grown from seed, it can be used as an annual in warm climates, but if a more permanent planting is desired, strike cuttings and replace every few years, as soon as it gets straggly. In a well-drained, leaf-rich soil, it makes a wonderful rockery subject in hot dry areas, growing very fast to 3, even 5 feet (1–1.5 m) with soft, drooping, pinnate foliage in shades of grey-green. The drooping orange pea flowers are followed by puffy green pods which give the whole plant a festive appearance.

Though it was at one time believed to be a promising cure for cancer, the promise remains unfulfilled. Reasonably frost resistant, *Sutherlandia* self-seeds freely.

Symphoricarpos

(sim-for-i-**kah**-pos)   ☼ ☀ Ⓒ Ⓣ
Snowberry, Waxberry,
St Peter's Wort
*Summer; 3 ft/1 m; arching stems;
deciduous*

CAPRIFOLIACEAE

'Hello, suckers!' cried the great entertainer Texas Guinan—but she was not, unfortunately, referring to these showy cold-climate shrubs, for sucker they do and at a great rate.

Native to cold areas of North America and China, the curious *Symphoricarpos* produces hollow arching stems which bend almost double in winter under the weight of puffy white or pink-tinted berries. These are very useful for winter decoration.

Snowberries are deciduous, like rich, acid soil and filtered sun, and can be planted out from divisions in spring. In *S. occidentalis* the berry crop is preceded by small pink flowers in quite large terminal and axillary clusters.

Symphoricarpos occidentalis. Snowberry, St Peter's Wort. W. North America

Synadenium

(sin-a-**den**-ee-əm)   ☼ ☀ Ⓦ Ⓗ
African Milkbush
*All year; 8–12 ft/2.5–3.5 m; succulent;
evergreen*

EUPHORBIACEAE

Grown mostly for its decorative form, and as a foliage subject, the *Synadenium* is a fleshy, succulent plant from Central Africa, looking much like a Plumeria. Its flowers, however, are scentless and insignificant, appearing in small cymes. The lightly patterned leaves are quite large, wavy-edged, over 6 in/15 cm in length and widest towards the tip.

Synadenium grantii. African Milkbush.
Tropical Africa

All parts of the bush flow with a milky sap said to be poisonous, typical of the family Euphorbiaceae.

S. grantii is grown from quite large cuttings, which should be allowed to dry out thoroughly before they are planted in a dryish, sandy mix. S. grantii has several varieties with purple and deep red foliage. Away from the tropics and subtropics they are occasionally seen as house plants.

Synaphea

(**sai**-naf-ee-ə)   ☼ T W
Spring; to 2½ ft/75 cm; spreading; evergreen

PROTEACEAE

An interesting small genus of the family Proteaceae, but quite unexciting when compared to the wondrous Protea and Dryandra, *Synaphea* are principally noted for their rather vicious foliage which seems like a modern sculpture made up of fish-hooks. The flower spikes, bearing small, tubular, golden blooms, are interesting only in a mass.

Growing *Synaphea* from cuttings is not easy; seed seems more of a possibility when available. Good drainage and full sun are advisable, and the plants certainly grow better with a layer of limestone chips beneath their roots. Regular water makes a difference in the growing season.

Syringa

(si-**rin**-jə)   ☼ C T
Lilac
Spring; 6–12 ft/2–3.5 m; vigorous; open; deciduous

OLEACEAE   FRAGRANT

In their native northern hemisphere, the 30-odd sweet-scented species of *Syringa* would have to be springtime's

Syringa persica. Persian Lilac.
Iran to China

favourite shrub genus. Found naturally only in Europe and north-east Asia, they are perhaps even more popular in America's winter-frigid mid-western states where they are among the few shrubs that can be relied on to produce a mass of springtime blossom year after year.

The reason is simple. Lilacs thrive on cold. Unless they go cold dormant, they may not bloom at all the

Syringa vulgaris. Common Lilac. E. Europe

Synaphea spondulosa. Western Australia

Murray Fagg

Syringa vulgaris CV 'Vestale'. White Lilac. Hybrid

following spring. The only alternative (and not a good one at that) is to plant them in semi-shade and force them into dormancy by drying them right out. But really, you'd be better off choosing a plant more suited to your climate.

Lilacs take up a lot of room and in small gardens they are often grafted onto rootstock of the related Privet which do not sucker (see Ligustrum). Lilacs can be propagated from seed

Syringa vulgaris CV 'Sensation'. Variegated Lilac. Hybrid

Syringa X josiflexa. Hybrid Lilac. Hungary

which often produces 3-lobed leaves. All species yield dense panicles of 4-petalled flowers from ends of branches. These may be any shade of purple, mauve, white, pink, red, violet or, occasionally, primrose yellow.

Syringa CV 'Souvenir de Ludwig Spaeth'. Purple Lilac. E. Europe

Syringa X 'Maréchal Foch'. Lilac cultivar

but will take up to 10 years to bloom and may not come true to type. The gardener in a hurry will either graft onto Privet stock or propagate from early summer tip cuttings struck in sandy soil. In mature specimens, excessive suckering should be controlled by pruning most away, *below* soil level. Spent flower heads should be removed to prevent seed formation and a few older shoots can be cut away each year. A leaf-rich, friable loam grows the best lilacs, but over-acid soil must be sweetened with a ration of lime. A pH of 6–6.5 is ideal.

Lilacs are deciduous but produce only a mild display of autumn colour. They mostly bear simple, medium-sized, oval leaves. An exception is *Syringa persica*, the Persian Lilac,

Syzygium wilsonii var *wilsonii*. Wilson's Eugenia. Queensland

Syzygium
(*syn.* EUGENIA)

(si-**zij**-ee-əm) ☼ ☀✶ W H
Wilson's Eugenia
Spr–Sum; 7 ft/2 m; rounded; evergreen

MYRTACEAE   FRAGRANT

The true species of *Syzygium* are well known under a variety of names: Acmena, Eugenia, Jambosa, Myrtus, Phyllocladyx and Stenocalyx, according to the fashion in nomenclature when they were first classified. The latest division has all species of Eugenia from Africa, Asia and Australia classed as *Syzygium* for reasons involving the seeds, but they are still often labelled Eugenia.

There are about 500 species, most of them trees, all with evergreen foliage and often brilliantly coloured new leaves. The flowers are mostly creamy white or pink, a mass of stamens and very attractive to bees. In all principally grown species, these are followed by vividly coloured fruits, often pink and delicately sweet.

The illustrated species is something of a rarity, though it can be grown in any warm-temperate to subtropical climate. Its deep wine-red inflorescences, up to 4 in/10 cm in diameter, appear in spring and early summer. The fruits are white and ½ in/1 cm in length.

Propagate from seed, and grow in a lightly shaded, well-composted position. Although young plants are hardy, they often take some years to bloom.

Tabebuia
(*syn.* BIGNONIA)

(tab-ae-**boo**-yə) ☼ ☀✶ T H
Whitewood
Summer; 20 ft/6 m; treelike; deciduous

BIGNONIACEAE

Beside the taller *Tabebuia* species, *T. riparia* can pass as a shrub, for its spectacular South American jungle relatives may reach 100 ft/30 m and more. But where there's no room for them, this shrubby species can perhaps be accommodated.

Tabebuia riparia. Whitewood. Jamaica

Easy to grow from seed or cuttings, it does best in fairly rich soil that has good drainage. It flowers while quite young. *T. riparia* is known as Whitewood and hails from Jamaica where it may reach its true tropical height of 20 ft/6 m. Its compound leaves have oblanceolate leaflets, and the 2½ in/7 cm flowers are pure white with a rich yellow throat.

Away from the tropics, the Whitewood may be briefly deciduous.

Tabernaemontana coronaria. Ceylon Moonbeam. India

Tabernaemontana

(*syn.* CONOPHARYNGIA, ERVATAMIA, NERIUM)

(tab-ur-nae-mon-**tah**-nə)   ☼ ☀ Ⓦ Ⓗ
Ceylon Moonbeam, Nero's Crown, Red Bay, Cape Jasmine, Butterfly Gardenia, Mock Gardenia
Summer; 8 ft/2.5 m; dense; evergreen

APOCYNACEAE	FRAGRANT

The lovely shrubs known these days as *Tabernaemontana* have a predica-

Tabernaemontana divaricata
CV 'Grandifolia'. Butterfly Gardenia. India

ment. There are some 160 species, all with fragrant white Gardenia-scented flowers, but like the gentlemen in the American Express commercials, nobody knows who they are! Perhaps if they had a simpler name? But having started out as Conopharyngia and Ervatamia they seem to have got even worse.

They are all shrubs or small trees from 3 ft/1 m in height. All need a semi-tropical or warmer climate, a sheltered, sunny spot and a soil mixture of sand, loam and peat to flourish. Unlike many tropicals, water is appreciated all year. The single flower type is rarely seen outside its native South-east Asia, but the double is quite common in warm-climate gardens anywhere.

Tarchonanthus

(tah-koh-**nan**-thəs)   ☼ Ⓣ Ⓦ
Guitar Wood
Summer; 15 ft/4 m; weeping; evergreen

ASTERACEAE	AROMATIC

A strong smell of balsam or camphor helps identify *Tarchonanthus camphoratus*, one of a small genus of decorative daisy shrubs endemic to Africa. Their narrow lanceolate foliage is grey and sage-like; the greyish raggedy daisy flowers are borne on 10 in/25 cm long terminal and axil-

lary panicles. Propagation is from cuttings struck in early summer. Plant out in full sun in a fibrous, peaty loam.

Though not often referred to, the *Tarchonanthus* yields a hard wood used in decorative work or musical instruments, hence the popular name.

Tarchonanthus camphoratus. Guitar Wood. S. & Tropical Africa

Tasmannia

(*syn.* DRIMYS)

(tas-**man**-nee-ə)   ☀ ☀ Ⓒ Ⓦ
Pepperbush
Summer; 6–7 ft/2 m; dense; evergreen

WINTERACEAE	AROMATIC

Every time I see this montane plant from the Barrington Tops and other high-altitude areas of New South Wales, I am reminded of the movies' aviation serials in the 1930s, when the hero's flight of single-engined prop planes came roaring down the canyon. The *Tasmannia*'s curious flowers really do look like a flight of twin-bladed Pratt and Whitney Wasp

Tecoma X *smithii*. Bigeneric hybrid

Tecoma garrocha. Orange Trumpet Bush.
Argentina

Tasmannia purpurascens. Pepper Bush.
Montane N.S.W.

Tecoma stans. Yellow Elder. Florida to South America

aero-engines. Thank heaven they
don't make the same noise!

T. *purpurascens* is a splendid foliage
plant with glossy dark green leaves
spreading from red stems. You can
grow them from seed or cuttings and
raise them in leaf-rich soil. All parts
of the plant have an aromatic, spicy
flavour, and the dried fruits have
actually been sold as a condiment.

Tecoma
(*syn.* STENOLOBIUM, BIGNONIA)

te-**koh**-mə)   ☼ ✸ W H
Yellowbells, Tecomaxochitl, Yellow
Elder, Orange Trumpet Flower
*Spr–Aut; 6–16 ft/2–5 m; treelike;
evergreen*

BIGNONIACEAE

It is not often remembered that the
Aztecs were great gardeners—though
perhaps with a rather garish taste in
colour. Dahlias they grew, and
Zinnias and Bougainvillea, and
another of their favourites has come
down to us with much of its Aztec
name. *Tecomaxochitl*—or *Tecoma* as
we call them. These splashy shrubs
are found from Mexico right down to
Argentina, and their gorgeous golden

bell flowers are features of the landscape right through the warm weather.

Smallest-growing of the group is the brilliant *T. garrocha*, an orange-scarlet flowering evergreen for frost-free gardens. Its leaves are composed of deeply veined, pointed and sharply-toothed leaflets, and from midsummer every branch is tipped with a large panicle of 1¼ in/3 cm bell flowers. These feature a 2 in/5 cm orange-yellow tube flaring into deeper orange petals.

Tecomaria capensis. Cape Honeysuckle. South Africa

Tecoma alata. Yellowbells. Hybrid

Related *T. alata* flowers in a richer yellow (though often tinged orange) and its buds may be quite red. Tallest is yellow-blooming *T. stans*, often sold as Stenolobium or Yellow Elder. It grows to 16 ft/5 m and catches every eye with its display.

All species do best in a warm sunny spot, but once established they'll stand the odd light frost. Well drained to sandy soil with added organic matter is the ideal growing medium. *Tecoma* can be increased by soft-tip or semi-hardwood cuttings taken during the warmer months. Light pruning of the flowered shoots right after bloom helps keep *Tecoma* shapely.

Tecomaria

(tek-oh-**mear**-ee-ə)   ☼ Ⓦ Ⓗ
Cape Honeysuckle
Sum–Aut; 7–10 ft/2–3 m; part climbing; evergreen

BIGNONIACEAE

The brassily-blooming Cape Honeysuckle, *Tecomaria capensis*, is technically classed as a shrubby climber, but can easily spring either way. Given a fence, it will climb; but if a shrub is preferred it must be pruned hard annually to control any trailing growth. It is particularly useful in temperate coastal areas, although it will tolerate inland drought as well as moist salt air, and is hardy down to 28°F/–2°C.

The flowers, which appear in terminal sprays, are tubular and usually vivid orange. There is a less-common yellow CV 'Aurea' which grows more slowly, needs more heat. Blooming begins in late summer and continues until autumn turns chilly. Grow *Tecomaria* from layers or semi-hardwood cuttings taken any time.

Tecomaria is actually related to the Tecoma, and will hybridize with them. *Tecoma alata* is believed to be such a cross.

Telopea

(tel-**oh**-pee-ə)   ☼ ☀ ☀ Ⓣ Ⓦ
Waratah
Spring; 10–20 ft/3–6 m; becomes treelike; evergreen

PROTEACEAE

Floral emblem of the Australian State of New South Wales is the gorgeous *Telopea speciosissima*, largest and most beautiful of the 4 *Telopea* species. Its bright red 6 in/15 cm spring flowers can be seen at a good distance, and that is the meaning of both its botanical and Aboriginal names—'seen from afar'. None of the Waratah species is commonly grown in their homeland, and they're rarely seen abroad except as *very* expensive cut flowers. It's not that they're not worthwhile (their blooms are treasured throughout the world), but they do have a reputation for being difficult.

Waratahs really only do well in damp, sandy loam covered by a thick mulch of coarse organic matter such as fallen twigs, leaves and bark. And if you can provide a cool root-run by placing a few large flat stones around the trunk, so much the better. In nature they are understorey shrubs in open forest, and while they accept

Telopea speciosissima. Modern Hybrids from University of N.S.W. Breeding Programme

Telopea oreades X *speciosissima*. Hybrid Waratah

Telopea oreades. Gippsland Waratah.
N.S.W., Victoria

full sun, bright dappled shade probably suits them better. Waratahs are hardy down to at least 17°F/−8°C and can be kept compact by regular tip-pruning and cutting of flowers.

The cone-like red inflorescence consists of many curved florets surrounded by common bracts, and there is a rare white form of *T. speciosissima* which is being used in a breeding programme by the University of New South Wales. Related *T. mongaensis*, *T. oreades* (the Gippsland Waratah) and *T. truncata* (the Tasmanian Waratah, which has a yellow form) are sometimes grown by enthusiasts. A fine new hybrid, *T. oreades* X *speciosissima* is a vigorous 10 ft/3 m spreading shrub said to be the easiest of all to grow.

Templetonia

(tem-pel-**toh**-nee-ə)   ☼ ☀ Ⓦ Ⓗ
Coral Bush, Cockies' Tongues
Spring; 7 ft/2 m; spreading; evergreen

FABACEAE

This showy dry-climate shrub is grown in America's southwest, and would seem a strong possibility for many drought-prone areas of the temperate world. It is, however, endemic to Australia's southern and western deserts. *Templetonia retusa* is a sparse-growing shrub which may reach 6 ft/2 m in height and much more in diameter. It likes gravelly, alkaline soil that is well drained and includes some leaf litter.

Propagated from scarified seed or hardwood cuttings, it looks better for a light overall trim of recently flowered shoots. The sparse foliage drops in extremely dry weather, the dull coral pea flowers appear in early

Telopea speciosissima. N.S.W. Waratah

Templetonia retusa. Cockies' Tongues.
South & Western Australia

spring. *Templetonia* is hardy down to
27°F/ – 3°C, and in areas of acid soil
will be improved by an overlay of
limestone chips. On the coast, it does
well in a sheltered position, for while
it doesn't mind salt, it is easily damaged by coastal winds.

Ternstroemia
(*syn.* CLEYERA)

(turn-**stroh**-mee-ə)   ☼ ✹ W H
Jungle Tea
*Summer; to 30 ft/9 m in nature, 7–10 ft/
2–3 m in gardens; evergreen*

THEACEAE   FRAGRANT

One glance at the foliage of a
Ternstroemia and you'd be almost
right in identifying it as a Camellia.
Almost, but not quite! The 45 species
belong to the same family, Theaceae,
but are found over a much wider
tropical range from India through
Indo-China and coastal China to
Japan. Raised from cuttings, they
enjoy acid, leaf-rich but well-drained
soil and grow rather slowly.

They range from low shrubs to
quite large trees. The glossy, leathery
leaves are quite handsome and
bronzy-red when young. Mature
leaves may be deep green in the
shade, bronze-green or even purplish

in a sunny aspect. The fragrant
flowers, yellowish-white and only
½ in/1 cm across, hang singly on
stems from the leaf axils and are not
very eye-catching.

Ternstroemia gymnanthera. Jungle Tea.
Japan to India

Tetrapanax

(tet-rə-**pan**-aks)   ☼ ✹ W H
Chinese Ricepaper Plant
*Aut–Win; 10–15 ft/3–4.5 m; multi-
trunked; large-leafed; evergreen*

ARALIACEAE

The Chinese Ricepaper Plant, *Tetrapanax papyrifera*, is one of the largest
members of the Aralia family, growing to well over 10 ft/3 m tall. Its
huge, deeply lobed, felted leaves may
be 16 in/40 cm across and provide
useful shelter from summer sun for
smaller plants. Whitish when young,
the leaves turn a rusty colour with
age. The fluffy greenish-white flowers
are pleasant enough, appearing from
late summer onwards in great 3 ft/
1 m panicles.

Tetrapanax is far too large for pots,
but is popular in courtyard plantings.
It is particularly useful in seaside

Tetrapanax papyrifera. Chinese Ricepaper Plant.
S. China, Taiwan

gardens, since it resists salt-laden
winds and grows well in sandy soil.
Needs lots of water year round.
Hardy down to 22°F/ – 5°C.

Tetrapanax self-seeds constantly,
and the many unwanted suckers
should be dug out as they appear.

Tetratheca ericifolia. Black-eyed Susan.
S.E. Australia

Tetratheca

(tet-rə-**thee**-kə) ☼ ◑ T W
Black-eyed Susan
*Spring; 1–2 ft/30–60 cm; heathlike;
evergreen*

TREMANDRACEAE FRAGRANT

Although the black centres of the small drooping flowers of most *Tetratheca* species are rarely seen due to their hanging habit, they have attracted the name Black-eyed Susan. Found all over Australia, their masses of showy pink, mauve or purple bell flowers hang on fine red

Tetratheca ciliata. Pink Bells. South Australia

Tetratheca ericifolia (white form). White Susan. S.E. Australia

stems; most species also have rarer white forms. *T. ericifolia* is the fine-leafed common pink type, and as with the other species, cuttings of half-hardened wood are used to propagate.

All *Tetrathecas* are low, understorey Australian shrubs, bringing long-lasting splashes of spring colour to areas with light, sandy soil. They enjoy sun or part shade and thrive only in well-drained places totally free of lime or animal manure (though they do appreciate a leaf mould or growing carpet mulch).

Teucrium

(**tyoo**-kree-əm) ☼ T W
Germander, Shrubby Germander
Spr–Sum; 5–9 ft/1.5–2.5 m; sparse, wiry, grey-foliaged; evergreen

LAMIACEAE AROMATIC

Useful for the grey-foliaged garden, hardy *Teucriums* come in over 300 species mainly from the Mediterranean area and Asia Minor. Aromatic *T. fruticans* is the commonly seen shrubby type, growing to 8 ft/ 2.5 m and spreading equally wide. It is often trimmed as a neat, low hedge, or used in sheltered seaside gardens. Hardy down to 28°F/–2°C, it can be grown in a wide range of climates, where its all-grey foliage contrasts effectively with delicate mauve flowers that have one greatly enlarged petal.

Teucrium fruticans. Shrubby Germander. S. Europe

A member of the mint family, Germander thrives in any moderately rich, well-drained soil. Propagate *Teucrium* from cuttings taken with a heel in spring or summer. Trim spent flowers away to promote new growth.

Thevetia thevetioides. Yellow Oleander. Mexico

Thevetia

(thə-**vee**-shə) ☼ W H
Be-still Bush, Yellow Oleander
Sum–Aut; 12 ft/3.5 m; treelike, evergreen

APOCYNACEAE

The dangerously beautiful *Thevetias* are poisonous in every part, from their milky sap to their gorgeous golden trumpets. In this they resemble the related Oleanders, which they also copy in habit if not in colour.

The most commonly seen is *T. peruviana*, sometimes called the Be-still Bush from the constant air movement of its spidery, short-stemmed leaves. It grows to 30 ft/10 m in height, bears fragrant 2 in/5 cm golden trumpet flowers followed by angular red fruits, which ripen black. Its variety *aurantiaca* has salmon-orange flowers; *alba*, blooming in white, is also grown.

Closely related *T. thevetioides* bears much larger, more open flowers of a clear yellow, but rarely exceeds 15 ft/ 4.5 m in height. Forms with orange flowers are also known.

All are increased from seed or cuttings and enjoy well-watered, sandy soil. Mature plants tolerate a few degrees of frost.

Thomasia macrocarpa. Woolly Thomas. Western Australia

Thunbergia
(*syn.* MEYENIA)

(thun-**berg**-ee-ə) ☼ W H
King's Mantle, Bush Clock Vine
Spring; 7 ft/2 m; sparse; evergreen
ACANTHACEAE

A genus of gaily-flowered plants from warm climates, *Thunbergias* come in many forms—perennial, shrubby and climbing—with the latter most commonly seen. The shrub versions with which we deal here are a bit of a puzzle, acting like climbers waiting to climb, and this is probably true. I have often noticed for instance that *T. battiscombei* tends to throw out ground-hugging trailing shoots that look as if they'd grab you by the leg and twine all the way up—but they never actually do it! And the several

Thomasia
(*syn.* LASIOPETALUM)

(tom-**ass**-ee-ə) ☼ ☀ W
Woolly Thomas
Spring; 2 ft/60 cm; spreading; evergreen
MALVACEAE

Endemic to Western Australia, several of the 28 species of *Thomasia* are useful subjects where the weather is mild and the humidity low. They enjoy a sandy soil with some peat. Since the flowers hang downward, they should be planted in a raised bed where you can look up at them. Most species are propagated from cuttings, but seed is a possibility for those with seed-raising experience.

Illustrated *T. macrocarpa* is most widespread in cultivation, having felt-textured, deeply divided leaves and lilac-pink flowers up to 1 in/2 cm wide. These are petalless, but the calyx lobes have adapted to take their place. Dappled shade, please, in hot areas.

Thryptomene

(thrip-toh-**mee**-nee) ☼ ☀ T W
Heath Myrtle
Win–Spr; 3 ft/1 m; spreading; evergreen
MYRTACEAE   FRAGRANT/
                   AROMATIC

A spicy myrtle-fragrance on winter days leads one quickly to Australia's

delicate Heath Myrtle or *Thryptomene*. Grow them anywhere the soil is well-drained and acid, preferably a little on the shady side. Regular water and sunshine are necessities for all of the 21 species. Flowering in varied shades of pink, white and lavender. The blooms are cup-shaped and under ¼ in/5 mm across, the leaves tiny and heath-like. Both are borne on slender, arching stems which make them just fine for cutting.

T. calycina is the hardiest white-flowering type, *T. saxicola* 'E. C. Payne' the best pink. Propagate from semi-hardwood cuttings during the warmer weather. Water lightly at all times and tip-prune all over after bloom. *Thryptomenes* benefit from a year-round mulch.

Thryptomene saxicola 'E.C. Payne'. Heath Myrtle. Western Australia

Thunbergia battiscombei. King's Mantle. Tropical Africa

Thunbergia erecta alba. White Clock Vine. Tropical Africa

varieties of *T. erecta*, while definitely shrubby in habit, look as if they might easily take off, up and away, if only the climate were a little warmer. The answer is probably a regular, light pruning and plenty of food and water to prevent their becoming too leggy.

Propagate from hardwood cuttings or seeds, and keep growing in a rich soil. Though nominally evergreen, the *Thunbergias* tend to become semi-deciduous away from the tropics.

Thymus

(**tai**məs) ☼ C T W
Thyme, Lemon-scented Thyme
Summer; 6–12 in/15–30 cm; mat-forming; evergreen

LAMIACEAE   AROMATIC

Let the good Thymes roll! Set them out along path edges or in rock pockets in well-drained, dryish soil, and away they go. There are some 100 species of Thyme, and it comes as something of a surprise to discover that these dainty, mat-forming plants really are shrubs. (Well, some of them are classed only as sub-shrubs, it's true.)

Easy to grow from divisions at almost any time of the year. Divided plants should be replanted at once and watered well but if the division

Thymus serpyllus. Thyme. Europe, Britain

must take place in summer, set the cuttings out in a cold-frame and grow on for a year.

These days we grow the original *Thymus vulgaris* for the kitchen but prefer its lemon-scented hybrid *T. X citriodorus* in the flower garden. Thyme likes a well-drained position (a bank is ideal) and is relatively hardy except in a severe winter. Water lightly in drought-stricken times. In summer, Thyme becomes a mass of tiny, pale lilac flowers, and bees come from all directions.

Thymus X citriodorus 'Archer's Gold'. Lemon-scented Thyme. Hybrid

Tibouchina heteromalla. Glory-bush. Brazil

Tibouchina

(*syn.* PLEROMA, RHEXIA)

(tib-oo-**shee**-nə) ☼ W H
Lasiandra, Glory-bush, Quaresma, Princess Flower
Aut–Spr; 7–10 ft/2–3 m; rounded; evergreen

MELASTOMATACEAE

Lasiandras, as they are commonly called, are gaudy South American shrubs for acid soil that is rich and well-drained. They produce extraordinary colour effects at many times of the year. New growth is shaded with bronze and red, quickly turning to a rich, velvet green. The plants are

Tibouchina granulosa rosea 'Kathleen'. Pink Glory-bush. Brazil

basically evergreen, but odd leaves may turn scarlet or yellow in cold weather. The magnificent flowers most commonly appear through summer and autumn, though some species bloom in spring. While they are generally a rich glowing purple, pink and white types are known.

There are 150 or more species in

Tibouchina 'Alstonville'. Princess Flower. Hybrid

Tibouchina clavata alba. Quaresma,
Silky Glory-bush. South America

Tibouchina laxa 'Skylab'.
Climbing Lasiandra. Peru

early autumn. Its cultivar 'Rosea' is similar, except the flowers are soft pink and less profuse.

T. *macrantha* grows to 10 ft/3 m at most. Its flowers are a deep royal purple, and, though not as generously produced, can be 4 in/10 cm across. Flowering will begin in autumn and a well-grown specimen may still be in bloom at winter's end.

Tibouchinas can be grown from fresh seed or soft-tip cuttings taken any time during the warmer months. The plants grow best in full sun, but in very hot areas dappled shade is acceptable. Keep consistently moist all through spring and summer and pinch out the growing tips regularly

Tibouchina macrantha. Lasiandra. S. Brazil

the wild, though cultivars of only three or four of these are widely grown. *Tibouchina granulosa*, one of the most popular species, can develop into a small tree 30 ft/10 m tall, but is usually kept pruned to smaller size. Flowers are rich, almost iridescent violet-purple, and produced in incredible profusion for many weeks in

to promote bushiness. Even so, plants are inclined to be leggy and the brittle branches soon broken by strong winds. Some species will take the odd light frost, but they're best planted under eaves or large trees where winters are regularly frosty.

More unusual species are *T. clavata alba* which has long-stemmed white flowers. Its cultivar 'Elsa' is popular in Australia. 'Jules' is a low, bushy cultivar suitable for rockery work, and 'Skylab' a CV of *T. laxa* which may reach 10 ft/3 m in height.

one year. The brilliant 4 in/10 cm flowers appear in winter. It is easily propagated from seed or hardwood cuttings, and does not seem fussy as to soil so long as the drainage is good. It is certainly not hardy and is best treated like Poinsettias, which come from the same area. To prevent the whole plant becoming straggly, it is best cut back to the ground after bloom. Then, with regular moisture, it will sprout up again, its coarsely-toothed, lobed leaves remaining beautiful until next winter's flowering cycle.

Trevesia sundaica. Snowflake Aralia. Java, Sumatra

Tithonia

(tai-**thoh**-nee-ə) ☼ Ⓦ Ⓗ
Tree Marigold
*Winter; 15 ft/4.5 m; leggy; open;
evergreen*

ASTERACEAE

If South Africa could name a daisy after dawn-goddess Aurora, it was a sure bet some taxonomist would remember her mythical boyfriend Tithonus. So we have *Tithonia*, a small genus of annuals, perennials and shrubs notable for their big, bright, daisy flowers.

T. diversifolia, the Tree Marigold, is a clump-forming shrub whose canelike stems can reach 12 ft/4 m in

Trevesia

(tre-**vee**-see-ə) ☼ ☀ Ⓦ Ⓗ
Snowflake Aralia
*All year; 25 ft/7.5 m; multi-trunked;
evergreen*

ARALIACEAE

Smaller species of *Trevesia*, the Snowflake Aralia, are grown indoors as house plants. But in frost-free areas *Trevesias* can be grown outdoors, and the illustrated *T. sundaica* is a popular choice for tropical foliage effect.

A large shrub (or small tree) 20–25 ft/6–8 m tall, it has big, glossy, deeply lobed leaves and prickly branches. Fortunately the leaves are attractive year-round, for the sum-

mer flowers must be among the most unremarkable produced by any plant—thick-stemmed clusters of tiny greenish blooms.

Trevesias are easy to grow from cuttings struck under glass. A leaf-rich, sandy soil will keep them growing so long as you can keep the humidity high.

Trichostema lanatum. Woolly Blue Curls. California

Tithonia diversifolia. Tree Marigold. Central America

Trichostema

(trik-oh-**stem**-mə)   ☼ W
Woolly Blue Curls, Romero
*Spr–Sum; 1½–3½ ft/45–100 cm; erect;
evergreen*

LAMIACEAE   FRAGRANT

One of California's most attractive wildflowers, *Trichostema lanatum* or Woolly Blue Curls is the one shrubby species of a 16-member genus in the mint family. It can be grown in any dryish climate. It is raised from seed, grows 3 ft/1 m in height in a well-drained sandy loam, and needs little water, especially in summer.

The foliage is very like that of Rosemary, though hairy on the underside; but the mauve flowers are borne as 6 in/15 cm spikes of up to 20, and their buds are covered with striking woolly hairs shading from pink to crimson to purple. *Trichostemas* have a spicy, sage-like fragrance, and are important bee plants.

Triplochlamys

(*syn.* PAVONIA)

(**trip**-loh-klam-is)   ☼ W H
Shooting Stars, Pavonia
*Summer; 6 ft/2 m; multi-stemmed;
evergreen*

MALVACEAE

In spite of their paucity of numbers, (only half a dozen species) what a splash these showy-flowered plants make in a warm-climate garden! Brazil is their homeland, so that really does mean subtropical conditions at least, with moisture available all year.

Shooting Stars like leaf-rich, well-drained soil, and can be grown from seed or cuttings where the temperature and humidity are high. Growth is fast, and the leaves are simple, spear-shaped and slightly toothed. In *T. multiflora* the flowers appear in terminal corymbs, each bloom shaped like a comet, many-petalled and crimson in colour.

Triplochlamys multiflora. Shooting Stars. Brazil

Tristania neriifolia. Watergum. N.S.W.

Tristania

(tris-**tan**-ee-ə)   ☼ ☀ W
Watergum
*Summer; 10 ft/3 m; open; treelike;
evergreen*

MYRTACEAE

Tristania was never a large Australian genus, but now it's even smaller, since the 'splitters' have created Lophostemon and Tristaniopsis from within its ranks. Still we are left with the Watergum, *T. neriifolia*, and a handsome shrub it is too. Upright in habit, it produces erect branches from a short trunk and may reach 10 ft/3 m in time, with a spread of about half that.

The flowers appear in clusters at every branch end during summer; each cluster relatively small, but enough are produced for a very worthwhile display—especially in a partly shaded area of the garden. Grow in leaf-rich, well-watered and drained soil in part or full shade. Propagate from seed, kept constantly damp.

Trochocarpa

(troh-koh-**kah**-pə)   ☼ ☀ ☀ W H
Tree Heath
Summer; to 20 ft/6 m; dense; evergreen

ERICACEAE

If you live in Australia, and there are bowerbirds in your district, you're not likely to retain much of a berry display from this shrub. Attracted as they always are to blue objects, the bowerbirds will make short work of the display in no time at all. But even without the fruits, *Trochocarpa laurina* is an attractive foliage shrub—so attractive it's hard to believe it is only an oversized member of the Australian Heath family, Epacridaceae.

New spring foliage turns from red

Trochocarpa laurina. Tree Heath. Qld, N.S.W.

Murray Fagg

to pink before settling on a light green. Spikes of dainty white heath flowers open in summer and are followed by the aforesaid fruits. *Trochocarpa* can be propagated from seed or cuttings, but is never a plant in a hurry. It does best in a well-drained compost that is not too rich.

Turnera ulmifolia. Sage Rose. Tropical Asia

Turnera

(**tur**-nur-ə) ☼ ☀ W H
Sage Rose, Marilopez,
Yellow Alder, West Indian Holly
Spring; 9 ft/3 m; dense; evergreen

TURNERACEAE

The yellow *Turnera* species seen in warm-climate gardens all over the world is only one of about 100 species in cultivation. *T. ulmifolia* grows naturally from Mexico through the Caribbean to many parts of South America. It is a much-branched, shrubby plant, easily mistaken for a yellow Hibiscus when in bloom, though in fact it belongs to quite a different botanical family, named rather incestuously after itself.

Strictly for the frost-free climate, *T. ulmifolia* is propagated from seed or cuttings, and grows best in light,

well-drained, sandy soil. It needs high humidity, but even then looks better with midday shade from the full sun. The simple leaves are toothed and rather pleated, like an elm's, hence the specific name *ulmifolia*.

Other *Turnera* species have been identified in Malagasy, Mauritius and South Africa, but they are only cultivated locally.

Ugni

(syn. EUGENIA, MYRTUS)

(**ug**-nee) ☼ ☀ T W
Chilean Guava, Chilean Cranberry
*Spr–Sum; 7 ft/2 m; dwarf; open;
evergreen*

MYRTACEAE   FRAGRANT

This smallish genus in the myrtle family is native from southern Mexico to Peru, Venezuela and Chile according to species, and is greatly valued for its small-scale fruit, which are edible and quite delicious. Chilean *Ugni molinae* is particularly valued for this purpose in cooler areas and is used to make jam.

Best planted from division or cuttings, it should be set in acid to neutral soil and kept moist at all times. Pinkish myrtle flowers appear in the leaf axils and are succeeded by the fragrant blue-black berries.

Ugni molinae. Chilean Guava. Chile, Bolivia

Pamla Toler

Ulex europaeus. Gorse. Western Europe

Ulex

(**yoo**-leks) ☼ C T
Gorse, Furze, Whin
Win–Spr; 3–7 ft/1–2 m; dense; evergreen

FABACEAE   FRAGRANT

Quickly spreading into impenetrable, viciously-spined thickets in open, temperate areas, Gorse can only be trusted in cold-climate city gardens, where it can be kept under control. It is a hated pest in farmers' fields of New Zealand and a proclaimed noxious weed in parts of Australia. But in northern Europe and the cooler parts of North America, it is a compact shrub to 7 ft/2 m that makes a marvellous security hedge.

Small, bright yellow, fragrant flowers cover the plant in spring, except in warmer climates where bloom is more than usually continuous. *Ulex europaeus* flowers best in poor soil, for in good conditions it bolts to leaf—or rather to spine, as true leaves are found only on young plants. Hardy to 5°F/−15°C.

Uncarina grandidieri. Catechu. Madagascar

Urena lobata. Uren. India

Murray Fagg

Uncarina

(un-kah-**ree**-nə)   ☼ Ⓦ Ⓗ
Catechou, Uncarina
Summer; 10 ft/3 m; dense; evergreen

PEDALIACEAE

To paraphrase Oscar Wilde, 'why is it that whenever some new plant appears, it is said to have been seen sometime in Madagascar?' Why indeed? That exotic island, now known as Malagasy, does seem to be home to a disproportionate number of remarkable plants, among them the showy *Uncarinas*.

These are soft-foliaged, red-stemmed, evergreen shrubs from dry parts of the island that seem to have no thirst at all. *U. grandidieri* is rare in its native land, but grown elsewhere for the gorgeous golden-yellow flowers, all of 4 in/10 cm across. It likes light, well-drained soil. Propagate from seed if you can get it.

Urena

(yoo-**ree**-nə)   ☼ ✳ Ⓦ Ⓣ
Uren, Aramina
Summer; 2–7 ft/60 cm–2 m; tough-stemmed; evergreen

MALVACEAE

Cultivated in some parts of the world for its stem fibre (which is used for making coffee bags, due to its strength), *Urena lobata* is a useful and quite pretty member of the mallow family, Malvaceae. The red-centred, pink mallow-type blooms appear in clusters at the leaf axils, enclosed in a 5-part calyx. Grown from seed or cuttings, *Urena* is classed as an under-shrub and develops 5- to 7-lobed leaves. It originates in India where it is known as Uren.

Vaccinium

(*syn.* CYANOCOCCUS, HERPOTHAMNUS, OXYCOCCUS, POLYCODIUM)

(vak-**sin**-ee-əm)   ☼ ✳ ✸ Ⓒ Ⓣ
Blueberry, Cranberry, etc
Spr–Sum; 1 ft/30 cm; dense-foliaged

ERICACEAE

Scattered throughout North America, Europe and Asia, the genus *Vaccinium* covers most of the favourite cool-climate berries. These include Blueberry, Bilberry, Cranberry, Huckleberry, Deerberry, Whortleberry, Whinberry, Grouseberry, Moorberry, Cowberry, Foxberry and

Lingon. There are 150-odd species in all including both evergreen and deciduous shrubs, vines and even small trees. The deciduous species have dazzling autumn colour. Small flowers (which may be borne singly or in clusters or racemes) may be white, green, red, purple or black.

V. myrtilloides and *V. corymbosum* are the principal commercial Blueberries but there are many cultivars and hybrids. *V. macrocarpon* (syn. Oxycoccus) is the main Cranberry species, though most of those grown commercially are cultivars. Some *Vacciniums* are raised as garden ornamentals, others are colonized in wild areas and grown for their edible fruits. Most of them need peaty or sandy acid soil and do not like lime. The Cranberry types are raised in acid bogs or swamps.

Vaccinium corymbosum 'Northeast'. Hybrid Blueberry

Verticordia nitens. Shiny Feather-flower. Western Australia

Verticordia grandis. Scarlet Feather-flower. Western Australia

at home anywhere the humidity is low and the soil sandy and leaf-rich. Perfect drainage and full sun would seem essential, and you might try growing them in raised beds. Still, at present, it must be confessed they are shrubs for the connoisseur — and the skilled one at that! Though seed fertility is low, semi-hardwood cuttings can be struck in a warm place with misting.

The *Verticordia*'s profusion of bloom has made them popular in Australia's cut-flower industry, so it's not surprising to find that the name *Verticordia* is from the Latin, meaning 'to turn a heart'.

V. plumosa is a small, open shrub to 1½ ft/50 cm. Its pink flowers appear singly or in groups towards the ends of branches. *V. nitens* grows erectly, bearing golden yellow flowers in broad terminal corymbs. *V. grandis* may reach 3–4 ft/1 m in height, topping its branches with clusters of fiery red blossom.

Verticordia plumosa. Juniper Myrtle. Western Australia

Verticordia

(vur-ti-**kor**-dee-ə)   ☼ T W
Feather-flower, Morrison, Juniper Myrtle
Spr–Sum; 1½–5 ft/50 cm–1.5 m; open; low growing; evergreen

MYRTACEAE

Endemic to Western Australia, *Verticordia* is a genus of 50-odd shrubs that are not often seen in cultivation outside that state. This is a great shame, because they should be

Murray Fagg

Vesselowskya rubifolia.
New South Wales

Vesselowskya

(vess-el-**off**-skee-ə)   ☼ ✹ W H
Vesselowskya
*Spr–Sum; 20 ft/6 m; erect; branching;
evergreen*

CUNONIACEAE

This handsome plant from the New
South Wales coastal rainforests might
easily be mistaken for one of the
Protea family, so much do its foliage
and flowers resemble those of
Macadamia and Buckinghamia. But
it really belongs to the Cunoniaceae,
which includes Callicoma, Ceratopetalum and Weinmannia.

Vesselowskya can be propagated
from seed or cuttings, grows in deep,
rich soil in a shaded position. Evergreen, it would seem to have a great
future as an indoor plant. The handsome leaves are pinnate with 3 to 5
serrated leaflets up to 4 in/10 cm in
length. The profuse panicles of
flowers open in spring.

Vestia

(**vess**-tee-ə)   ☼ ✹ C T
Chilean Heath
*Summer; 12 ft/4 m; many-branched;
evergreen*

SOLANACEAE   ILL-SCENTED

Although Chilean Heath may be
from Chile, a heath it is not, in spite
of its popular name. Its claim to botanical fame is as a member of the
Solanaceae or tomato family. I must
say, you could have fooled me!

Vestia lycioides. Chilean Heath. Chile

The plant is erect-growing and
many-branched, its leaves oblong
and about 1 in/3 cm in length. The
distinctively heath-type flowers consist of a 1 in/3 cm long tube of
yellow-green ending in 5 spreading,
triangular lobes. These are quite ill-
scented and are followed by small
urn-shaped fruits about 1 in/3 cm in
length. In spite of its odour, *Vestia
lycioides* is popular in many parts of
the world. A monotypic genus, *Vestia*
is closely related to Cestrum. Grow
Vestia from cuttings in good, loamy
soil and if you live away from a
warm-temperate climate, consider
raising it in a greenhouse.

Viburnum trilobum (fruit).
Cranberry Bush. N. North America

Viburnum

(vai-**bur**-nəm)   ☼ ✹ ✹ C T
Snowball Tree, Cranberry Bush,
Guelder Rose, Laurustinus
*Spring; 6–13 ft/2–4 m; dense; some
deciduous*

ADOXACEAE   FRAGRANT

Dare one claim a single genus of
shrubs as the most beautiful and
varied of all? It could only be said of
the *Viburnums*—120 species and
many more named varieties, short or

Viburnum erubescens. Blushing Viburnum.
W. China

Viburnum plicatum CV *tomentosum* 'Roseum'.
Double-file Viburnum

tall, some with brilliant autumn foliage and colourful fruits that birds adore. Some, including *V. tinus*, *V. X burkwoodii* and *V. X carlcephalum* have a honeysuckle-like fragrance.

Viburnums are almost equally divided between deciduous and evergreen, but the division can become blurred in some climates. Of the evergreens, *V. X burkwoodii* usually reaches 6 ft/2 m and bears 4 in/10 cm wide globular clusters of flowers that open pinkish but soon fade to white. The Laurustinus (*V. tinus*) grows to 10 ft/3 m; its tiny, pinkish flowers are clustered together in heads.

Viburnum X *carlecephalum*.
Spice Flower. Hybrid

Viburnum opulus sterile. Guelder Rose. Europe, N. Africa, N. Asia

In most species, at least some autumn colour can be expected, even if it is only in the fruits. But where autumns are frosty, gardeners can be assured of an extravagant display of scarlet and gold from the deciduous species. First among these is the gorgeous Guelder Rose (*V. opulus*). Its spring display consists of flat heads of Hydrangea-like white blossoms and in the preferred variety, *V. o. sterile*, these are formed in great 3 in/8 cm spheres that have suggested the common name Snowball Tree. It grows to around 17 ft/5 m. *V. plicatum* var *tomentosum* may reach 10 ft/3 m with a much wider spread. It has sterile, relatively large, open, single blooms in white blushed pink surrounding the tiny, insignificant fertile flowers.

All species demand moderately rich, well-drained soil and plenty of

Viburnum X *burkwoodii.*
Burkwood Viburnum. Hybrid

Viburnum tinus. Laurustinus. Mediterranean

moisture throughout spring and summer. They are mostly hardy; of those shown, *V. tinus* is the least so, being able to tolerate temperatures only as low as 0°F/–18°C. *Viburnums* are not difficult to propagate as all but a few sterile hybrids bear seed and these often germinate naturally. Otherwise it is quite easy to strike cuttings of half-ripened shoots (most easily with gentle bottom heat) or to set layers. Dead flower heads should be removed regularly and an annual light pruning is wise if the plants are to be kept controlled. Spider mites and mildew are common pests.

Vinca major 'Variegata'. Periwinkle. Europe

Vinca

(**vin**-kə)   ☼ ☀ ☀ T W
Periwinkle, Blue-buttons,
Cut-finger
Spr–Aut; 6–12 in/15–30 cm; mat-forming; evergreen

APOCYNACEAE

Shrubs? Well, sub-shrubs anyway, though even then I have my doubts about the classification of this popular plant. *Vincas* or Periwinkles are the universal groundcover in temperate climates, useful for shade, semi-shade, flat areas, steep embankments or almost anywhere else. They are easily increased by divisions planted out in deep soil. These then send out a mass of suckering shoots which

take root wherever they rest on the ground so that the spreading process starts all over again.

There are single and double blooming varieties in shades of purple, blue and white. The marbled-leaf type shown, *V. major* 'Variegata', is particularly effective. Keep *Vincas* moist at all times.

Vitex

(**vai**-teks)   ☼ T W
Blue Vitex
*Summer; 20 ft/6 m; low-branching;
evergreen*

LAMIACEAE   AROMATIC

A large genus (over 250 species) of trees and shrubs in the Mint family, *Vitex* are mostly native to subtropical areas of all continents. Several are grown as ornamentals for their aromatic foliage and the showy panicles of bloom, resembling Buddleia. They thrive in good soils, can be raised from seed, cuttings or layers.

V. trifolia, the Blue Vitex from Asia and Australia, is a shrubby, low-branching plant with mauve-tinged foliage. Each leaf consists of three leaflets; young growth is purple. The lavender-blue flowers borne in 5 in/12 cm trusses resemble Lilac.

Vitex trifolia. Blue Vitex.
Australia to Asia

Warscewiczia

(var-se-**vitch**-yə) ☼ W H
Wild Poinsettia, Chaconia
*Spring; to 20 ft/6 m; straggly or treelike;
evergreen*

RUBIACEAE

This gorgeously blooming plant was described as a tree in a book I read some time ago. I really do hope it never goes that far, since I've been recommending it to the tropically situated for years, but I have never seen it more than scrambly shrub size.

Warscewiczia coccinea. Wild Poinsettia. Trinidad to Brazil

It produces shining evergreen leaves and arching terminal flower clusters. In our picture, the orange rosettes are groups of flowers, while the scarlet 'leaves' are enlarged calyx lobes and appear one to a flower.

Apart from its craving for tropical heat, it has two other disadvantages for the average garden. One, it is supposed to need 60 in/1.5 m of rain a year (which is nonsense) and two, it is not frost hardy. Seed germinates uncovered in 10 days under glass.

Weigela

(syn. DIERVILLA)

(**Wai**-gee-la) ☼ ☀ C T
Fairy Trumpets, Weigelia
*Spring; 6–7 ft/2 m; fountain shaped;
deciduous*

CAPRIFOLIACEAE

Leggy, woody *Weigela* bursts into life for one short period in spring, opening sheer masses of red, white or pink trumpet flowers. Then, as the leaves form in the summer sun, and the flowers fade, they are often cut right back to avoid untidiness. The leaves

Weigela florida 'Variegata'. Fairy Trumpets

Weigela florida. Weigelia. N. China

Weigela florida 'Bristol Ruby'. Ruby Weigelia

fall early without a colour display and the shrubs are bare for a long time in cold weather. In severe winter climates they are often burned right back by frost and may be of limited use.

But in spite of all the above bad news, the *good* news is that they make a gorgeous flower display (though without much fragrance) and the arching stems cut well for large arrangements.

Grow *Weigela* in rich, well-drained soil and keep up the water during the growing season. Propagate from winter cuttings of year-old hardwood. *W. florida* is the preferred species; its hybrids include 'Abel Carrière' (rose-pink), 'Bristol Ruby' (crimson), 'Candida' (white), 'Eva Kallike' (crimson) and 'Boskoop Glory' (rose-pink).

Weigela florida 'Alba'. White Weigelia

Weinmannia racemosa. Kamahi.
New Zealand

Weinmannia

(wain-**man**-nee-ə) ☼ T
Kamahi
Spring; to 60 ft/20 m; dense; evergreen

CUNONIACEAE

A large tree under rainforest conditions, New Zealand's handsome *Weinmannia racemosa* can remain shrubby in the garden and should, in any case, be pruned to restrict it. The simple, shiny, evergreen leaves are like those of a beech, while the spring flower display consists of densely flowered, bottlebrush type racemes, which are long lasting in the mass. These are usually creamy white but may be pink on some plants.

   Weinmannia is propagated from seed or cuttings; it likes deep, rich soil with plenty of leaf mould and moisture.

Westringia grandifolia. Coast Rosemary.
Queensland

Westringia fruticosa 'Morning Light'.
Variegated Rosemary. Hybrid

Westringia

(west-**rin**-jee-ə) ☼ T W H
Coast Rosemary
Spr–Sum; 6 ft/2 m; bun-shaped; evergreen

LAMIACEAE

The reputation of the *Westringia* genus has become tarnished for me at the hands of get-rich-quick builders. Lookalikes for the European Rosemary (see Rosmarinus), their problem is that they grow not wisely but too well. Set a planting of them around some newly built houses and in six months you have a garden (albeit a colourless one!). But when the

builder has moved on, suddenly the short-lived bushes die away and half-dead branches appear everywhere.

   The solution is to confine them to the well-drained coastal garden and prune lightly and often to keep them dense and compact. Queensland's *W. grandifolia* is the showiest species, *W. fruticosa* the most common.

Westringia fruticosa. Coast Rosemary.
New South Wales

Wigandia

(wig-**an**-dee-ə) ☼ ☀ W H
Stinging Shrub
Spring; 10 ft/3 m; multi-trunked; evergreen

HYDROPHYLLACEAE

Wigandia species are used for pseudo-tropical plantings because of their very large, fleshy leaves. The 5 species

Wigandia macrophylla. Stinging Shrub.
Mexico

form a very small genus from mountainous areas of South America. The handsome Stinging Shrub, *W. macrophylla*, is grown from seed or cuttings at a temperature of 55°F/13°C and may be treated as an annual at the back of the mixed border. But as it is actually a shrub, it can be grown to its full height of 10 ft/3 m and pruned back again and again.

The heavy, doubly toothed leaves can be irritating to some people, so best scrub your hands after handling them. The violet flowers resemble giant forget-me-nots.

Wistaria
(*syn.* WISTERIA)

(wis-**tear**-ee-ə)   ☼ ✹ C T W
Chinese Kidney Bean,
Chinese Wisteria
Spring; to 6 ft/2 m (as a shrub); deciduous

FABACEAE   FRAGRANT

These marvellous plants, commonly seen as twining climbers, were named for the American Professor Caspar Wistar, thus making nonsense of the alternative spelling used by many horticultural writers. They form a small genus found naturally in the Far East and North America, but make up for their lack of numbers with the sheer beauty of their display. All look similar, but if you're onto a good thing, why change the design?

Most versatile plants, they can be trained as vines, hedges, standard shrubs, even as container plants. All species are completely deciduous, dropping their pinnate leaves early and generally not developing new foliage until after flowering. This is a very sudden event, beginning in my climate on the very first day of spring every year—I could set a clock by it!

All species may be grown from seed but this is very slow. The alternatives are cuttings or suckers. I have had best results from root cuttings, which generally grow at a great rate in the loamy, acid soil *Wistaria* needs. And don't let up on water during the actual flowering period—water and sun are their two great needs.

Chinese *W. sinensis* is the common type with fragrant, pale mauve pea flowers in 10 in/25 cm panicles. With patience, it can be trained to any shape you like, starting with a strong support for the trunk—iron rather than wood is to be preferred. Constant pruning of the trailing stems back to two axillary buds each will ultimately cause the plant to give up all ideas of being a climber and turn into the loveliest shrub you ever saw. The specimen in our picture is at Bowral, New South Wales.

Woodfordia floribunda. Red Bell Bush. India

Woodfordia
(*syn.* GRISLEA)

(wood-**ford**-ee-ə)   ☼ H
Red Bell Bush
Spring; 1–6 ft/30 cm–2 m; spreading; deciduous

LYTHRACEAE

A popular shrub in Indian gardens, the *Woodfordia* is also highly regarded as a source of dye and medication. It flowers in mid-winter in India but not till spring in cooler climates.

Grown from seed or cuttings, it develops a rather spreading habit, produces simple, lanceolate leaves with a rather pronounced curve at the tips. The orange-scarlet bell flowers appear either singly or in short panicles at the leaf axils. They are tubular and 6-petalled with exserted stamens of the same reddish colour. *Woodfordia* is monotypic, does well in a dry, well-drained spot.

Wistaria sinensis. Chinese Wisteria. China

Woolsia

(wool-zee-ə) ☼ ☀ T W H
All year; 5 ft/1.5 m; erect; evergreen
EPACRIDACEAE

Spiky *Woolsia* is a monotypic genus within the Australian Heaths, Epacridaceae. It is an erect plant, seldom more than 5 ft/1.5 m in height and occasionally consisting of a single stem branched near the ends. The stiff, prickly leaves are closely placed along the stems in a clasping mode, the 4-petalled flowers white or sometimes pink.

Woolsia is almost always propagated from cuttings, which must be transplanted with care for the roots are fine and easily broken. They seem to enjoy poor, gravelly soil so long as the drainage is good. In nature, it is often found in coastal areas, close to seepage but not actually growing in it. Flowers and leaves continue to appear for many months as the stems elongate. In cultivation, it looks best in a rockery.

Zauschneria cana. Hummingbird Flower. California Coast

Woolsia pungens. S. Queensland to
S. New South Wales

Zauschneria

(*syn.* EPILOBIUM)

(zoush-**neer**-ee-ə) ☼ W H
California Fuchsia,
Hummingbird Flower
Summer; 2 ft/60 cm; spreading; evergreen

ONAGRACEAE

This popular shrub from California's driest areas is also widely grown in the damp climates of England and Ireland.

Grow *Zauschneria* from seed, cuttings or sections of underground runners, and plant in poor, gravelly, well-drained soil. But as the plant self-sows regularly, none of this may be necessary. Water is not needed except during droughts and, in fact, regular water and rich soil can turn the plant into something of a monster. The evergreen (or evergrey) silvery foliage and spikes of dainty scarlet flowers attract birds—particularly hummingbirds—from miles around. There are four species of *Zauschneria* but none of them is really hardy.

Zenobia

(*syn.* ANDROMEDA)

(zen-**oh**-bee-yə) ☼ ☀ C T
Virginia Heather
*Spring; 4–6 ft/1–2 m; low; open;
deciduous*

ERICACEAE   FRAGRANT

I guess one of my most favourite historical heroines was Zenobia, the almost fabulous Queen of the east who ruled from Palmyra. Poor Zenobia! Through her ambition she lost both her kingdom and her liberty and passed the years in exile with her sons at Tivoli. What a surprise to find her name given to this lovely North American shrub—as yet, the connection quite eludes me.

Zenobia, the shrub, is propagated from offshoots, seed, cuttings and layers, all with relative ease. Like most of the family Ericaceae, it thrives in any well-drained soil, provided lime is absent. It is rather an untidy grower and needs to be thinned out from time to time.

The leaves are alternate, blunt, variable in shape and covered with a whitish bloom; deciduous, but partly evergreen in a mild climate. The

Murray Fagg

glistening white flowers have a hint of green and hang pendent in clusters on the upper or leafless parts of the previous year's growth.

Zenobia pulverulenta. Virginia Heather. Virginia, South Carolina

Zieria veronicea. Sandfly Bush. S.E. Australia, Tasmania

Zieria

(zee-**eər**-ee-ə)   ☼ ☀ Ⓒ Ⓦ
Stinkwood, Sandfly Bush
Spring; 6 ft/2 m; woody; compact; evergreen

RUTACEAE   AROMATIC

All 20 species of *Zieria* are larger, woodier relations of the dainty Boronia and are endemic to southeast Australia and Tasmania. They grow easily from cuttings and romp in shaded areas. The crystalline textured leaves of *Z. veronicea* are highly aromatic. The ½ in/1 cm flowers vary from white to deep pink, with the darker shades being more highly valued. Almost any soil seems to suit, so long as the drainage is above suspicion.

Both *Z. veronicea* and *Z. arborescens* are found naturally in Tasmania, Victoria and South Australia, yet are rarely seen even in specialized nurseries of Australian plants. Height rarely passes 6 ft/2 m, but a regular, light pruning after bloom will help keep them dense and compact.

Ziziphus

(syn. ZIZYPHUS, CONDALIA*)*

(**ziz**-i-fəs)   ☼ ☀ Ⓦ Ⓗ
Indian Jujube
Summer; 13 ft/4 m; treelike; evergreen

RHAMNACEAE

Jujubes are native mostly to warm-temperate areas of the northern hemisphere, from the Balkans eastward to India and China. They bear a most popular fruit, particularly where the soil is sharply alkaline.

The 40 species are about equally divided between shrubs and trees, both deciduous and evergreen. *Ziziphus mauritianus* is commonly evergreen, with the leaf undersides rusty and woolly. The fruit are globose, 1 in/3 cm or less in diameter and a great favourite in Arab countries where they are preserved and made into many sticky confections—presumably the origin of our own jubes and jujubes.

According to legend, *Z. spina-christi* from North Africa and Asia Minor was the bush from which Christ's crown of thorns was woven. It is indeed widely spread and bears grape-sized fruits which are quite edible.

Ziziphus mauritianus. Indian Jujube. Asia

ACKNOWLEDGEMENTS

Though the plants to be included in this book had been in my mind for several years, many of them proved surprisingly elusive when I came to track them down with camera in hand. These particularly included North American shrubs which were, at one time at least, grown widely in Australia (my home base) – perhaps making the voyage out with the families of miners in the days of the great gold rushes. I am indebted to many friends both old and new who helped locate my chosen subjects, or even supplied photographs of them. These include (from the United States) Pamela Harper, R. A. Jaynes, Dr. Mildred Matthias of UCLA; (from the United Kingdom) Gillian Beckett and Pamla Toler; (from South Africa) Una van der Spuy; (from Australia) Murray Fagg, Pamela Jane Harrison, Jean Johnson, the late E. E. Lord, Michael Morcombe, the late H. A. Morrison, Reg Morrison, Rosemary Purdie, Dr. Tony Rodd, Dr. James H. Willis. Their contributions will add immeasurably to the international usage of this book.

Unpaid assistants who jotted down the names and details to aid in identification at a later date include:

in Australia
Sir Alexander Beattie, Geoffrey Burnie, Trish and Steven Clifton, Brian Donges, Eddy Graham, Peter Landers.

in France
Mme. R. P. Jeanneret, Arnaud de Vinzelles.

in Hawaii
the late Dr. Horace Clay, Bill, Owen and Ruth Farrior, Milton I, Loy Marks, Dr. William Stewart.

in Hong Kong
Mrs. Gloria Barreto, Albert Chin.

in Japan
Hirofumi Chonan, Peter Okumoto.

in Tahiti
Jacques Rentier, Teama Teriipaia.

in the United Kingdom
Group Captain and Mrs. Bryan Burley, Miss Lucy Burley, Kim Clifton, David Garde.

in the U.S.A.
Margaret Davis OBE, Dave and Barbara Goux, Betty Klein, Jim Lichtman, Al and Ginny Littau, Professor Milton Meyer, John Winston, David Wittry.

The greater number of plants were photographed at the following gardens:

Adelaide Botanic Gardens, S.A.
Ala Moana Park, Honolulu
Albany, W.A.
Alstonville, N.S.W.
Arnold Arboretum, Boston, Mass.
Atherton Tableland, Queensland
Australian National Botanic Garden, Canberra, A.C.T.
Bagatelle, Paris
Balboa Park, San Diego, Calif.
Bangkok Hilton Hotel
Bang Pa-in, Thailand
Bantry House, Cork, Eire
Beauchamp Park, Chatswood, N.S.W.
Bellingen, N.S.W
Belvedere Palace, Vienna
Berlin-Dahlem Botanischer Garten
Berlin '85 Stadtlich Gartenschau
Beth Chatto Garden, Essex, U.K.
Bilbery House, Midleton, Cork, Eire

Bodnant, North Wales
Brooklyn Botanic Garden, New York
Butchart Gardens, Vancouver Island, British Columbia
Cambridge Botanic Garden, U.K.
Chelsea Flower Show (several years)
Chelsea Physic Garden, London
Cranebrook Native Nursery, N.S.W.
The Dandenongs, Victoria
Descanso Gardens, Sacramento, Calif.
Disneyland, Anaheim, Calif.
Disneyland Hotel, Anaheim, Calif.
Echo Point, Katoomba, N.S.W.
Edinburgh Botanic Garden, U.K.
E. G. Waterhouse Memorial Camellia Garden, Yowie Bay, N.S.W.
Eklinge, Udaipur, Rajasthan
Eryldene, Gordon, N.S.W.
Everglades National Trust Garden, Leura, N.S.W.
Ewanrigg, Leura, N.S.W.
Exbury House Estate, Sussex, U.K.
Flecker Botanic Garden, Cairns, Q.
Foster Garden, Honolulu, Hawaii
Giverny, Ile de France
Glasgow International Garden Festival, 1988
Great Dixter, Sussex, U.K.
Haddon Hall, Derbyshire, U.K.
Hibiscus Park, Warriewood, N.S.W.
Hidcote, Gloucestershire, U.K.
Hilton Hotel, Abu Dhabi, U.A.E.
Hong Kong Botanic Garden
Huntington Gardens, San Marino, Calif.
Hyatt Hotel, Anaheim, Calif.
Hyatt Regency Hotel, New Delhi
Ilnacullin, Garinish, Cork, Eire
Irish National Botanic Garden, Glasnevin
Jardin Botanique de la Ville, Lausanne, Switzerland
Jardin Botanique de Tahiti
Jardin Botanique, Geneva, Switzerland
Jardin des Plantes, Paris
Jardim Lou Lim Ioc, Macau
Kadoorie Botanic Garden, Tai Po, Hong Kong
Kapiolani Park, Honolulu, Hawaii
Kew Palace, Richmond, Surrey, U.K.
King's Park, Perth, W.A.
Kingsway Cottage, St. Osyth, Essex
Kumamoto Province, Kyushu, Japan
Kyoto Gardens, Kyoto, Japan
La Brea Park, Los Angeles, Calif.
Lafayette, Calif.
Lal Bagh, Bangalore, India
La Source, Orleans, France
L'Hay-les-Roses, Paris
Limberlost Nursery, Cairns, Q.
Lindfield Park, Mt. Wilson, N.S.W.
Living Desert, Palm Springs, Calif.
Los Angeles State and County Arboretum, Arcadia, Calif.
Louvre, Paris
Lyon Arboretum, Honolulu, Hawaii
Malmaison, Paris
Marriot Hotel, Palm Springs, Calif.
Maurya Sheraton Hotel, New Delhi
Meiji Shrine Garden, Tokyo
Menlo Park, Calif.
Mildred Matthias Garden, UCLA, Calif.
Milton Park, Bowral, N.S.W.
Mount Coot-tha Botanic Garden, Brisbane, Q.
Mount Usher, Wicklow, Eire
Muckross House, Killarney, Eire
Mughal Sheraton Hotel, Agra
Munich Botanischer Sammlung
Nagoya Botanic Garden, Japan

National Botanic Garden, Canberra, A.C.T.
Neels Nursery, Rancho Mirage, Calif.
Nishat Bagh, Kashmir
Nooroo, Mt. Wilson, N.S.W.
Nymans, Sussex, U.K.
Oasis, Brisbane, Q.
Old Botanic Gardens, Brisbane, Q.
Orange Botanic Gardens, N.S.W.
Orto Botanico, Padua, Italy
Pacific Coast Botanic Garden, Calif.
Pacific Tropical Botanic Garden, Kauai, Hawaii
Parc Florale, Paris
Pine Crest, Leura, N.S.W.
Port Douglas, Q.
Powerscourt, Wicklow, Eire
Pruhonice, Czechoslovakia
Pua Laki, Kauai, Hawaii
Quail Botanic Garden, Calif.
Queen Mary's Rose Garden, London
Rancho Santa Ana, Palm Springs, Calif.
Rarotonga, Cook Islands
R.H.S. Garden, Wisley, Surrey, U.K.
Ritz Carlton Hotel, Laguna, Calif.
Rizal Park, Manila, Philippines
Rockhampton Botanic Gardens, Q.
Rogers Nursery, Newport, Calif.
Royal Hawaiian Hotel, Honolulu
Royal Botanic Garden, Hobart, Tasmania
Royal Botanic Garden, Kew, London
Royal Botanic Garden, Melbourne, Vic.
Royal Botanic Garden, Sydney, N.S.W.
Royal Botanic Garden Annexe, Mt. Tomah, N.S.W.
Sandy Bay, Hobart, Tasmania
Savile Garden, Windsor, U.K.
Santa Barbara Botanic Garden, Calif.
Schönbrunn Palace, Vienna
Seiwa-en, Singapore
Shalimar Bagh, Kashmir
Shinjuku Go-en, Tokyo
Singapore Botanic Garden
Sissinghurst Castle Garden, Kent, U.K.
Society for Growing Australian Plants Shows, Castle Hill, N.S.W.
St. Bernards Hotel, Mt. Tamborine, Q.
Stirling Ranges, W.A.
Stony Range Reserve, Dee Why, N.S.W.
St. Osyth Priory, Essex, U.K.
Strybing Arboretum, San Francisco
Suan Pakkad Palace, Bangkok, Thailand
Sunset Gardens, Menlo Park, Calif.
Sydney Harbour National Park, N.S.W.
Sydney Wildflower Nursery, Terrey Hills
Syon Park, London
Timoleague House, Cork, Eire
Toowoomba, Q.
Townsville Botanic Gardens, Q.
UCLA Japanese Garden, Bel Air, Calif.
University of British Columbia, Vancouver, B.C.
University of Hawaii, Honolulu
University of the Philippines, Los Banos, Luzon
Vatican Gardens, Vatican City, Rome
Villa d'Este, Tivoli, Italy
Villa Fiorentina, St Jean, Cap Ferrat, France
Villa Marlia, Lucca, Italy
Villa Taranto, Pallanza, Lago Maggiore, Italy
Virginia Robinson Garden, Bel Air, Calif.
Wahiawa Botanic Garden, Oahu, Hawaii
Waimea Falls Park, Oahu, Hawaii
Wakehurst Place, Sussex, U.K.
Wallington National Trust Garden, U.K.
Westaway Garden, The Esplanade, Cairns, Q.
West Head, Pittwater, N.S.W.
Yu Hwa Yuan, Singapore

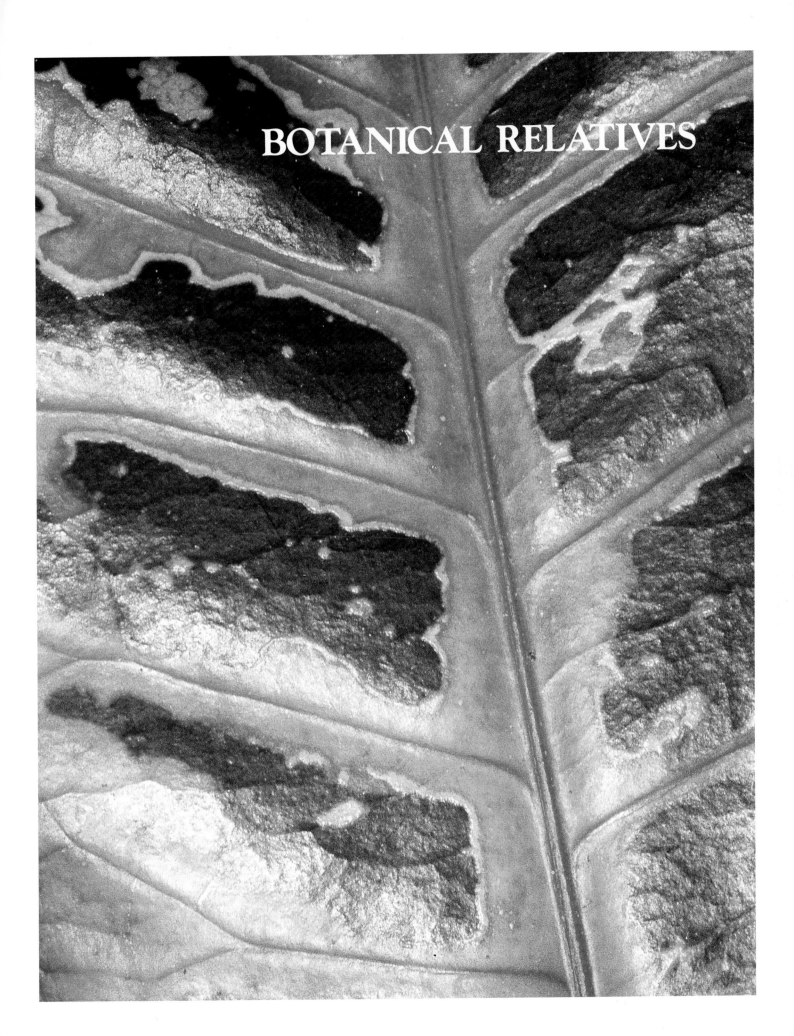

BOTANICAL RELATIVES

Many popular flowering shrubs belong to botanical families which include a number of close relatives that often do well in the same garden or climatic conditions. Immediately following is a list of the principal 57 families, together with the names of all members of those families included in the book (where two or more genera are included). Also, we show a small colour illustration of a popular, typical member of each family. An additional 70 or so monogeneric families are not illustrated or listed.

ACANTHACEAE

The Acanthus family, mostly tropical in origin, are noted for their spikes of two-lipped flowers, often in colourful bracts. Leaves are opposite.

Aphelandra	*Pseuderanthemum*
Asystasia	*Ruspolia*
Barleria	*Ruttya*
Crossandra	*Sanchezia*
Drejerella	*Strobilanthes*
Duvernoia	*Thunbergia*
Eranthemum	
Graptophyllum	
Justicia	
Mackaya	
Megaskepasma	
Odontonema	
Pachystachys	

Aphelandra

ADOXACEAE

Formerly classified with the honeysuckles (Caprifoliaceae), now split as a family on its own.

Sambucus
Viburnum

Sambucus

APOCYNACEAE

The Dogbane family; mostly tropical shrubs with milky sap. Leaves opposite, flowers tubular with 5 petals (lobes), usually highly fragrant.

Acokanthera	*Carissa*
Adenium	*Kopsia*
Allamanda	*Nerium*
Alstonia	*Pachypodium*
Alyxia	*Rauvolfia*
Strophanthus	*Tabernaemontana*
Thevetia	*Vinca*

Nerium

ARALIACEAE

The Ginseng family; perennial herbs or shrubs from temperate or tropical regions. Leaves palmately divided, small flowers massed in compound umbels.

Fatshedera
Fatsia
Polyscias
Schefflera
Tetrapanax
Trevesia

Fatsia

ASCLEPIADACEAE

The Milkweed family; herbs, shrubs or vines, mostly from the sub-tropics. Flowers single or in umbels, 5 petals, 5 stamens.

Calotropis
Hoya
Sarcostemma

Hoya

ASPARAGACEAE

Includes many species formerly classified under the Liliaceae.

Cordyline
Ruscus

Cordyline

ASTERACEAE

The Daisy family; over 20,000 species. Composite, densely clustered heads of tiny, simple flowers surrounded by ray florets or petals to form a typical daisy shape.

Artemisia	*Montanoa*
Asteriscus	*Olearia*
Baccharis	*Osteospermum*
Brachyglottis	*Santolina*
Calocephalus	*Senecio*
Chrysanthemoides	*Tarconanthus*
Chrysocoma	*Tithonia*
Encelia	
Eriocephalus	
Eupatorium	
Euryops	
Felicia	
Gamolepis	

Chrysanthemoides

BERBERIDACEAE

The Barberry family; 10 or more genera from the N. temperate zone. Leaves simple or compound, flowers solitary or in racemes, bisexual, sepals and petals similar. Stamens as many as petals to twice as many. Fruit a berry.

Berberis
Mahonia
Nandina

Berberis

BIGNONIACEAE

The Bignonia family; mostly showy sub-tropical plants, often climbing. Flowers are 2-lipped with a 5-toothed calyx and 4 stamens.

Chilopsis
Delostoma
Tabebuia
Tecoma
Tecomaria

Chilopsis

BORAGINACEAE

The Borage family; mostly temperate growing herbs but some shrubs. Flowers arranged in a cyme. These have a 5-lobed corolla, 5-toothed calyx and 5 stamens. Most flowers blue or purple.

Cordia	*Heliotropium*
Echium	*Lithodora*
Halgania	*Moltkia*

Echium

CACTACEAE
The Cactus family; mostly spiny succulents, often branched and with ribbed stems. Bisexual flowers, often stalkless and brilliantly coloured.
Hatiora
Pereskia

Pereskia

CAESALPINIACEAE
A division of the family once named Leguminosae or Beans and including most species with irregularly shaped flowers (not pea-shaped) and with prominent clusters of 10 or fewer stamens.
Bauhinia
Cadia
Caesalpinia
Cassia
Cercis
Lysiphyllum
Parkinsonia
Patalostylis
Schotia

Bauhinia

CALYCANTHACEAE
The Calycanthus family; 2 genera, bark aromatic, leaves opposite, entire. Flowers solitary, bisexual. Sepals and petals many, stamens 5 to many on flower tube.
Calycanthus   Chimonanthus

Calycanthus

CAPRIFOLIACEAE
The Honeysuckle family; shrubs mostly from the N. temperate zone. Flowers tubular, often fragrant, borne in flat-topped cymes or clusters, bisexual.
Abelia
Diervilla
Dipelta
Kolkwitzia
Lonicera
Symphoricarpos
Weigela

Abelia

CHENOPODIACEAE
The Goosefoot family; shrubs of wide distribution. Leaves alternate and simple. Flowers small and inconspicuous, often bracted having no perianth or a 4-5 lobed calyx, stamens 1-5. Includes several vegetables.
Atriplex
Rhagodia

Atriplex

CISTACEAE
The Rock Rose family; about 8 genera mostly native to Mediterranean regions. Leaves mostly opposite, simple, hairy. Flowers solitary or in cymes or racemes, regular. Sepals 3-5, petals 5 soon deciduous.
Cistus
Halimium
Helianthemum

Helianthemum

DILLENIACEAE
The Dillenia family; 11 genera, mostly trees or shrubs mostly from tropical America or Australia. Leaves alternate, flowers yellow or white, sepals and petals 5, stamens many. Fruit a follicle or berry-like.
Dillenia
Hibbertia

Hibbertia

ELAEAGNACEAE
The Oleaster family; 3 genera of shrubs or trees covered with silvery scales. Leaves alternate, opposite or whorled, simple. Flowers solitary or in clusters, bisexual. Fruit drupaceous, the achene enclosed by the fleshy flower tube.
Elaeagnus
Hippophäe

Elaeagnus

ERICACEAE
The Heath family; possibly the most popular family of flowering shrubs from the northern hemisphere. Leaves simple, alternate. Flowers bisexual, borne singly or in terminal inflorescences, 5-7 petalled, often urn-shaped. Now includes about 30 genera of the the Southern Heath family (formerly classified as Epacridaceae); native to Australia and New Zealand.

Agapetes	Leiophyllum
Andersonia	Leucothoë
Andromeda	Lyonia
Arbutus	Manihot
Astroloma	Menziesia
Azalea	Pentachondra
Azaleodendron	Pernettya
Calluna	Phyllodoce
Cassiope	Pieris
Cavendishia	Rhododendron
Chamaedaphne	Richea
Comarostaphylis	Sprengelia
Cyathodes	Styphelia
Daboecia	Trochocarpa
Dracophyllum	Vaccinium
Enkianthus	Woolsia
Epacris	Zenobia
Epigaea	
Erica	
Eupatorium	
Euryops	
Gaultheria	
Gaylussacia	
Kalmia	
X Ledendron	
Ledum	

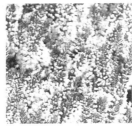

Erica

EUPHORBIACEAE
The Spurge family; a very large group of variable shrubs with poisonous white sap, often Cactus-like or with small flowers subtended by colourful bracts.
Acalypha   Codiaeum

Euphorbia
Jatropha
Macaranga
Omalanthus
Pedilanthus
Ricinocarpus
Ricinus
Synadenium

Pedilanthus

FABACEAE

The Pea or Pulse family; a vast group of plants featuring butterfly-shaped blooms with a large petal or standard and the two lower petals united to form a keel. A pod follows in which the seeds are attached alternately to either side. Pinnate leaves.

Acacia	*Jacksonia*
Amicia	*Lespedeza*
Amorpha	*Lupinus*
Anthyllis	*Mimosa*
Aotus	*Mirbelia*
Brachysema	*Ononis*
Burtonia	*Piptanthus*
Calliandra	*Podalyria*
Calpurnia	*Prosopis*
Caragana	*Pultenea*
Chorizema	*Retama*
Clianthus	*Robinia*
Colutea	*Sophora*
Coronilla	*Spartium*
Crotalaria	*Sutherlandia*
Cytisus	*Templetonia*
Dalea	*Ulex*
Daubentonia	*Wistaria*
Daviesia	
Dillwynia	
Erythrina	
Eutaxia	
Genista	
Gompholobium	
Goodia	
Hamamelis	
Hovea	
Indigofera	

Eutaxia

GOODENIACEAE

The Goodenia family; mostly native to Australia and mostly shrubs. Flowers irregular, bisexual. Calyx and corolla 5-lobed, stamens many. Closely allied to the Lobelias.

Goodenia	*Scaevola*
Lechenaultia	

Lechenaultia

HAMAMELIDACEAE

The Witch-Hazel family; mostly deciduous Asiatic shrubs. Bisexual blooms with 4-5 strap-like sepals, petals 0-5. Fruit a woody, 2-beaked capsule.

Corylopsis
Disanthus
Fothergilla
Hamamelis
Loropetalum

Loropetalum

HYDRANGEACEAE

A family which is widespread in the Northern Hemisphere and includes 17 genera.

Dichroa
Hydrangea
Jamesia

Hydrangea

LAMIACEAE

The Mint family; usually aromatic shrubs with square sectioned stems, 4-ranked leaves. Flowers in cymes in the axils of opposite leaves 4-6 lobed, 2-lipped.

Clerodendrum	*Salvia*
Colquhounia	*Teucrium*
Conradina	*Thymus*
Faradaya	*Trichostema*
Holmskioldia	*Vitex*
Hyptis	*Westringia*
Hyssopus	
Iboza	
Lachnostachys	
Lavandula	
Leonotis	
Lepechinia	
Phlomis	
Pittyrodia	
Prostanthera	
Rosmarinus	

Clerodendrum

LYTHRACEAE

The Loosestrife family. About 22 genera, widely distributed. Leaves opposite or whorled, entire. Flowers bisexual, calyx lobes 4-6 alternating with 3-5 triangular appendages. Petals 3-16i. Stamens few to many.

Cuphea	*Punica*
Lagerstroemia	*Woodfordia*
Lawsonia	

Cuphea

MALVACEAE

The Mallow family; perennial and shrubby, with mostly palmate leaves. Flowers with regular 5-lobed calyx. 5 petals, stamens united into a single column.

Abutilon	*Malacothamnus*
Alyogyne	*Malvaviscus*
Commersonia	*Phymosia*
Corynabutilon	*Rulingia*
Dombeya	*Sida*
Entelea	*Sparmannia*
Fremontodendron	*Thomasia*
Goethea	*Triplochlamys*
Gossypium	*Urena*
Grewia	
Guichenotia	
Hibiscus	
Howittia	
Keraundrenia	
Lasiopetalum	
Lavatera	

Lavatera

MELASTOMATACEAE

The Melastoma family; mostly tropical shrubs. Leaves, opposite and hairy. Flowers bisexual, regular, usually with 5 petals, 5 stamens.

Centradenia
Distictis
Medinilla
Melastoma
Osbeckia
Tibouchina

Osbeckia

MYRTACEAE

The Myrtle family; mostly from the tropics and Australia. The showy flowers mostly consist of massed stamens as in Callistemon, the petals being absent.

Actinodium
Angophora
Astartea
Austromyrtus
Backhousia
Baeckea
Balaustion
Beaufortia
Callistemon
Calothamnus

Eugenia

Calytrix
Chamelaucium
Darwinia
Eremaea
Eucalyptus
Eugenia
Feijoa
Homoranthus
Hypocalymma
Kunzea
Leptospermum
Lhotzkya
Melaleuca
Metrosideros

Micromyrtus
Myrtus
Phymatocarpus
Pileanthus
Psidium
Regelia
Rhodomyrtus
Syzgium
Thryptomene
Tristania
Ugni
Verticordia

OLEACEAE

The Olive family; temperate trees or shrubs with simple, opposite leaves. Flowers regular, bisexual or unisexual. Calyx and corolla commonly 4-lobed.

Abeliophyllum
Forsythia
Jasminum
Ligustrum
Osmanthus
Syringa

Osmanthus

ONAGRACEAE

The Evening Primrose family; annuals, perennials and shrubs of various habit. Flowers mostly with 4 sepals, 4 petals, 8 stamens, very showy. Most are from the Americas.

Fuchsia
Hauya
Zauschneria

Fuchsia

PHYLLANTHACEAE

Contains about 2000 species of 50-60 genera, including some formerly classified in the Euphorbiaceae.

Breynia
Phyllanthus

Breynia nivosa

PITTOSPORACEAE

The Pitch-seed family; evergreen trees and shrubs with shining foliage. 5-petalled fragrant flowers in panicles. Seeds very sticky.

Billardiera
Bursaria
Pittosporum
Sollya

Billardiera

PLANTAGINACEAE

Recent taxonomic studies have increased the size of the Plantain family to about 1700 species in 90 genera.

Galvezia
Globularia
Hebe

Galvezia

POLEMONIACEAE

The Phlox family; Mostly annual or perennial, but a few shrubs. Bisexual sun-loving flowers in axillary or terminal cymose clusters.

Cantua
Leptodactylon

Cantua

POLYGALACEAE

The Milkwort family; about 10 genera of mostly shrubs, often climbing. Leaves alternate, flowers solitary or panicled; Irregular. Sepals 4-7, petals 3-8, stamens 5-8.

Nylandtia
Polygala

Nylandtia

PROTEACEAE

The Protea family, found exclusively in the three southern continents. Trees and shrubs mostly from South Africa and Australia. Leaves alternate, often lobed. Flowers in clusters or showy, branching heads.

Adenanthos
Banksia
Bellendena
Conospermum
Dryandra
Embothrium
Franklandia
Grevillea
Hakea
Isopogon
Lambertia
Leucadendron
Leucospermum
Lomatia
Orothamnus
Persoonia
Petrophile

Protea
Serruria
Stirlingia
Synaphea
Telopea
Xylomelum

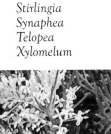

Grevillea

RHAMNACEAE

The Buckthorn family; about 55 genera. Leaves mostly alternate and simple. Flowers usually in axillary corymbs or cymes, mostly blue, but sometimes white, green or pink. Small, regular or bisexual. Sepals and petals 5, stamens 5. Fruit sometimes winged.

Ceanothus
Collettia
Cryptandra
Discaria
Phylica
Rhamnus
Zizyphus

Ceanothus

ROSACEAE

The Rose family; mostly shrubs with alternate leaves, often compound flowers, regular with 4 or 5 or more petals and sepals. Fruit is a berry, pome or drupe.

Adenostoma
Amelanchier
Aronia
Chaenomeles
Cotoneaster
Exochorda
Heteromeles
Holodiscus
Kerria
Malus
Neillia
Neviusia
Osteomeles
Photinia
Physocarpus
Potentilla
Prunus

Pyracantha
Raphiolepis
Rhodotypus
Rosa
Rubus
Spiraea
Stephanandra
Stranvaesia

Amelanchier

RUBIACEAE

The madder family; chiefly subtropical shrubs, trees and vines. Leaves simple, opposite. Flowers in cymes. Corolla usually 4-5 lobed, more rarely 6-9 lobed.

Adina	Psychotria
Bouvardia	Rondeletia
Burchellia	Rothmannia
Cephalanthus	Serissa
Coffea	Warscewicza
Coprosma	
Carphalea	
Gardenia	
Hamelia	
Ixora	
Luculia	
Mussaeanda	
Pavetta	
Pentas	
Posoqueria	

Ixora

RUTACEAE

The Rue family; mostly evergreen shrubs with alternate glossy leaves. Flowers mostly unisexual with 3-5 each of sepals and petals. Fruit a lealthery-skinned berry, as in citrus.

Adenandra	Orixa
Agathosma	Phebalium
Asterolasia	Philotheca
Boronia	Ptelea
Choisya	Ruta
X Citrofortunella	Skimmia
Citrus	Zieria
Coleonema	
Correa	
Crowea	
Eremocitrus	
Eriostemon	
Fortunella	
Geleznowia	
Microcitrus	
Murraya	
Nematolepis	

Boronia

SALICACEAE

Contains more than 50 genera, including the Willows.

Azara
Salix

Azara

SAXIFRAGACEAE

The Saxifrage family; herbs or shrubs with alternate leaves. Blooming in many flowered clusters or panicles usually with 4-5 petals.

Carpenteria	Deutzia
Escallonial	Itea

Deutzia

SCROPHULARIACEAE

The Figwort family; mostly cool-climate plant with soft, puffy flowers that are typically irregular, often two-lipped.

Alonsoa	Selago
Buddleia	Sutera
Calceolaria	
Galvezia	
Hemichaena	
Jovellana	
Leucophyllum	
Myoporum	
Nicodemia	
Parahebe	
Phygelius	
Russela	

Calceolaria

SOLANACEAE

The Nightshade family; herbs or shrubs, trees or vines, mostly from South America. Stems often prickly, leaves usually alternate. Flowers bisexual with 5-lobed calyx and 5-lobed corolla. Many species are poisonous.

Anthocercis	Vestia
Brugmansia	
Brunfelsia	
Cestrum	
Cyphanthera	
Duboisya	
Fabiana	
Iochroma	
Lycium	
Solanum	
Streptosolen	

Cestrum

STYRACACEAE

The Styrax family consists of 6 genera of shrubs and trees. Leaves alternate, simple. Flowers regular bisexual, calyx 4-5 lobed, petals 4-8 united at base. Stamens 14-16.

Pterostyrax
Sinojackia
Styrax

Styrax

THEACEAE

The Tea family. Large shrubs and trees with simple, leathery leaves. Axillary, bisexual flowers petalled in multiples of 5. Many stamens. The Camellia is typical.

Camellia
Cleyera
Franklinia
Gordonia
Stewartia
Ternstroemia

Camellia

THYMELAEACEAE

The Daphne family; mostly shrubs with simple, alternate entire leaves and a strong fragrance. The petalless flowers have a 4-5 lobed calyx, 4-8 stamens. Fruit sometimes appears in the form of a berry.

Däis
Daphne
Dirca
Edgworthia
Gnidia
Pimelea

Daphne

TREMANDRACEAE

The Tremandra family; about 3 genera of heathlike shrubs native to Australia and Tasmania. Leaves small, simple. Flowers bisexual. Sepals and petals 4 or 5 of each, stamens 8-10. Fruit a seed.

Platytheca
Tetratheca

Platytheca

VERBENACEAE

The Verbena family; mostly tropical herbs, shrubs and vines with opposite leaves. Flowers often small and irregular, in showy clusters.

Aloysia
Callicarpa
Caryopteris
Congea
Duranta
Gmelina
Lantana
Petraea

Callicarpa

GLOSSARY

Botanists have adopted many specialized words and terms to describe precisely the different parts of a plant, and their appearance, colour, shape and texture.

It is difficult to write any garden book without using at least a few of these words. As some are not much used in everyday English, and others have a specialized botanical meaning, we include this glossary for the plant lover who is not taxonomically minded.

Most unfamiliar words used in this book (or for that matter, in other garden books) will be found here, together with their meanings.

Achene a small, dry, one-seeded fruit with an undivided outer wall.

Acid said of soil that is deficient in lime — hence **Acidity**.

Acuminate (of a leaf), tapering with slightly concave sides to a point.

Acute (of a leaf), tapering with straight sides to a point.

Adventitious occurring away from the usual place — e.g., aerial roots, a flower centred in a leaf.

Aerial root a root appearing above soil level, often from a branch. Used for both support and feeding.

Alate (of a stem or seed), with wing-like projections.

Alkaline said of soil that is rich in lime — hence, **Alkalinity**.

Alpine said of elevated habitats where snow covers the ground for much of the year.

Alternate (of leaves), arranged singly on different sides of the stem, and at different levels.

Angiosperm a plant that has its seeds enclosed in an ovary — as any flowering plant.

Anther the pollen-bearing top of a stamen.

Apex (of a leaf or stem), the tip — hence, **Apical, Apiculate**.

Appendage an attached secondary part, as a projecting or hanging bract.

Areole a raised or sunken spot on the stem in Cacti — site of one or more spines or flowers.

Articulate (of a stem), jointed or with nodes where it can easily be separated.

Asymmetrical not evenly balanced.

Attenuate (of a stem or leaf), very gradually long-tapering.

Axil the upper angle that a leaf-stem makes with the stem from which it appears. Site of many shoots and flower buds — hence, **Axillary**.

Bark the tissues of a woody plant outside the cambium layer.

Basal at the bottom; e.g., a basal shoot appears near the trunk base.

Berry a pulpy, generally small fruit containing one or more seeds, but no true stones.

Bicolor a flower or leaf with two distinct colours borne at the same time.

Biennial a plant which completes its life cycle in a two-year period — growing the first year, flowering the second.

Bigeneric said of a hybrid between two genera of plants, as opposed to more common hybrids between species or varieties.

Bipinnate (of a leaf), doubly pinnate, the primary leaflets being again divided into secondary leaflets, as in a *Jacaranda*.

Black spot a fungus disease, principally affecting roses, in which the leaves first become spotted black, later dropping altogether.

Bisexual having organs of both sexes functioning in the same flower.

Bloom (a) a flower; (b) a fine powdery coating on some plants or leaves.

Boss a roundish protuberance on some part of a plant — generally describing a compact mass of central stamens projecting above the plane of the petals.

Bract a modified leaf at the base of a flower, often the most colourful part, as in a Poinsettia or *Mussaenda*.

Break (in a flower), a spontaneous change in colour or pattern (e.g., streaking), as the result of a beneficial virus.

Budding grafting by inserting a stem-bud of one plant into the cambium layer of another.

Budworm an imprecise description of the many small caterpillars which invade and destroy flower buds.

Cactus a generally spine-bearing plant, found almost exclusively in the Americas. Often with magnificent blooms.

Calcareous chalky, containing or like calcium carbonate.

Calcifuge a lime-hating plant.

Calyx the outer covering of a flower bud, usually consisting of united sepals. Often decorative. Plural, **Calyces**.

Cambium layer a layer of growing cells beneath the bark or skin of a stem. These develop both inside and out, causing a stem or root to increase in size.

Campanulate (of a flower), shaped like a bell.

Cane (a) the developed, jointed stem of a large grassy plant, e.g., bamboo; (b) the long, arching growth of many plant genera, e.g. raspberries, roses, *Abelias*.

Capsule a dry, divisible fruit composed of two or more sections.

Carpel one of the units comprising a pistil or ovary.

Catkin a scaly-bracted, usually hanging inflorescence.

Chlorophyll the green colouring substance of leaves and plants, necessary for the production of carbohydrates by photosynthesis.

Chlorosis an abnormal yellowing of a plant, most commonly due to a lack of iron in the soil.

Cladode a flattened stem having the form and function of a leaf.

Clone any plant propagated by vegetative means, such as division, budding, cuttings, layers. These methods are widely used for plants that do not come true from seed.

Column the structure formed by the union of style and stamens, as in the Orchid family.

Companioning or **Companion planting** a horticultural theory (by no means universally accepted) which proposes that certain plant genera grow better in proximity to certain others, each genus conferring some benefit on the other. For instance, garlic is supposed to protect roses from their natural pests.

Compost a mixture of broken-down organic elements that will stimulate a plant's growth; sometimes, loosely, a potting mix.

Composite like a daisy. That is, a dense grouping of tiny single flowers surrounded by a single row of petals.

Compound (of leaves), a leaf composed of two or more leaflets.

Cone a dense construction of seed-bearing scales on a central axis, often woody and elongated.

Cordate (of a leaf), heart-shaped.

Corolla the inner circle or second whorl of petals in a flower.

Corona (in a flower), a crown or circle of appendages — e.g., the outer circle of stamens as in *Hymenocallis*; an outgrowth of the perianth as in *Narcissus*.

Corymb a more or less flat-topped inflorescence, the outer flowers opening first.

Cotyledon the first leaf to emerge from a germinated seed.

Creeper a trailing plant that roots at intervals.

Crenate (of a leaf), with shallow, rounded teeth, or scalloped edges.

Crown (a) the corona; (b) the base of a plant where stem and root meet; (c) part of a rhizome with a bud, suitable for propagation.

Cultivar a plant strain, apparently produced only in cultivation, and capable of propagation.

Cutting an amputated section of a plant or tree which will develop new roots and become self-sufficient. These may be taken from stems, branches, sometimes roots or leaves.

Cyme a type of broad, flat-topped inflorescence in which the centre flowers open first.

Damping off disease causing abrupt death of apparently healthy seedlings induced by fungi in the soil.

Deadhead to remove faded flower heads and prevent their seeding. This forces the plant to make new growth, more blooms.

Deciduous a plant or flower that sheds all its leaves or petals at a particular stage of its growth — generally in autumn.

Defoliate to strip or deprive a plant of its foliage or leaves.

Dehiscence the method of opening of a seed capsule, generally splitting along an existing seam; hence, **Dehiscent**.

Dentate (of a leaf), toothed.

Dieback a variety of fungal diseases which kill part or all of a plant by causing the tissues to die back from a tip or cut branch.

Digitate (of a leaf), resembling a hand; compound with all divisions arising from a single point.

Dioecious with unisexual flowers, male and female blossoms borne on separate plants.

Disbudding removing side flowerbuds to concentrate growth in a single flower and enlarge it.

Disc in the family Asteraceae, the central area of the flower head, being composed mostly of florets.

Dissected (of a leaf), deeply cut into numerous segments.

Divide to separate a clump of perennial plants into smaller clumps; hence, **Division**.

Divided (of a leaf), separated nearly to the base or the midrib.

Dolomite the mineral Calcium magnesium carbonate, a form of lime much used to improve soil without greatly affecting its acidity.

Dormancy the time when a plant makes minimum growth, usually but not invariably in winter. Often when a plant is bare of foliage; hence, **Dormant**.

Drift a loose term for an informal planting of the bulbs.

Drupe a fruit containing one (rarely two) woody-skinned seeds, e.g., a peach.

Ecology science of interaction of organisms and their environment.

Elliptical like a flattened circle with its widest part at the centre.

Endemic native to a particular, restricted area.

Entire (of a leaf), with a continuous, unbroken margin.

Epiphyte a plant growing on another tree or shrub, using roots for support only and feeding from the chemicals in water and decaying plant or insect tissue, not from its host.

Espalier a shrub, tree or vine trained formally in two dimensions only — generally against a wall.

Evergreen having foliage that remains green and growing throughout the whole year.

Exotic in botany, a plant which is foreign to the country in which it grows, as opposed to native.

F1, F2 hybrid respectively, the first and second generation offspring from a given parent plant.

Fall one of the outer petals of *Iris* and related plants, often drooping.

Family a group of related botanical genera.

Fasciation abnormal growth in which normally cylindrical stems or roots become flattened.

Fastigiate with branches or stems erect and more or less parallel.

Fertilizer any material used to enrich the soil and encourage plant growth — by understanding, generally a concentration of chemicals.

Fibrous-rooted with roots of the same order with no single root dominant.

Filament a thread-like organ, especially a stamen supporting an anther.

Flat a shallow box of wood or plastic, used for raising seedlings; in common usage, a commercially-raised box full of such seedlings.

Floret a very small flower, particularly one component of a composite cluster.

Flower bluntly, the specialized apparatus developed by a plant to enclose the sexual organs, and to attract insects and other pollinators needed for fertilization.

Foliage collective term for leafy units making up crown of plant.

Friable (of soil), easily crumbled or reduced to a fine texture.

Frost tender describes a fleshy plant which may be destroyed when the unprotected sap freezes.

Fruit the developed ovary of a seed plant, together with its contents, as a tomato, nut or pod — but not necessarily edible.

Fungicide a chemical preparation for the destruction of any type of fungus.

Fungus a parasitic organism with no chlorophyll, and usually without leaves.

Gall any abnormal vegetable growth or excrescence on plants — a plant's natural reaction to injury caused by various insects, viruses, etc.

Generic name a plant's first scientific name, indicating the genus to which it belongs.

Genus a clan or group of closely related species. Plural, **Genera**.

Germinate to begin to grow from a seed or spore. Sometimes, to sprout or put forth shoots.

Gesneriad a member of the botanical family Gesneriaceae which includes African Violets and Gloxinias.

Glabrous smooth, without hairs of any kind.

Gland an organ or appendage which produces various functional secretions.

Glaucous (of foliage), covered with a waxy bloom which is easily rubbed off or marked.

Globose globe-shaped or nearly so.

Glochid a minute barbed spine, often occurring in tufts on Cacti.

Grafting when a bud or shoot is severed from its parent plant and joined to a rooted section of another. Used for rapid multiplication of woody plants.

Greenhouse a structure largely of glass, built for the protection and cultivation of delicate plants.

Gymnosperm a plant bearing its seeds naked, not enclosed in an ovary.

Habit in plants, the manner of growth, or tendency constantly to grow in a particular way.

Half-hardy a plant which will resist a moderate degree of frost in a sheltered position.

Halophyte a plant tolerant of salt in the soil or atmosphere.

Hardwood cutting a cutting taken for propagation from a stem which is at least a year old.

Hardy tough or sturdy, but by botanical definition, fully frost-resistant.

Heeled cutting a cutting of new wood, still attached to portion of the hardened, previous year's growth.

Herb (a) any non-woody plant; (b) a plant grown for flavouring, perfumery, etc.

Herbaceous perennial a non-woody plant which dies back to the roots in winter, sending up new growth in spring.

Herbicide a chemical which will destroy growing plants or weeds.

Humus the rich debris resulting from the rotting of vegetable and other organic matter.

Hybrid the result of cross-fertilization of different kinds of parent plants.

Incised (of a leaf), deeply and irregularly slashed.

Indigenous native to a particular country or area.

Inflorescence (a) the flowering part of a plant, irrespective of arrangement; (b) the arrangement of blooms in a flower head.

Insecticide a chemical mixture designed to destroy insects. There are both specific and general types.

Irradiate to treat or change by exposure to radiation; used to produce some hybrids.

Invasive said of a plant which grows quickly and spreads to occupy more than its allotted space, usually to the detriment of surrounding plants.

Involucre one or more whorls or close groups of small leaves beneath a flower or inflorescence.

Jointed (of a stem), with nodes, where separation is most likely to take place.

Juvenile (of leaves), the second pair to appear from seedlings, often quite different from leaves of the adult plant.

Keel (a) in a pea-type flower the joined, lowermost petals; (b) a central ridge on the top part of a flower.

Labellum the lip of an orchid, differing strongly from the other petals.

Labiate formed like a lip.

Laciniate (of a leaf), slashed into slender lobes.

Lanceolate (of a leaf), lance-shaped, long and gradually tapering.

Lateral on or at the side; e.g., a side-branch produced from a main stalk or trunk.

Latex a milky sap produced by many plants such as the *Euphorbias*.

Lath house a shade house in which light levels are reduced by a canopy of wooden laths. Largely superseded by structures covered with shade cloth.

Layering propagation by pinning a partly-cut branch down to the ground until it produces roots.

Leaflet one of the smaller units of a compound leaf.

Leaf axil the acute angle produced at the junction of a leaf with its stem.

Leaf-cutting a method of propagating many tropical plants from portions of their leaves.

Leaf-well the hollow produced by the spiral overlapping arrangement of leaves in (for instance) a Bromeliad.

Legume a plant which produces pea-type seeds attached alternately to both sides of a pod.

Lignotuber a subterranean bulblike storage chamber of many eucalypts which enables them to regenerate after fire.

Limestone chips fragments of rock consisting principally of calcium carbonate — used as a mulch or dressing around lime-loving plants.

Linear (of a leaf), long and narrow, with sides almost parallel, as in a blade of grass.

Lithophyte a plant which grows on rocks in almost no soil, extracting nourishment principally from the atmosphere, as in many orchids.

Loam a friable topsoil containing sand, clay and silt particles, with the addition of organic matter; hence, **Loamy**.

Lobe a major segment of an organ, representing a division halfway or less to the middle of that organ.

Malathion (Maldison) an effective but foul-smelling insecticide, banned in some areas.

Marginal in popular botany, a plant grown in over-wet, even soggy conditions around the margins of a pool or watercourse.

Mealy see Glaucous.

Membrane a thin, pliable layer of vegetable tissue, often lining an organ or connecting parts.

Microclimate a purely local combination of climatic conditions.

Mildew several whitish fungi affecting plants exposed to over-humid conditions; downy mildew and powdery mildew are the most common. They distort and disfigure new growth and must be controlled by spraying with fungicide.

Mite any one of a number of small spider-relatives that are parasitic on plants and animals. To gardeners, the red spider mite is the worst pest, sucking plant tissues to the point of desiccation and death. Controlled with a special miticide (e.g. Kelthane). They are not insects.

Miticide a chemical compound formulated to destroy mites, as opposed to insects.

Monoecious (of flowers), unisexual, both male and female flowers on the one plant.

Monopodial used of a plant in which the main stem continues to grow indefinitely without branching, as in orchid genera like *Vanda*.

Monotypic said of a genus which has but a single species.

Moraine a special type of garden reproducing the fast-draining material left behind a glacier: a thick deposit of boulders, gravel and sand. Essential for growing many alpine plants.

Mulch a soil-covering to conserve moisture or prevent root damage by heat and frost. May be of organic matter, pebbles, even plastic.

Mutant, Mutation a variant, differing genetically and often visibly from its parent or parents and arising spontaneously.

Natural cross a hybrid which has occurred between two distinct but usually related plant species, without human help.

Naturalize the process by which plants are left in casual groups to spread and multiply year after year.

Nectar gland or **Nectary** a nectar-secreting gland, often appearing as a protuberance.

Needle a specialized elongated leaf, as in conifers.

Node the place on a stem where one or more leaves are attached.

Nodule a small rounded mass or lump, especially on the roots of some plants.

Noxious harmful or injurious to health.

Nut a fruit containing a single seed in a hard shell.

Nutrient deficiency a deficiency of nourishment.

Oblanceolate (of leaves), the opposite to lanceolate — several times longer than broad, but with the widest point more than halfway from the stem.

Oblong (of a leaf), longer than wide, with the sides nearly parallel most of their length.

Obovate (of a leaf), ovate, but with the widest part more than halfway from the stem.

Obtuse blunt, rounded.

Offset a small outside division from a mature clump-forming plant.

Opposite (of leaves), two at each node, on opposite sides of the stem.

Organic composed of live or formerly living tissue.

Osmunda fibre stem fibre from the mature *Osmunda* fern, a component of composts used for orchid growing and seed raising.

Ostiole a minute opening or orifice, as in the fruit of *Ficus* species.

Oval egg-shaped, an ellipse wider at one end than the other.

Ovary the lower, seedbearing part of a plant's female organ.

Ovate (of a leaf), oval, with the broadest end at the stem.

Palmate (of a leaf), roughly hand-shaped, with three or more lobes radiating fanwise from a common point.

Panicle a branching cluster of flowers.

Papilionaceous literally, like a butterfly; applied to a flower of the family Papilionaceae.

Pappus The bristle, scale or hair frequently crowning the achene or fruit of a member of the Asteraceae (daisy) family.

Peat-moss organic material used particularly in composts. Very acid and water retentive.

Pedicel the stalk of an individual flower.

Peduncle the stalk of a flower cluster.

Pendent (of a leaf or stalk) drooping, hanging downwards.

Perennial a plant with a life-cycle spread over a variable number of years. Not necessarily permanent, however, in certain climates.

Pergola a structure formed of horizontal beams or trellis work, supported on columns or posts, over which climbing plants are trained.

Perianth a collective term for the entire floral envelope consisting of calyx, corolla, petals and sepals.

Petal one decorative segment of a flower's corolla.

Petiole the stalk of a leaf.

Phallic shaped like a male organ.

pH balance the degree of acidity or alkalinity in soil.

pH scale a soil's balance of acidity or otherwise is divided into 14 parts, the number 7 being the centre point and indicating neutrality. Numbers below 7 indicate degrees of alkalinity, those above, acidity.

Phonetic pertaining to speech sounds and their pronunciation.

Phyllode an expanded, leaf-like stalk with no true blade, as in many *Acacia* species.

Picotee a flower variety in which the petals have an outer margin in a contrasting colour, usually red or white.

Pinch back, pinch out to prune soft leading shoots with the fingernails to encourage branching.

Pinnate (of leaves), like a feather; specifically with leaflets arranged on both sides of a stalk.

Pip (a) a small seed, especially of a fleshy fruit; (b) a rooted growth-bud of certain plants, as Lily of the Valley.

Pistil the prominent female organ of a flower, generally surrounded by male stamens and projecting beyond them.

Planter a large pot, generally designed to hold an arrangement of growing plants.

Plicate (of a leaf), pleated.

Plume imprecisely, a feather-like inflorescence, as in many grasses.

Pod a dehiscent fruit, usually of the pea family.

Pome The fleshy fruits typical of the apple and pear division of the rose family.

Pollen the spores or grains borne by an anther, containing the fertilizing male element.

Prick out to transplant seedlings from the boxes in which they were germinated.

Procumbent used of a plant which trails without rooting at intervals.

Propagate originally, to reproduce a plant by means of cuttings or divisions to ensure it came absolutely true to type. But today the word also refers to reproducing from seed or spores.

Prostrate a general term to indicate lying flat on the ground.

Protead characteristic of a bloom of the family Proteaceae.

Prune to cut, lop or sever excess or undesired twigs, foliage or roots from any plant, generally with the idea of directing growth, reducing size or improving fruit or flower yield.

Pubescent covered with fine, downy hairs.

Pyramidal (of a plant), loosely pyramid or cone shaped, tapered from a wide base to a pointed apex.

Pyriform pear-shaped.

Raceme a stalk with flowers along its length, the individual blossoms with short stems, e.g., *Delphiniums*.

Radical arising from the root or its crown, said of basal leaves.

Ray or **Ray flower** a strap-shaped flower with a tubular base, forming one petal of the corolla of a flower in the daisy family, Asteraceae.

Reed (a) any tall grass-like plant of the family Poaceae; (b) the stalk of any tall grassy plant.

Reflexed bent abruptly downward or backward.

Reniform kidney shaped.

Reticulate (of a leaf), having net-like veins or nerves.

Rhizomatous possessing or developing rhizomes.

Rockery, Rock garden loosely, a mound of earth and rocks designed to reproduce the ideal growing conditions for mountain or alpine plants.

Root cuttings a method of propagating *Wistarias* and other plants from small sections of root.

Root run the total area beneath which a plant's roots spread.

Rootstock a rooted section of plant used as the base onto which a scion from another plant is grafted.

Rose sick said of soil in which the nutriment has been exhausted by the growing of roses. It must be replaced completely before roses are grown again in the same position.

Rosette an arrangement of leaves radiating from a crown or centre, usually close to the earth.

Runner a trailing stem which takes root at intervals.

Rust any of various plant diseases caused by fungus infections, in which leaves or stems become spotted with rust-coloured marks, or turn altogether rusty-brown. Treated with a fungicide and by removal of affected foliage, etc.

Sagittate (of leaves), shaped like an arrowhead.

Sap the juice or circulating fluid of a woody plant.

Saprophyte a parasitic plant, usually lacking chlorophyll, and living on dead, organic matter.

Scale (a) a small vestigial stem-leaf on certain plants; (b) the protective covering of many so-called scale insects which suck vital fluids out of plant tissue. They are variable in form and colour and treated in many different ways; (c) a segment of lily bulb which may be detached for propagation.

Scape a leafless stem arising from the ground. It may bear one or many flowers.

Scarify to weaken the covering of some hard-cased seeds to hasten germination. Large seeds can be nicked with a knife, smaller seeds rubbed between coarse sandpapers.

Scion the bud or shoot which is grafted onto the stock of another plant.

Scorch variant of scarification. To hasten germination of hard-cased seed by the application of heat.

Scoria a coke-like cellular rock used in crushed form as the growth medium for certain plants, especially Cacti and *Bougainvilleas*.

Scree in horticulture, a raised bed of gravelly growing medium reproducing the natural conditions preferred by many alpine plants.

Secondary next in importance after the main; e.g., a secondary branch or trunk.

Seed a ripened (and usually fertilized) ovule containing the embryonic plant.

Self-seeding the method by which many seed-scattering plants reproduce without human intervention.

Sepal the individual segment of a calyx, an outer petal.

Serrate (of a leaf), saw-toothed, with the teeth pointing away from the stem.

Sessile without a stalk.

Shadehouse a structure for growth or propagation of shade-loving plants in which the amount of light is reduced by a roof and/or walls of shade cloth.

Shear to prune, usually to produce a relatively smooth plane surface.

Sheath any more or less tubular structure surrounding an organ or part; sometimes the leaf which surrounds the stem of a palm.

Shoot immature combination of leaf and stem.

Shrub a woody plant, usually with multiple trunks, and remaining lower in height than a tree. Not a specific term.

Sideshoot see Lateral.

Simple (of a leaf), having a single blade; the opposite of compound.

Sinuate (of a leaf), wavy-edged.

Slip imprecise term for a stem cutting.

Softwood unripened, immature tissue of any woody plant. Used for propagation in some species.

Spathulate (of a leaf), spatula shaped.

Species the basic or minor unit in plant nomenclature.

Specific name a plant's second name.

Sphagnum the dried parts of a moisture-loving moss, used in pot culture. Very water retentive.

Spike a series of stalkless flowers on a single stem.

Spine a stiff, sharp-pointed growth from a stem or leaf.

Spire a tall stalk or sprout of a plant.

Spore the reproductive cell of ferns and mosses, differing from a flower's seed.

Spray loosely, a single branching stem or twig with its leaves, fruit or flowers. May be growing or detached.

Stake a strong stick or post pointed at one end. Driven into the ground, it is used to support a plant.

Stamen the pollen-bearing or male organ of a flower.

Standard one of the more or less erect petals of a flower.

Stellate starlike or star shaped.

Stem the main leaf-bearing and flower-bearing axis of a plant.

Sterile (a) non-functional; (b) not bearing flowers or producing fruit.

Stigma that part of the flower which receives the pollen.

Stock the parent plant onto which the scion or cutting is grafted.

Stolon a shoot that runs along the ground, taking root at intervals and giving rise to new plants.

Stoloniferous reproducing by stolon.

Stomata the leaf-pores through which a plant breathes.

Stone a hard-shelled seed of certain fruit, e.g., a peach or plum.

Strain a loose term for a group of plants· distinguished from others of the variety to which they belong by some intrinsic quality, such as a more colourful flower.

Stratify to treat dormant seeds by chilling under moist conditions to effect germination — hence **stratified**.

Strike cause a cutting to take root.

Sturdy tough, resilient, not necessarily hardy.

Style the part of the pistil between the ovary and stigma, often elongated.

Sub-shrub a very low shrub, usually treated as a perennial, or a woody-based perennial.

Subspecies a major subdivision of a species, ranking above a variety.

Subtend to stand close to and below, as a bract just below a flower.

Subtropical pertaining to a region intermediate between tropical and temperate.

Succulent (of a leaf or plant), juicy, fleshy and often thick.

Sucker an adventitious stem arising from the roots of a woody plant, often from the stock rather than the scion of a grafted plant.

Suffruticose very low and shrubby.

Symbiosis the living together of two plants or other organisms with some advantage to both.

Sympodial having growth of the stem or rhizome periodically terminated, with prolongation of the axis continued from a lateral branch — as with some orchidaceous genera such as *Cattleya*.

Syncarp a compound fruit, composed of the coalesced fruit of a number of flowers, as in a pineapple or *Pandanus*.

Systemic said of a poison or other chemical substance which destroys sucking pests by circulating through the sap system.

Tanbark the shredded bark of certain trees used for its acid content as a mulch or fertilizer.

Taproot a main root extending downward from the plant and giving off small lateral roots.

Taxonomy the science of plant classification, hence **Taxonomist**.

Temperate a mild climate, often coastal.

Tendril a twisting, threadlike extension by which a plant clings to a support. It may be part of a leaf or stem.

Terminal (of a shoot), at the tip or end; hence, **Terminally**.

Ternate in threes, or divided into threes, hence a ternate leaf.

Terrestrial plants which grow on the ground, in contrast to tree-dwelling or epiphytic varieties, e.g., of orchids, bromeliads, etc.

Tetraploid having four rather than the usual two sets of chromosomes.

Thorn a sharp, woody, spine-like outgrowth from the wood of a stem.

Thrips sap-sucking insects, colonies of which rapidly disfigure leaves and flowers. Best controlled with systemic insecticides.

Tip cutting a cutting of new growth, used for the propagation of carnations and perennial daisy plants particularly.

Tip prune pruning of immature growth to force lateral shoots.

Tomentose woolly.

Trapeziform (of a leaf), asymmetrically four-sided.

Trellis a frame or structure of latticework.

Trifoliate having three leaves.

Trifoliolate (of a leaf), having three leaflets to each leaf.

Trigeneric a hybrid crossed from three different species.

Tripinnate (of a leaf), bearing leaflets on the leaflets of its leaves.

Triploid having three rather than the usual two chromosome sets.

Truncate appearing as if cut straight across at the end, as with the leaf of a *Liriodendron*.

Truss a compound terminal cluster of flowers borne on one stalk.

Tube (a) a hollow organ; (b) the extension of a corolla between the opened petals and the calyx; hence, **Tubular**.

Tubercle a small, warty excrescence on a leaf or other plant part.

Tuft (a) a bunch of short hairs, linked or joined at the base; (b) a cluster of short-stemmed flowers growing from a common point.

Turgid swollen and distended with fluid.

Twig the current season's growth of a woody plant or shoot.

Twiner a plant which climbs by winding around itself or other plants.

Type the common species of a plant, as opposed to its variety or cultivar.

Umbel a group of flowers growing from a common point in a stem; hence, **Umbellate**.

Undulate (of a leaf) having a wavy surface.

Unilateral one-sided.

Unisexual of one sex.

Urceolate (of a flower), urn or pitcher shaped.

Variegated a condition of any plant when the natural green of foliage or stems is broken by other colours.

Varietal name a plant's third scientific name.

Variety (officially **Varietas**) (a) the subdivision of a species; (b) a recognizably different member of a plant species capable of cultivation.

Vegetation the normal plant cover of any area.

Velutinous velvety.

Vermiculite a light-weight, inorganic substance, used to lighten potting composts and enhance soil moisture.

Verrucose warty.

Vine (a) any climbing plant bearing long trailing, climbing or twining stems; (b) any species of the genus *Vitis*.

Viscid sticky.

Volubile twining.

Whorl a circle of three or more flowers or branches appearing around a stem, branch or trunk at the same level.

Windbreak a specialized planting (generally of trees or shrubs) designed to protect smaller and more delicate plants from prevailing winds.

Wing a thin, dry or membranous extension of an organ.

Woodsy suggestive of or associated with the woods or forest.

Xerophyte a plant adapted to growing in dry regions.

Zygomorphic bilaterally symmetrical, capable of being divided into two equal halves in one plane only, as in many flowers.

INDEX

Page numbers in **bold** type indicate photographs.